WHEN THE
IRISH
INVADED
CANADA

WHEN THE
IRISH
INVADED
CANADA

*The Incredible True Story of the Civil War
Veterans Who Fought for Ireland's Freedom*

Christopher Klein

DOUBLEDAY ⚓ NEW YORK

Book design by Michael Collica
Jacket images: The Battle of Ridgeway, June 2, 1866; courtesy of the Library of Congress, Washington, D.C. Harp: Atlaspix / Shutterstock
Jacket design by Michael J. Windsor

Library of Congress Cataloging-in-Publication Data
Names: Klein, Christopher, author.
Title: When the Irish Invaded Canada : the Incredible True Story of the Civil War Veterans Who Fought for Ireland's Freedom / Christopher Klein.
Description: New York : Doubleday, 2019.
Identifiers: LCCN 2018032572 (print) | LCCN 2018042393 (ebook) | ISBN 9780385542609 (hardcover) | ISBN 9780385542616 (ebook)
Subjects: LCSH: Canada—History—Fenian Invasions, 1866–1870. | Fenians. | BISAC: HISTORY / Military / Other. | HISTORY / Europe / Ireland. | HISTORY / North America.
Classification: LCC F1032 (ebook) | LCC F1032 .K54 2019 (print) | DDC 971.04/8—dc23
LC record available at https://lccn.loc.gov/2018032572

MANUFACTURED IN THE UNITED STATES OF AMERICA

1 3 5 7 9 10 8 6 4 2

First Edition

For Erin

CONTENTS

AUTHOR'S NOTE

Spellings of some words in quotations have been Americanized from the British versions for consistency and ease of reading. Italics have been maintained to preserve the original emphasis.

Prior to July 1, 1867, present-day Canada was referred to as "British North America." For the sake of clarity and simplicity, this book employs the term "Canada" in place of "British North America."

WHEN THE
IRISH
INVADED
CANADA

PROLOGUE

T HIRTEEN MONTHS AFTER Robert E. Lee laid down his sword at Appomattox Court House, former Confederate rebels slipped on their gray wool jackets. Union veterans longing to emancipate an oppressed people donned their blue kepis. Battle-hardened warriors from both the North and the South returned to the front lines, but not to reignite the Civil War. Instead, the former foes became improbable brothers in arms united against a common enemy—Great Britain.

Entwined by Irish bloodlines, the private army that congregated on the south side of Buffalo, New York, on the night of May 31, 1866, shared not just a craving for gunpowder but a yearning to liberate their homeland from the shackles of the British Empire. For seven hundred years, British rulers attempted to extinguish Ireland's religion, culture, and language, and when the potato crop failed in the 1840s and 1850s, causing one million people to die, some Irish believed that the British were trying to exterminate them as well.

Many of the two million refugees fleeing the Great Hunger washed ashore in the United States, where the newcomers continued to face the scorn of nativist Know-Nothings who believed the Irish had no intention of assimilating into American culture but plotted to take handout after handout while imposing papal law on their adopted home. Even from a distance of nearly fifteen years and three thousand miles, the trauma remained raw for many of the insurgents who enlisted in the self-proclaimed Irish Republican Army. Radicalized by their collective ordeal, these Irish American Civil War veterans viewed their service in the bloody crucibles of Bull Run, Antietam, and Gettysburg as training for the real fight they wanted to wage—one to free Ireland.

Wearing green ribbons tied to their hats and fastened to their buttonholes, eight hundred Irish paramilitaries who had traveled from as far away as New Orleans emerged from the boardinghouses and saloons of Buffalo's Irish enclave, the First Ward, on a clear spring night. Carrying green flags sewn by their wives, girlfriends, and mothers and hauling nine wagons laden with secretly stockpiled rifles and ammunition, the Irish Republican Army set off on one of the most fantastical missions in military history—to kidnap Canada.

❧

Bred to hate the British, the thirty-two-year-old colonel John O'Neill was fulfilling his boyhood dream as he led the Irish Republican Army on its march northward. "The governing passion of my life apart from my duty to my God is to be at the head of an Irish Army battling against England for Ireland's rights," he declared. "For this I live, and for this if necessary I am willing to die."

O'Neill could neither forgive the British for the unspeakable horrors that he had witnessed as a boy coming of age during the Great Hunger nor forget his grandfather's soul-stirring tales of seventeenth-century ancestors who dared to take up arms against the Crown. Although they did not deliver freedom to Ireland, the young lad learned that just the mere act of fighting the British could render an Irishman a hero.

Even after taking a Confederate bullet in defense of the Union, O'Neill never forgot the plight of his homeland. Lured by its plan to strike the British province of Canada, which was directly ruled by London, he enlisted in the Irish Republican Army after the Civil War. O'Neill saw the logic in targeting the British Empire at its most accessible point—on the other side of America's porous northern border—instead of an ocean away in Ireland, a plan that had failed repeatedly over the centuries.

"Canada is a province of Great Britain; the English flag floats over it and English soldiers protect it," he wrote. "Wherever the English flag and English soldiers are found, Irishmen have a right to attack."

❀

Far from some whiskey-fueled daydream, the plan for the Irish invasion of Canada had been carefully crafted for months by veteran Civil War officers, including the one-armed general Thomas William Sweeny. Keen students of military history, the Irishmen knew that attacking Canada had been as time-honored an American tradition as fireworks on the Fourth of July. In fact, even before John Hancock affixed his signature to the Declaration of Independence, the Continental army had launched its first major assault of the American Revolution by storming into Quebec.

In the first American century, the United States and Canada were hardly peaceful neighbors. Old-timers in Buffalo could recall when British soldiers breached the border during the War of 1812 and burned the nascent village to the ground in retaliation for similar measures by U.S. forces. American anger toward Canada surged during the Civil War, when the British colony became a haven for draft dodgers, escaped prisoners of war, and Confederate agents who plotted covert operations including raids on border towns, the firebombing of New York City, and the assassination of President Abraham Lincoln.

Given Great Britain's tacit support for the Confederacy and American hopes that Canada would become the next territory to be absorbed as the country continued to fulfill its Manifest Destiny, President Andrew Johnson was more than willing to let the Irish Republican Army twist the tail of the British lion. The U.S. government sold surplus weapons to the Irish militants, and Johnson met personally with their leaders, reportedly giving them his implicit backing. The Irishmen had been free to establish their own state in exile—complete with its own president, constitution, currency, and capitol in the heart of New York City.

While the Irish Republican Army believed its invasion could spark an Anglo-American war or force the British to redirect troops from Ireland, leaving it more vulnerable to an internal rebellion, what it sought, in essence, was to capture the British colony on America's northern border, hold it hostage, and ransom it for Ireland's independence.

In what is now a little-known coda to the Civil War, Irish Americans invaded Canada five times between 1866 and 1871 in what are collectively known as the Fenian raids. They attacked New Brunswick, Ontario, Quebec, Quebec again, and Manitoba in a series of incursions that eventually devolved into a mix of farce and tragedy. From the Atlantic Ocean to the Great Lakes to the vast prairie, the Fenian raids sowed panic along the border and generated front-page news on two continents.

Before their conclusion, the Fenian raids would prove instrumental in the creation of a new nation—just not the one that Irishmen intended. In the process, however, O'Neill and his brethren would achieve the first Irish military victory over the British since 1745, make the United States a key player in Anglo-Irish affairs, and forge a transatlantic framework that proved pivotal in providing the financial and military support that led to Ireland's eventual liberation from British rule.

The Irish invasions of Canada drew in some of the most notable figures from the Civil War—such as Ulysses S. Grant, George Meade, Edwin Stanton, and William Seward—as well as a colorful cast of characters that included a British spy who successfully infiltrated the Irish Republican Army, a turncoat targeted for assassination, and a radical Irish revolutionary who staged his own funeral to evade capture by the British. No man, however, would become as consumed by the improbable scheme of holding Canada hostage as O'Neill.

❧

After leading the Irish Republican Army on their six-mile march through Buffalo, O'Neill halted his troops at a dock near the Pratt & Co. blast furnace, where the distance across the Niagara River was among its narrowest.

As the Irish colonel surveyed his ragtag force clad in blue, gray, and green, he saw grizzle-bearded men and fair-skinned boys, Catholics and Protestants, Yankees and Rebs. As O'Neill squinted into the darkness, he could faintly make out the enemy territory one thousand yards across the river. Awaiting the troops were two steam tugs and four canal boats, which had been procured by an Irishman posing as a foundry owner seeking to transport his employees to a company picnic on Grand Island.

With Canadian defense forces stationed miles away, the Irishmen easily slipped across the international boundary. The soldiers shook the American dust off their boots and planted their feet firmly on the soil of the British Empire.

The Irish Republican Army's invasion of Canada had begun.

1

The Young Irelanders

WHILE HIS COUNTRYMEN wept at the news of his death, James Stephens absorbed the view from atop Ireland's highest mountain. He might not have been in heaven yet, but the young rebel was closer to it than any man in Ireland.

Shot twice and left to die during a failed uprising against the British Crown, Stephens somehow escaped both death and the enemy that had occupied his beloved island for seven centuries. An outlaw in his own land, he hid from the authorities in the mist-shrouded Macgillycuddy's Reeks, where he followed in the footsteps of Finn McCool, the mythical Celtic warrior who hunted deer with his five hundred Irish wolfhounds in these mountains. Now, in the summer of 1848, Stephens and his fellow Irish patriots were the prey, with the world's foremost superpower in pursuit.

To throw the police off the chase, friends and family in the fugitive's hometown of Kilkenny spread the erroneous news of his death. The *Kilkenny Moderator* ran an obituary for "poor James Stephens," who "proved a martyr in the true sense of the word." To further the ruse, the Irishman's father staged a mock funeral. In the shadows of Kilkenny's St. Canice's Cathedral, which had been ransacked by the British forces of Oliver Cromwell two hundred years earlier, broad shoulders bore a coffin laden with stones. They laid the casket in the turf and erected a simple gravestone that bore the inscription "Here Lies James Stephens."

The deceased, however, was very much alive as he traversed vast bogs, overgrown moors, and mountain streams swollen from summer downpours on a journey across the south of Ireland—one that he knew could conclude at the end of a noose. A stout man of average height, Stephens had fair skin and noticeably small hands and feet, which gave him an effeminate appearance. A voracious reader, he had few close acquaintances apart from his beloved books, perhaps because of his shifty appearance, thanks to an involuntary twitch in his left eye that caused him to wink constantly.

James Stephens, the founding member of the Irish Republican Brotherhood, never wavered in his opposition to any invasion of Canada.

Covering as many as forty miles a day on raw, blistered feet, Stephens left behind a trail of blood drops from County Tipperary to County Kerry and the summit of Ireland's tallest peak. Surely, he thought, the British combing the countryside for insurgents would not bother to look on the roof of Ireland. From the top of Carrauntoohil, Stephens gazed out at a wondrous panorama of glimmering lakes and rain-scoured mountains.

The beautiful facade, however, belied the rotting death that lurked below the surface of Ireland's green sod. The same newspapers that had printed the rebel's obituary also reported that the dreaded "potato disease" had returned for the fourth straight year. Potatoes that had appeared perfectly healthy just weeks earlier now bled a putrid red-brown mucus. A closer inspection of the scenery from Carrauntoohil's summit revealed a horrific landscape of abandoned potato ridges, walking skeletons, and deserted homes.

Along his trek, Stephens had encountered families dressed in rags and farmers who locked their cows and sheep inside their hovels at night to save them from slaughter by desperate neighbors with empty stomachs. He witnessed his starving countrymen withering away and feared that the revolutionary spirit of the Irish might be wilting too.

❀

For seven centuries, the luck of the Irish was nothing to be coveted. A geographic accident had placed them in the backyard of the most powerful empire in world history. Ever since the Englishman Nicholas Breakspear, who inherited the throne of Saint Peter to become Pope Adrian IV, purportedly granted his countryman King Henry II his divine blessing to invade the island in 1155, Ireland had been occupied—and abused—by its neighbor.

While English politicians watched the richest, most modern economy on earth flourish across the Irish Sea from the poor, starving potato people who spoke a foreign language and practiced an exotic religion, they wrestled with what they called the "Irish problem." The problem with the Irish, of course, was that they weren't English.

For nearly a millennium, the English sought to reshape the Irish in their own image and Anglicize what they saw as a savage land populated by people who lacked the intellect and initiative to govern themselves. Following the Reformation, Presbyterians from Scotland and Anglicans from England were transplanted to the north of Ireland. The 1690 defeat of the forces of King James II, the deposed Catholic monarch, at the Battle of the Boyne secured the Protestant ascendancy in Ireland.

That wasn't enough for the Crown, however. It inflicted extra vengeance upon the conquered by attempting to annihilate their Celtic culture. Under the Penal Laws that passed beginning in 1695, Irish Catholics could not openly worship their God. They could not vote or hold public office. They could not send their children to Catholic teachers—or employ Catholic teachers to come to them. They could not own firearms or hold military commissions. They could not own horses valued at more than £5. They could not purchase or inherit land from a Protestant. In fact, they could not inherit anything from a Protestant. They were permitted to own a knife—as long as it was chained to a table to be of no threat to the police.

The English also required inheritances of Catholic-owned land to be subdivided equally among sons, which resulted in Irish Catholic farmers clinging to progressively smaller and smaller parcels of land. An eldest son, however, could take full ownership of his father's land by converting to the Anglican church. Even in death the Irish could not be free, because their colonial overlords prohibited priests from presiding over graveside services, forcing them to bless handfuls of dirt that they gave to mourners to sprinkle over the deceased.

While they were gradually dismantled during the eighteenth century, the last of the Penal Laws endured until 1829. By that point, Anglo-Irish landlords owned four-fifths of the island, which was ruled directly from London after the abolition of the Irish Parliament by the 1801 Act of Union.

Stubbornness ran deep in Ireland's old clans, however. Try as the English might to exterminate the proud, ancient Celtic culture, the defiant Irish refused to conform. No matter how many laws were passed, there was one thing no government could take from the Irish—their will to resist.

In parishes across Ireland, hatred of the English was in the mother's milk. Huddled around fireplaces, boys like Stephens listened to tales of great Irish rebels like Hugh O'Neill, Theobald Wolfe Tone, and Robert Emmet who dared to raise arms against the Crown. The heroes in the stories might not have liberated Ireland, but they achieved immortality by their willingness to resist and fight in the face of overwhelming odds.

❧

For millions of poor Irishmen, the potato was the ultimate superfood. Laden with vitamins, minerals, protein, and carbohydrates, the nourishing tubers flourished in Ireland's cool, moist soil. The Irish ate potatoes for every meal—breakfast, lunch, and dinner. The average adult workingman in Ireland consumed a staggering fourteen pounds of potatoes, equivalent to three thousand calories, per day. The average adult Irishwoman a little over eleven pounds.

Because they required less space to grow than other crops, potatoes became ever more vital to survival as British policies continued to constrict farm sizes at the same time that the island's population nearly doubled to over eight million people between 1800 and 1845.

In the first days of September 1845, farmers reported that the early potato harvest had never been better. Then, without warning, from County Donegal in the north to County Cork in the south, one-third of the island's wonder crop suddenly failed. Black spots scorched potato plant leaves. Stalks withered. Bewildered farmers excavated potatoes pockmarked with lesions. Even those tubers that appeared healthy on the outside contained a putrid mush inside.

When the horror reappeared in 1846, the devastation was near total, with more than three-quarters of the crop lost. The potato blight exposed Ireland's dangerous dependence on a single crop and sparked one of the worst famines in Western European history.

The harsh winter months of early 1847 presaged a year so ghastly that it would go down in history as "Black '47." Frantic farmers sprinkled holy water on their fields. Rats feasted on the corpses of the famished who died on the sides of roads as they wandered in search of food. Emaciated figures, tired of a diet of grass and seaweed, dug their frostbitten fingers into the rocky ledges above the crashing Atlantic as they scaled cliff sides to harvest seagull eggs.

The pestilence had arrived in Europe aboard vessels that departed American ports in 1843 carrying the microorganism *Phytophthora infestans.* After infecting the lowlands of the European continent, the deadly potato spores crossed the English Channel to the British Isles. Ireland's damp conditions proved a superb breeding ground, and the island's dependence on the potato greatly magnified its impact.

Through the duration of the Great Hunger, between 1845 and 1852, approximately two million people fled Ireland. They sailed to England, North America, and beyond. Another one million people perished from starvation and diseases such as typhus and dysentery. Jail populations in Ireland exploded as the starving broke the law just so they could dine on the guaranteed meals given to inmates. All of Ireland, however, had become a vile prison, and the truly desperate decided to escape.

❀

In the months following the first appearance of the potato blight, the British prime minister, Sir Robert Peel, reacted quickly with relief measures that prevented mass starvation. Peel's government established relief commissions, purchased significant amounts of American corn for controlled sale, and persuaded Parliament to repeal tariffs on imported grains. His actions, however, brought about the downfall of his government in June 1846, because merchants complained about government meddling in the marketplace.

Reluctant to interfere with the invisible hand guiding the free market, the ensuing government under Lord John Russell took a much different path toward Irish relief. It kept stores of corn shuttered. Vowing that "Irish property must support Irish poverty," the government transferred full responsibility for funding workhouses and relief programs to Ireland's property owners and tenants. The resulting spike in taxes further exacerbated the problem, because debt-ridden landlords forced out unproductive farmers, causing the eviction rate to soar nearly 1,000 percent between 1847 and 1851. Other landlords found it cheaper to ship tenants abroad than pay for their relief, which forced many of Ireland's poor into exile.

The British government did feed the starving—as long as they worked for their sustenance. Through a new public works program, the hungry toiled for ten or more hours a day, often on useless tasks. The Irish hammered big rocks into smaller ones. They built roads connecting two points in the middle of nowhere. Projects were grueling and monotonous—intentionally so. Charles E. Trevelyan, the British civil servant in charge of relief measures, didn't want Irish stomachs to become too full, lest they become dependent on government handouts. "Relief ought to be on the lowest scale necessary for subsistence," he advised.

Like others in Britain, Trevelyan saw the Great Hunger as a long-sought divine opportunity to depopulate Ireland and transform it from a backward agrarian economy into a modern, dynamic one, like Britain itself. "The judgement of God sent the calamity to teach the Irish a lesson," Trevelyan wrote. "That calamity must not be too much mitigated." Who was he, a mere civil servant, to combat the will of God? The solution to the "Irish problem" had finally been delivered.

Many Irish Catholics believed the British were more concerned about the spread of moral deprivation and idleness than of hunger and disease. For seven centuries, the British had taken away Ireland's land, its rights, and its independence. Now, as a final indignity, they took away Ireland's food under armed guards at a time when it needed it most. Although far more food was imported into Ireland than was exported during the Great Hunger, it still galled the Irish that wheat, oats, barley, and other grains left its ports to England and other destinations.

Conditions worsened in 1848, and anger and frustration sprouted from Ireland's barren fields. A microorganism might have caused the potato blight, but many Irish Catholics, tired of being second-class citizens in their own homeland, placed the blame for the disaster elsewhere.

⚜

As the Great Hunger continued to gnaw away at Ireland, support swelled for a movement of youthful, middle-class intellectuals that came to be known as Young Ireland. They embraced Celtic literature, history, and mythology and advocated for a revival of the Irish language. Their weekly newspaper, *The Nation,* published poems and ballads along with book reviews and articles. Young Ireland was not a sectarian movement but a union of both Protestants and Catholics. The Protestant intellectual Thomas Davis, the first editor of *The Nation,* was its most powerful voice before his untimely death of scarlet fever at the age of thirty in 1845.

While Young Ireland didn't preach physical force, it also didn't disavow its use. The collection of poets, journalists, and barristers believed in the power of words but knew that sometimes action was needed as well. That led to a break with the more moderate Repeal Association headed by Daniel O'Connell, the stalwart nationalist who preached nonviolent constitutional resistance. As nationalists watched Ireland's people perish or flee in the wake of the British government's feeble response to the Great Hunger, they grew more radicalized and increasingly viewed O'Connell's preference to compromise with the British as capitulation.

While O'Connell—known as "the Liberator" for his successful campaign to repeal the last of the Penal Laws and gain the right of Catholics to sit in the British Parliament—advocated the eradication of the 1801 Act of Union and restoration of the Irish Parliament, Young Irelanders sought nothing less than a fully independent republic.

Few Young Irelanders were more militant toward the British than John Mitchel, the son of a Presbyterian minister. When Mitchel's rhetoric grew too hot for *The Nation,* he started his own broadsheet, *The United Irishman.* It sizzled with accusations against the Crown, which he held directly responsible for the Great Hunger.

In his columns, Mitchel advocated a "holy war to sweep this island clear of the English name and nation." He published directions for street warfare. He referred to Britain's lord lieutenant as "Her Majesty's Executioner-General and General Butcher of Ireland" and argued that food grown in Ireland should stay in Ireland.

After seeing famished children as he traveled between Dublin and Galway, he wrote, "I saw Trevelyan's claw in the vitals of those children; his red tape would draw them to death; in his government laboratory he had prepared for them the typhus poison."

The British were feeding three million people per day at the height of the Great Hunger, and it permitted hundreds of thousands of refugees to resettle inside Great Britain. Still, Mitchel's accusations of genocide took root. The seven-hundred-year history of English rule had fueled Irish nationalism—at home and abroad with the diaspora—and would for decades to come.

In the first months of 1848, another contagion swept across Europe that eventually settled in Ireland. That February, the French overthrew King Louis Philippe in a relatively bloodless affair that led to the establishment of the Second Republic. The political earthquake sent shock waves across the Continent as liberals revolted against monarchies and absolutist governments in Berlin, Vienna, Rome, Prague, and Budapest.

The "springtime of the peoples" shook the British government and inspired members of Young Ireland to launch their own revolution. Their bitterness toward the British, always at a low simmer, finally bubbled over.

By May 1848, the British government had heard enough from Mitchel. It introduced a new crime—treason felony—just to lock him up. On July 22, the British Parliament suspended habeas corpus, allowing authorities to imprison rebels indefinitely. They raided *The Nation* and issued warrants for the arrest of Young Ireland's leaders.

The rebels were determined to resist. Irish republicans weren't going to starve like dogs. If they were going to die, it would be on the battlefield.

❧

The sound of iron striking iron rang across the Irish countryside during the summer of 1848 as blacksmiths hammered out pikes on their anvils. By the light of the summertime moon, Stephens and his fellow rebels gathered on Moll Mackey's Hill outside the medieval town of Kilkenny to perform military drills and practice formations. Few of the Irishmen owned rifles or muskets, so they armed themselves with improvised spears, pitchforks, and scythes they had grabbed from their barns.

On the evening of July 25, Stephens attended a Young Ireland meeting at Kilkenny's town hall and became swept up by patriotic fervor. He heard that the British had suspended the right to bear arms in cities such as Dublin, Cork, and Kilkenny. Persuaded to lend his voice to the cause, Stephens delivered his maiden speech as a rebel. "Treasure your arms as you would the apples of your eyes, and bury them safely in the hope of a happy resurrection!"

After the meeting, Stephens heard a rumor that a detective had arrived in town with a warrant for the arrest of William Smith O'Brien, a Young Ireland founder who had fled to Kilkenny and its environs. The time for action had arrived. Stephens returned home, grabbed his dagger, and rushed out into the Irish night.

Accompanied by other rebels, Stephens found O'Brien the next morning in Cashel at the house of the Young Irelander Michael Doheny. A longtime member of the British House of Commons, the forty-four-year-old O'Brien had an atypical pedigree for an Irish revolutionary. Although descended from the medieval Irish high king Brian Boru, who defeated the Vikings at the Battle of Clontarf in 1014, the Cambridge-educated, Protestant landlord looked, talked, and worshipped more like an Englishman than an Irishman. The patrician was a politician, not a soldier. Yet while other Young Irelanders urged him to delay any uprising until after the harvest, O'Brien wanted to wait no longer. He asked for volunteers, and Stephens stepped forward.

❧

Even in battle, O'Brien adhered to a set of manners. He first targeted a police barracks in the County Tipperary village of Mullinahone. Stephens, who had been named an aide-de-camp, stormed through the door with O'Brien and another rebel, taking the six constables inside by surprise. The chief constable begged the rebels to return with a larger force because he and his fellow officers would lose their jobs if they surrendered to only three rebels. His appeal to O'Brien's sense of decency worked. O'Brien ordered his men to leave and come back in fifteen minutes with more insurgents. Sure enough, as soon as the rebels departed, the policemen darted out a back door, never to return.

Two days later, Stephens took charge of thirty Young Irelanders in Killenaule when news arrived of an approaching cavalry. Clad in a white coat, Stephens cut a conspicuous figure as he ordered the construction of a makeshift barricade of turf carts and timber beams. As the cavalry galloped up to the barrier, Stephens pointed the rebels' only rifle at the commanding officer of the dragoons. The captain insisted he didn't have a warrant for O'Brien's arrest and simply wanted to pass through.

Stephens ordered his men to hold, but they craved a fight. "General, in the name of Jesus and the Blessed Virgin, will you give the word?" one of them implored. "Steady," whispered Stephens, who faced the decision of whether a gunshot would strike a blow for Ireland or lead to more deaths of his fellow citizens. He lowered his gun and allowed the authorities to pass through one at a time.

The villagers hailed Stephens as a hero for getting the troops to back down without firing a shot. "We want the little man in the white coat!" they shouted. "Fellow countrymen," Stephens replied, "this is not the time for words but for deeds."

⁂

The next day, Stephens crouched along the road to Ballingarry, where the rebels had erected another blockade. He watched as a forty-five-man unit of the Irish Constabulary, the British-controlled paramilitary police force, approached, then suddenly swerved at a fork in the road. Armed with pikes, pitchforks, and two dozen guns, the rebels ran in pursuit of the police, who took refuge inside a two-story gray stone farmhouse on a small crest.

To barricade the farmhouse's entryways and windows, the police smashed doors and broke apart wooden furniture. Outside, eighty rebels surrounded the house and hurled rocks behind the protection of a five-foot garden wall. Stephens and Terence Bellew MacManus, a Liverpool shipping agent who packed up his green-and-gold uniform and abandoned his business when he heard of the planned uprising, took cover in the stables in the rear of the house. MacManus dragged hay bales to the back door with plans to set them ablaze, in order to smoke out the enemy, only to find that his ragtag insurgents lacked matches. Instead, MacManus fired his revolver into the hay, until a spark caused the bales to smolder.

O'Brien immediately ordered the fire doused, explaining that the house's owner, the widow Margaret McCormack, had arrived in hysterics because five of her young children were trapped inside. The Young Ireland leader opted instead to tramp through the widow's cabbage garden, approach the parlor window, and shake hands with the police through a firing gap in the barricade.

Young Ireland rebels including James Stephens exchange gunfire with policemen during the 1848 rebellion in what became derided as the Battle of Widow McCormack's Cabbage Patch.

"We are all Irishmen, boys. I am Smith O'Brien, as good a soldier as any of you," he said before demanding their guns. The police refused the order. As O'Brien backed away, a voice from the mob yelled, "Slash away, boys, and slaughter the whole of them!" The rebels fired rocks, and the police fired their guns. Although at a disadvantage in ammunition, the Young Ireland leader refused to call a retreat. "An O'Brien never turned his back on an enemy!" he declared. Displaying cooler heads, Stephens and MacManus forcibly removed their commander from the line of fire as bullets kicked up dirt all around them.

As the rebels scattered, Stephens spotted a mounted policeman on the scene. He forced the officer to dismount, swapped his nondescript hat for O'Brien's flamboyant green-and-gold one, and told him to gallop away from danger.

Stephens directed the remaining rebels to hide on both sides of the road in order to ambush arriving police reinforcements. In the ensuing gunfire, Stephens watched two rebels drop dead next to him. He felt a searing pain in the fleshy part of his right thigh and another on his left hip. Stephens crumpled to the ground with two gunshot wounds, playing dead until the policemen continued their march.

Having survived what was sardonically called the Battle of Widow McCormack's Cabbage Patch, Stephens recovered at a friend's house. But with the authorities closing in, he went in search of another Young Irelander, a man who would become a brother in arms for the next twenty years.

⚜

Stephens had met John O'Mahony at a war council the night before the shoot-out at the Widow McCormack's. With handsomely chiseled features and shaggy dark brown hair flowing toward his broad shoulders, the thirty-three-year-old O'Mahony was an athletic man and an excellent horseman. His admirers still told the tale of the time many years earlier when he wrestled a bull to the ground with his bare hands. He was descended from the chieftain of the O'Mahony clan, and the peasants in the mountainous region on the border of County Cork and County Tipperary still considered him "Chief of the Comeraghs."

Following the example of his grandfather, father, and uncle who were local leaders of Wolfe Tone's United Irishmen in 1798, O'Mahony supported the Repeal Association and then Young Ireland after it broke apart. The Great Hunger had further hardened him against British rule. While O'Mahony subscribed to *The Nation,* like Stephens, he had not been active in Young Ireland until recent weeks. "I kept away from any public adhesion to the party," O'Mahony recalled. "I wished to wait until the time for action had come."

That time had now arrived. When Stephens limped to the door of his Ballyneale farmhouse, O'Mahony's most immediate concern was getting him to safety. The pair spent the night in the house of one of O'Mahony's plowmen before venturing to the cabin hideout of the Young Ireland compatriot Doheny. The three rebels ventured to greater safety in the more remote Comeragh Mountains, where most of the population was loyal to O'Mahony. There they would make a vow.

While Stephens, O'Mahony, and Doheny remained on the run, the Crown arrested O'Brien and other Young Irelanders. Their rebellion quickly petered out. In the midst of starvation, Ireland was simply too weak to rise up against the British. It would take years before the spirit of Ireland's discouraged people could be rekindled, but the three fugitives pledged to devote their lives to the expulsion of the British from their land.

❀

By August 13, with arrests continuing, O'Mahony determined it was no longer safe for Doheny and Stephens to remain in the mountains. The pair left O'Mahony and began a journey on foot across the south of Ireland as Stephens's friends spread the erroneous news of his death. The rebels spent nights sleeping in haystacks, churchyards, and rude mountain cabins. They begged for food and a place to dry out their sodden clothes and warm themselves around a fire.

Although two decades separated them in age, Stephens and Doheny forged a bond on their trek. Stephens lifted the older man's spirits by singing tunes as they hiked west from the Irish Sea in County Waterford to the Atlantic Ocean in County Kerry. Faced with the threat of execution, the two realized that their journey might be their last in Ireland, so they soaked in the beauty of the island, from the Lakes of Killarney to the peaks of Macgillycuddy's Reeks.

Finding shelter in Kenmare with a sympathetic attorney after nearly a month battling storms, mosquitoes, and hunger, Stephens finally found a means to escape Ireland. He would disguise himself as a servant boy and accompany to London the lawyer's sister-in-law, the popular poet Mary Downing, who signed her works as "Christabel." (Stephens rejected a notion that he dress up as a maidservant, although Doheny wrote that "he was well fitted for such disguise, being extremely young and having very delicate features.")

On September 12, Stephens ascended the plank to a waiting ship in Cork Harbor. He had cause to worry. His twitching left eye could quickly arouse suspicion. In addition, two weeks earlier, MacManus had been snatched off the deck of an American ship in Cobh just as he was ready to escape Ireland, leading to a conviction for high treason and banishment to Tasmania.

Assuming the identity of Mr. Thomas Cussens from Tralee, Stephens carried a little boy in his arms, looking as best he could like a doting father, although he couldn't help but monitor the policemen eyeing every passenger boarding the vessel. "All the time that I appeared so much taken up with the child, my eye continued to watch the movements of these beasts of prey," he wrote. Safely aboard the ship, he watched Ireland fade from view.

❀

After traveling across England, Stephens arrived in Paris on the night of September 16. Paris became a home in exile for Stephens, who still suffered from his wounds and feared his foot might need amputation. He immersed himself in books and culture during his seven-year stay in France. He learned French and attended logic and metaphysics lectures at the Sorbonne. He wandered the galleries of the Louvre and the gardens of Versailles. He imbibed Kant and Descartes. He taught English and found work as a translator and journalist.

Several months following Stephens's arrival, he was reunited with O'Mahony, who took refuge in Paris after leading an unsuccessful guerrilla campaign against police barracks and military posts in Tipperary, Waterford, and Kilkenny. In August 1849, O'Mahony and Stephens became roommates in a rickety boardinghouse on Rue Lacépède, a narrow, crooked street in the Latin Quarter. Inside their derelict room, two broken stools flanked the ends of a three-legged table, propped against a plaster wall covered with charcoal diagrams. They slept on straw woven into a rug. They lived in poverty, but they consumed the riches of knowledge evidenced by the books and piles of paper littering a corner of the apartment.

Following the political upheaval that engulfed Europe in 1848, the French capital teemed with revolutionary groups that, according to Stephens, offered him a useful education in plotting his next rebellion. "Once I resolved that armed insurrection was the only course for Ireland," he recalled, "I commenced a particular study of continental secret societies." Whether or not the Irishmen mounted the barricades to prevent the fall of the Second Republic in Louis-Napoleon's 1851 coup d'état, they witnessed the activity as bullets flew.

For his portion, O'Mahony scratched out a living teaching Irish, Latin, Greek, and English and occasionally contributing to French newspapers. Four years of a Parisian exile, however, did nothing to banish the misery of the Great Hunger from his mind, and once Louis-Napoleon proclaimed himself emperor of France, Paris was no longer so hospitable to democrats and revolutionaries such as O'Mahony.

By the end of 1853, the Irishman wanted to shift his exile elsewhere. O'Mahony packed up his few belongings and set sail for the most Irish metropolis in the world outside Dublin.

Bold Fenian Men

J OHN O'MAHONY FOLLOWED in the wake of one million Irishmen who washed up on North American shorelines during the years of the Great Hunger in one of the largest migrations in human history. Many of the castaways sailed aboard former slave ships and hastily converted cargo vessels. The hunger and disease that they thought they had left behind in Ireland clung to them like the lice that spread cholera below deck. Mortality rates soared as high as 30 percent aboard these aptly nicknamed "coffin ships." Along with the pails of garbage and excrement, crews tossed overboard dead bodies, wrapped in cloths and weighted down by rocks. Some emigrants reported that so many corpses splashed into the ocean that sharks stalked their ships, awaiting their next meals.

After recruiting his fellow Young Irelander James Stephens to lead the Irish Republican Brotherhood, John O'Mahony became the head of the Fenian Brotherhood in the United States.

Upon landing in New York City in January 1854, O'Mahony was greeted by a cacophony of noise and a hash of foreign languages. Manhattan might have been a Babel of an island, with the majority of its denizens foreign-born, but the arrival of every ship laden with poor, hungry Irishmen made it increasingly an emerald isle. By the 1850s, more than a quarter of the city's residents had been born in Ireland.

Too destitute to venture any farther than their feet would take them, the Irish who arrived in New York huddled inside rickety, disease-riddled tenements in neighborhoods such as the notorious Five Points. They lived in unventilated attics where they suffocated in the summer and froze in the winter. They lived belowground in dark cellars that routinely flooded with sewage and rainwater. Breathing putrid air, lacking running water, and still suffering the ill effects of the Great Hunger and their voyage, the Irish died at a rate of seven times their fellow New Yorkers. A rural people now found themselves in the midst of one of the world's most densely populated cities. Their farming skills rendered useless, they took low-paying, manual labor jobs. They dug ditches. They unloaded ships. They cooked and sewed.

The winter of 1854 was a uniquely bad time to be an immigrant, a Catholic, and an Irishman in America. The year ahead would be only worse.

❦

With immigration controls left primarily to the states and cities, more than 1.4 million foreigners poured through U.S. borders in the 1840s, a figure that doubled in the 1850s. Native-born Americans feared the torrent of foreigners would dilute their culture and pilfer their jobs. The cry of "America for Americans!" echoed across the country.

A secret society of native-born Protestants coalesced in the 1850s to form the anti-Catholic, anti-immigrant American Party, whose members were dubbed Know-Nothings for their parroted response, "I know nothing," when questioned about their activities. Know-Nothings advocated an increase in the waiting period for American citizenship from five to twenty-one years and sought to restrict eligibility for elective offices to native-born Americans—as long as they weren't also Catholic.

Although hostile toward most immigrants, the Know-Nothings reserved their worst scorn for the Irish, who not only came in unprecedented numbers but were unlike any newcomers that the

United States had seen before. They were not immigrants seeking political or religious freedom but refugees of a humanitarian disaster. Although most certainly tired and poor, the Irish did not arrive in America yearning to breathe free; they merely wanted to eat.

To nativist eyes, these immigrants had no love of American culture, no respect for its laws. They had no intention of becoming productive members of society. They came only for the handouts and then ungratefully complained about their mistreatment. They were desperately poor and sickly, uneducated and unskilled. They brought crime and disease.

Many didn't even speak English. According to some scholars, more than a quarter of the Great Hunger exiles arriving in the 1850s spoke Irish, and the majority of them were illiterate. They exhausted the capacities of jails, asylums, and orphanages and strained welfare budgets. Even worse, they imported their strange religion.

Anglo-Saxon Protestants whose ancestors explicitly crossed the ocean to escape papism and ensure their worship was cleansed of any remaining Catholic vestiges feared that the Irish would impose the Catholic canon as the law of the land. Rumors even spread that the pope and his army planned to overthrow the U.S. government and establish a new Vatican in Cincinnati.

The religious tension boiled over just weeks after O'Mahony's arrival. In March 1854, Know-Nothings seized a marble block gifted by Pope Pius IX for construction of the Washington Monument and threw it into the Potomac River, suspecting it was a signal from the pontiff to launch an immigrant uprising in the United States. That summer, anti-Catholic rioters in Bath, Maine, smashed the pews of a local church recently purchased by Irish Catholics before setting it ablaze. Farther up the Maine coast in Ellsworth, a Protestant mob blew up a Catholic chapel with gunpowder before tarring and feathering the Jesuit priest John Bapst because he denounced the use of the King James Bible in local schools.

That fall, the Know-Nothings scored major victories at the ballot box, in particular in Massachusetts, where they captured every statewide office and all but three of the 380 seats in the legislature. They mandated the reading of the King James Bible in public schools, prohibited the teaching of foreign languages, and systematically deported thousands of destitute Irish back to the British

Isles. They disbanded Irish American militia units and launched surprise inspections of Catholic convents and schools amid rumors of lascivious sexual behavior by clerics. Know-Nothings also won the governorships in Pennsylvania, Connecticut, Rhode Island, and New Hampshire as well as legislative majorities in Indiana and Maine.

O'Mahony could encounter signs of the discrimination against his kind all around New York, including in the help-wanted advertisements in the city's newspapers that stipulated "Irish need not apply" or "any country or color except Irish." In popular magazines such as *Punch*, cartoonists sketched the Irish as simian creatures with monstrous countenances and jugs of alcohol tethered to their sides. In the city's theaters, audiences howled at depictions of the Irish as drunken, pipe-smoking buffoons with overwrought brogues.

After spending seven centuries under the thumb of the British, the Irish who came to America found themselves again subservient to an Anglo-Protestant ruling class. "This is an English colony and its people inherit from their ancestors the true Saxon contempt for everything Irish," said one disappointed exile.

The more threatened the Irish felt, the more they turned inward, like a snake coiling itself for protection. Always a tribal people, they grew fiercely communal in their urban enclaves. They clung together in church parishes and fraternal organizations such as the Ancient Order of Hibernians.

The Irish had never assimilated with the English. That's how their culture had survived centuries of colonization. Why should they behave differently in the United States?

❊

In some respects, the diaspora who crossed the Atlantic became even more radical than those who stayed in Ireland. They bore not only the scars of the Great Hunger but the disdain of the Know-Nothings. Plus, they enjoyed the protections of the U.S. Constitution, which gave them a haven from which they could operate beyond the reach of British laws. In America, they had the freedom to assemble, bear arms, and speak out against their enemy.

No Irish revolutionary in America exercised his newfound freedom of speech more vigorously than John Mitchel, the incendiary onetime publisher of *The United Irishman*. While imprisoned in

Tasmania for his role in the uprising, Mitchel engineered an escape, fleeing to New York City in November 1853 in the footsteps of his fellow convict Thomas Francis Meagher, who had done the same a year earlier.

Banishment to Australia had done nothing to douse Mitchel's fiery rhetoric about the British government and its role in the Great Hunger. In the pages of his newly established weekly newspaper, *The Citizen*, he printed the accounts of his years as a political prisoner, continuing to accuse the British of genocide.

Mitchel's fire-breathing pen, however, began to set collateral targets ablaze. Still smarting from what he saw as the clergy's betrayal of Young Ireland, he clashed with New York's archbishop, John Joseph Hughes, a County Tyrone native. Mitchel's broadsides against hypocritical abolitionists—such as Theodore Parker, who wrote that the Irish had "bad habits, bad religion, and worst of all, a bad nature"—turned into vehement defenses of slavery. Shortly after, in 1855, Mitchel abruptly shuttered his newspaper and moved to Tennessee, where his pro-slavery views found a more welcoming audience.

This left O'Mahony abandoned. It had been Mitchel's arrival in New York that had spurred his resettlement. He joined with Michael Doheny, his compatriot in exile years earlier in the mountains of Ireland. Doheny had resumed practicing law after his own arrival in New York in 1849. Together with fellow Young Irelanders, they formed the Emmet Monument Association. Its moniker alluded to Robert Emmet's famous speech in the dock before his hanging. The Irish rebel leader implored, "When my country takes her place among the nations of the earth, then, and not till then, let my epitaph be written."

The men took practical steps toward the liberation of Ireland. Members drilled weekly with an Irish regiment that Doheny organized as part of the New York State Militia. Their activities in New York drew the concern of the British ambassador to the United States, who complained to the U.S. secretary of state, William Marcy, about "the existence of clubs composed of the Irish population in that city for the purpose of enlisting and drilling volunteers to effect an insurrection in Ireland."

British unease grew when authorities arrested twenty Irish Americans in Cincinnati in 1856 and charged them with plotting an assault in Ireland, in violation of the U.S. Neutrality Act of 1818. The court acquitted the Irishmen, but not before Judge Humphrey Howe Leavitt warned the exiles that they were first and foremost Americans. "There can be no such thing as a divided national allegiance," he said. "The foreigner who takes the oath of fidelity to our government necessarily renounces his allegiance to all others."

The Irishmen could be forgiven if they thought that launching operations against foreign governments was a quintessential American activity. Two decades earlier, Americans poured across the border of the Mexican province of Texas and eventually declared it an independent republic. They did the same in California in 1846. During the 1850s, "filibusters" launched expeditions to Central and South America with the intent of adding more slave states to the Union and lining the pockets of multinational corporations. The Venezuelan-born Narciso López used New Orleans as a base for attacking Spanish-controlled Cuba, while the American William Walker captured the Mexican city of La Paz in Baja California and later conquered Nicaragua, reinstituted slavery, and named himself president, a move recognized by President Franklin Pierce.

Through the efforts of O'Mahony and his fellow exiles, the transplanted Irish revolutionary movement took root in American soil. Back in Ireland, however, its prospects were as dim as ever.

❧

Residents of Ireland spotted a dead man walking the island's roads in 1856. Eight years after the *Kilkenny Moderator* printed his obituary, James Stephens quietly returned home from the European continent. A year earlier, the Young Ireland veteran Charles Gavan Duffy had reported, "There seems to me no more hope for the Irish cause than for the corpse on the dissecting-table." Stephens chose to judge for himself.

He had lost hair and gained weight during his eight-year exile. Some doubted he was who he claimed to be. Even his local Catholic priest did not recognize him.

Out of touch with his family since taking flight from Ireland, Stephens learned the devastating news that his father and sister had died shortly after his departure.

Further disheartening the rebel, support for Irish independence appeared to have likewise perished. With its people still processing their trauma and survivors' guilt, Stephens wrote of his fear that Ireland "had given up the ghost, and was at last, to all intents and purposes, one of England's reconquered provinces."

To get a better sense of whether the same attitude permeated the rest of the island, Stephens embarked on what he later claimed to have been a three-thousand-mile ramble, in a circuit of Ireland. Smoking his pipe and leaning on his walking stick, he spoke with farmers, peasants, and laborers. He slept in their homes and supped around their tables. He learned about their hardships—low pay, landlord oppression, rising rents, and high taxes to support a government and a church in which they had no faith.

But he detected a faint nationalist pulse among poor Catholic farmers and laborers, in particular the Ribbonmen, a secret agrarian society that terrorized landlords by burning barns, damaging property, and harming livestock. "The cause is not dead but sleeping," he reported.

Stephens warned, however, that "if another decade was allowed to pass without an endeavor of some kind or another to shake off an unjust yoke, the Irish people would sink into a lethargy from which it would be impossible for any patriot, however Titanic in genius, or, for any body of patriots, however sincere and zealous, to arouse them into anything like a healthy existence."

On the other side of the Atlantic, O'Mahony felt the same urgency to act. He wrote to Stephens that he had grown "sick of Young Ireland and its theatrical leaders" who did little more than bloviate about the British colonization of Ireland. Unlike the "tinsel patriots" he derided, O'Mahony set about to forge a new Irish republican movement, one that would be as revolutionary in its structure as it would be in its mission.

❦

At the close of December 1857, a young Irishman named Owen Considine called on Stephens at his Dublin residence. He bore a letter from the United States signed by four exiles, including O'Mahony and Doheny. It called upon him to form an organization in Ireland that would work in conjunction with them to secure independence.

It would be a transatlantic effort, unlike previous movements. The Irish would take advantage of the revolutionary zeal and freedoms of the United States to raise money, ship arms, and plot military operations, while kindred rebels in Ireland would supply manpower and coordinate logistics.

Stephens dispatched Joseph Denieffe as a messenger to the United States with his enthusiastic agreement to take on the task—but on two conditions that reflected his growing arrogance. In addition to £80 to £100 per month, he demanded to be "perfectly unshackled; in other words, a provisional dictator. On this point I can conscientiously concede nothing." For his part, Stephens vowed within three months to recruit ten thousand men, fifteen hundred armed with guns and the rest with pikes.

Stephens couldn't take it as anything but an encouraging sign that Denieffe returned to Dublin on March 17, 1858, with the first monetary installment and an agreement to his terms. As Ireland commemorated its patron saint, Stephens read the document signed by Doheny, O'Mahony, and fourteen other Irish American leaders, appointing him "Chief Executive of the Irish Revolutionary movement" and granting him "supreme control and absolute authority over that movement in Ireland."

That night, Stephens gathered with his fellow nationalists Considine, Denieffe, Peter Langan, Garrett O'Shaughnessy, and Thomas Clarke Luby to inaugurate the secret revolutionary organization that would come to be known as the Irish Republican Brotherhood (IRB). As the head of the conspiracy, he was first to take the oath drawn up by Luby.

To maintain secrecy, Stephens organized the IRB into cells known as "circles." A "head center," referred to as an "A" and equal in rank to a colonel, was to lead each circle. Head centers selected nine B-level members, equivalent to captains, who each selected nine C-level personnel, equivalent to sergeants, who each selected nine D-level members, equivalent to privates. A fully staffed circle would include 820 members. In theory, members would know only the identities of those directly above or below them in the organization, with only captains knowing the identity of the head center.

Stephens and Luby went right to work traveling south of Dublin to recruit members for their new organization. Stephens excelled as an organizer, combining his mind for numbers with his vision of a free Ireland. "He seemed to have me under a spell," Denieffe recalled. "There was earnestness in his every move."

In the United States, the venture did not get off to as smooth a start. With America deep in the throes of the financial panic of 1857, fund-raising proved difficult, and most of April's £90 payment to Ireland had to be shaken out of the personal pockets of the Emmet Monument Association's leaders.

In spite of a promise that the second installment would reach Ireland in April, summer arrived without any money from America, forcing Stephens and Luby to abandon their recruiting only shortly after it had begun.

Stephens again dispatched Denieffe to the United States, but he returned with only £40 this time, along with an ominous warning. "The Irish-Americans will not subscribe until they are obliged to," he said. "They have been humbugged so often that they have lost confidence, and at present have no faith in attempts for the regeneration of Ireland." Disappointed at his lack of support from the United States, Stephens took matters into his own hands. He decided to cross the Atlantic himself, to prime the cash flow and lobby fellow Young Ireland veterans to join the new organization.

⚜

When Stephens arrived on American soil for the first time, on October 13, 1858, his legs buckled and his stomach churned from his time at sea. It was only the start of the Irishman's relentless litany of complaints, about both his health and the United States itself, during his five-month stay. In his diary, Stephens described a "land of self, greed, and grab" that abounded with "debasing influences." He found a country putting on a facade as grotesque as the "dirt-colored stone and piss-streaked marble" facings that covered up the slender brick walls of the mansions he passed on Fifth Avenue. Even the brightly colored autumn leaves he found to be "tiresomely monotonous."

During his tour of America's Irish enclaves, Stephens traveled to the nation's capital and met President James Buchanan. Stephens was not any more impressed with Buchanan than with the country he governed. He wrote that "Old Buck" had "the expression of a

philandering tom-cat" and was little better than "a Yankee development of the Artful Dodger."

Upon their reunion, Doheny found little evidence of the young
man who sang tunes and quietly endured his gunshot wounds while
on the run in Ireland in 1848. Embracing the role of the "provisional
dictator," Stephens had grown condescending. His relationship with
Doheny cooled, but Stephens found much to admire in O'Mahony,
whom he called "far and away the first patriot of the Irish race."

"In loving Ireland *he* loves more than a principle of justice," Stephens wrote. "Intensely, passionately he loves the Irish race. The
memories of times gone by and hallowed by the deeds of the men
of his blood, the language, the literature, the monuments, speak to
him as to no other."

At a meeting inside New York's Tammany Hall, Stephens officially
appointed O'Mahony the head of the IRB's branch in the United
States, designating him the "supreme organizer and director of
the Irish Revolutionary Brotherhood in America." In early 1859,
O'Mahony would dub the American counterpart to the IRB the
Fenian Brotherhood, a name that harked back to the legendary
Celtic warriors with whom the Gaelic scholar had spent long days and
nights in 1857 as he translated Geoffrey Keating's *History of Ireland*
from Irish into English. The word "Fenian"* was an Anglicized ver-
sion of the Irish word *Fianna,* the band of mythical Gaelic heroes
from pre-Christian times commanded by Finn McCool. Although
members of the IRB were distinct from those in the Fenian Brotherhood, the term "Fenian" would come to refer to both groups, and
eventually Irish republicans in general.

Similar to the IRB, the oath-bound Fenian Brotherhood adopted
a military-style organizational structure. The group started with
approximately forty members, all of them in New York. (Significantly,
their ranks didn't include two prominent Young Irelanders—Mitchel
and Meagher.)

Stephens returned to Ireland in March 1859 with £600 and,
according to a document drafted by the Irish Americans, a further
assurance of "supreme control and absolute authority over that

---

* To this day, the term "Fenian" is wielded as both a derogatory term of sectarian
abuse and a badge of honor by both sides of the divide in Northern Ireland.

movement *at home and abroad.*" He also left with growing concerns about whether O'Mahony was the right man to lead the American operation. "Should I perish, the cause is lost," he wrote. "For I fear that even he lacks many of the essentials of a leader."

❁

As a new decade dawned, membership in both the IRB and the Fenian Brotherhood grew more slowly than Stephens or O'Mahony had hoped. A major obstacle to recruiting Irish Catholics on both sides of the Atlantic was their fear not so much of dying at the hands of the British as of the eternal damnation that would follow. Although most Americans believed the Fenian Brotherhood was a papist organization, clergy across the United States railed against its members from their pulpits. Secret societies—particularly those willing to use violence—ran afoul of church teaching, and priests threatened to withhold sacraments from anyone who recited the Fenian oath. American bishops also accused the Fenians of preying on the gullible Irish.

The Vatican might have cloaked its stance toward the Fenians in its opposition to clandestine societies, but it had little affinity with those preaching the gospel of popular uprising, particularly when it was itself at war with Italian revolutionaries. Pope Pius IX appealed to his Irish subjects to join the fight for the Papal States against Italy's rebels. He had no use for those doing the same for their homeland.

The opposition of Dublin's powerful archbishop, Paul Cullen, and other clerical leaders in Ireland slowed the growth of the IRB, particularly in rural areas of Ireland where the church was most powerful. Even though its parishioners were treated as second-class citizens, the Roman Catholic Church in Ireland was comfortable with its position in relation to the Crown. It was the Fenians who threatened its status in their espousal of the separation of church and state.

Stephens and O'Mahony believed the clergy had overstepped their bounds by becoming involved in political matters during the Young Irelander Rebellion, and they vowed not to let it happen again. "Those who denounce us go beyond their duty as clergymen," O'Mahony wrote.

Stephens urged his followers to obey the clergy on spiritual matters, but when it came to other subjects, to treat them as fellow citizens. "It was necessary to get the people, in my mind, to distinguish between the twofold character of the priest," he wrote, "to distinguish between their temporal and spiritual character."

❈

While generations of rebels in Ireland had been forced to drill with pikes and pitchforks by the light of the moon, the Fenians in America gained valuable military training with firearms. They served in volunteer militias, which became prevalent in the United States after the Mexican-American War. Irish American militia groups sprouted across the country.

By November 1859, O'Mahony had organized forty military regiments and companies with connections to the Fenian Brotherhood. However, he was no evangelizer. He rarely traveled from New York City to recruit new members, which led to growing tensions between him and Stephens. Meanwhile, Stephens boasted so often of his superior organizing efforts in Ireland that O'Mahony grew distrustful of the IRB leader's accounts.

O'Mahony traveled to Ireland at the end of 1860 to check on the rebellion's progress himself. After welcoming his counterpart to Dublin, Stephens immediately "reproached him in words of the most cutting sarcasm, telling him of his shortcomings, feebleness and insincerity," according to Denieffe. He capped the tirade with a reminder of how he "had dragged him out of obscurity and put him in a position he never dreamed of." The solidarity between the two men shaken, O'Mahony sailed for home in March 1861. He returned to a nation that had been divided in two.

3

The Civil War

THE FIRST BLOODSHED in the Civil War was Irish.

While the Union soldiers stationed at Fort Sumter all survived the thunderstorm of Confederate mortar shells and cannonballs that marked the start of the Civil War on April 12, 1861, they didn't emerge from the surrender ceremony unscathed. An accidental explosion during the firing of a one-hundred-gun salute to the Stars and Stripes killed two Irishmen.

The cause of death might have been a fluke, but the fatalities of two Irishmen in a Union outpost were not just some stroke of bad luck. Irish natives not only accounted for half of the sixteen-thousand-man regular army but outnumbered American-born soldiers inside Fort Sumter.

The fatalities reinforced John O'Mahony's worst fears that the Irish would perish while battling both fellow Americans and fellow Irishmen, instead of their true enemy, a concern shared by one Dublin newspaper. "Ireland will be more deeply, more mournfully, affected by the disasters in America, than any other country in the world. The lives of her exiled children will be offered in thousands," predicted *The Nation*.

Feeling a kinship with fellow rebels, approximately 20,000 Irish Americans joined the Confederate forces, while according to some estimates more than 200,000 Irishmen fought for the United States when factoring in volunteers in American territories, the Union army, and the Union navy—in which as many as 20 percent of the sailors were Irish-born.

Irish on both sides of the Mason-Dixon Line enlisted not just out of a sense of duty to the new land that took them in but to silence nativists who questioned their patriotism. For many, though, hungry stomachs and empty pockets offered the only necessary motivation. The Irish still struggled at the bottom of the American economy with unemployment among Irish males 25 percent higher in 1861 than during the panic of 1857. Sure, the job could bring death, but at least it paid.

To many Fenians and Irish republicans, enlistment offered the opportunity to gain valuable training for the eventual revolution they planned to launch in Ireland. The County Kilkenny native John O'Keeffe wrote that he joined the Union army to "learn the soldier trade in the hope that the knowledge we acquired might, in the future, be of service to the old land."

The Young Ireland veteran Thomas Francis Meagher echoed the sentiment. "It is a moral certainty that many of our countrymen who enlist in this struggle for the maintenance of the Union will fall in the contest. But, even so; I hold that if only one in ten of us come back when this war is over, the military experience gained by that *one* will be of more service in the fight for Ireland's freedom than would that of the entire ten as they are now."

O'Mahony, however, could be excused if he didn't quite see the long-term benefit of the Civil War as a proving ground for an Irish revolutionary army—not if it wiped out all of Ireland's Celtic warriors. Membership in both the Irish Republican Brotherhood and the Fenian Brotherhood had already stagnated, and now war pitted Irishman against Irishman. Fenianism appeared to teeter—until a dead man arose from the grave to give it new life.

❧

Even those who loathed the Irish could grudgingly admit one thing: They sure knew how to throw a funeral. Few good-byes in Irish history, however, rivaled the one the Fenians gave to Terence Bellew MacManus, the Young Irelander who fought alongside James Stephens in Widow McCormack's cabbage patch.

MacManus had also escaped from his captivity in Tasmania, having settled in San Francisco. There, the fifty-year-old bachelor died in poverty on January 15, 1861. Although his passing drew little notice outside Irish American newspapers, MacManus would not be permitted to rest in peace in San Francisco's Calvary Cemetery. The Fenian Brotherhood circle in San Francisco decided that the Irish patriot should be buried in native soil, and O'Mahony and Stephens foresaw the propaganda benefits of staging a transatlantic funeral procession with MacManus as the lifeless star of a Fenian pageant.

On August 19, 1861, seven months after the exile's burial, they excavated his grave and placed his remains inside a lavish rosewood coffin. Following a funeral Mass and a procession through the streets of San Francisco lined with many of the city's ten thousand Irish-born residents, the patriot's body sailed to New York City. On September 16, Archbishop John Joseph Hughes—in spite of past run-ins with Young Irelanders such as Meagher and John Mitchel—delivered remarks at a funeral Mass inside old St. Patrick's Cathedral, a task he was willing to undertake because MacManus never swore an oath to join the Fenian Brotherhood.

A month later, the corpse of MacManus sailed home to Ireland. On the cold, wet Sunday morning of November 10, Dubliners who knelt to their God in the morning stood for hours to venerate an Irish rebel's bones in the afternoon. According to Stephens, 150,000 people watched the massive funeral procession slog through ankle-deep mud along the seven-mile route to Glasnevin Cemetery, the vast necropolis on Dublin's northern outskirts where the city's Catholics had finally found the freedom and dignity in death that the British had so long denied them in life. In enveloping darkness, one of history's longest Irish wakes finally ended with the burial of MacManus beneath the gaze of the 160-foot-tall traditional Irish round tower that soared above the tomb of Daniel O'Connell, the great nationalist leader at whose behest the burial ground was established in 1832, at a time when the city's Catholics had no cemeteries in which their graveside services were permitted.

The Fenians basked in the largest outpouring of Irish nationalism since O'Connell's funeral fourteen years earlier. "The facecloth is removed from the dead nation, and lo! instead of a dead face the living lines of strength and resolve are seen! It was a great triumph," an ebullient Stephens wrote to O'Mahony.

❧

While the MacManus funeral invigorated IRB membership abroad, it had less of an impact in the United States, where Irish pocketbooks were understandably consumed by the Civil War. Unaware of the full extent of the difficulties confronting O'Mahony, Stephens continually ridiculed his American counterpart and demanded more money. "*One hundred and thirteen pounds from the whole American organization in a whole year!* I should look on this as a small sum *monthly*," Stephens castigated O'Mahony in April 1862. "It would pain you to hear all that is said about the American branch, and to know that *I* cannot conscientiously defend the conduct of our brothers yonder, especially since the funeral."

The conspiratorial mind that proved so adept in organizing a secret society failed Stephens in his relationships with American Fenians. Like a jealous lover, Stephens grew paranoid at what he considered long periods between the Fenian leader's communications. "No other living man would bear what I am bearing," he once complained about O'Mahony's infrequent letters.

Stephens grew so disgusted at the slow fund-raising pace that he took an unusual step for a secret society: He launched a newspaper. Hardly bothering to hide the enterprise, Stephens opened its offices mere steps away from Dublin Castle, the center of British power in Ireland. Stephens expected the newspaper to generate £5,000* a year. If it couldn't, he warned with typical bombast that the whole IRB could collapse. "The establishment of the paper had become a *necessity—a matter of life or death to the organization*," he later wrote.

The Irish People debuted on November 28, 1863, and all ten thousand copies sold out quickly. It was the IRB leader's second major undertaking that month. On November 11, he got married, shocking his followers who thought that Ireland was his only true love,

---

* The sum of £5,000 in 1863 is equivalent to more than $580,000 today. See www .uwyo.edu.

remembering his discouragements of nuptials or even lovemaking until the establishment of the Irish Republic.

Marriage proved an easier go than the newspaper business as *The Irish People* struggled to make money. The anticlerical tone of the sixteen-page newspaper caused the clergy to pressure parishioners not to sell copies in their retail establishments. Oftentimes, it lost money, forcing Stephens to tap his meager private funds to keep the printing press going.

❧

Although Stephens had stayed true to his demand to be a "provisional dictator" when the Fenians launched their transatlantic structure five years earlier, O'Mahony chafed at his subservient role. He wanted the Fenian Brotherhood to be more than simply the arsenal and money box for Ireland. He wanted a greater say in formulating policy.

Unwilling to submit to the "dictatorial arrogance" of Stephens any longer, O'Mahony decided to liberate himself and the Fenian Brotherhood. "As chief officer of the American organization, my powers must be put upon an even level with his authority over the Irish," he wrote of Stephens. "I will no longer consent to be accountable to him for my official conduct. We must treat as equal to equal, when it is necessary for us to treat at all." On October 19, 1863, O'Mahony resigned his position as supreme organizer and director of the IRB in America.

"I am sick—almost to death—of the man and his ways," Stephens wrote of O'Mahony. He complained that the Fenian Brotherhood leader had become a "standing drag-chain and stumbling-block" to the revolutionary efforts, and a growing number of Irish Americans agreed with him. A group of impatient Fenians, including James Gibbons of Philadelphia and Michael Scanlan of Chicago, who called themselves "men of action," forced O'Mahony to call the Fenians' first general convention.

On November 3, 1863, eighty-two delegates from twelve states and the District of Columbia, including a soldier who had recently lost a limb at the Battle of Gettysburg, gathered inside Chicago's Fenian Hall and proclaimed "the Republic of Ireland to be virtually established." Accordingly, the Fenian Brotherhood reorganized itself along the lines of a proper republican government by drafting a constitution that made several structural changes. The head center would now be an elected position and the executive and financial departments separated. Delegates unanimously returned O'Mahony to the head center position and approved his nominations of Gibbons, Scanlan, and three others to a new central council.

The Fenian Brotherhood also agreed to abandon its semisecret status. O'Mahony hoped the decision would put the Fenian Brotherhood "beyond the reach of hostile churchmen," but the changes did not appease the archbishops of Chicago and Philadelphia, who continued to condemn the Fenian Brotherhood as a secret society afoul of Catholic doctrine. Archbishop Peter Richard Kenrick of St. Louis reinforced to his flock that any members of the Fenian Brotherhood would be barred from receiving the sacraments of the church.

The structural changes did not satisfy these "men of action," either. Still frustrated at the slow pace of activity and fund-raising in the United States, they organized the Irish National Fair in Chicago in the early spring of 1864 without consulting O'Mahony. The two-week fair raised $54,000 for the purchase of weapons through the sale of handmade Irish goods—from blackthorn walking sticks to carved bog art—as well as Irish republican relics such as a window shutter handle from Theobald Wolfe Tone's Dublin residence and the silver crucifix placed on the coffin of MacManus when it lay in state.

The success of the fair bolstered the spirits of Stephens, who had accepted a personal invitation to attend. Departing Chicago, the IRB leader maintained a grueling recruiting and fund-raising schedule, with a new city each night—Milwaukee, Detroit, Toledo, Cleveland, Buffalo. Buoyed by the support he encountered on his tour, the Irishman felt confident enough to repeatedly declare to his American audiences, "Next year will be the year of action." Under the code name Captain James Daly, he visited Union army camps and, like many Fenian organizers, found them to be fertile recruiting grounds.

❧

Fenian circles arose in the Armies of the Potomac, Tennessee, and Cumberland and on the decks of the navy steamers USS *Port Royal* and USS *Brooklyn* as well as the frigates USS *New Ironsides* and USS *Huntsville*. Soldiers dropped their spare change into Fenian cash boxes nailed to trees, and the Union army even permitted Fenians to lay down their arms to attend their conventions.

While the Army of the Potomac made its winter quarters in Falmouth, Virginia, during the winter of 1863, an Irish newspaper editor serving as an emissary of Stephens—presumably Thomas Clarke Luby—rowed across the Rappahannock River from a Confederate camp and wandered into the Union camp with the permission of both Secretary of War Edwin Stanton and the Confederate secretary of state, Judah Benjamin. Several nights later, members of the Potomac circle were ushered from camp to a nearby ravine guarded by a Union sentry at one end, a Confederate sentinel at the other. Men in both blue and gray who had shot at each other a few weeks earlier during the fierce Battle of Fredericksburg now shook hands, pledged not to mention the Civil War, and listened to the emissary discuss where they could act in unison to strike the British.

As the war progressed, however, Irish Americans who buried their brethren by the thousands became increasingly disenchanted in its aims. The 1863 enactment of the Emancipation Proclamation had altered the stated goal of the conflict to include the liberation of the slaves, an unwelcome prospect for many poor Irish who feared that millions of African Americans would flood the labor market and take their unskilled jobs. Rather than empathize with another oppressed people, too many Irish let their fears blind them to the irony of their opposition to emancipation. After the institution of conscription in 1863, which allowed the wealthy to buy their way out of military service for $300, Irish frustrations with the war and their economic status boiled over in the New York City draft riots.

Through their sacrifice and service, the Irish demonstrated their patriotism to Americans. They just didn't expect to have to die in such numbers to do so. Even in a holocaust of unthinkable losses, the Irish suffered disproportionally terrible casualty rates, placed on the front lines to serve often as little more than cannon fodder. Much as it had in South Carolina at the start of the Civil War and on battlefields across the continent for four years, Celtic blood also soaked the Virginia soil at the war's conclusion, with an Irishman being the last Union general killed in the war.

❧

Five days after General Robert E. Lee's surrender, General Francis Frederick Millen boarded the steamship *Etna* on a mission to Ireland. The "year of action" promised by Stephens had now entered its spring, and the IRB head continued to insist he would launch the rebellion in Ireland by the end of 1865. O'Mahony and the Fenian Brotherhood's central council, however, remained skeptical of his claims to have 100,000 men ready to take the field within twenty-four hours.

O'Mahony dispatched three different soldiers to report on the IRB's true state of affairs. The arrival of the American inquisitors enraged Stephens, who told the Fenian Brotherhood leaders that he considered it "the deadliest blow ever aimed against us."

Stephens wrote that the choice facing the IRB was either war with the British in 1865 or dissolution. "The pledge given to the people must be redeemed. Else the movement is lost and with it, I am convinced, the cause of our race for ever." On the other side of the Atlantic, the Irish who fought for both the Union and the Confederacy also looked ahead to the next war, the one they truly wanted to wage. And as the Civil War drew to its conclusion, the Irish were not the only ones eager to point their guns at the British.

❧

The United States had contracted a severe case of Anglophobia as a result of the tacit support given by Great Britain to the Confederacy. Relations first soured in May 1861, when the British declared their neutrality during the Civil War, which granted belligerent rights to the Confederacy. Six months later, war nearly broke out between the United States and Great Britain after an American frigate seized two Confederate envoys from the unarmed British mail steamer *Trent* while in international waters.

In spite of their professed neutrality, the British built blockade runners that kept Southern ports supplied and forged Armstrong guns that mowed down Union troops. Shipyards in Liverpool built, equipped, and armed Confederate warships that seized American goods and burned their whalers. British crews sporting fake Southern accents even manned the vessels.

British hands had built the most fearsome ship afloat, the CSS *Alabama*. For nearly two years, the Confederate warship had prowled the seven seas in search of nautical prey. As part of a guerrilla war against Union merchant shipping, the commerce raider flying both the Confederate Stars and Bars and an English flag terrorized Union shipping lanes from Newfoundland to Sumatra until it sank in a June 1864 naval battle outside Cherbourg, France. The half-Confederate, half-English crew captured or destroyed more than sixty American ships and inflicted more than $5 million worth of losses. By the end of the Civil War, the United States demanded millions of dollars in reparations from Great Britain—the so-called *Alabama* claims—for the damage inflicted by the Confederate warships built in their ports.

Further inflaming Americans' attitudes toward their former motherland, the British colony of Canada harbored not only Union draft dodgers but also Confederate spies and operatives who exported terror across the border. From their safe haven in Canada, Confederates launched raids on border towns in Maine and Vermont. They carried out a failed attack by arson squads to set New York City aflame, and some suspected their involvement in President Abraham Lincoln's murder. Eyewitnesses claimed to have seen the assassin John Wilkes Booth in Montreal days before he shot the American president, and authorities found a bank receipt from the Royal Ontario Bank in his possession after the assassination. In the days following the shooting, the conspirator John Surratt Jr. fled north, where a Catholic priest in southern Quebec gave him sanctuary before he absconded to Liverpool.

By the end of the Civil War, Anglo-American relations were at their worst since the redcoats torched the nation's capital half a century earlier. When Queen Victoria sat down to her diary on February 12, 1865, she noted that during the day she had discussed "America and the danger, which seems approaching, of our having a war with her as soon as she makes peace; of the impossibility of our being able to hold Canada."

Much of the Union sought to engage with the British. But the United States was exhausted after four years of war, and it faced the daunting job of healing wounds and reintegrating the South. In the Fenians, however, America had a perfect vessel through which it could outsource its revenge. The British Empire had a debt to pay, and the Americans weren't above using the Fenians as leverage in order to collect it.

4

Torn Between Brothers

As James Stephens continued to promise "war or dissolution in 1865," General Francis Frederick Millen reported to John O'Mahony that "between June and September barely a steamer arrived" in Ireland "that did not bring fifteen of these fighting Irishmen." According to Millen, some of the Civil War veterans were experienced officers; "others had lived loafing round the bar-rooms and engine-houses of New York—equally ready to cut a pack of cards or a throat."

When the British government became aware of the influx of Fenians, it began to screen Irish-looking passengers arriving on steamers from the United States. If their accents didn't betray the Fenians, their fashion often did. British authorities kept such watchful eyes for the double-breasted vests, felt hats, and square-toed shoes so popular in America that Colonel Thomas Kelly urged Fenians to leave those items at home to avoid suspicion.

On September 15, the police stormed through the front door of *The Irish People,* seizing books and ledgers. Across Dublin, the authorities arrested more than a dozen *Irish People* staffers and Irish Republican Brotherhood leaders, including Thomas Clarke Luby. In a drawer of Luby's nightstand, police found an envelope of incriminating IRB documents that would lead to several convictions, including his own. The authorities charged the Fenians with treason felony and attempting to levy war upon the Crown, which was later increased to high treason, punishable by death. In addition to decapitating the IRB leadership, the authorities seized £5,000 of the Fenians' money and froze the IRB's bank account.

Stephens managed to evade capture, fleeing to a safe house in the Dublin suburbs. His advisers urged him to launch his uprising before the British could cripple the entire organization, but Stephens decided now was not the time for action. "Had we been prepared," he wrote to O'Mahony the day after the raid, "*last* night would have marked an epoch in our history. *But we were not prepared;* and so I had to issue an order that *all should go home.*"

With a £2,300 reward for his capture, Stephens went into hiding. He had given clear instructions to O'Mahony in the event of his taking. "Once you hear of my arrest, only a single course remains to you," he wrote. "Gather all the fighting men you [can] about you, and then sail for Ireland."

※

General Thomas William Sweeny picked up his pen with his left hand (his only hand), dated his letter October 12, 1865, and requested a twenty-day leave of absence from the Union army to attend to private business in New York. After the granting of his petition, the veteran of two American wars departed Nashville to attend to his affairs, which were hardly private and not in New York but in Philadelphia, where more than six hundred delegates assembled for the Fenian Brotherhood's third general convention.

Few Americans embodied the spirit of the "fighting Irish" more than Sweeny. Leaving Ireland as an eleven-year-old, he survived thirty minutes in the Atlantic Ocean after being washed overboard during a storm on his voyage to the United States. After joining the nearly five thousand Irish-born soldiers who fought for the U.S. Army in the Mexican-American War, "Fightin' Tom" rose to the rank of second lieutenant. During the 1847 Battle of Churubusco, Sweeny took a bullet to the groin, but still he refused to abandon his men. Minutes later, a ball pierced his right arm so completely that it had to be amputated.

Rather than wallow in self-pity, Sweeny simply folded over the empty right sleeve of his uniform jacket and continued to serve in the Second U.S. Infantry, even whipping his commanding officer in a fistfight with just his one good arm. During the Civil War, Sweeny rose to the rank of brigadier general and, according to General William Tecumseh Sherman, "saved the day" commanding a brigade at the 1862 Battle of Shiloh in spite of taking two gunshots to his remaining arm and one to the leg.

The career officer joined the Fenian Brotherhood while on garrison duty in Nashville. He wrote that his military service was "a school for the ultimate realization of the darling object of his heart"—Irish independence.

When he entered the convention hall in Philadelphia in the middle of October, Sweeny was the highest-profile Civil War general to align himself with the

The one-armed general Thomas Sweeny left the U.S. Army to serve as the Fenian Brotherhood's secretary of war and draw up plans for the invasion of Canada.

Fenian Brotherhood. Assembling just blocks away from where the Founding Fathers drafted the Declaration of Independence ninety years earlier, he and his fellow Fenians hoped for inspiration in their efforts to cast off the same tyrannical government across the ocean.

The convention's record attendance testified to a surge of interest in the Fenian cause after the Civil War's conclusion, particularly among those like Sweeny who were drawn to the more militant "men of action" and who sought democratic reforms to check O'Mahony's power. In addition to approving a new constitution with a familiar-sounding preamble, "We, the Fenians of the United States," the congress replaced the central council, whose members had been nominated by the executive, with an unpaid fifteen-person senate elected by the delegates. To curb the power of the executive, whose title changed from head center to president, the senate was given the ability to approve cabinet nominations and overrule presidential decisions with a two-thirds vote.

Delegates reelected O'Mahony as their executive. In case of his death, impeachment, or resignation, power would now fall to the president of the senate, a role filled by William Roberts, a splendid orator and one of the "men of action." The thirty-five-year-old had arrived in New York in 1849. After working for nearly a decade for A. T. Stewart's dry-goods emporium, Roberts launched his own successful store. His Crystal Palace Emporium on the Bowery advertised "cheap goods, at the real cost price, and no humbug."

As he filled out his cabinet, O'Mahony appointed Sweeny his secretary of war and general commanding the "Army of the Irish Republic." He was relieved to have an experienced hand to pull together the plan for the invasion of Ireland, which might have to be implemented soon if the British tracked down Stephens.

For his part, Sweeny asserted his belief in striking where the enemy "was most vulnerable and where victory would give us the most real positive advantage," a notion with which O'Mahony could hardly disagree. However, unlike his fellow Fenian, Sweeny wasn't referring to Ireland.

❧

Sweeny believed the idea of launching a transatlantic operation to support an uprising in Ireland would be logistically impossible, particularly because the Fenians lacked a navy.

So why not strike the British where they were closer, more vulnerable, and more easily attacked? "The Canadian frontier, extending from the mouth of the St. Lawrence River to Lake Huron, a distance of more than 1,300 miles, is assailable at all points," Sweeny wrote. The lightly defended border with Canada, which had only one-tenth of the population of the United States, was a lawless no-man's-land frequented by counterfeiters, transnational criminals, and outlaw gangs smuggling alcohol, produce, opium, and even livestock by wagons, boats, and sleighs. The migration of fugitive slaves, draft dodgers, and Confederate agents to Canada during the Civil War proved just how porous it was.

Sweeny's idea, backed by Roberts and the "men of action," called for the Fenians to establish a foothold in Canada that would allow it to be granted belligerent rights by the United States, and to issue letters of marque to privateers to attack British merchant ships. They could then use Canada as a base of operations to launch a naval program that could be successful in attacking the British overseas.

The Canadian plan offered several scenarios that could result in Ireland's independence. An attack could divert British army troops from Ireland, increasing the chances of a successful IRB uprising. It could perhaps even trigger a war between Great Britain and the United States, which had cast its land-hungry eyes northward after having expanded west and south in the prior three decades. Under another scenario, the Fenians could seize Canada and trade the colony back to the British in return for Ireland. In essence, a geopolitical kidnapping of Canada, with its ransom being Ireland's independence.

Even the plan's proponents understood that the chances of success weren't in their favor. But the odds would be against the Irish no matter what they did. A slim chance is all Ireland ever faced when challenging the British over the past seven centuries. The likelihood of failure might have been high, but it was guaranteed if they did nothing at all.

⚜

Invading Canada might have sounded outrageous to some, but it followed a long American tradition of attacking the British colony. In fact, the United States had yet to even declare its independence from Great Britain when the Continental army attacked Canada in the late summer of 1775.

After marching north from Lake Champlain and seizing Montreal, the Dublin-born general Richard Montgomery continued on to the outskirts of Quebec City, where in December 1775 he united with Colonel Benedict Arnold, who had marched north through Maine. With the enlistments of many soldiers expiring the next day, the Continental army attacked during a New Year's Eve blizzard and suffered a terrible defeat, failing to gain a stronghold on the St. Lawrence River to control the movement of goods and troops. The patriots erroneously expected to receive the support of the French Canadians in their operation, a mistake that Americans would often repeat.

After declaring war on Great Britain in 1812, the United States planned a three-pronged invasion of Canada in which it expected to be greeted as liberators, not marauders. "The acquisition of

Canada . . . will be a mere matter of marching," promised the former president Thomas Jefferson. It wasn't.

The U.S. general William Hull's attack across the Detroit River in the first weeks of the War of 1812 proved disastrous, and he surrendered his entire army without firing a single shot. General Henry Dearborn abandoned his plans to strike Montreal before the attack could even be launched, while General Stephen Van Rensselaer's attack across the Niagara River ended in defeat at the Battle of Queenston Heights.

A quarter century later, Americans became involved in a series of failed populist uprisings that killed hundreds in Canada in the Patriot War of 1837 and 1838. In Quebec, Francophones excluded from power rebelled against English-speaking elites, while reformers in Ontario rebelled against the aristocracy over political patronage and corruption.

Rebel leaders who fled to the United States during the Patriot War found considerable support for their democratic aspirations. Secret "Hunters' Lodges" dedicated to liberating Canada from British rule sprouted along the northern border of the United States, causing President Martin Van Buren to warn American sympathizers to obey the country's neutrality laws. In November 1838, approximately three hundred "Hunter Patriot" insurgents, soldiers originally from both sides of the border, crossed the St. Lawrence River, only to be defeated at the Battle of the Windmill.

In the ensuing years, farcical disputes with equally ridiculous names flared along the border. In the final days of 1838, American lumberjacks spotted their Canadian counterparts chopping down trees in disputed territories of Maine and New Brunswick near the Aroostook River, setting off the bloodless Pork and Beans War (named for the lumberjacks' meal of choice). Both Maine and New Brunswick sent militias to the border region, followed by the arrival of British forces from the Caribbean and congressional authorization for the dispatch of a fifty-thousand-man force. The arrival of Brigadier General Winfield Scott finally defused the tension, but the dispute led to a negotiated settlement of the border between the United States and Great Britain under the 1842 Webster-Ashburton Treaty.

Farther west, other portions of the boundary between Canada and the United States remained in dispute. The war cry "Fifty-four forty or fight" carried James Polk to the White House in 1844 as expansionists sought a far-northern latitude for the Oregon Territory. The subsequent Oregon Treaty settled on the 49th parallel as the international boundary, but it did not address the status of the San Juan Islands between Seattle and Vancouver, which continued to be claimed by both Great Britain and the United States.

In June 1859 on San Juan Island, the American Lyman Cutlar shot dead a pig dining on the potatoes in his garden that belonged to a ranch manager for the Canadian Hudson's Bay Company. The situation quickly escalated. British authorities threatened Cutlar with arrest and evicted seventeen of his countrymen from the island. President James Buchanan sent troops in response. The British retaliated; their arms race continued until five hundred American troops and two thousand British aboard five warships kept watch over San Juan Island.

While the British governor of Vancouver Island urged an attack, the British rear admiral Robert L. Baynes refused to "involve two great nations in a war over a squabble about a pig." And once again, General Scott was dispatched to calm the situation, serving as a military sedative to soothe the frayed nerves. Great Britain and the United States eventually agreed to a joint occupation of the island until the settlement of the water boundary.

At the close of the Civil War, the Fenians weren't the only Americans thinking about an attack on Canada. After Appomattox, Senator Zach Chandler of Michigan developed a plan to dispatch 200,000 Civil War veterans—100,000 each from Grant's and Lee's armies—to confiscate Canada as compensation for the *Alabama* claims.

"If we could march into Canada an army composed of men who have worn the gray side by side with the men who have worn the blue to fight against a common hereditary enemy," Chandler said, "it would do much to heal the wounds of the war, hasten reconstruction, and weld the North and South together by a bond of friendship." Thirty senators signed off on the plan, but it derailed after Lincoln's assassination.

This is all to say that in the 1860s an American invasion of Canada might not have sounded as ridiculous to American ears as it does to those today. It would receive a further shot in the arm from an unlikely and influential source.

The Civil War had decimated John Mitchel, much as it had his newly beloved South. He lost two sons in 1863, one at Fort Sumter and the other at Gettysburg. A third boy lost his arm in the war. The news, however, could not dampen his fiery rhetoric toward the American government, which arrested him in June 1865 on the vague charge of "aiding the rebellion" and consigned him to Virginia's Fortress Monroe, where he was jailed with his friend the former Confederate president Jefferson Davis, whom he had visited frequently at the Confederate White House.

Even those who vehemently disagreed with the Irishman's slavery stance had to wonder why General Lee remained free while Mitchel languished behind bars. Having gained O'Mahony's approval, the St. Louis Fenian Bernard Doran Killian traveled to the nation's capital to personally lobby President Andrew Johnson and the U.S. secretary of state William Seward for his release.

During his White House audience on October 13, Killian raised the prospect of a hypothetical Fenian invasion of Canada and seizure of Canadian territory south of the St. Lawrence River, in order to gauge the potential reaction of the American government. According to Killian's account (the only one that exists), the pair told him that they would "acknowledge accomplished facts," in spite of American neutrality laws. In other words, they wouldn't endorse a Canadian invasion per se, but they wouldn't interfere with one either.

For its part, the Johnson administration saw value in a Fenian invasion. It could be used to pressure Great Britain in the government's quest to extract millions of dollars in reparations for the *Alabama* claims. Plus, with the future of Reconstruction at stake, Johnson saw a chance to earn the goodwill of the country's 1.6 million Irish voters.

The Fenians would hang their expectation of American support on Killian's account of the White House meeting, which he brought back to the Philadelphia convention along with news of Johnson's agreement to release Mitchel, who subsequently spent a year in Paris as a financial agent funneling money from the Fenian Brotherhood to the IRB. Their nascent idea was gaining life.

The most wanted man in the British Empire slumbered as a posse of policemen surrounded his hideout around 6:00 a.m. on November 11. A suspicious neighbor had noticed that "Mr. Herbert," said to be a well-to-do gentleman of private fortune and a son of a Kilkenny reverend, made only nocturnal excursions, while numerous parcels arrived for him every day. When police began to monitor the house, they saw the fugitive's wife, Jane Stephens, entering and exiting the villa.

Scaling the high wall surrounding the property, the police closed in as Inspector Hughes rapped on the door. Eventually, they heard the voice of Stephens from the other side of the door asking if it was the gardener. When he heard that it was the police, Stephens ran to a front window and saw the house surrounded. With no escape, he opened the door and was taken into custody. Mrs. Stephens asked her husband whether she could visit him in prison, which he quickly dismissed. "You cannot visit me in prison without asking permission of British officials," he barked, "and I do not think it becoming in one so near to me as you are to ask favors of British dogs. You must not do it—I forbid it."

The police loaded Stephens and three Fenians sleeping in adjacent rooms into a police van and galloped away to Dublin Castle before the IRB leader's transfer to Richmond Bridewell Prison. While past political prisoners such as William Smith O'Brien, Thomas Francis Meagher, and Daniel O'Connell resided in the governor's residence at Richmond Bridewell Prison, Stephens received no such privilege. He remained with the general population, which was subjected to the particularly cruel Victorian punishment of the treadwheel, a contraption on which prisoners walked in place on the planks of a large paddle wheel that turned gears pumping water or crushing grain. Over the course of a monotonous eight-hour shift, a prisoner could scale the equivalent of seventy-two hundred feet, twice the height of Ireland's tallest peak.

Two weeks after his arrest, Stephens heard a key rattling in his cell door. John Breslin, an orderly in the prison hospital and brother of an IRB member, entered and handed Stephens a six-chambered revolver. Along with the prison turnkey and IRB member Daniel Byrne, Breslin had taken beeswax impressions of the six keys needed to get Stephens outside and given them to an optician to manufacture duplicates, which he filed down until they worked.

Fleeing through the prison yard, Stephens scaled the prison wall, using a knotted rope that had been thrown over by a nine-man rescue team led by Kelly, the American envoy who had become a Stephens confidant. Stephens hauled his body up and saw the drop on the other side. Although he was nervous, the rescue team told him to jump, so Stephens fell into the arms of his fellow Fenians.

It was a daring and effective escape, but Stephens's comportment affected at least one of its participants. He "shook like a dog in a wet sack," reported John Devoy, a twenty-three-year-old IRB operative who had recruited the rescue team. It was in that moment he began to question the IRB leader's nerve.

❀

The news of Stephens's escape shook the British Isles. Not only was the man who promised a rebellion by the end of the year free once again, but the authorities wondered if there was any place in Ireland that the Fenians had not infiltrated.

The authorities offered a £2,000 reward for the Irishman's capture. They papered Dublin with his description, oddly citing his twitching left eye, as well as that his hands and feet were "remarkably small and well formed." Just as in 1848, Stephens was a fugitive.

He didn't take flight into the Irish countryside this time. Far from it. In fact, not only did he remain in Dublin, but he could see the prison from which he had just escaped from the chamber window of his temporary hideout.

Stephens's top advisers, especially the Fenians who had traveled to Ireland from the United States, implored him that this was the moment to fight. But the IRB leader stalled. Just like when he stood on the barricade in 1848 with a rifle in his hand, just as he had the night of the *Irish People* raid, Stephens didn't take the shot.

The Fenians, particularly those who had come from America, felt betrayed. "I do not know him to be a liar at all, though I do not take him to be very scrupulous about the truth," wrote John O'Leary. "I'd believe little he said on his mere word, but that is because I believe he very easily deceives himself."

The decision not to fight sparked not just incredulity among some Fenians but also the rumor that Stephens must be a British spy who was given his freedom in return for becoming a double agent. It was, many felt, the most plausible explanation for how he managed to break out of Ireland's most secure prison and elude arrest.

Stephens alone had pledged that 1865 would be the year of action. Instead, Irish republicans resigned themselves to yet another year chained to the British. In Ireland and abroad, a restlessness began to grow.

❧

Like a lodestar at night, a green Fenian banner emblazoned with a golden sunburst whipped in the November sky from atop a four-story brownstone. It guided O'Mahony to his organization's palatial new headquarters at 32 East Seventeenth Street on the northern edge of Manhattan's Union Square.

Tasked by the Fenian senate with leasing a new headquarters commensurate with its self-importance, Roberts, Sweeny, and Killian chose Moffat Mansion, one of New York's plushest properties. In mid-November, the Fenians moved uptown from their cramped Duane Street quarters, huddled among saloons, tattoo parlors, and boardinghouses. Now they rubbed shoulders with the elegant Everett House hotel.

Sunlight poured through Moffat Mansion's stained-glass windows, casting colorful rays on the frescoes, sculptures, paintings, and coats of arms adorning the walls. Behind the great glass folding door of the reception room sat cabinet secretaries and senators eager for an audience with the president. In adjoining rooms, treasury department clerks counted incoming donations and paid bills.

The Fenians thought their opulent accommodations were symbolic of their emergence on the world stage. Respectability came at a price, however. They leased the "Fenian White House" for eighteen months at a cost of $18,000 paid in advance. They also emptied the treasury of $5,000 to be placed as a security against damages. On top of the rent, the Fenians spent several thousand dollars to purchase rosewood desks, luxurious carpets, and armchairs upholstered in green and gold.

For a man comfortable wearing threadbare clothing and living in rude apartments like the one he shared with Stephens in Paris, O'Mahony could only shake his head at the lavish expense and mutter to a friend that he feared "it might prove the tomb of the

In November 1865, the Fenian Brotherhood moved
its headquarters into the plush Moffat Mansion on
the north side of Manhattan's Union Square.

Fenian movement." On the second floor, O'Mahony navigated his
way through the traffic of scurrying clerks filing correspondence and
transmitting presidential orders and entered his private office. While
Sweeny and the ordnance bureau, corps of engineers, and rest of
the war department on the third floor pored over maps, organized
a secret service corps in Canada, and crafted the plan for attacking
America's northern neighbor, O'Mahony followed the directive that
Stephens issued two months earlier to gather all the fighting men
he could and sail for Ireland as soon as he learned of his capture.

Like any self-respecting government, the provisional government
of the Irish Republic in exile now had its own declaration of independence, its own constitution, its own president and senate, its
own army, and now its own grand capitol. The Fenians even issued
their own bond notes in denominations of $10, $20, $50, $100, and

$500. Printed in green and black, the bonds featured patriotic symbols including a harp, an Irish round tower, and portraits of Irish nationalist heroes such as Robert Emmet and Theobald Wolfe Tone. In the center of the bond, a woman representing Erin, with an Irish wolfhound at her feet, pointed with her left hand to a distant sunburst rising over Ireland and with her right to an unsheathed sword on the ground, about to be grasped by an Irish soldier. The bonds could be redeemed six months after the establishment of the Irish Republic with interest at 6 percent a year.*

Despite its grand appearances, all was not well at Moffat Mansion, which was rife with tension from the day the Fenians first arrived. O'Mahony continued to feud with the senate over its war strategy. Stephens learned of the estrangement, and he threw his backing behind his fellow Young Irelander, no matter what grievances he might have had with him. Stephens condemned Sweeny's proposed Canadian foray as a "traitorous diversion from the right path."

The division erupted into an irreparable schism over the issue of the Fenian bonds. After O'Mahony ordered Killian, the Fenian treasurer, to deny Sweeny's request for money to purchase guns for a Canadian attack, the Fenian bond agent, Patrick Keenan, resigned his position at the senate's behest, meaning that no further bonds could be issued.

Believing the situation in Ireland to be an emergency, O'Mahony proceeded to issue bonds with his signature on them, although he lacked the constitutional authority to do so. The senate drew up articles of impeachment against O'Mahony in response, charging him with violating the Fenian constitution, engaging in financial irregularities, and lining his own pockets by drawing the $1,200 annual salary of the bond agent in addition to the president's $2,000 yearly payment. The senators accused O'Mahony of extravagant spending, pointing to Moffat Mansion as the prime example (although the decision to rent the property was clearly more theirs than his).

The Fenian Brotherhood had managed to survive the Civil War

---

* Following the establishment of the Irish Free State in 1922, there were bondholders who unsuccessfully lobbied the new government to honor the bonds issued by the Fenian treasury.

intact, only to now tear itself apart. Meeting in special session, the senate removed O'Mahony from the presidency for eleven specific violations of his oath of office and replaced him with Roberts, the senate president. Having shepherded the Fenian Brotherhood since its inception, O'Mahony was hardly about to step aside without a fight. He retaliated by expelling Roberts and Keenan from the Fenian Brotherhood, seizing control of the treasury and the keys to Moffat Mansion. The so-called Roberts wing formed its own competing Irish Republic government in exile, with headquarters on Broadway, just around the corner from Moffat Mansion.

The Irish Republic might not have had land of its own, but it now had two headquarters, two presidents, and two divergent plans for freeing Ireland.

❦

Across North America, the Fenian movement cleaved into competing circles: those loyal to Roberts or O'Mahony. While East Coast Fenians tended to remain with O'Mahony, the Roberts wing found its base of support in the Midwest. For some, the decision was not easy. F. B. McNamee reported that his circle in Montreal was "ready to 'go in,' for which ever party is in the field first."

Although the Fenian movement was pulling itself apart, the British remained concerned with the American government's coddling of the Irishmen, in particular the War Department's decision to grant Sweeny a leave of absence from the military to plot an attack against them. "It seems to me that he ought to be called to choose between the North American and the Irish Republic," Sir Frederick Bruce, the British minister to Washington, D.C., complained to Seward. "The effect of his acting as Secretary of War is to confirm the Fenian dupes in the belief that the Government of the United States favors the movement."

The British protest might have been what led to the denial of Sweeny's request for a six-month leave of absence and his dismissal from the Union army on Christmas Day. Sweeny had given twenty years of his life—and one limb—in service of the United States, but the call of his homeland was powerful enough that he was willing to walk away.

One day after celebrating the arrival of the new year of 1866, six hundred delegates of the O'Mahony wing congregated in New York's Clinton Hall. The convention rescinded the Fenian constitution, which had been agreed to in Philadelphia just four months earlier, and reverted to the prior one drafted at the 1863 convention in Chicago. This meant that O'Mahony would be reinstated as head center, advised by a five-man council elected by the congress. The convention also approved a resolution endorsing war in Ireland— and only Ireland.

❁

Sweeny and Roberts—both Protestants—captured headlines as they visited Irish enclaves from New York to Illinois to Tennessee, loudly pronouncing their intention to attack Canada by July. The duo relished these public events. Sweeny's charisma combined with Roberts's oratorical skills generated excitement and sold out theaters.

By the time the Roberts wing held its own convention behind the closed doors of Pittsburgh's Masonic Hall in February, it had stolen the headlines from the O'Mahony wing. Many Irish Americans agreed with Sweeny that the Roberts wing had "the only feasible plan to the liberation of Ireland." Sweeny there unveiled his war plan to attack Canada. The measure was overwhelmingly adopted. "We promise that before the summer sun kisses the hilltops of Ireland," Sweeny thundered, "a ray of hope will gladden every true Irish heart, for by that time we shall have conquered and got hostages for our brave patriots at home."

Following the convention, the Roberts wing grew its membership through a

A native of Ireland, the dry-goods magnate William Roberts favored an invasion of Canada and led the senate wing after its break with John O'Mahony, who advocated a Fenian uprising in Ireland.

network of salaried recruiters and organizers who evangelized for the Fenian cause in hopes of getting the Irish to open their wallets and establish new circles. These "missionaries" visited mining towns and mill cities for weeks at a time, traveling by train to a different locale each night. They tugged on the emotional strings of the Irish in events that mirrored revival meetings, with brass bands and Irish jigs as entertainment.

The Fenian Brotherhood held a particular appeal to Irish immigrants in rural areas of the Midwest and the West that lacked the political machines, parishes, and immigrant aid societies that bound the Irish together in the big cities of the East. Like other Irish fraternal organizations, the Fenian Brotherhood offered a sense of community. While some joined out of a desire to free their homeland, others did so primarily to maintain their ethnic identity and meet fellow Irishmen.

Fenian organizers, though, continued to battle clerical opposition. In Sharon, Pennsylvania, fifteen young men had been ready to start a circle until, as one Irishman reported, "Father O'Keefe spoke of the Fenians last Sunday and call[ed] us children of hell and said that he was ordered by the Bishop of Erie to stop our progress."

Thanks to the work of the organizers, the momentum in the Irish republican movement resided with the Roberts wing in early 1866. Events in Ireland, however, would give both American factions a jolt of energy.

❦

Nearly three months after his prison escape, Stephens remained on the loose, hundreds of Civil War veterans from America loitered about Ireland, and the British government remained fearful of a possible uprising. On February 17, 1866, the British government suspended habeas corpus in Ireland, allowing suspicious persons to be detained without reason. The British prime minister, Lord John Russell, told Parliament the move was necessary to address the threat of violence being imported from the United States.

The following morning, a squad of nearly fifty detectives met at dawn and fanned out around Dublin rounding up Irish Americans, many of whom had no apparent employment yet never seemed to lack for money as they stayed at respectable hotels. Colonel John W.

Byron was even arrested at a Lower Gloucester Street brothel. In Dublin alone, authorities locked up 150 Irishmen, one-third of them natural-born or naturalized American citizens suspected of Fenian activity. Similar scenes occurred in Tipperary, Limerick, Cork, Belfast, and Sligo.

The crackdown further inflamed anti-British passions among Americans, causing Seward to lodge a protest about the treatment of his fellow citizens. O'Mahony called on all Irishmen in the New York area to attend a massive protest at the Jones's Wood estate, a popular Manhattan picnic ground along the East River, on the Sunday afternoon of March 4. That morning, New York's archbishop, John McCloskey, had denounced the Fenians from the pulpit of old St. Patrick's Cathedral and called on all God-fearing Catholics to stay away from the afternoon's event, which he called "a profanation of the Lord's Day." He warned that attendance would provoke "the anger of God."

If he was right, the Almighty would have been quite upset that afternoon. Even on a wintry day, 100,000 Fenians—most of them members of the Catholic flock—gathered in the pastures of Jones's Wood. "When the priests descend into the arena of worldly politics they throw off their sacred robes," O'Mahony had asserted. The turnout showed that the Fenians had succeeded in training many Catholics to disregard the clergy in political matters.

As snowflakes began to fall and the wind grew more biting, Fenians reached into their pockets, purchasing bond after bond to fund the establishment of the Irish Republic. Mass meetings were held in many other American cities, and for days afterward money poured into Moffat Mansion.

❖

Nothing happened along Canada's frontier with the United States without Gilbert McMicken knowing about it. During the Civil War, he had organized Canada's first secret service to monitor Confederate activities along the frontier. Now the spymaster had been directed by John A. Macdonald, the province's joint premier, to keep a close surveillance of all Fenian activities.

Having dispatched agents to infiltrate Fenian circles—and even going undercover himself to a Fenian congress—McMicken had received reports of suspicious-looking Irishmen crossing the border in advance of an imminent invasion. One of his agents monitoring the Fenians said that they planned to attack on March 17— St. Patrick's Day.

Rumors flew that the Fenians planned to dispatch three ironclads to Halifax, poison the reservoirs of Montreal, and infect Canadian hogs with trichinosis. President Johnson had been less than transparent when he assured Bruce in January 1866 that the Fenians "met with no sympathy on the part of the Government, which on the contrary was anxious to discourage it." Canadians were skeptical of such claims. In response to the reports, authorities called out ten thousand volunteers, and civic authorities in Toronto, Ottawa, and Montreal canceled their official St. Patrick's Day parades.

At the White House, the cabinet debated how to handle the situation. Secretary of War Edwin Stanton advocated for Johnson to issue a presidential proclamation warning citizens against violations of the neutrality laws, much as President Martin Van Buren had done during the Patriot War of 1837. Secretary of the Navy Gideon Welles argued that Lieutenant General Ulysses S. Grant should instead be consulted and sent to the Canadian frontier.

Welles had his way and the task fell to Grant, who ordered Major General George Meade, the hero of Gettysburg who now served as commander of the Military Division of the Atlantic, to "use all vigilance to prevent armed or hostile forces or organizations from leaving the United States" and attacking Canada. Not that Grant was enthusiastic about the mission. "During our late troubles neither the British Government or the Canadian officials gave themselves much trouble to prevent hostilities being organized against the United States from their possessions," Grant wrote to Meade. "But two wrongs never make a right and it is our duty to prevent wrong on the part of our people."

Meade directed Major General Joseph Hooker to seize arms, munitions, and contraband of war that could be found along the frontier, though he didn't see how he could stop an Irish invasion without very considerable reinforcements, because there were fewer than four hundred soldiers along the border in New York and none in New England.

When St. Patrick's Day arrived, America's northern border

remained quiet. The only Irishmen marching through the streets of Montreal did so to greet the governor-general, the queen's representative in Canada, with cheers. Canadians breathed a sigh of relief as the Fenian threat appeared to pass. "I do not think Sweeny will trouble you for some time to come. Your preparations have evidently dampened the Fenian ardor," wrote Edward Archibald, the British consul in New York, to a Canadian official.

Canada might have remained quiet on March 17, but the Irish celebrated loudly on the streets of New York. The first St. Patrick's Day since the end of the Civil War slaughter always promised to be enthusiastic, but the British suspension of habeas corpus in the homeland had put an extra determination in the steps of the thirty thousand Celtic marchers. It appeared that every Irishman in New York was joining in the celebration—except for one notable Fenian.

5

The Eastport Fizzle

FEW IRISHMEN IN New York were having a less enjoyable St. Patrick's Day than John O'Mahony. While the cheers of revelers and the melodies of military bands fluttered through Moffat Mansion, the Fenian head center remained sequestered inside, engaged in a tortured grapple with his soul.

On front pages and on balance sheets, O'Mahony's faction had been eclipsed by the Roberts wing, which offered the Irish a more immediate return on their investments with its plan to attack Canada. Around the corner from Moffat Mansion, the Broadway headquarters of William Roberts and his radical upstarts remained open eighteen hours a day, money gushing through the door. Just the day before, a *New York Herald* reporter watched as $3,000 in donations arrived in just twenty minutes.

O'Mahony had heard the complaints from impatient members who warned that his lack of action could doom their wing of the Fenian Brotherhood. He felt his movement slipping away.

In no mood to parade along with his fellow members of the Ninety-Ninth New York Regiment, O'Mahony chaired an emergency meeting of the central council to figure out how to regain the upper hand. The head center's closest adviser told him he had a solution, but it meant doing the one thing he pledged never to do.

Behind the doors of the Fenian White House, O'Mahony listened as Bernard Doran Killian proposed a drastic change in strategy. The portly treasury secretary told the Fenians they should seize Campobello Island, which sat in Canadian waters across a narrow channel from the far-northeastern corner of Maine. During the American Revolution, the island provided a sanctuary for British Loyalists, and after betraying his country, the traitor Benedict Arnold oversaw a vast smuggling operation from its shores.

Killian argued that the Fenians could use the island of fifteen hundred people as a base from which to launch an invasion of Ireland. It could allow them to gain belligerent status, just as the Confederacy had, to issue letters of marque to privateers without violating international law or the U.S. Neutrality Act. By moving first, a successful venture would preempt the Canadian plan of Thomas Sweeny and Roberts and allow the O'Mahony wing to regain its place at the vanguard of the revolutionary movement.

Killian reportedly assured the central council that Campobello Island was "neutral territory, claimed alike by Great Britain and the United States, while no clear title to its ownership had been established by either." (Little research would have been necessary to confirm that this was incorrect. It most definitely belonged to the British.)

Having spent months concocting his plan, Killian assured his fellow Fenians they would find sympathetic allies in New Brunswick, where one-third of the province's residents had Irish roots. Many of them had fled from the north of Ireland during the Great Hunger and still carried bitter memories of the British. Killian also believed they could expect help from those who opposed a growing movement to unite the provinces of Ontario, Quebec, Prince Edward Island, Newfoundland, New Brunswick, and Nova Scotia in a semi-autonomous confederation and instead favored annexation by the United States. Killian also reminded his colleagues that no less than President Andrew Johnson and Secretary of State William Seward had signaled their support at their White House meeting in the fall by saying they would "acknowledge accomplished facts."

The head center hesitated. O'Mahony was a scholar, not a soldier. He acted on reason, not emotion, and this plan appeared to go against his better thinking. The Fenian Brotherhood had just paid $30,000 for a former Confederate ship auctioned by the U.S.

Customs Service with plans to sail it to Ireland once it was repaired. Only a week earlier in Lowell, Massachusetts, he had told his fellow Irishmen that "the men who propose to invade Canada have no right to call themselves Fenians." How could he now order a raid across the northern border without losing all credibility?

Killian argued that the political reality was exactly the opposite. Given that the suspension of habeas corpus foreclosed any imminent invasion of Ireland, O'Mahony would lose credibility if he *didn't* fight in North America. "In my opinion, the real reputation of the F.B. [Fenian Brotherhood] in America can be revived only by *striking a blow* and *making a fight*," Killian asserted.

According to O'Mahony, he reluctantly approved the plan, but only if it was part of a larger movement on Ireland and not an isolated expedition. The head center tried to convince himself that he had found a workable compromise between his sound judgment and the fervor of the "men of action." Revolutions are rarely won, however, by choosing the middle ground.

❀

General Bernard F. Mullen couldn't believe his ears when he learned of O'Mahony's decision. It was bad enough that the Fenian secretary of military and naval affairs, who replaced Sweeny inside Moffat Mansion, had not been asked for his input on the plan, but O'Mahony gave command of the expedition to Killian instead of him. The war secretary had served in the Mexican-American and Civil Wars; the treasury secretary had hardly any military experience at all outside an eighteen-month stint with the Missouri militia during the Civil War.

Mullen protested to O'Mahony that the one-ship "navy" he was so eager to employ was barely seaworthy. The rigging was in miserable condition, its sails even worse. The ship lacked hammocks, cooking utensils, and coal supplies but had its fill of seawater that had seeped inside. "A target for artillery practice could not be more successfully painted—black hull and straw-colored wheel-house," he informed O'Mahony. The head center was unmoved.

Killian supervised the loading of the Fenian arms onto their dilapidated naval vessel. He sealed the sailing papers with his own hand on April 4, before departing New York separately with just short of one hundred men. He planned to reunite with the weapons upon his arrival in Eastport, Maine, and attack Campobello Island the following day.

When readers of New York's newspapers awoke the next morning, they might have been confused as to Killian's destination. Fed wild counterintelligence from Moffat Mansion, *The New York Herald* told its readers that an enormous Fenian force had left the city to capture not Campobello but another British island—Bermuda. The *Herald* reported that Killian departed with three thousand desperadoes, all army veterans, on three iron steamers, while Colonel Patrick J. Downing led another twenty-five hundred on two other ships. In other newspapers, the Fenians planted the even more absurd claim that seven warships carrying a ten-thousand-man army were en route from California to Bermuda.

The New York *World,* however, had it correct: Killian and five to six hundred Fenians in small squads were en route to strike Campobello Island. But even that report became grossly inflated. According to *The World,* the Fenians would establish a provisional government on the island, elect O'Mahony president, and use it as a base to launch an army of twenty-five thousand men to conquer New Brunswick and rechristen it the "Republic of Emmetta" in honor of the Irish patriot Robert Emmet. Even the most romantic of Fenians, however, failed to conjure such a glorious dream.

❀

On April 6, "General" Killian and the first wave of Fenian soldiers arrived in Eastport. The fishing port of thirty-seven hundred people at the mouth of the St. Croix River was the nearest American city to Ireland, and there was much to remind Killian of his homeland. The British had dubbed this northeast corner of Maine "New Ireland" when they conquered it during the American Revolution and the War of 1812, and it featured its own collection of emerald isles sprinkled on the sapphire waters of Passamaquoddy Bay.

Killian had no time for soaking in the views because he immediately encountered a problem upon disembarking in Eastport. The Fenian naval vessel laden with his supplies hadn't arrived, but the British had.

Within days of O'Mahony's approval of the Campobello venture, British authorities knew all about it. Rumors of a possible Fenian raid on New Brunswick had circulated as early as December 1864, and when Canada called out its volunteers in early March, Canadians assumed Campobello Island among the probable targets.

By March 20, the lieutenant governor of New Brunswick and his counterpart in adjacent Nova Scotia had been informed of the Fenian invasion plan, given that each Canadian province was responsible for its own defense, and six days later the entire volunteer force of New Brunswick was ordered to report to the border town of St. Stephen, twenty-five miles upriver from Eastport, "armed and equipped for active service."

Canadian journalists reported that someone inside Moffat Mansion had been spilling secrets to the British. O'Mahony suspected that Killian himself might have been the mole, particularly after the New York *World* revealed that a high official of the O'Mahony government was a close friend of one of the most singular and significant Irish voices in all of Canada.

❧

Even by the standards of Young Ireland, Thomas D'Arcy McGee had been a wunderkind. Born north of Dublin in the village of Carlingford in 1825, McGee might have been the most intellectually gifted of the Young Ireland rebels. A brilliant orator and a gifted poet and journalist, he had spoken forcefully against the British occupation of Ireland, signing his letters "Thomas D'Arcy McGee (A traitor to the British Government)."

During the Great Hunger, he accused the British government of two million "ministerial murders" and argued that the Irish were being "exterminated as a people." After the failed uprising in 1848, McGee fled to Philadelphia and founded a string of Irish American newspapers. He grew disenchanted with the United States, however. In addition to the Know-Nothing scourge, he saw something amiss in the poverty, corruption, and intemperance in American cities that he believed was destroying Irish faith and families.

McGee believed his countrymen were no better off in the United States than they had been in Ireland. He came to see a better future for the diaspora instead in Canada, where he believed minorities found greater liberty and tolerance under the British parliamentary system. In 1857, he joined the sizable Irish community in Montreal and launched a newspaper, *The New Era,* as well as a political career, being elected to the provincial assembly.

In his rhetoric, McGee grew more conservative and conciliatory to Great Britain. Although he once called upon the United States to annex Canada, he became a vocal supporter of Canadian confederation—to defend itself from the threat from south of the border. He called Fenianism "a foreign disease" and "political leprosy," a movement that was too secular and too republican. They were, he said, a secret society, no better than the despised Know-Nothings.

To the Fenians, he was a traitor who had abandoned all his previous ideas for political expediency. They wouldn't have been shocked if it was true that McGee was colluding with Killian, an old newspaper colleague, to merely pretend that a Fenian invasion was imminent in order to force the United States to enforce its neutrality laws and sabotage Sweeny's plan to strike Canada.

The head center ordered Downing to keep a close watch on Killian. Unfortunately for him, O'Mahony harbored no suspicions about the true double-dealer in his midst.

❧

James McDermott might have been named to the Order of St. Sylvester by Pope Pius IX for his heroism while serving the Papal Brigade, but he was no angel. Nicknamed "Red Jim" for his crimson hair, he was described by the Fenian John Devoy as "a handsome fellow, glib-tongued and ready-witted, but wholly without principle, moral sense or moral scruples." Born illegitimately in Ireland, McDermott blackmailed his biological father, a prominent Dublin attorney who lived on St. Stephen's Green, threatening to reveal the man's secret.

James Stephens and other Fenians who knew the blustery McDermott in Ireland warned O'Mahony about him before his arrival in the United States in 1863. Still the Fenian head center made him an organizer and took him in as one of his closest confidants. "He became O'Mahony's evil genius and acquired a strange influence over him," Devoy wrote. O'Mahony lacked a skeptic's eye, perhaps an admirable quality for leading daily life but not for leading a paramilitary organization. "I notice *you seem not to examine* into character closely," Downing warned O'Mahony. "This trusting disposition will create a thousand vexations for you."

He was right. McDermott was selling Fenian secrets to Britain's consul in New York, Edward Archibald.

Indeed it was hardly just McDermott who had infiltrated the Fenians. The American, Canadian, and British governments all had informants inside the organization. "Wherever there are three Fenians there are two informers," an Irishman quipped to a *New York Times* correspondent. So many double agents prowled Moffat Mansion that spies were reporting on the activities of other spies, unaware of their informant status. In some cases, the British government had more knowledge of Fenian plans than the Fenians themselves.

Being on the British payroll, McDermott was truly a professional troublemaker. Devoy thought him more responsible for the split in the Fenian Brotherhood than any other person. "He was constantly fomenting trouble by lying stories which he put in circulation or told 'confidentially' to numbers of people." He would heckle Sweeny at rallies one day and then plant lies about O'Mahony the next.

McDermott had accompanied Killian to Eastport as adjutant general of the expedition, where he continued to show his true colors. One editor of a St. Stephen newspaper described him as a "rough Irish lad, evidently lacking in brains, judgment and experience, as quiet as a mouse in the presence of his master, but garrulous and bombastic when the latter is out of sight."

For a group condemned by the Roman Catholic Church as a secret society, the Fenians weren't particularly adept at keeping secrets. The British didn't need spies, just a newspaper subscription. The Fenians regularly announced their intentions at public meetings and in interviews with reporters. "No news travels so freely or so fast as the 'secret' doings of the Fenian Brotherhood," quipped Mark Twain. "In solemn whisperings at dead of night they secretly plan a Canadian raid, and publish it in the 'World' next morning."

❧

When it became clear that the secrecy of the Campobello expedition had been compromised, O'Mahony recalled the naval ship and stopped several hundred Fenians in Boston from going to the border. Left without a portion of his arsenal and his army, Killian discovered that the $10,000 O'Mahony had promised to forward was not waiting for him in Eastport either.

Meanwhile, packs of Irishmen who left their jobs and families continued to arrive in Eastport and the surrounding towns. *The St. Croix Courier* reported that they appeared to be "the most villainous cut throat individuals we ever laid eyes on—men who would be in their native element in the midst of rapine and murder."

In a city of fewer than four thousand people, the four hundred Fenians filled every vacancy in Eastport's hotels and rooming houses. While some stayed with local Irish families or camped on the banks of the St. Croix River, Killian and his officers shared the same lodgings as the British consul, British detectives, and the U.S. marshal, which made for tense interactions.

As Killian waited for his cases of arms to arrive, he tried to sow dissension north of the border. He hired Eastport's Trescott Hall and announced that the Fenians had come there to stage a convention to rally against Canadian confederation. Although dwarfed by Ontario and Quebec, New Brunswick was the keystone of confederation. Without its inclusion, Nova Scotia would be severed from the other provinces, and the entire enterprise might not be viable. So, with two printing presses he'd brought to Maine, Killian published a proclamation offering Fenian support to the citizens of New Brunswick, who remained lukewarm about the idea of confederation.

While Killian tried to whip up public sentiment against the British in New Brunswick, he did the same with the edgy fishermen of Maine. The most senior of Eastport's citizens could remember that the War of 1812 lasted until 1818 in their city, because the British occupied the border community they believed to be theirs for an extra three years after the signing of the Treaty of Ghent. More recently, Confederates had used New Brunswick as a haven to attempt a raid on a bank in the border town of Calais, Maine.

Some Mainers enjoyed seeing Canadians panic for a change. "The Provincials are terribly frightened," the *Machias Republican* reported, "which is pleasant for us to contemplate. They are now reaping what they sowed a little time ago." However, many in Eastport were tired of Irishmen armed with revolvers and bowie knives loitering around their waterfront. The St. John *Telegraph* reported that a decent portion of the city was "much opposed" to the Fenians because "the whole summer's trade would be ruined if they remained much longer."

Every day seemed to bring a new obstacle to Killian's plans. On April 9, eighty Fenians left Portland aboard the steamer *New Brunswick*, but the steamship company said it lacked the space to haul dozens of cases of rifles and boxes of ammunition. Killian chartered a schooner and dispatched it to Portland to retrieve the weapons from the company's warehouse. The following day, Michael Murphy, founder of the Hibernian Benevolent Society of Canada, and six fellow Fenian sympathizers were arrested by Canadian authorities en route to Eastport.

The delays had given the British navy time to make a show of force in Passamaquoddy Bay. By April 11, two British warships guarded the waters between Eastport and Campobello Island. The military buildup continued over the next week until there were five British ships and five thousand British and New Brunswick troops in the vicinity.

The Fenians did not let the British warships deter them. On April 13, two boatloads of Fenians, led by the Calais head center Dennis Doyle, attempted a nighttime landing a mile below St. Stephen, before retreating when townspeople spotted them and sounded an alarm. In the spirit of Paul Revere, "Old Joe" Young mounted his horse and rode up and down the road flanking the St. Croix River, pounding on front doors, rousing people from their sleep, and yelling, "Arm yourselves! The Fenians are upon you!" As Young's hoofbeats receded in the distance, some of the panicked Canadians hid their valuables, packed their belongings, and fled to the American side of the border.

Doyle caused further mischief on another night when he stacked piles of wood along a four-mile stretch of the St. Croix River between Calais and Milltown, then set them ablaze under the cover of darkness and fired shots into the air to give the appearance of a large Fenian army amassing around a string of campfires. Confusion tore through St. Stephen as nervous residents kept watch for the invaders until daylight revealed the ruse.

Killian's men, however, grew impatient. They were ready to finally plant their boots on British soil.

❁

Near midnight on April 14, James Dixon heard a violent rap on the front door of the customhouse on New Brunswick's Indian Island, sandwiched between Eastport and Campobello Island in the middle of Passamaquoddy Bay. The deputy customs collector had spent the day much more consumed with thoughts about his sick wife than any looming Fenian threat. One of the two women attending to Mrs. Dixon went to the door and, without opening it, asked who was on the other side.

"We want that English flag!" came the shout on the other side. "Give it quickly, or we will burn down the house!"

In a panic, the unarmed Dixon threw on his clothes and darted down the stairs. He opened the door to be greeted by the barrels of pistols pointed squarely in his direction and the sound of a pack of men attempting to tear off his window shutters. Nine Irishmen had come ashore on the unguarded island after being lowered in a boat from a Fenian privateer and rowing with muffled oars right beneath the nose of the HMS *Pylades.* The frightened Dixon readily surrendered the Union Jack waving over the customhouse. Satisfied with their war trophy, the Fenians departed the island in triumph, causing no damage nor firing a single shot.

Aside from the midnight game of capture the flag, Killian made no move toward Campobello Island. He continued to rattle nerves, though. One thousand people, many of them curious Canadians, packed St. Croix Hall in Calais on the evening of April 16 to listen to Killian deliver a one-hour address in which he claimed the Fenians had no thoughts of invading New Brunswick and would respect American neutrality laws. However, he also said that the Fenians had no intention of leaving. He vowed that the "convention" would remain in session on the border until the idea of Canadian confederation died, pledging that the Irishmen would save the residents of New Brunswick from having Great Britain "force" confederation upon them. "If the people of the Provinces wish, the Fenian Brotherhood stand ready to help them resist England," Killian told his audience. "We are ready to establish an Irish Republic in New Brunswick."

Back in Washington, D.C., Secretary of War Edwin Stanton and Lieutenant General Ulysses S. Grant had been monitoring the Fenian buildup along the border. They decided to move American forces into Passamaquoddy Bay, in order to enforce American neutrality laws. Secretary of the Navy Gideon Welles dispatched the side-wheel gunboat USS *Winooski,* and the revenue steamer *Ashuelot* also sailed into the bay to monitor the situation. In addition to the naval power, it had come time to dispatch the hero of Gettysburg to keep the peace.

❦

Less than a year earlier, Major General George Meade had been consumed by thoughts of the Confederacy. Now, improbably, the commander of the Military Division of the Atlantic was being asked to concentrate his attention on a bunch of unruly men up north.

On April 16, Meade received a telegram from Stanton instructing him to leave his Philadelphia home and proceed to Eastport and prevent any incursion onto British territory. The "Old Snapping Turtle" might not have inspired enthusiasm, but he commanded respect, and Stanton hoped the presence of the great-grandson of an Irish immigrant might deter the Fenians from doing anything rash.

As Meade traveled north from Philadelphia the following day, the telegrams continued to arrive in Washington, D.C., at a steady clip. On the evening of April 17, Secretary of the Navy Welles received a message informing him that the Fenian-chartered schooner *E. H. Pray* had arrived at Eastport from Portland and was being detained.* Aboard were 129 cases of arms containing fifteen hundred Springfield and Enfield muskets, carbines, knapsacks, canteens, and 100,000 ball cartridges.

Five minutes later, Secretary of State Seward's son arrived and handed Welles an envelope of papers forwarded by his father, including telegrams from Sir Frederick Bruce, Britain's minister to the United States, "urging that the arms and the Fenians should not be permitted to meet."

---

* Welles in his diary refers to the ship as the *Ocean Spray.* Meade and other communications refer to it as *E. H. Pray.*

Welles couldn't help but notice that Seward and Stanton appeared more concerned about alienating the increasingly powerful bloc of Irish voters than enforcing American neutrality laws. Welles was also content to do nothing. He left the matter in the hands of the commander of the USS *Winooski* and the local authorities—at least until Meade showed up in Eastport.

Although dressed in civilian clothes rather than his Union blues, Meade commanded a presence when he arrived on April 19 in Eastport, where he found four hundred Fenians, as well as an equal number in Calais and surrounding towns. The general immediately ordered his soldiers to seize the arms aboard the *E. H. Pray* and remove them to Fort Sullivan, situated on the hill above Eastport, where they would be under guard. He also told the leaders of the Fenian expedition in no uncertain terms that any violation of the neutrality laws would result in their immediate arrest.

Killian told Meade an unlikely tale: His fellow Irishmen, he said, were there on a fishing expedition and had brought their rifles in light of the run-ins between American and Canadian fishermen. The explanation was laughable, but Meade still vowed to "prevent the departure of any *armed* fishing party."

Without any weapons and short on money, Killian made one last appeal for resources from Fenian headquarters. The reply was terse: "Requisition cannot be filled." Hours later, he departed Eastport on a boat bound for Portland. He later admitted that he had "considered the chance of a successful movement over" more than a week earlier.

❦

Abandoned by their leader, the Fenians who remained in Eastport were desperate to attempt some sort of maneuver across the border to justify their expedition. On the night of April 20, they landed once again on Indian Island, which remained unguarded, and lit up the night by torching four stores, including a British customs warehouse.

Their victims were not all British subjects, however. Reflecting the interconnected commerce on the border, a pair of Americans bore the brunt of the attack. The Fenian inferno charred one store owned by Eastport's Robert Burns and spread to an adjoining cooperage and wholesale liquor and grocery store leased by another Eastport resident, John Shiels. The fire destroyed scores of fish barrels and casks of whiskey, gin, brandy, and port wine—a total loss calculated by Shiels to be $2,315.25.

Two nights after the raid on Indian Island, approximately fifty Fenians decided to finally make an attempt on their original target— Campobello Island. Carrying several cases of muskets, they boarded the schooner *Two Friends,* which Killian had arranged to lease for $10 a day. When the schooner's captain refused to transport a squad of armed men, the Fenians put a pistol to his head, causing him to reconsider.

After loading the weapons and provisions, the Fenians set sail. They soon found British warships in pursuit. After rounding one of the islands, they approached another schooner, which the revolver-wielding Fenians captured "in the name of the Irish Republic." They then sank the *Two Friends* in order to throw the British off the chase, before retreating to safety again on the American mainland.

Making one last attempt to retrieve their guns, now in government custody, Colonel James Kerrigan called upon Meade. A former congressman, Kerrigan had fought in the Mexican-American War and filibustered with William Walker in Nicaragua before serving with the Twenty-Fifth New York Volunteer Infantry Regiment during the Civil War. In spite of his political and military résumé and affiliation with the Fenians, the former congressman claimed to be just a New York merchant, and he protested the government seizure of his private property.

Meade reported to Grant that Kerrigan disclaimed any Fenian connection or intent to violate the neutrality laws, but the Irishman couldn't "explain grounds on which he, a stranger, expected to find a market in Eastport for such articles—nor the coincidence of his arrival with his goods simultaneously with the concentration here of the Fenians." Meade agreed to return the arms to Kerrigan if he provided a $10,000 bond pledging that they would never be used to violate the country's neutrality laws.

With Passamaquoddy Bay locked down by both American and British forces, the discouraged rank-and-file Fenians were left with no choice but to follow Killian's lead. They set sail for home. As it turned out, the only successful armed invasion launched by the Fenians occurred on their return trip home from Eastport, aboard the crowded steam packet *New Brunswick*. Upset that they could only find seats in steerage after paying for more expensive cabin tickets, 170 disgruntled Fenians drew their revolvers and annexed the most comfortable accommodations aboard the ship.

By early May, most of the Fenians had departed from Passamaquoddy Bay. General Meade, who had caught a severe cold and was confined for several weeks by the threat of pneumonia, finally left on May 2.

The whole episode crushed O'Mahony's reputation. He had gone against his long-held belief and now had nothing to show for it except ridicule. Newspapers lambasted the "Moffat Mansion farce," while members of the Roberts wing chortled at the "Eastport fizzle."

❀

Killian had claimed that the Fenians traveled to the New Brunswick border in order to help defeat the plans for Canadian confederation, but their Down East fiasco had exactly the opposite effect. It caused some Canadians to reconsider the benefits of confederation. The Irish menace showed if anything that union was necessary for the region's defense. The Nova Scotia assembly, which had previously opposed confederation, overwhelmingly adopted a resolution in favor of it on April 17. In New Brunswick, pro-confederation forces won decisively at the polls, just weeks after the last of the Fenians returned home.

Thomas D'Arcy McGee couldn't help but be thrilled by the simultaneous advancement of confederation and the weakening of the Fenian Brotherhood. It was so effective, in fact, that to some it reeked of conspiracy. "The failure of this project has been so complete and so ruinous to O'Mahony as well as disgusting to his supporters and dupes, that it appears difficult not to believe that Killian deliberately played the part of a traitor in order to break up the organization," Britain's consul in New York wrote to the Earl of Clarendon, secretary of state for foreign affairs.

Alas, they gave O'Mahony, Killian, and their men too much credit. With the collapse of the Campobello venture, the Fenians returned to the fighting they did best—among themselves.

❀

Many of the disappointed and embarrassed Fenian fighters who returned from Eastport shared the sentiment of William H. Grace, an organizer from Portsmouth, New Hampshire, and expedition captain who denounced O'Mahony as "an imbecile and a fraud on the public." Grace blamed the head center for not delivering the resources he had promised and instructed his circle to switch its allegiance and send no more money to Moffat Mansion. "Let us unite under the leadership of General Sweeny, and carry out the pledge that we have taken before God and man," he urged.

New York Fenians returning from Maine carried their frustrations with them. Two leaders of the Eastport foray stormed into the Fenian White House on April 28 and demanded compensation from O'Mahony for their loss of employment—not to mention their transportation costs—due to the futile expedition. When the head center refused any payment, the soldiers locked the doors of Moffat Mansion to prevent his escape and pointed their pistols at his head until he handed over $30 to each man.

The following day, the district center of Manhattan called together 132 of his circles inside their headquarters at 814 Broadway. The irate Fenians demanded to examine the accounts of Moffat Mansion and appointed a select committee to interrogate O'Mahony about the Eastport debacle.

O'Mahony heard every taunt as he entered the room to answer questions. "Imbecile!" "Killian's dupe!" "Where is the invasion of Ireland now?" For nearly two hours, he subjected himself to a rigid cross-examination. He grew increasingly exasperated. He was the one who had founded this organization and tended to its growth. Who were these people to question his commitment to do what he thought best for the liberation of Ireland? O'Mahony asked his fellow Fenians to judge his entire record. "Am I to be destroyed for this, the one great mistake of my life?"

The shout from the gallery, however, reflected the lack of mercy in the room: "You are a servant of the Fenian Brotherhood, not the master any longer!"

The tribunal discovered that the Campobello expedition had cost the Fenian Brotherhood $26,000, and the only thing they had to show for it was one captured Union Jack. It found O'Mahony guilty of gross mismanagement in financial and military affairs and incompetent leadership and concluded that "nearly all—if not all—the frauds thus perpetrated on the Brotherhood by the various officials at Headquarters were indirectly, if not directly, the result of this *incapacity, imbecility,* and *total unfitness* of the Head Center." In addition, even without proof of a conspiracy with McGee, the Fenian investigators tried Killian on the charge and found him guilty.

Before he could be expelled from the organization he had founded, however, O'Mahony played his last card. He showed his fellow Fenians a letter he had received from Stephens announcing that he had departed France and was due to arrive shortly in New York. With this news, the tribunal granted him a last-minute reprieve. Stephens would be allowed to determine O'Mahony's fate.

Erin's Boys

ON THE NIGHT of James Stephens's return to New York, well-wishers filled an entire city block of Broadway outside his quarters at the Metropolitan Hotel. Although the press believed him to be in Paris for the five months since his prison break, Stephens had been in the heart of Dublin the entire time.

Since Eastport, John O'Mahony had been just as besieged as Stephens, but instead by irate Irishmen who demanded their contributions back. Donations to Moffat Mansion had dropped 70 percent, and bond sales had stopped. The sullen O'Mahony exchanged a cordial greeting with Stephens when they saw each other that night, but he said little before the strains of "Hail to the Chief" filled the room as a band outside delivered an impromptu serenade. Stephens appeared on the hotel's balcony as women yelled and men flung hats into the air. In a brief address, he assured them that he intended to unite the Irish in America. He offered no words of support for his fellow Young Irelander.

O'Mahony read the writing on the wall. He resigned as head center of the Fenian Brotherhood the following day. "In consenting to the recent disastrous attempt to capture Campo Bello, I violated my duty, not alone to the Fenian Brotherhood and the Irish Republic, but to the best interests of the Irish race, as also to my previous unvaried policy," he wrote in his resignation letter.

Stephens made no attempt to change O'Mahony's mind. "In sanctioning this divergence from the true path you not only gave a proof of weakness, but committed a crime less excusable in you than in any other man; for you should have known that your project would have resulted in our ruin," he asserted.

It was a brutal blow for the man who had invited Stephens to lead the Irish republicans in the first place. After eight years of disagreements with his fellow Young Irelander, it was an invasion of Canada, a strategy he didn't even believe in, that brought about his downfall. O'Mahony remained a part of the Fenian Brotherhood, but he would never regain the same level of influence.

❦

Stephens selected himself as O'Mahony's replacement. The "provisional dictator" now ruled directly over the Irish republican movement in the United States—or at least half of it. To make the Fenian Brotherhood whole once again, Stephens would have to reach an agreement with William Roberts, whom he met face-to-face for the first time on the same day as O'Mahony's departure. Dictators, however, make poor negotiators. Stephens wanted unity with the Roberts wing, as long as the Roberts wing changed its position to agree with him. "The objective point is Ireland, not Canada, Japan, or any of those distant regions that do not concern Irishmen," Stephens insisted. He called any raid on Canada a "suicidal movement," something he believed the "mad and most inglorious fiasco" at Eastport had proven. The failure of the O'Mahony wing, however, had not deterred the Roberts wing. It only made them redouble their efforts, in the hopes of reclaiming the good name of the Fenian Brotherhood.

Reunification prospects further dimmed upon the release of a letter in which Stephens had urged O'Mahony to jettison the Roberts wing and "cut and hack the rotten branches around you without pity." Only four days after meeting Roberts, Stephens called on him to follow O'Mahony's lead and resign. For his part, Roberts accused the IRB leader of being on the payroll of the British government.

Stephens found Moffat Mansion to be about as empty as the Fenian Brotherhood's coffers. The twenty-eight clerks working in the headquarters had dwindled to only a straggler or two. Layers of dust coated the chandeliers that remained unlit over empty desks. With circles no longer sending money, only $500 remained in the treasury. Stephens moved the Fenian headquarters back downtown into the *Daily News* headquarters on Chatham Street and allowed financial vultures to pick through the carcass of the O'Mahony wing, auctioning off its lavish furniture.

❧

After hearing news of the O'Mahony wing's expedition to Maine, the Fenian senate unanimously passed a resolution on April 16 ordering Sweeny to take "immediate action." The Fenian secretary of war, who favored a wintertime attack when ice would hamper British gunboats and allow the Irishmen to cross rivers on foot, registered his objection to an accelerated timetable that he thought reckless. Senators, however, told him that if he didn't invade at once, the Fenian Brotherhood would collapse. Sweeny wrote that he "reluctantly yielded, preferring the chances of an honorable failure in the field, to the disintegration of the organization."

So, with the burden of the Fenian Brotherhood's survival on his shoulders, Sweeny studied the war plans employed against Canada during the American Revolution and the War of 1812. He envisioned a three-pronged attack.

To the west, he placed a left wing of three thousand Fenians, under Brigadier General Charles Carroll Tevis, an 1849 West Point graduate with Irish roots who fought as a soldier of fortune in the Turkish, Egyptian, and French armies before serving in the Civil War. The left wing would sail across the Great Lakes from Chicago and Milwaukee and advance directly on to London, Ontario. The Fenians would then occupy Port Stanley on Lake Erie to provide an entry point for receiving supplies and reinforcements.

A center wing made up of upwards of five thousand men would cross Lake Erie from Cleveland and attack the Niagara Peninsula near Port Colborne, Ontario, under Brigadier General William Francis Lynch, a trusted confidant who led the Fifty-Eighth Illinois Volunteer Infantry Regiment as part of Sweeny's brigade at the Battle of Shiloh. They would march toward Hamilton and seize the Welland Canal, the vital connection between Lakes Erie and Ontario, in order to disrupt British troop movements and cripple trade between eastern and western Canada.

Sweeny anticipated that the center wing's advance on Toronto would force the British to move defense forces from Montreal—leaving the Fenians' true target exposed for the main attack of seventeen thousand men under Brigadier General Samuel Perkins Spear, a Boston-born veteran of the Mexican-American War who served with the Second U.S. Cavalry and the Eleventh Pennsylvania Cavalry during the Civil War. While Lynch made his diversionary attack, the "Right Wing of the Army of Ireland" would advance with seventeen infantry and five cavalry regiments from northern Vermont and upstate New York in order to capture Canada's liquid lifeline—the St. Lawrence River.

Following the well-trodden path of the Continental army in 1775 and American forces in 1812, a Fenian force, under Brigadier General Michael C. Murphy, would march straight up the Lake Champlain valley in two columns flanking the Richelieu River and seize garrisons in Quebec before capturing the Great Victoria Bridge, which connected to the island of Montreal. One unit would continue north to the Canadian capital of Ottawa and seize government buildings and ministers who would serve as hostages to ransom for Fenian prisoners in England.

While a small expedition would prevent the arrival of reinforcements from New Brunswick and Nova Scotia, Murphy's men would move east along the Grand Trunk Railway toward Quebec City in order to control the lucrative shipping lanes of the St. Lawrence River. "With the revenues of the Canadas to pay our expenses," Sweeny predicted, "we can confidently look forward to the realization of our dreams." If Spear could not reach Quebec City or Montreal, he was to concentrate his force in the corridor bounded by the St. Francis and Richelieu Rivers and establish the capital of the Irish government in exile in the city of Sherbrooke.

In addition to the three thousand sworn Fenians in Canada, dozens of operatives north of the border provided intelligence back to the headquarters in New York City. Once the invasion was launched, these agents would destroy bridges to cut off communication and transportation between Ontario and Quebec.

Sweeny didn't believe the Fenians would be fighting alone once they breached the border. He expected that most of Canada's quarter million Irish Catholics would greet the Fenians as liberators and join in the fight. He believed that the ten thousand members of the Canadian military who were Irish by birth or descent would refuse British orders to repel the attack. Based on reports from Fenian agents, Sweeny also felt confident that Quebec's French Canadians—fellow Catholics with similar grievances against British imperialism—would, if not assist, at least remain neutral, as they had done during the American invasions of 1775 and 1812.

It was an audacious plan, fantastical even. A private army without uniforms or a commissariat—let alone a country—would strike the world's most powerful empire and make it bend to its will. The odds of success were undeniably long, but so were the litany of outrages suffered by the Irish.

Sweeny knew, however, that his plan had no chance to succeed if his men didn't carry modern weapons into battle. History had shown that pikes and pitchforks would not free Ireland. They needed guns. Luckily for the Fenians, there was a supply to match their demand.

❧

The Civil War had been good for the killing business. The smokestacks of weapon factories and federal arsenals worked around the clock to fulfill orders for ammunition and arms on both sides of the conflict. When the guns finally fell silent, the Union army had more than one million surplus muzzle-loading rifles, which were rapidly becoming outdated with the advent of breech-loading rifles that allowed for quicker shots.

Fenian operatives could purchase surplus equipment such as uniforms and knapsacks at government auctions. They needed to be more circumspect, however, in the acquisition of arms and ammunition for the self-proclaimed Irish Republican Army. While many of the Fenian Brotherhood members who served in the Civil War took advantage of the Union army's offer to demobilized soldiers to purchase their rifles and gear for $6, Sweeny also dispatched Tevis to Philadelphia to buy Springfield rifles, many rebuilt from mix-and-match parts. The Fenians ultimately acquired more than four thousand muskets produced at the Bridesburg Armory and shipped them to twenty-two contacts in locations from East St. Louis, Illinois, to Watertown, Massachusetts.

Sweeny did not acquire artillery or naval vessels, though not for a lack of interest. The Fenian war secretary even went down to the depths of Manhattan's East River in pursuit of a secret weapon. Twice he participated in the successful testing of an experimental, hand-cranked submarine that was dubbed the *Intelligent Whale*. According to one account, Sweeny even left the submerged craft, outfitted in a diving suit, to plant a twenty-five-pound explosive beneath a test target. Sweeny, however, had enough difficulty paying for the outfitting of an army, let alone a navy. His original plan called for an outlay of at least $450,000, but due to the schedule acceleration he had only $100,000.

For weeks leading up to the planned attack, Sweeny stealthily distributed the guns and ammunition to locations along the Canadian border, where the Fenian army would await the invaders. He feared that because of the compressed time frame and a lack of promised funds, his arsenal was wholly inadequate for the job. Still, the time had come for the commander in chief to summon the Irish Republican Army to the front.

※

Among those called to invade Canada was John Charles O'Neill. He had been born eight days before St. Patrick's Day in 1834 in the small Ulster parish of Clontibret, where the bad blood ran deep. Straddling the fault line between Protestant loyalists to the north and Catholic republicans such as the O'Neill family to the south, the surrounding hills and vales of rural County Monaghan remained a "bandit country" that regularly required the British military to intervene in sectarian clashes.

O'Neill's father died of scarlet fever five weeks before the boy's birth, and his single mother, Catherine, left him and his two older siblings behind in Ireland when she moved to the United States in 1840. Three years later, O'Neill's mother sent for his older brother and sister, leaving the youngest in the care of his grandparents.

Catherine's devoutly republican father, George Macklin, instilled in his grandson a strong devotion to the Roman Catholic Church and an even fiercer fidelity to hating the British. O'Neill learned the Irish language and studied the history of his native land and its folk heroes who dared to pick up the sword. "I wept over the speeches of her orators, and asked myself whom of the Irish patriots I would seek to emulate. I decided that eloquence will not do unless it be that which flashes from the cannon's mouth," O'Neill recalled of his childhood.

O'Neill's grandfather stirred his soul with epic tales of two of Ireland's most revered rebels with whom he shared a last name and bloodline. The young boy listened intently to the story of Hugh O'Neill, the Irish chieftain who in 1595 routed the troops of Queen Elizabeth I in the hills and bogs not too far from his front door at the Battle of Clontibret, although his rebellion ended with a devastating defeat in the 1601 Battle of Kinsale. A generation later, the vanquished chieftain's nephew, Owen Roe O'Neill, led another Catholic revolt against English rule.

Young John O'Neill worshipped his ancestors and rebel leaders, who sacrificed themselves on the altar of Irish freedom. That they all failed to achieve their goal of Irish independence didn't matter. O'Neill learned from his grandfather that the mere act of fighting the English rendered them heroes. Their glorious failures had transformed them into immortals who fulfilled the words of Emmet on the eve of his execution: "The man dies, but his memory lives."

Just after O'Neill's eleventh birthday, he watched his village wilt along with its harvest. O'Neill's family owned a farm of about three acres and struggled along with everyone else as the pastoral landscape morphed into a wasteland of abandoned cottages, desolate potato ridges, and crumbling stone walls. The Great Hunger struck with particular virulence in south Ulster. At least thirteen thousand people died from starvation and disease in County Monaghan between 1847 and 1850 alone. Clontibret lost over 17 percent of its population between 1841 and 1851, and O'Neill was among those forced to flee.

After five years apart from his mother and siblings, the fourteen-year-old O'Neill reunited with his family when he immigrated to the United States in 1848. He worked as a clerk in the family's Elizabeth, New Jersey, grocery business and then as a traveling sales agent for a publishing house. After struggling as a Catholic bookstore owner in Richmond, Virginia, the impulsive O'Neill suddenly enlisted in the U.S. Cavalry in 1857 and headed west to Utah to serve in a standoff with Mormon settlers.

For a young soldier in search of battlefield glory like that of Hugh or Owen Roe O'Neill, the Mormon War proved a bitter disappointment. The impatient Irishman craved combat but grew so frustrated at the lack of action that he deserted to San Francisco to pursue riches. There the twenty-five-year-old O'Neill began a romance with Mary Ann Crowe, an Australian girl ten years his junior whose Irish parents had chased the promise of wealth in the California gold rush. The young girl persuaded the stubborn O'Neill to return to the U.S. Army in July 1860 after a two-year absence. His reputation as a solid soldier—and probably more so the army's need for manpower in the West—saved him from a court-martial, and the military restored him to duty without trial.

After the United States turned on itself in 1861, O'Neill returned east to join the Union army's First U.S. Cavalry as a sergeant. No longer would he complain about a lack of battle action. He had a horse shot out from underneath him during the Peninsular Campaign, and in December 1863 he sustained severe injuries during the siege of Knoxville as a first lieutenant with the Fifth Indiana Cavalry.

Although the Irishman could endure wounds to his flesh on the battlefield, he was far more vulnerable to bruises to his ego. After being bypassed—unfairly in his estimation—for a promotion to colonel, the thin-skinned O'Neill resigned his commission in November 1864 and quickly settled into domestic life. He opened a real estate and claims office in Nashville, where he had last been detailed, and married Mary Ann, who had spent the war working as a servant in a San Francisco mansion.

John O'Neill, who immigrated to the United States during the Great Hunger, thought it his life's purpose to lead an Irish army against the British Empire.

Given his upbringing, O'Neill was a natural recruit for the Fenian Brotherhood. But it was not until the Roberts wing proposed the attack on Canada that he paid his $1 initiation fee and quickly rose to become the organizer of Nashville's circle. His military experience proved valuable in drilling the men of his private militia, the Thirteenth Tennessee Regiment.

O'Neill had had enough of the ceaseless proclamations and speeches by some Fenian leaders, who used their gifts of gab but little else. "If resolutions could give liberty to a people, the Senate of the F.B. [Fenian Brotherhood] would long ago have made Ireland the freest nation on the globe," O'Neill groused. Body counts—not word counts—would liberate Ireland from its oppressor. "A firm believer in steel as the cure of Irish grievances, I was attracted to the ranks of the organization for no other reason than it proposed such a remedy," O'Neill wrote.

He believed that remedy best administered in Canada. "There is no spot of earth on the habitable globe where I would rather fight England than on Irish soil, but if it is not practicable to fight her there then I am in favor of fighting her wherever we can reach her."

So militant had O'Neill become from his boyhood experiences that when a secret telegram arrived ordering him to take up arms against the British Empire at the end of May 1866, he did not waver at leaving behind a budding business, which he estimated to be worth $50,000, as well as his new wife and two-month-old son. Although the odds were against him, previous generations of O'Neill warriors had demonstrated that no glory could ever be found in doing nothing at all. Striking a losing blow was better than striking no blow at all.

Along with the 115 men of his Thirteenth Tennessee Regiment, Colonel O'Neill collected his belongings and marched to Nashville's railroad station. The Irish soldiers proceeded north to Cleveland, the staging point for an amphibious invasion of Canada across Lake Erie.

Similar scenes played out across America as Fenians left their homes, their families, and their jobs for assigned locations along the border, including Port Huron, Michigan; Toledo, Ohio; Sandusky, Ohio; Erie, Pennsylvania; Buffalo, New York; and Dunkirk, New York.

On the plains of Nebraska, John O'Keeffe received his order from O'Neill: "Come at once the hour for action has arrived." The second lieutenant with the Second U.S. Cavalry asked for a sixty-day leave of absence, which was given only reluctantly because, as he wrote, "the Indians were gathering for the war path." Riding for five days on horseback through a country occupied only by "wild animals and wild men" to the nearest Union Pacific Railroad station, O'Keeffe traveled more than one thousand miles to report for duty.

In Anderson, Indiana, Father John McMahon paid little heed to the Vatican preachings against the Fenians and boarded a train with members from the local circle, including the parochial school teacher John Finley. Born in Clontibret like O'Neill, the pioneer priest had arrived in the United States in 1840 and supervised the construction of Anderson's first church. Knowing their pastor had limited means and wanted to travel to Montreal to check on business affairs left behind by a late brother, his parishioners offered him free railroad passage as far as Buffalo, as well as a chance to serve them as a spiritual adviser.

As O'Neill rode north from the heart of Dixie, each stop along the way added more Fenians to the cause. In Louisville, Colonel Owen Starr and 144 men of his Seventeenth Regiment boarded the train carrying their furled banners. At Indianapolis, another 100 soldiers under Captain James Haggerty joined the convoy.

Line officers donned military overcoats and carried swords, but most Fenians wore their everyday working clothes in order to reduce suspicion. It was impossible, however, for such a large collection of Irishmen to escape prying eyes and probing questions. When asked where they were going, the Fenians parroted the cover story that they were soldiers en route to California, even if the fact that they were traveling due east at the moment suggested otherwise. "Everything in connection with them is veiled in mystery," reported a Cleveland newspaper. On the night of May 28, four hundred soldiers arrived at the rendezvous point in Cleveland, where they planned to cross Lake Erie as part of Lynch's five-thousand-man force.

The following day, Sweeny's orders arrived. He instructed Lynch to commence his attack. The Fenians, however, lacked three key elements to carry out Sweeny's plan—five thousand men, boats, and even Lynch himself.

In response, Sweeny ordered the Fenians to abandon Cleveland for Buffalo, where his assistant adjutant general, Captain William J. Hynes, had been dispatched with instructions. Tevis, who had proceeded to Chicago to organize troops from surrounding states in the Midwest, reported back that he was short by two thousand muskets.

Sweeny could only wonder if his war plan was breaking down before it even had a chance to begin.

❧

Among the most Irish patches of turf in the United States, the working-class Irish Catholic neighborhood of the First Ward offered the Fenians the perfect sanctuary. Home to most of Buffalo's ten thousand Irishmen, the south-side neighborhood could easily absorb hundreds more without attracting suspicion or causing alarm. The Irish brogues that lilted out of the neighborhood's open windows carried a familiar tune. Home amid the Whalens, Ryans, and McNamaras, the Fenians found that family, faith, and work tightly knit the enclave together.

After the Civil War, many of Buffalo's Irish American veterans formed the Seventh Regiment of the Irish Army of Liberation and for months prepared for an attack against the British. Little did they expect that they would be able to walk to the battlefront.

The women of the First Ward supported the cause as well. Wives, daughters, and sweethearts raised money with balls, bazaars, and picnics. The Celtic versions of Clara Barton and Betsy Ross in the Buffalo chapter of the Fenian Sisterhood collected medicines, bandages, and nursing supplies necessary for the battlefield and wielded their needles to hand sew silk battle flags. To the Seventh Regiment, they presented a dark green silk flag nine feet long and six feet wide with heavy gold fringe and a golden sunburst painted in the upper left-hand corner.

The torrent of cargo that regularly flowed through Buffalo by sea and rail made it easier for the Fenians to ship weapons into the city. Fenian sympathizers who worked for the New York Central Railroad packed and labeled crates of the organization's guns and ammunition simply as "merchandise"—which was true, but not true enough—and stored them in their warehouse.

Many of the crates of firearms ended up in the crowded Pearl Street warehouse of the auctioneer Patrick O'Day, a fat, fussy man and leader of Buffalo's Fenian circle. O'Day's business offered a splendid cover for the Fenians to stash away their guns. Week after week, cases of muskets, pistols, and other war equipment arrived at his warehouse and were lowered into the cellar under the guise of being stored for a forthcoming auction.

Unbeknownst to O'Day, however, his every move was being monitored by the enemy. His bookkeeper, Alexander McLeod, was a British spy who kept the Canadian government apprised of the activities inside the auction room. From a desk outside O'Day's office, McLeod overheard his boss concocting secret plans. He described watching the "ignorant little Irishman" as he converted his cellar into a drill room where two hundred men at a time could practice. "I was astonished to see those men go through their drill as easy as if they were drinking a glass, their double quick and charge brought applause," McLeod informed his superiors. "It seems the whole city encourages them on."

Indeed, after looking over its collective shoulder in fear of Confederate raiders descending from Canada during the Civil War, Buffalo delighted in delivering a fright of its own to those on the other side of the Niagara River. "We don't wish them any ill," reported the *Buffalo Courier,* "but a little healthy scaring won't do them any harm. So soon does time make all things even."

As the date for the attack approached, the *Buffalo Courier* carried an advertisement announcing O'Day's preemptory sale of surplus army supplies—muskets, rifles, swords, knapsacks, tents, blankets, and overcoats. The advertisement, however, was only a cover to minimize suspicion surrounding his stockpiling of arms. The auctioneer had no intention of staging the sale. Those guns were due to be carried onto Canadian shores in the hands of the Fenian army.

❦

Until midnight on May 30 in Buffalo, hundreds of insurgents gathered inside the Fenian Brotherhood's local headquarters, Townsend Hall.

Buffalo's anti-Irish mayor, Chandler J. Wells, telegraphed the mayors of both Toronto and Hamilton in Ontario and warned them that six hundred Fenians had left Cleveland for his city. "This town is full of Fenians," an alarmed H. W. Hemans, the British consul in Buffalo, informed the Canadian spymaster Gilbert McMicken.

Still, Canada left its border with the United States unguarded. No

Canadian or British forces were positioned within fifty miles of the Niagara River. The false alarm that had sounded on St. Patrick's Day had wasted both the money and the goodwill of Canada's volunteer infantrymen. Government officials disbelieved the latest fevered reports of an imminent attack. "I cannot conceive it within the bounds of a reasonable probability that Sweeny will attempt any demonstration upon Canada now," McMicken reported.

For its part, the United States was reluctant to intervene, fearing that by doing so, it might inflame the situation. The U.S. attorney William A. Dart told Hemans that his government "looked upon the Fenian project as so wild and absurd that it preferred leaving it to die a natural death, rather than give its dishonest originators the power of ascribing their failure to official interference."

Back in New York, on May 31, Sweeny grew frenzied. Tevis had sent word from the left flank that no boats could be secured in either Chicago or Milwaukee and only half of the promised three thousand men had shown up. While another two hundred Fenians arrived in Buffalo, the fighting force for the central flank was still only about one thousand men—well short of the five thousand for which Sweeny had planned.

Even worse, illness and cowardice had sidelined the Irish Republican Army's expected leaders. With the planned invasion only hours away, O'Neill returned to headquarters after a fruitless search for Lynch and reported to Hynes that the commander who had been absent in Cleveland could not be found in Buffalo either.

Hynes held in his hands an urgent telegram from Sweeny telling him to find the most senior officer in Buffalo and give him command of the expedition. Hynes looked at O'Neill and knew his new "Commander of the Armies of the Irish Republic in Canada" was standing in front of him. Given only hours to prepare for the invasion planned for that night, the descendant of Hugh and Owen Roe O'Neill would be the man to lead the Irish Republican Army into Canada.

❧

As speculation grew among newspaper reporters and government officials that the still-unarmed Fenians might board a midnight train either east or west to the true invasion point where weapons awaited, John McLaughlin, one of McMicken's detectives, suspected otherwise. He hurried to O'Day's auction house and watched as the Fenians secretly loaded crates of ammunition and rifles onto nine large furniture wagons and began to march north through the streets of Buffalo.

Word of the Irish Republican Army's mobilization flew across the city and landed at the foot of Ferry Street, where Captain Andrew Bryson ordered the USS *Michigan* to raise anchor and patrol the Niagara River separating the United States and Canada and stop any Fenian incursion. When the sailors swarmed the deck of the U.S. Navy gunboat, however, the one indispensable man could not be found.

Unbeknownst to Bryson, the Irishmen had infiltrated his vessel. Mate William Leonard had recruited seventeen crew members whom he reported to be "good and true to the cause" of Ireland. Leonard and his fellow sailors knew the ship could safely navigate the Niagara River's tricky shoals in the dark only with the steady hand of its experienced pilot, Patrick Murphy.

No man, not even Bryson, knew the old paddle steamer better than the forty-three-year-old career sailor, who not only worked as an original crew member when the USS *Michigan* was first commissioned in 1844 but also helped build the boat with his own hands. The Waterford-born Murphy was certainly a proper Irishman— a Patrick married to a Bridget no less—but he was no rebel. In fact, he had spent his teenage years faithfully serving in the Royal Navy.

Knowing that appeals to the pilot's Irish roots would prove fruitless, the insurgents turned to sabotage. While the Irish Republican Army mobilized, the USS *Michigan*'s assistant engineer James Kelley introduced Murphy to the attractions of Buffalo's waterfront. Fueled by cigars, liquor, and the company of a "lady friend," the pair indulged in debauchery inside a string of seedy saloons. As Kelley and Murphy staggered down Main Street singing "The Wearing of the Green," the powerless Bryson stewed as his warship remained tethered to the dock.

❧

With the only potential obstacle in their path removed, the Irish Republican Army paraded northward to Canada. As clock hands slipped past midnight, the soldiers marched by the brick mansion of Millard Fillmore, no friend of the Irish. Throughout his political career, the former president had doggedly courted nativists, who blamed the Great Hunger refugees for importing poverty, crime, disease, and a strange religion to the United States. Fillmore accused "foreign Catholics" of engineering his defeat in the 1844 New York gubernatorial election, and a dozen years later he accepted the presidential nomination of the anti-immigrant Know-Nothings in an unsuccessful bid to reclaim the White House.

After their two-hour trek through Buffalo, the Irish Republican Army arrived at its rendezvous point in the suburban neighborhood of Black Rock. O'Neill received the count that only six hundred men had made it to the end of the six-mile march. Two hundred Irishmen had vanished into the Buffalo night, some dissuaded by second thoughts, others lured into passing saloons by the gratification awaiting at the bottom of a whiskey bottle.

O'Neill looked out upon his motley army. Starr's Seventeenth Infantry wore blue Union army jackets with green facings. The New Orleans company of the "Louisiana Tigers" were clad in gray military caps and Confederate tunics as well as belt plates emblazoned with the initials "C.S.A." The Eighteenth and Nineteenth Ohio Regiments from Cincinnati and Cleveland sported green shirts and caps. Most, however, were dressed like their leader in civilian clothes.

Although an accidental commander, O'Neill had supreme confidence in his pedigree and ability to lead the largest independent Irish army into combat since 1798. Over the span of seven centuries, the Irish who had challenged the British had repeatedly achieved immortality but never independence. By daring to fight, O'Neill knew—win or lose—greatness would be his. He gave the order for Starr to make the first crossing of the Niagara River.

A native of County Tyrone and a veteran of the Second Kentucky Cavalry, the twenty-eight-year-old Starr urged his men from Kentucky and Indiana across the river, where they landed on Canada's Niagara Peninsula. To a chorus of cheers, the color-bearers of the Seventeenth Infantry scrambled up the riverbank and pierced the British soil with three green Fenian battle flags, marking the one tiny corner of the British Empire that was now controlled by the Irish.

A Lawless and Piratical Band

O N THE NIGHT of May 31, 1866, the University of Toronto undergraduate David Junor was studying for his final examinations when a knock at his door brought the welcome news that he would be allowed to pass his remaining tests without having to take them. Any relief, however, was tempered by the news that he might have to sacrifice his life in return.

As a member of the Queen's Own Rifles volunteer militia, Junor received orders to report for active service at the regiment's drill shed by 4:30 a.m. The private was among the dozens of students who enlisted in the University Rifles company, which had been formed by professors when war with the United States beckoned during the *Trent* affair. The University Rifles had been called upon to help defend Canada from the Fenians in March, and there was nothing to dissuade Junor from thinking that this was yet another false alarm. He packed more for a holiday than a battle, stuffing his satchel with clothes, photographs, and letters that he planned to drop off at his home before returning to Toronto to graduate with the class of 1866.

With his heavy baggage in tow, the young man discovered the streets outside the drill hall teeming with anxious Toronto residents. The burden of defending Canada fell squarely upon volunteer militias like Junor's, soldiers perhaps more poorly provisioned than the Irish Republican Army. Although many militiamen brought their personal luggage to the drill shed, they lacked food, blankets, tents, medical provisions, and even canteens. Some received only five rounds of ammunition.

The volunteers also lacked the Irishmen's military experience. Some had never even fired a gun. The new commander of the Queen's Own Rifles, Lieutenant Colonel John Stoughton Dennis, was a forty-five-year-old wealthy land surveyor who had never so much as drilled with his battalion on a parade ground, let alone led it into battle.

What the young men of the Queen's Own Rifles lacked in training, they had in enthusiasm. They sang songs as they marched from the drill shed to the wharf at the foot of Yonge Street. Boisterous cheers accompanied Junor and the twenty-seven other volunteers of the University Rifles as they boarded the steamer *City of Toronto* for a three-hour trip across Lake Ontario to Port Dalhousie. There, they boarded a train to Port Colborne to protect the Lake Erie entrance to the Welland Canal, knowing that would be the Fenians' likely target.

While the volunteers mobilized to the border, British troops remained in their barracks. Not until 2:00 p.m. did the professional British army officer in command of the operation against the Fenians, Lieutenant Colonel George Peacocke, board a train from Hamilton, Ontario, toward Niagara Falls, with seventeen hundred troops from the Sixteenth and Forty-Seventh Regiments of Foot and a six-gun field battery.

When news of the Fenian breach of the border reached Ottawa during the day on June 1, Governor-General Lord Charles Monck sounded incredulous in his call for all volunteers west of Toronto to repel the enemy. "The soil of Canada has been invaded, not in the practice of legitimate warfare, but by a lawless and piratical band in defiance of all moral right, and in utter disregard of all the obligations which civilization enforces on mankind." The assault on Canada would not go undefended.

❀

After making the first landing, Colonel Owen Starr left a small unit to hold the dock for the arrival of the rest of the Irish Republican Army and marched the bulk of his men three miles south to the ruins of Old Fort Erie—hallowed ground for the British, who lost more than one thousand men there during the War of 1812 in a series of battles with American forces. Above the moss-grown rubble of the fortress, which had absorbed the most blood ever spilled on Canadian soil, Starr's Indiana and Kentucky troops hoisted an Irish flag where the Union Jack once waved.

Two hours after Starr's crossing of the Niagara River, John O'Neill stepped ashore around 3:30 a.m. in the village of Waterloo. The Fenian colonel might have lacked food, horses, artillery, and even a map, but he had plenty of self-confidence. As his first order, O'Neill directed one party of men to pull up tracks and burn a railway bridge to Port Colborne, while he marched south to the town of Fort Erie and directed his troops to cut the telegraph wires connecting it to the rest of Canada while keeping those in communication with Buffalo intact. Using axes stolen from a barn, the Irishmen chopped the village's forest of telegraph poles to the ground.

O'Neill summoned Fort Erie's mayor, Peter Kempson, and requested food for his men. The villagers quickly offered the Irishmen not just food to break their fast but plenty of flasks filled with good cheer, perhaps as an enticement to impair the invaders. The Fenian John O'Keeffe turned away the free-flowing liquor. "I prevailed on the mayor to tell his people to give no man a flask," he wrote. "Knowing what was coming I wanted sober men."

Gathering together all the adult men in the village, O'Neill ordered the reading of a proclamation that had been penned and distributed to the press by General Thomas Sweeny to assure Canadians that the Fenians had come to evict the British, not pillage their homes. "We have no issue with the people of these provinces, and wish to have none but the most friendly relations," read the document. "Our weapons are for the oppressors of Ireland. Our blows shall be directed only against the power of England; her privileges alone shall we invade, not yours." Sweeny's proclamation also called upon Irishmen, his "countrymen," throughout Canada "to stretch forth the hand of brotherhood in the holy cause of fatherland." O'Neill pledged that his men would behave honorably, and he threatened to shoot a soldier who stole a woolen shawl from an inn. The Irish Republican Army did seize food and tools necessary for their campaign, along with upwards of fifty horses. However, they didn't take any saddles or stirrups and instead rode bareback. They offered Fenian bonds or scrip notes in return for the property taken, a proposal that, unsurprisingly, had no appeal to the Canadians.

Around 10:00 a.m., the Irish Republican Army made its camp amid an apple orchard four miles north of Fort Erie. The Fenian-contracted tugs ferried provisions across the Niagara River throughout the morning, but by 11:00 a.m. the USS *Michigan* had steamed out of Buffalo, shutting down the supply line.

As the sun set on the Irishmen's first day in enemy territory, O'Neill received reports that five thousand troops were advancing on him in two columns—one from Chippawa, fifteen miles to the north, and one from Port Colborne, fifteen miles to the west. The Fenian colonel ordered his camp broken. When he mustered his men around 10:00 p.m., however, he found a smaller army than he had arrived with hours earlier. Scores of soldiers who thought O'Neill too green to lead them into battle deserted the army, hiding in friends' houses in Fort Erie or rowing back to the United States in stolen boats.

Left with three hundred surplus muskets, O'Neill ordered them destroyed so they didn't fall into enemy hands. The Irishmen burned their extra rifles and smashed them against apple trees. They marched north along the Niagara River before turning inland, in hopes of intercepting one of the two advancing columns before they had a chance to unite.

The march proved difficult—even for the many Civil War veterans among the Irishmen. Recent rainstorms had turned the roads into mud. The more grizzled soldiers took off their sodden stockings and shoes, tied the laces over the barrels of their guns, and walked barefoot.

O'Neill's men were weary and famished. They couldn't forget, however, the suffering they or their forebears had endured during the Great Hunger.

"Terance, I'm awful hungry," groused one soldier to another.

"Shut up, man, you don't know what hunger is!"

❀

By 7:00 a.m. on June 2, the sun's rays alighted on Starr's advance guard, promising a hot day to come for the men as they marched toward the village of Ridgeway. For Junor, too, who was then disembarking from his train in the same village, with the Queen's Own Rifles. The university student and the rest of his company had arrived only hours earlier in Port Colborne, where they found the rest of the regiment on a freight train eating a frugal breakfast of bread and red herring.

Already, the Canadians had shown their inexperience. Without Peacocke's approval, Dennis and seventy-two artillerymen and sailors of the volunteer Welland Canal Field Battery and Dunnville Naval Brigade had departed Port Colborne at 4:00 a.m. in an armed tugboat bound for Fort Erie to cut off Fenian supply lines and prevent their retreat. Lieutenant Colonel Alfred Booker, an English-born auctioneer who headed the volunteer Thirteenth Infantry Battalion that had traveled south from Hamilton to Port Colborne, assumed command as the ranking officer. Booker had no battle experience, and his men were perhaps even more untried than the Queen's Own Rifles. Sixty percent of his 250 men were under the age of twenty. Seventy of his men had never fired live ammunition.

Shortly after Dennis's departure, Peacocke ordered Booker to meet him in Stevensville, halfway between Chippawa and Port Colborne. Booker planned to make the thirty-minute train ride to Ridgeway, running along the north shore of Lake Erie, before marching north for the four and a half miles to Stevensville.

As the Canadian volunteers disembarked from the Buffalo and Lake Huron Railway in Ridgeway, Booker could not locate any wagons to transport their stores, including their ammunition, so he sent the supplies back to Port Colborne. Junor and his fellow students piled their baggage in a heap at the station, "expecting to return and get it after we had annihilated the Fenians," he wrote.

While the Irish Republican Army might have been foreign invaders, O'Neill arguably had more local knowledge than his Canadian rivals, thanks to the information supplied by Fenian intelligence officers such as Major John C. Canty, who had spent six months living in Fort Erie performing reconnaissance work. The Irishmen took a position on a long ridge of limestone three miles north of Ridgeway. O'Neill made his headquarters in the house of seventy-three-year-old Henry Angur, a veteran of the War of 1812 and of the Patriot War of 1837 who refused to leave his house, declaring that he had survived two wars and liked his chances in a third.

From his perch on the bluff known as Limestone Ridge, O'Neill overlooked the surrounding fields. He could see troop movements for miles. The Fenians saw the familiar, hated red coats on the backs of the Thirteenth Infantry, but the green uniforms worn by the Queen's Own Rifles presented a jarring target for the Irishmen. Around 8:00 a.m., O'Neill watched the Queen's Own Rifles march north on Ridge Road at the head of a column trailed by the Thirteenth Infantry and the York and Caledonia Rifle Companies. The enemy force was at least three times the size of his army. The odds were against the Irish once again.

Booker's men approached a crossroads populated by a tavern and a few scattered buildings. He placed Company Five of the Queen's Own Rifles in the lead because they carried the most state-of-the-art weaponry. Their Spencer seven-shot repeating rifles allowed for quicker shots than the muzzle-loading Springfield rifles carried by the Fenians and the muzzle-loading British Enfield rifles used by the rest of the Canadian forces. The men of Company Five, however, had received the unfamiliar firearms only the previous day, along with just twenty-eight rounds of ammunition per man.

O'Neill advanced two companies in skirmishing formation along the ridge. They formed a battle line behind a temporary breastwork, constructed with pieces harvested from the split-rail fences that dissected the fields parallel to the enemy line and the road to Fort Erie. As the enemy skirmishers came into view, sharp fire cracked the air. O'Neill watched as the white puffs of smoke from his forward skirmishers blossomed, followed a split second later by the reverberation of their gunshots. Biting into the end of their cartridges, the battle-hardened Irishmen would once again taste that familiar acrid gunpowder before loading the shot into their rifles.

Officers with swords raised in the air shouted orders to fire over the din. Junor heard the command: "With ball cartridge, load." With every gunshot they heard, the inexperienced Canadians instinctively ducked. Although more than a year removed from the Civil War, the Union and Confederate veterans were used to the whistle of bullets flying over their heads. "To most of us who had been in the war, it was soon evident that fighting was new to our opponents," O'Keeffe recalled.

The Canadian skirmishers advanced through fields of young wheat and tree stumps. They dashed from stump to stump, throwing themselves flat on the ground still wet with morning dew as a deluge of bullets struck the stumps and rattled the orchards, sending a shower of apple blossoms down upon the heads of the Canadians. Once the Fenians had emptied their single shots and worked to reload, the Canadians rose to fire their repeating rifles. The Canadian skirmishers advanced so far in front of their main body that they began taking on gunshots from both the front and the rear.

As they progressed through the fields toward the Fenian lines, the Canadians had to climb over or through a new fence every fifteen or twenty yards. With loaded rifles and bayonets at their sides, this took considerable effort and left them exposed. Not only did the terrain prove an obstacle course for the advancing Canadians, but Booker's men also started to run out of their limited ammunition.

The Canadians, however, maintained a steady advance to dislodge the Fenians from the thick timber that protected the center of their line. O'Neill feared that the enemy flanks had become so prolonged that his men could be enveloped. Knowing that he was outmanned, the Fenian colonel decided to undertake a risky maneuver, one that could be tried only with experienced troops. O'Neill ordered his men to slowly fall back a few hundred yards to coax the Canadian center and form a new line. They acted, and believing the Irish in retreat due to the relatively small size of their force, the Canadians became bold with their attack. They charged ahead until they found themselves practically in a valley at the base of Limestone Ridge.

With their center uncovered, O'Neill waited until the Canadians were within one hundred yards. "Charge!" he suddenly shouted. The Fenians took the Canadians by surprise, unleashing a terrific volley. They sounded a chorus of wild Irish whoops as they advanced behind the green flag given to them by the Fenian Sisterhood, the brunt of their attack falling upon the University Rifles.

On their horses, O'Neill and Starr appeared in the rear of the center of their line. Whether Booker saw those officers or other horsemen cresting Limestone Ridge, the inexperienced commander panicked. "The cavalry are coming!" came the cry from the Canadians. Bugles ordered the Canadian militiamen to form a square, a textbook defensive position against a cavalry attack, which the militia had drilled on the practice ground.

There was no cavalry, however, and even if the Irishmen had one, the battlefield terrain with its obstacles was hardly conducive to a charge of horsemen. All the maneuver did was leave the Canadians exposed to withering fire because the Fenian infantry had a target on which to focus. A succession of soldiers fell to the ground with bullet wounds. "We were all called to form [a] square—that awful square," lamented the Canadian A. G. Gilbert. "No cavalry came, for there was none to come."

Once Booker realized there was no cavalry, the Canadians tried to form a line, but the fire was just too much. Officers made futile attempts to rally their forces until the bugle sounded their retreat. After nearly two hours of fighting, the Canadians ran for their lives, throwing aside muskets, overcoats, knapsacks, and anything that could slow them down. Lying in the dirt by the roadside was the flag of the Queen's Own Rifles.*

Junor ran along the crossroad as he joined in the sprint to safety. He heard a dull, heavy blow as his twenty-one-year-old fellow student William Tempest fell face-first into the road. The tall, promising medical student was in his final year of studies, preparing to join his father's medical practice. Junor knelt over his fallen colleague for a moment and saw the bullet wound to the head. There was nothing he could do. Tempest was dead. Moments later, the Fenians took Junor prisoner.

At the same time, Edward Lonergan, a ship carpenter and lieutenant with the Seventh Regiment, came upon Private R. W. Hines of the Queen's Own Rifles. He declared him, too, a prisoner. The Irish soldier seized the Canadian's rifle and swore it would never shoot another Fenian. But when he smashed the rifle butt of the weapon on a stone in an attempt to destroy it, the impact released the rifle's hammer, which fired. The bullet pierced Lonergan's throat and exited the back of his head, killing him immediately on his twenty-first birthday.

The Irish kept the enemy on the run through the town of Ridgeway until O'Neill called off the pursuit after a mile on the other side of the village. The Irishmen collected as many of their wounded

---

* The banner would star as a trophy of war at Irish gatherings in Chicago for years to come.

as could fit in their wagons. They left the rest in the care of local civilians, who also promised to bury the Fenian dead. Some of those wounded and left behind would eventually be arrested by British authorities.

This lithograph dramatizes the Irish Republican Army's advance during the Battle of Ridgeway while Canadian defense forces retreat.

On the Canadian side, seven of the Queen's Own Rifles died in action. Three more succumbed to wounds received in battle, and six would die of disease contracted in service. Twenty-eight Canadians were wounded at Limestone Ridge. Between six and eight died on the Fenian side, including the spy Canty.

For the first time since the 1745 Battle of Fontenoy, an Irish army had emerged victorious against forces of the British Empire. News of the Battle of Ridgeway consumed citizens on both sides of the international border. Toronto newspapers issued extra editions hourly, while *The Boston Herald* sold more copies of its edition covering the Fenian raid than it had after Lee's surrender at Appomattox.

O'Neill's victory incited joy among the Irish diaspora and in Ireland itself. *The Nation* in Dublin exulted in the news that "the red flag of England has gone down before the Irish green" and reported that the news "fills our people with tumultuous emotions impossible to describe, impossible to conceal." *The Detroit Free Press* shook its head. "It is difficult to believe that any body of men who are not insane, have from this country invaded and committed acts of depredation or war against a nation with which we are at peace."

The news stirred Irishmen across the United States, who now saw the Fenian Brotherhood was more than just bluster. From Louisiana to Maine, hundreds grabbed their rifles and boarded trains to Buffalo to join in the fight. Momentum was finally on their side.

O'Neill took no time to bask in the glow of his historic victory. He knew his position remained precarious, given the small size of his army and the advance of Peacocke's force, which remained nearby. He wondered where his reinforcements were—both those from the United States and those from Canada. The Fenians had expected Canadians to join them in casting off the British, not take up arms against them. They assumed any colony of Great Britain sought liberation as they did. Plus, the Irishmen in Canada had yet to accept their "hand of brotherhood in the holy cause of fatherland" that was offered in their proclamation.

"I decided that my best policy was to return to Fort Erie, and ascertain if crossings had been made at other points," O'Neill recalled, "and if so, I was willing to sacrifice myself and my noble little command for the sake of leaving the way open."

In the wake of their victory, O'Neill maintained order among his men. The Irishmen shared pipes with their newly captured prisoners and requested water for them from passing houses on their march to Fort Erie. They even purchased glasses of beer for their captives at a roadside tavern.

The Irishmen arrived back at the village around 4:00 p.m. In absence of the Fenians, Canadians had repossessed Old Fort Erie, capturing Irishmen as they returned from Ridgeway, some fifty in all.

When the Fenian captain Rudolph Fitzpatrick galloped into Fort Erie on his stolen steed, a gunshot rang out from the upper window of a dwelling house. Fitzpatrick drew his pistol and returned fire. The Fenian infantry rushed to join the fight. This time, it was the Canadians who were outnumbered. They held the Fenians at bay for about twenty minutes but no longer. The Canadians took shelter in any house where they found an open door. They hid behind piles of cordwood and fences. The twenty-five village blocks of Fort Erie became the scene of street fighting as gunfire emanated from the collection of two-story frame houses, stores, hotels, taverns, and boardinghouses. This was house-to-house guerrilla combat. O'Neill ordered his men to break down the doors of houses containing the enemy and smoke them out with burning straw thrown into broken windows. As many as thirty of the Canadian troops fled into the house of the postmaster George Lewis and fired from its windows. Bullets pierced the home's clapboard exterior and plaster walls until the Fenians set the building ablaze, forcing a quick surrender.

The skirmish had an international audience. Gathered on the banks of the opposite shore, curious Buffalo residents watched the gunfight unfold from Squaw Island. Not only could they hear the staccato of gunfire, but eyewitnesses also reported bullets whistling over their heads and puncturing the walls of the island's flour mills. One Irishman with a long gray beard danced in frantic excitement with his revolver, which he fired at the enemy across the river. "Give it to them, give it to them," he shouted, cheering on the Irish Republican Army.

With his men pushed back to the waterfront, Dennis ordered a steamship boarded with his Irish prisoners to cast off into the Niagara River and sounded the retreat—every man for himself. For his part, he took shelter in a friend's house, shaved off his distinctive whiskers, donned a disguise, and escaped.

The only escape route for Captain Richard King of the Welland Canal Field Battery was to swim to the steamship before it departed. He ran to the dock and jumped into the water, but a Fenian gunshot shattered his leg in the process. The wounded captain would survive, though his leg would be amputated.

O'Neill emerged victorious on enemy soil once again, with the Fenians taking forty-five of the enemy prisoner. O'Neill dispatched one hundred men to guard the road to Chippawa and took the rest of his command to the old fort. He had triumphed, but the colonel knew his situation was growing direr by the minute.

❧

At 6:00 p.m., O'Neill sent word to Captain William J. Hynes and the other Fenians in Buffalo that an enemy force of five thousand men remained on the Niagara Peninsula and could have them surrounded by the following morning. After fighting two battles and marching nearly forty miles in less than twenty-four hours, the Irish Republican Army now grappled with hunger and fatigue.

The Fenian colonel was still willing to fight if reinforcements were on the way. However, the disappointing word arrived from Buffalo that no other Fenians had been able to cross over, due to the USS *Michigan* and federal revenue cutters keeping a constant vigil on the Niagara River. The Fenians might have been advancing on Canada, but it was the United States by which they were now stymied.

Without Canadian support, the Irish Republican Army had no options. Around 10:00 p.m., Hynes rowed across the Niagara to order O'Neill to retreat while he worked to furnish transportation as soon as he could to take the Fenians back to the United States. Although weary, the Irishmen had remained jovial. They danced to keep warm as the temperature began to drop and even cracked jokes with their prisoners, tearing into biscuits and raw pork. O'Neill approached O'Keeffe, pulled him aside, and broke the disappointing news: "Johnny, I have orders to evacuate."

Around 2:00 a.m., Junor and the rest of the prisoners were roused from their sleep and ordered to form a line. The thought crossed a few Canadian minds that they were about to be shot. Instead, they were placed into marching order and then taken to the bank of the Niagara River. O'Neill directed his men to board a waiting barge tied to a tugboat as he began the river evacuation.

A number of Fenians didn't return with their comrades. Thirteen were killed or died of wounds received at Ridgeway and Fort Erie, while another twenty-eight were wounded. Some of the most seriously injured had to be left behind in the houses of sympathizers in Fort Erie.

After the last of his able-bodied men embarked, O'Neill proceeded down the line of the nearly two dozen Canadian prisoners, shaking hands with each of them. He said his good-byes, informed them that they were again free men, and promised to return to Canada soon—this time with a larger force.

A tug hauled the barge with its disappointed Fenian cargo back across the river they had crossed in the other direction just forty-eight hours earlier. Once the tug reached American waters, the *J. C. Harrison,* a steam launch for the USS *Michigan,* fired its twelve-pound pivot gun across the bow of the tugboat and threatened to sink it unless the Irish Republican Army surrendered. Behind the steam launch lurked the USS *Michigan* with extra maritime muscle. Its captain, Andrew Bryson, wasn't about to let the Fenians elude him a second time.

As a Union army veteran, O'Neill strictly followed orders from the U.S. government and offered no resistance. "We would have as readily surrendered to an infant bearing the authority of the United States," he wrote.

The thirteen Fenian officers were taken to relatively comfortable quarters aboard the USS *Michigan,* but the 367 rank-and-file soldiers remained confined to the barge. When daylight arrived, curious men and women came by the thousands to the Black Rock waterfront to gawk at the Irish Republican Army floating in the Niagara River.

On the opposite riverbank, the Fenians watched as the redcoats reclaimed the village of Fort Erie. A detachment of Tenth Royals found Fenian stragglers in the woods and their dead and wounded hidden in the homes of sympathizers.

When the British troops searched the late Canty's hilltop residence, they discovered Father John McMahon hiding in a cupboard dressed in his Roman collar, long black coat, and well-worn plug hat. Inside his carpetbag, the troops found Holy Eucharist and consecrated oils for administering last rites to dying soldiers, but no weapons. McMahon claimed that he was on his way to visit the bishop of Montreal and denied that there were Fenians on the premises. However, the British found two wounded Irishmen elsewhere in the house and more out back in the barn and a nearby haystack. Inside the barn they also found the body of Lonergan, dead from his self-inflicted wound and taken from Ridgeway by his fellow soldiers.

In all, the British captured fifty-eight Fenians in Fort Erie, including fourteen Protestants, one German, and seven Canadians. A third of them were under the age of twenty-one. They then took a tug to the USS *Michigan* and demanded that the Americans turn over the hundreds of Fenians detained on the barge. Bryson refused. They would remain in American custody.

⚜

Just weeks after he had departed Eastport, Maine, Major General George Meade had once again been summoned to prevent any further incursions over the Canadian border. With his recommendation to impose martial law in states along the border rejected, Meade instead ordered Major General William F. Barry to prevent any further border incursions and seize all Fenian weapons he believed would be used in an attack on Canada.

With reports arriving of Irishmen amassing in both northern Vermont and upstate New York, Meade posted nine companies along the border from Buffalo to St. Albans, Vermont. Satisfied that O'Neill's brief invasion had been a feint, Meade departed on June 3 to Ogdensburg in upstate New York, having spent only a few hours on the ground in Buffalo.

Inside the White House, Andrew Johnson wavered about what to do with the ship-bound Irish Americans. Secretary of the Navy Gideon Welles had grown frustrated with the reluctance of anyone inside the administration to take action because Johnson and his cabinet knew that any measures taken against the Fenians would anger the Irish vote. Meanwhile, Secretary of War Edwin Stanton, a Radical Republican sympathizer who often clashed with the Democratic president, remained passive in the hopes that Johnson would be forced to take unpopular action.

However, days had passed without any word from the president, who hoped a military man would put an end to the Fenian uprising so that he could be absolved from blame. "This is a war on the Irish in which he, Stanton, and Grant fear to do their duty," Welles wrote of Johnson.

⚜

Just four days after the bells of Toronto had pealed to summon volunteers to battle, they now tolled in mourning on June 5. Inside the undergraduate lounge at the University of Toronto, students had filed past the open caskets containing the bodies of their classmates, still in their muddy, bloodstained uniforms. Now the Queen's Own Rifles assembled once again in its drill shed as the city gathered to bury five of its heroes killed at the Battle of Ridgeway.

City businesses, banks, and public buildings shuttered early, while flags drooped at half-mast. The Union Jack and other flags adorned the rough pine coffins that were processed to St. James Cemetery for burial. In a city raw with grief, six Fenian prisoners captured at Fort Erie had the unfortunate timing of being paraded through the streets of Toronto on the same afternoon as the funeral. Sorrow turned to anger as the handcuffed prisoners were marched up Parliament Street under heavy guard. Crowds returning from the funerals rushed the captives. "Lynch them!" they hollered. "Give us back our dead!" they cried. A Canadian cavalry dashed to drive the crowd back and escort the prisoners safely to jail. Eventually, sixty-five Fenian prisoners would be held behind bars in Toronto.

The Toronto *Globe* reported that the deaths of the province's young men at Ridgeway bound Canadians closer together with resolve not to join the Fenians or the Americans. "The autonomy of British America, its independence of all control save that to which its people willingly submit, is cemented by the bloodshed in the battle on the 2nd of June."

❖

While the White House dithered, the captured Fenians continued to suffer. With barely enough room to turn around, the Irishmen stood on the open deck of the squalid barge, where they were alternately blistered by the sun and doused by heavy rains. Still, they found exposure to the elements preferable to the terrible odor and filth that lingered in the hold.

After visiting the prisoners, Dr. Edward Donnelly, a surgeon and zealous Fenian supporter, expressed his fear that an outbreak of disease was imminent. The situation grew so desperate that dozens dove into the water at night to swim ashore and make the barge's deck a little more comfortable.

Some prisoners cussed out Sweeny for their predicament, but all cursed Johnson for betraying them, cutting their supply lines in spite of his pledge to "acknowledge accomplished facts." The Irish Republican Army believed it could have, with reinforcements, seized the Welland Canal and advanced toward Toronto, particularly because every railway train arriving in Buffalo from the West deposited hundreds of Irishmen per day, some from as far away as Nebraska and Kansas.

At the end of their third day confined to the barge, the prisoners watched as a tug rounded the stern of the floating prison and sidled up to the USS *Michigan*. Aboard the boat, two American commissioners bore an order that the prisoners be released on their own recognizance. The Fenians launched their hats skyward and embraced each other at the prospects of being free men once again.

O'Neill and his fellow officers, however, were not so fortunate: They would be charged with violation of American neutrality laws. Three companies of U.S. artillery troops and large crowds of spectators escorted them to a nearby jail. The officers lacked money for a proper legal defense, but one of Buffalo's most eminent attorneys agreed to help. Having recently lost his first run for elected office, the attorney Grover Cleveland, after visiting with the Irishmen, agreed to take their case pro bono, even refusing the purse collected by Fenian supporters.

After appearing in court on June 6, O'Neill and Starr were released on $6,000 bail each, ordered to appear at the U.S. Circuit Court in Canandaigua, New York, on June 19. An estimated six thousand Fenians remained in Buffalo, many of whom escorted the Irish patriots to the Mansion House, clamoring to see and hear from O'Neill. The hero of Ridgeway stepped onto a balcony above Main Street, looked out over the crowd, and kept his remarks brief. "Gentlemen, you may not be aware that I am no speechmaker," he said. "The only kind of speeches I am accustomed to are such as are made from the cannon's mouth. Situated as I am at present, I can only advise you to retire to your homes, peacefully and in an orderly manner. Good-bye."

A modest proclamation, but all the same O'Neill had proven himself a born leader and an able tactician after being unexpectedly thrust into the role of commander. While detained on the USS *Michigan,* he received a promotion to brigadier general "for the gallant and able manner in which he handled the forces under his command, and for routing double the number of British troops at the battle of Limestone Ridge." He learned something about his fellow Fenians as well. "I saw at that time that Irish troops on

Canadian soil would fight with desperation and courage, and that carefully organized and properly disciplined, they would prove valiant soldiers," he said.

O'Keeffe saw the change in his commander. After the successes at Ridgeway and Fort Erie, he wrote of O'Neill, "the re-invasion of Canada was his day vision and his night dream."

Iron Wills and Brave Hearts

THE TOWNSPEOPLE OF St. Albans, Vermont, knew the look of a rebel when they saw one, for nothing could erase their memories of that terrible day when terror descended from Canada, just fifteen miles away.

It had started with a single shot from a Colt Navy revolver piercing the crisp afternoon sky, then the gunman's stunning cry: "I take possession of this town in the name of the Confederate States of America!" Without warning, the Civil War stormed into this northern Vermont hamlet on October 19, 1864, not with a broadside from the south, but with a sucker punch from the north.

Twenty-two raiders, led by Bennett H. Young, a Confederate cavalry lieutenant from Kentucky, relieved three St. Albans banks of their greenbacks, silver, and gold. They forced tellers and customers to swear allegiance to the Confederacy before locking them inside the banks' vaults. They held hostages at gunpoint on the village green. They even shot poor Elinus Morrison dead right in front of Miss Beattie's Millinery Shop before galloping back across the Canadian border on stolen horses with a haul of more than $200,000.

Canadian authorities arrested fourteen of the rebels in the border towns of Quebec, but the Crown refused to extradite them to the United States. St. Albans seethed further when the rebels walked out of a courtroom with not only their freedom but also $90,000 of their ill-gotten money, after a Canadian judge ruled that he lacked jurisdiction over citizens of the Confederate States of America. The outrage even drove President Abraham Lincoln to order his military staff to draw up invasion plans of Canada.

Perhaps worse than the miscarriage of justice to the six thousand citizens of St. Albans was that the self-proclaimed "Vairmont Yankee Scare Party" had violated the hospitality of their amiable little town. They posed as horse traders, fishermen, tourists, and members of a Canadian sportsmen's club. Wielding a Bible as a prop, the twenty-one-year-old Young pretended to be a theological student from Montreal on three separate reconnaissance visits. The village's most illustrious resident, then-Governor John Gregory Smith, even invited the scoundrel into his mansion for a tour. All the while as the infiltrators swapped stories with the citizens of St. Albans, they were secretly scouting the community and casing its banks.

Now, two years later, unfamiliar rebels were again wandering the still-jittery town. The seat of Franklin County had awoken on June 1 to find 350 men from Boston and the mill cities of Lowell, Massachusetts, and Rutland, Vermont, eating breakfast in its saloons and wandering Main Street's wooden sidewalks with carpetbags slung over their shoulders. Speaking in low voices, the strangers addressed each other as "colonel" and "captain" in between drags on their pipes. The outsiders were orderly, but then again, the Confederate invaders had been, too.

Throughout the morning, the suspicious Irishmen paid repeated visits to a tall, dignified man with a commanding military presence registered at the Tremont House. When a delegation of town authorities decided to pay the gentleman a social call as well, the tight-lipped guest volunteered only that he was awaiting friends, perhaps as many as five thousand of them, who were also "intending to take a journey for their health during the month of June."

That evening, sixty more Irishmen arrived by train. What did these strange men want? What kind of trouble did they seek?

Answers arrived over the telegraph wire when it was learned that John O'Neill had planted the green flag on British soil four hundred miles to the west. Now war had returned to St. Albans. With it clear that the village would again be on the front lines of the action, the mystery man lodging inside the Tremont House finally introduced himself: He was "Brigadier General Spear, senior commander of the right wing of the Fenian army."

The news was greeted with shock. Word of a possible invasion had spread, but few believed the Fenians would actually strike. That included many Fenians themselves. In cities across the United States, Irish eyes devoured the latest bulletins posted outside newspaper offices and upscale hotels. The news served as a recruiting tool and a fund-raising boon for the Roberts wing. Thousands of Irishmen abandoned their jobs and spent their last pennies for train fare to St. Albans, Buffalo, and other locales in upstate New York. The web of railroad tracks woven across New England carried carloads to the front, such as it was, along the Quebec border.

Edward Archibald, the British consul in New York City, reported "the excitement among the Irish caused by the news of a collision and bloodshed was everywhere manifest." A green flag waved from the front balcony of Tammany Hall, where secretaries scribbled the names of hundreds of new recruits. Women showed their solidarity by donning strips of green ribbons over their hearts. Even a group of African American veterans, casting aside any lingering animosity from the Irish violence directed toward them during the New York City draft riots, reportedly lent their services to the Fenians. (Their offer was declined.)

The New York Times devoted five front-page columns to "the border excitement" the day after the Fenians breached the international frontier, while *The New York Herald* made a much more blunt declaration: "WAR." *The Irish-American* tried with breathless hyperbole to rally readers to grab their guns. "The whole border from Maine to Michigan is bristling with Irish bayonets," it proclaimed. But not all Irishmen were so optimistic.

William Roberts basked in what *The Irish-American* called "startling but most intensely pleasurable news." For his part, though, Thomas Sweeny still feared that the entire operation would prove a disaster. A lack of manpower had plagued the initial steps in his plan and pushed back the start of the main attack on Quebec from its June 2 target. The Fenian secretary of war grew further annoyed to learn that his orders for troops to move from Detroit to divert enemy attention had not been executed. And he hadn't heard news from upstate New York in days.

Sweeny held out hope that the tide of Celtic recruits that swelled in the days after Ridgeway had yet to crest upon the Canadian border. While Roberts continued to rally the troops with a fusillade of proclamations, Sweeny departed for the front lines in upstate New York on June 4 to see for himself how many men were there to be rallied. What the general found would do little to improve his mood.

When the Fenian secretary of war stepped off the train in Malone, New York—a town of seven thousand that had been sacked by the British during the War of 1812—he expected to find nearly as many troops as villagers. However, out of the 16,800 troops his plan called for, he had barely more than 2,000. There was little sign of the five cavalry regiments to be commanded by Brigadier General Michael C. Murphy that he had ordered to Malone. Where were all the new recruits, and why hadn't he been told of the disappointing turnout?

An officer insisted that he had been, in six different telegraph messages. It seems the U.S. government had intercepted their dispatches. In fact, the federal authorities had seized more than just the Fenians' communications. Two weeks earlier, U.S. customs agents in Rouses Point, New York, confiscated thirty-two suspicious cases marked "machinery" that were addressed to Malone's Fenian leader, Edward J. Mannix, a County Cork native and Civil War veteran. Customs agents found forty muskets inside each box. Hours before Sweeny arrived, another thirty-one cases of Fenian arms had been seized. At Potsdam Junction, at De Kalb Junction, at Watertown, and at Malone, the federal government took possession of mysterious railroad shipments that Sweeny had purchased from Philadelphia's Bridesburg Arsenal and Troy's Watervliet Arsenal. The general was outraged. He had bought those munitions from the same government that was now seizing them.

Sweeny could feel the time to strike slipping away. He lost faith in the ability of the Fenians to launch an attack along the west side of the Richelieu River from upstate New York. With gunships now patrolling the St. Lawrence River and General George Meade lurking just sixty miles away in Ogdensburg, Sweeny decided on June 6 to move his post from Malone to a more inviting—and promising—locale.

※

St. Albans might have been named for the first recorded English martyr, but its scenery was pure Irish. Stone walls dissected emerald meadows dotted with sheep. Brooks trickled down from the Green Mountains to the east. To the west, the undulating tops of the distant Adirondacks floated above the cobalt surface of Lake Champlain. The tidy village's weekly butter market drew traders from as far away as New York City and Boston.

It was guns, not butter, though, that drew Sweeny's attention to St. Albans, home to one of Vermont's thirteen Fenian Brotherhood circles. John Fallon, the captain of the local Fenian Brotherhood circle, assured Sweeny that St. Albans was the "best town on the line" because it was not only just sixty-five miles from Montreal but also a major rail hub, which would aid in transporting guns and ammunition in advance of the attack.

Fallon thought he had a perfect front for making the secret arms shipments. Peter Ward, secretary of the Fenian circle in St. Albans and superintendent of the town's gasworks, was overseeing the plant's reconstruction after a devastating fire, which meant he was receiving "a great quantity of material every day." Beginning in late May, swords and rifles that Sweeny had purchased from the U.S. government were shipped to Ward's attention in crates marked "glass," "crockery," and "gas fixtures" and then hidden in barns and buried in the woods throughout the surrounding towns.

The watchful eyes of U.S. customs agents, particularly those on the British payroll as informants, grew too prying when one suspicious shipment of boxes marked "glass, with care" arrived on an express from Springfield, Massachusetts. After the rail workers tenderly lifted the boxes to the platform, they watched in shock as a pair of Irishmen threw the supposedly precious cargo onto a wagon before bolting away from the station.

Shortly after Spear arrived in St. Albans, so did the U.S. marshal Hugh Henry and three companies of the Third U.S. Artillery, which seized boxes and barrels at the train depot that were addressed to Ward, finding them to be brimming with sabers, carbines, and cavalry equipment. "The President approves of your action in stopping the arms," Secretary of War Edwin Stanton wrote to the local collector of customs. "You will detain them in your custody until further orders, and pursue the same course to any other lots."

The Fenians grew wise and began to toss boxes off railcars before reaching the St. Albans depot, retrieving them later, but the arms seizures threatened the invasion plan because many of the Fenians who arrived in northern Vermont lacked blankets or overcoats, let alone a revolver. "We Irishmen are determined and will fight," one veteran of Antietam and Gettysburg told a newspaper correspondent, "but we cannot do anything without an abundance of arms, and where are we to get them?"

❧

For nearly a week, a steady stream of Fenian fighters from New York and New England arrived by rail in St. Albans. Another 350 arrived on June 6. Most were young, some mere boys fourteen and fifteen years old. Some found open arms and open doors among Franklin County's sizable Irish population. Others camped in the woods and scrounged for provisions from local Fenians. The heavy spring rains that liquefied the dirt roads into mud, however, slowed their movement. Day after day, the sodden Fenian camp slogged toward the border—from Fairfield to Sheldon to East Highgate.

By the time Sweeny arrived in St. Albans, later on June 6, the registers of the town's hotels were inked with the names of Civil War correspondents from newspapers such as *The New York Herald,* the *New-York Tribune,* and the *Boston Journal* who were suddenly back on their old beat. Hundreds of government troops had converted the village green into a makeshift army camp, their white teepee tents offering badly needed coverage from days of deluges.

Sweeny convened a war council with the few Fenian officers remaining in St. Albans, including Brigadier General Spear. The general's handpicked man to lead the most crucial phase of the Fenian campaign had spent three decades in service of the United States, serving with distinction in the Civil War as a colonel with the Eleventh Pennsylvania Cavalry until sustaining a serious leg and head injury.

Spear reported to Sweeny that he had approximately one thousand men camping in the Vermont countryside "without supplies, commissary stores, or anything but good comfortable clothing." He couldn't help but wonder what had happened to the money donated to the Roberts wing to be used for precisely this moment. As in upstate New York, Spear found himself constrained by the government's seizure of their arms. He told Sweeny that he had been forced to "beg, borrow, or take such ammunition as can be found" while avoiding the watchful eyes of federal troops. Order had prevailed, but the men were getting uneasy and eager for action.

The good news was that for all the disruption to their town the citizens of St. Albans didn't appear too put out. "Never has there been congregated in St. Albans so large a number of strangers who have conducted themselves more orderly than the invaders of Canada," reported one of the town's newspapers. After touring the front lines, Vermont's governor, Paul Dillingham, said he would sooner "think of calling out the militia to put down a Quaker meeting as to resist the Fenian movement."

Aside from those Confederate raiders who had torn through their town two years prior, St. Albans had a bit of a soft spot for rebels. After all, Ethan Allen's Green Mountain Boys had declared independence not only from Great Britain during the American Revolution but from New York as well. For fourteen years, Vermont was its own independent republic with its own printed currency, much like the Fenian government in exile. St. Albans had refused to enforce the fugitive slave law, serving as one of the final depots on the Underground Railroad. The town's old-timers could even remember when they barred the late general Winfield Scott, dispatched as President Martin Van Buren's special envoy, from lecturing them about their "flaunting" of American neutrality laws by supporting the anti-British forces during the Patriot War of 1837.

The residents of St. Albans were even less willing to listen to any talk about neutrality laws after what had been done to them in October 1864. They might not have backed the Fenian cause, but they surely approved of the Irish delivering some equivalent discomfort to the British and the Canadians. Perhaps it shouldn't have been a surprise, as one newspaper reported, that "ninety-nine out of every one hundred of the people at St. Albans are friendly to the Fenian cause." But resistance was brewing just a few miles north on the other side of the international frontier.

❀

Scarlet-uniformed soldiers marched throughout the streets of Montreal to Bonaventure Station and boarded Grand Trunk Railway trains bound for cities such as Kingston, Cornwall, and Prescott along the St. Lawrence River and for towns in southern Quebec. A constant soundtrack of drums and bagpipes played as the Royal Artillery, Prince of Wales' Rifles, and Victoria Rifles marched in unison through a city guarded by armed militia and papered with placards calling for volunteers to take up arms to repel the marauders.

Many answered the call, and those who couldn't volunteer enlisted their voices to cheer on the men marching out of Montreal. "Good luck to you!" "Don't leave a mother's son of the villains alive!" they called out while cursing the pirates, bandits, and robbers who had thrown the city into a frenzy.

It was no small irony that the city in such a state of panic about lawless rebels violating neutrality laws still offered considerable sanctuary to leaders of the Confederacy. This was the city, after all, where news of President Abraham Lincoln's assassination was toasted and General George Pickett lived in a luxurious hotel and exchanged salutes with Confederate sympathizers. Boxes of official Confederate government documents were housed inside the vaults of the Bank of Montreal. The city even harbored the family of Jefferson Davis.

The news from Ridgeway had thrown Montreal into a particular panic because it feared the enemy within. Not fully convinced of the loyalty of the two Irish Catholic companies in the Prince of Wales' Rifles, soldiers in the Protestant "Orange Company" made sure to keep their rifles loaded at all times. Montreal's mayor, Henry Starnes, stoked fears further by announcing he had dismissed ten policemen who had refused to take an oath of allegiance tendered to all civic employees at the outbreak of trouble.

However, there were few outward signs of Fenian support among Montreal's Irish after O'Neill's raid. Thomas D'Arcy McGee, the staunch supporter of Canadian confederation, saw little nuance in the threat facing Canada. "Whoever is not with us is against us," he told Montrealers shoehorned into city hall on June 4. "Whoever has any sympathy with the invaders commits a crime." He assured his constituents that he was ready to travel to Ottawa and cast a vote in Parliament in favor of the suspension of habeas corpus.

Many in his audience were already shocked that the Johnson administration had done so little to enforce American neutrality laws and control the Irish menace. "You must allow me to say that I do not understand why the United States Government does not issue a proclamation warning people against joining in these proceedings," Sir Frederick Bruce, the British representative in Washington, wrote to Secretary of State William Seward. Sweeny and his men were just miles from the Canadian border, yet the White House remained silent.

But that was about to change.

❁

Seward and President Johnson might have tolerated the Fenians for a time, but the lark was over. The Irish succeeded in alarming British diplomats, who were increasing the pressure on their American counterparts to rein in their citizens. Lieutenant General Ulysses S. Grant had also had enough of the freelancing by his former soldiers, recommending to Stanton that Sweeny, Roberts, and other Fenian leaders be taken into custody and the Irish Republican Army be reeled in from the front.

On June 6, four days after the assault on Ridgeway, Johnson scrawled his signature on a proclamation that forbade the Fenians to carry on any further operations in violation of the country's neutrality laws and empowered "all judges, magistrates, marshals, and officers in the service of the United States" to arrest the Fenian ringleaders. That afternoon, as Sweeny was meeting with his war council in St. Albans, Johnson's words filtered through the telegraph wires to the front lines in upstate New York and Vermont. When Major A. A. Gibson, commander of the Third Artillery, received the notice in St. Albans, he had the words printed, posted around town, and distributed by couriers to the surrounding villages. He then gave the order for his men to take the Fenian officers in the village into custody.

Sweeny and his war council took no heed. They decided that they would cross the border at daybreak. The general had turned in for a few hours of restless sleep before his invasion when he heard a knock on the door of his hotel room around midnight. Offering no resistance, Sweeny was taken into custody along with his chief of engineers, Colonel John Mechan, to the officers' quarters.

The following morning, rather than leading the Irish Republican Army onto British soil, Sweeny found himself inside one of the spacious parlors of the Welden House hotel being arraigned on the "charge of aiding and abetting in the violation of the neutrality laws." Sweeny waived his examination, and bail was set for $20,000, which Sweeny could not furnish. Instead of being placed in jail, the general was confined to a room in the Welden House with two sentries posted at his door, pending his appearance before the U.S. District Court scheduled for the following month.

Soldiers swarmed the Tremont House five minutes too late to capture Spear. He had received word of the raid and was loaded into a horse-drawn wagon and whisked out of town. The Fenian general traveled nearly twenty miles before arriving around 8:30 a.m. at the Fenian camp in Franklin, barely two miles from the Canadian line. Spear found his rank and file singing and dancing, full of cheer that belied their restless night. The lucky ones had slept like animals— and next to animals—on the ground inside barns. Others found shelter from pelting rain in sheds and even outhouses, where they were forced to stand for the entire night.

They emerged at first light to continue their treacherous march. In some spots, the men sank ankle-deep in mud, pulling ill-fitting boots right off the men's feet. The local Fenians finally resurrected boxes of guns they had buried around St. Albans, distributing three hundred arms of various calibers. Their commissary, though, was still neglected. Some companies had one loaf of bread for every five or six men.

Spear convened his war council again, this time inside a Franklin hotel, where Brigadier General John Mahan and his officers had spent a more comfortable night than their regulars. The general had fifteen thousand fewer men than promised to strike Montreal—six hundred in the command of Colonel Louis Contri, three hundred under Colonel John Scanlan, and two hundred under Colonel Timothy O'Connor.

Mahan, a major with the Ninth Massachusetts during the Civil War and a member of the Massachusetts Legislature, briefed Spear that the lack of food and weapons combined with the abundance of mud and rain had driven many of his men home, but those who remained were eager to advance.

So too was Spear. Although he had but two horses, two twelve-pounder brass fieldpieces, and half an army without weapons of any kind, the Fenian general rallied his men. To a chorus of wild cheers, he ordered them to take Canada. President Johnson's proclamation and the White House's perceived backstabbing had only embold-ened the stubborn Irish to move ahead with their plans. The Fenian army was on the enemy's threshold, and once again it would find the front door wide open.

9

The Fenians Are Coming!

I N SPITE OF the panic that had gripped America's northern neighbor for more than a week and the Fenian threat that had lingered all year, not one British regular or Canadian volunteer could be seen as the Irish army marched to the border on the morning of June 7. The defense of Quebec's Missisquoi County had been ceded to the residents themselves in the form of a homegrown militia composed of two hundred residents under the direction of Captain C. W. Carter. Even compared with the defense forces at Ridgeway, the Missisquoi volunteers were an inexperienced lot. Most were farmers who had never fired a rifle.

Carter, a British army officer from Her Majesty's Sixteenth Regiment, had little faith in the fighting ability of his men, and when a scout returned from Vermont with a vastly exaggerated report that a Fenian army of two thousand men all armed with rifles was approaching the border, Carter ordered his men to fall back to St. Alexandre, fifteen miles from the frontier. The farmers groused at their captain atop his horse as they marched through the mud. In him they saw cowardice and capitulation personified. Many of them had been forced to abandon their fields at the critical planting time in the short growing season. Thanks to their captain, they were now leaving their homes, farms, and families in direct line of the Fenians without any defense.

Inside the Eastern Townships, the villages in southern Quebec across the border from Franklin, farmers buried their valuables, drove away their cattle, removed their deposits from banks, and sent their wives and children to safer locales—in many cases not farther north toward Montreal but actually south to Vermont, passing by the very army that was causing them to flee. In some respects, the Eastern Townships—initially settled by New Englanders seeking cheap farmland—had closer ties to their American neighbors than to Canada. It was common for members of extended families to live, work, and even celebrate the Fourth of July on both sides of the border.

As they marched the final miles to the boundary, the Fenian army passed their wagons, laden with household goods and furniture. Unlike the liquid boundary that John O'Neill traversed, the international border ahead of Samuel Spear and his men was visible only on a map and no more of an obstacle than a county line. There were no border guards. Customs officers resided in village centers miles from the dividing line, allowing the free movement of smugglers who could make $2.00 per gallon on spirits, $0.75 per pound on tea, and great prices on spices, medicine, and silks. By one estimate, the value of the property seized by customs agents in New York's St. Lawrence County was only 5 percent of the merchandise fraudulently imported.

Just after 10:00 a.m., British mud splattered across the boots of the Irish Republican Army, a lone iron post on the roadside the only indicator that they had crossed an international border. The men marched in a column four across as they entered Canada to cheers and a chorus of "The Wearing of the Green," the Hibernian street ballad evoking the memory of the Irish Rebellion of 1798.

Spear, standing before his men, looked out onto the most ragtag of armies. Some, like Colonel Louis Contri, had spent their entire lives attached to a gun, while others were so young they were incapable of growing a mustache. His cavalry hugged saddles in their arms in hopes of finding a horse to match. While some officers wore the blue coats of the U.S. Army, most of the soldiers lacked uniforms of any kind, and all were wet from the relentless downpour. About three hundred of the soldiers carried Enfield and Springfield muskets and three hundred held breech-loading carbines, but their lack of ammunition rendered many of them impotent. Those without rusty sabers and balky revolvers were armed with only their patriotism.

"You are now on British soil," Spear told his men. "I charge you to spare the women and children. I leave in your hands the enemies of your country." Spear proclaimed the establishment of the Irish Republic, setting off cheering. Colonel Contri stepped forward and unfurled a green silk emblem hand stitched by the Fenian Sisterhood circle in Malden, Massachusetts, planting it in the spongy turf. Spear then announced a $100 reward to the first man to seize the British colors. He ventured all of five hundred yards into British territory before establishing headquarters for the "Right Wing of the Army of Ireland" inside an old red farmhouse abandoned by the Eccles family. At the base of Eccles Hill, the Fenians erected a small tent city that they named Camp Sweeny in honor of their captured commander.

❧

"The Fenians are coming!" shouted the Canadian alarm riders sprinting through the Eastern Townships to alert any residents who still remained. The Fenians, though, largely discovered a vacant land of empty farmhouses and ghost towns. They found telegraph offices shuttered and the lines cut to hinder Fenian communications. They encountered few people, let alone any organized resistance.

Spear hoped to maintain his toehold in Canada until reinforcements and provisions could arrive. Most immediately, however, he needed to feed his starving army. "The cry was still—hunger," Spear wrote to Sweeny, who was receiving communications in spite of being under hotel arrest in St. Albans, as the sun began to set on his first night on enemy territory. "I had but one alternative—foraging parties were sent out."

Contri assured one Quebecer who came to the headquarters to ascertain the intentions of the invaders that his men "were not robbers, but soldiers." Contri said his army expected to pay for what it took "but that the Irish had been downtrodden by British power, and they had come to make war upon the forces of the Province, but not on the inhabitants." In some cases, the Irishmen handed out IOUs, such as the one given to one St. Armand farmer: "The Irish Republic promises to pay W. Stewart Holsapple 100 dollars for value received, six months later."

More often than not, however, the Fenians who raided the farms of the Eastern Townships stole cattle, sheep, and pigs—sometimes slaughtering and cooking them on the spot—without any intentions of repayment. The hungry army forced its way into empty farmhouses and confiscated copious quantities of butter and sliced hunks from cheese wheels with their bayonets. At one farm, the woman answering the door said she had milk "only enough for the pigs" and could not supply any to the soldiers. Seconds after closing her door, she heard squealing from the pen as the Irish eliminated the excuse for their denial.

Sentries armed with muskets and fixed bayonets patrolled the roads of southern Quebec. The occupying army distributed passes to local residents allowing them to travel. The soldiers demanded the British citizens take oaths of allegiance to the Irish Republic and warned they would hang from the first tree if they were found harboring British soldiers.

By evening time, twenty-two members of the Third Fenian Cavalry had marched into Frelighsburg, five miles from Camp Sweeny. They plundered two stores and ransacked the most prominent symbol of the Crown—the customhouse. The Irish removed official stamps and split the royal coat of arms to pieces. They confiscated the British ensign that had been bought by the villagers and raised a green flag with a golden harp in its place. The Fenian cavalry returned to Camp Sweeny with the first trophy of war and raised the British flag on the staff in front of the makeshift headquarters beneath the Harp of Erin.

Spear's second day in Canada brought with it a shipment of fresh beef from a contractor in St. Albans and the arrival of $500, but he continued to wait for his promised reinforcements. "Give me men, arms, and ammunition and I will subsist my command sumptuously off the country," Spear wrote to Colonel John Mechan. "I feel in most excellent spirits, and if I can hold my own until the 500 muskets and 100,000 rounds arrive, I shall have no doubts of success," the general wrote before adding one last plea to "hurry up those arms."

While O'Neill maintained stringent discipline over his men and operated by the strict rules of war, the same could not be said of Spear's army. His men were greener than O'Neill's. The Right Wing of the Irish Republican Army included fewer experienced soldiers and more youngsters caught up in the Fenian fever that swept through their cities after the victory at Ridgeway. Having gone nearly a week without a decent meal and with nary a dry day, they were in a situation more desperate than that faced by O'Neill.

As discipline broke down, the Fenians looted more than just food. When local farmers refused to sell them horses they could use to organize a cavalry company, the Irish stole them. They broke into locked houses to raid closets and rummage through drawers for clothes.

While only $6,000 of losses were reported at Fort Erie and Ridgeway, a Canadian government report found that Spear's army caused $15,463.83 in damages reported by 102 claimants. Compensation claims filed by the farmers, traders, innkeepers, and spinsters of the Eastern Townships listed bureaus, safes, and even the axes used to break into those safes among the damages. The Fenians apparently drank well in Frelighsburg, where there were considerable losses of high wine, old rye, and other liquors. Spear placed three of his men under arrest for looting in violation of orders, but officers excused the thefts as the work of "bummers" who had tagged along on the venture.

Blue skies had finally banished the rain clouds by June 9, but this brought little cheer to Camp Sweeny. Spear had yet to receive reinforcements or orders. Discipline and morale were eroding, as was the size of his force. Not only were individual men deserting, but in some instances colonels marched off with entire commands.

❧

News of Spear's raid wrecked nerves in Montreal. Fearful that the Fenians could commandeer a train into the city or signal an uprising of the city's Irish, five thousand people crammed inside Bonaventure Station to send off the Royal Guides, the governor-general's bodyguard in Quebec, to safeguard the city. Primarily populated with aristocrats from the Montreal Hunt Club, the voluntary cavalry unit was composed of the city's most elite horsemen who looked every bit the part, from their blue tunics with white froggings to their dragoon-style helmets punctuated with red horsehair plumes.

While the Royal Guides boarded trains for St. John's, Sir John Michel, commander of forces in Canada, dispatched four hundred men from a wing of the Twenty-Fifth Regiment to St. Alexandre, where Carter's two hundred volunteers had retreated.

On the morning of June 9, the Crown forces approached St. Armand, just a few miles from the Fenian camp. As the Canadian soldiers reached Pigeon Hill, they encountered five Fenian prisoners captured by local farmers. The Royal Guides were ordered to the front of the column as the regulars and militia cheered.

Fenian scouts brought news of the Canadian advance to Spear, who gathered his officers for a war council. They agreed to a man that they had only one course of action. At 9:30 a.m., Spear ordered a retreat.

It did not take long to break down a camp that had been erected only forty-eight hours earlier. While some men loaded looted goods on their backs and packed them in satchels, others erected protective barricades of brushwood on the road outside their headquarters at the base of Eccles Hill. Spear was among the last to leave camp as his men started to trudge south.

Fenians who never had the opportunity to take aim at a British soldier instead fired indiscriminately into the Canadian sky as their parting shot. They also fired off curses toward Andrew Johnson. A few even directed their verbal volleys at Sweeny for mismanaging the invasion. Many Fenians tossed aside their muskets, sabers, and ammunition before crossing the border—some to improve their ability to tote blankets, clothing, and any goods they might have pilfered during their Canadian foray. A line of U.S. regulars that flanked the Eccles Hill Road just across the international frontier relieved any Irish hands of their weapons as they returned to America.

While the Irish continued to straggle out of Canada, two hundred Fenians remained huddled behind the makeshift barricades when the Royal Guides suddenly turned right onto Eccles Hill Road just a few hundred yards in the distance. After dismounting and dismantling the barricades, the cavaliers of the Royal Guides came upon scores of enemy fighters running for the border.

As the Irish began to scatter, Captain D. Lorn MacDougall, a Montreal stockbroker born in Scotland, ordered the Royal Guides to charge with their sabers drawn. He yelled at his men to strike with only the flat of their swords as they attempted to cut off the Fenian retreat.

Gunfire broke out across Eccles Hill Road. Canadian forces began to take prisoners. The Canadian detective Anthony Sewell chased a band of armed Fenians into the woods near their headquarters and wounded Thomas Madden, a twenty-five-year-old immigrant from County Tipperary, in the right shoulder before arresting him. The Fenians rounded up by the Canadians were not grizzled Civil War veterans but, as one correspondent noted, "little scamps such as one sees about the streets of all great cities." Of the sixteen Fenians captured, three were fifteen years old.

When the Fenians were backed to within three hundred yards of the border, they tossed their weapons aside and made a run for it. With American troops flanked across the road on the other side of the border directly in front of them, the Canadians were afraid of a misfire that could strike the American picket and create an international incident. So exuberant were four of MacDougall's men, though, that they did not see the iron post marking the boundary and crossed two hundred yards onto American territory.

The Fenians returned to the United States weary and footsore, though the looters could at least lay claim to new suits, hats, and shoes. Spear and his officers were left with no choice but to surrender to American forces and were taken into custody for violating neutrality laws. Having given his word to report to Major A. A. Gibson in St. Albans, Spear was permitted to travel in his private carriage as the dispirited column filled the roads from Franklin to St. Albans.

Spear wept as he rode past his disheartened men resting by the roadside, partaking of a meager lunch of dry bread. The Fenian general declared "that he would rather have been shot than have left Canada in the manner he was obliged to."

After three days, the Eastern Townships were no longer Irish lands. The Right Wing of the Irish Republican Army returned to the United States with little to show outside the Union Jack it had seized in Frelighsburg. They milked the enemy ensign for all it was worth, parading their prized trophy around New York City. It was dragged through the muddy streets of Brooklyn as it trailed the hearse carrying the body of the nineteen-year-old Eugene Corcoran, who was killed accidentally in a Fenian camp in upstate New York.

The lone fatality from the Fenian incursion into the Eastern Townships occurred days after the Irish returned to the United States. With tensions remaining high, a picket guard of the Seventh Royal Fusiliers patrolled the border around Eccles Hill as it grew dark on June 10. Through the gloaming they spotted a shadowy figure moving through a pasture. The cloaked individual refused three calls to halt. With their commands unheeded, the picket opened fire. The suspected Fenian dropped to the ground, dead instantly from a shot to the head.

When the soldiers reached the body, a collective look of horror came over their faces. "My God, it is a woman," uttered one of the soldiers. The victim was seventy-one-year-old Margaret Vincent, born into a Loyalist family, who lived with her sister north of the international border near Eccles Hill. The former teacher at a one-room schoolhouse in Pigeon Hill had been fetching water from Chickabiddy Creek in spite of orders to remain inside after dark. She never heard the verbal warnings nor the shots that ended her life, because she was nearly deaf. Her gravestone at Pigeon Hill Cemetery was erected by the men who mistakenly killed her.

⚜

Following a long day of marching, the Fenian army returned to St. Albans as darkness descended. Outside the Welden House, where Sweeny remained in custody, General George Meade, who had just arrived in the town, was being serenaded by the Third Artillery's marching band and cheered by a crowd gathered in front of the hotel. "We will show the world that, no matter how we have been treated by others, we have but our rule of duty to do to them as we would be done by," he told his audience. "I am here as a soldier to fulfill all my duty, and whatever my sympathies are in regard to this movement, and those who are engaged in the scheme which has caused so much trouble, I have but my duty to perform and it must be done at all hazards."

Meade had come from upstate New York with an enticing offer for all the Fenians below the rank of field officers—free transportation home courtesy of the War Department for those destitute and willing to sign a parole in which they pledged to "abandon our expedition against Canada, desist from any violation of the neutrality laws of the United States and return immediately to our respective homes." Meade wrote that he trusted "these liberal offers will have the effect of causing the expedition, now hopeless, to be quietly and peaceably abandoned."

"Let no Fenian disgrace himself by accepting ignominious terms attached to proffers of governmental transportation," thundered the Fenian senator Michael Scanlan, who urged his brethren to refuse the government's offer. General Sweeny, however, told his men to accept it and go home. He telegraphed Roberts not to send any more troops.

Although bitter at the federal government for crippling their attack, most of the Fenians reluctantly accepted its hospitality because they lacked money for the return train fare. Within hours of returning to St. Albans, nearly all of the one thousand soldiers were gone on trains heading south. Spear and the officers remained in custody in the Vermont village where they were released under heavy bond the next day to await trial for violating the neutrality laws.

Similar scenes played out in towns such as Ogdensburg and Malone along the northern border of New York as the Tammany Hall kingpin, William "Boss" Tweed, and New York City's mayor, John Hoffman, footed the railroad bill for any Fenians who didn't want to accept the government's largesse.

The Fenian fighters last left Buffalo, the place where they first arrived. They fled by the hundreds on the night of June 15, to the relief of Buffalonians who had wearied of their guests. In all, the War Department provided transportation home to seven thousand Fenians.

"It grieves me to part with you so soon," the Fenian brigadier general Michael Burns told his men as he bade them farewell from Buffalo. "I had hoped to lead you against the common enemy of human freedom, England, and would have done so had not the extreme vigilance of the United States Government frustrated our plans. It was the United States, and not England, that impeded our onward march to freedom. Return to your homes for the present, with the conviction that this impediment will soon be removed by the representatives of the nation."

The final days of spring brought with them the conclusion of the Fenian raids of 1866. Although Ireland was no closer to freedom as a result of the failed attacks on New Brunswick, Ontario, and Quebec, Irish Americans were far from discouraged. The invasions had thrown a scare into Canada, and the victory at Ridgeway demonstrated that the Irish could defeat enemy forces—when given the chance to fight. The willingness of the soldiers of the Irish Republican Army to undertake such daring action energized the Irish diaspora in the United States.

The curtain had come down on the theaters of war. But, as Burns told his men departing from the border, the fight was not over; it would simply move to the political arena.

10

Hail the Vanquished Hero

WILLIAM ROBERTS HAD expected to be savoring the fleeting days of spring reigning over New Ireland from its new capital of Sherbrooke, Quebec. Instead, his dominion comprised four walls, two chairs, a small table, and a bed inside Manhattan's Ludlow Street Jail.

Hours after Sweeny had been taken into custody in St. Albans, federal authorities acting under Attorney General James Speed's orders arrested the Fenian president inside his Broadway headquarters on charges of violating the Neutrality Act and "disturbance of the peace between two nations." Far from offering resistance, Roberts could barely bottle up his excitement as he was led into a waiting stagecoach for the short trip downtown. He now had his opportunity to become a legitimate Fenian martyr.

As news of the arrest spread from one Celtic tongue to the next, eager Irishmen crowded into downtown streetcars bound for the U.S. District Court on Chambers Street. An overflow crowd clogged the hallways and stairwells outside the courtroom when Roberts appeared for examination before the U.S. commissioner George F. Betts. No fewer than a dozen Fenians—one even willing to post $40,000 bail for Roberts—begged to be their leader's bondsman. The Fenian president, however, refused all offers. "I will not give bail of any kind, nor will I, under any circumstances, give any bail to keep the peace against Great Britain; for that would interfere with my duties as an Irishman," said Roberts, who insisted that doing so would have been treasonous to his presidential oath.

Betts remanded Roberts to the custody of two deputy marshals as friends cursed his obstinacy. "He's making a damned ass of himself," one Fenian quipped to nodding heads as Roberts rode away from the courthouse. One man's martyr was another man's fool.

The government-furnished accommodations given to Roberts inside the lavish Astor House were considerably more comfortable and befitting of a president. The proprietors of New York's first luxury hotel, however, moved quickly to evict the prisoner after the property's insurers informed them that they could not cover damages if the Fenians attempted a jailbreak, as they had done for James Stephens.

They needn't have worried. Given the president's desire to be taken into custody, the Fenians weren't enthusiastic about assembling a force to break him out. "He got himself in there without any help," one Irish longshoreman grumbled, "an' I say let him get himself out."

For two days, the rowdy spectators who squeezed inside the Chambers Street courtroom hooted and hollered as if they were fans ringside at a boxing match. Prolonged cheering greeted Roberts when he entered the legal arena, and indignant hisses awaited any witnesses who gave testimony against their man.

From the opening gavel, the defense attorney John McKeon fought to keep the Fenian president's case out of court. He immediately identified the carpenter George Weishart as the "wretched informer" responsible for the arrest of Roberts, and he made sure to loudly divulge the tipster's Houston Street address, so it could be heard by all Fenians who wanted to administer their own form of justice.

One witness after the next withheld knowledge. The Fenian vice president James Gibbons refused to answer nearly every query, including a question about the location of the Fenian headquarters, on the grounds that he might incriminate himself. Even subpoenaed reporters from *The Sun*, the *Daily News*, the *Tribune*, and other New York broadsheets who covered Fenian affairs remained tight-lipped when called to testify. William Cole told the court he was a publisher but refused to divulge what exactly he published. The *New York Herald* reporter John Gallagher managed no recollections of what Roberts had said in a recent interview because "subsequent duties drove them from his mind."

Witnesses disclosed such a paucity of information that McKeon waived his opportunity to cross-examine them. He told the court that the government failed to prove anything, and he was right. After two days of ineffectual testimony, the proceedings, as *The New York Times* reported, "failed to connect in the slightest degree Mr. Roberts with the Fenian Brotherhood."

The district attorney, Samuel Courtney, faced an added complication: Fearing reprisal, witnesses had a tendency to disappear when officers came to collect them at their residences. Those concerns were not unfounded, for Courtney reported that a collection of Fenian roughs had shown up at Weishart's doorstep and chased him through the streets after McKeon broadcast his address. Courtney informed Betts that his star witness failed to show because he "found it necessary to change his place of residence, secretly, to escape the vengeance of a mob."

The obstruction and witness intimidation worked. Courtney decried "the utter impossibility of securing the service of subpoenas" and complained that witnesses were "deterred by threats or terrorism from giving testimony." In light of that, the district attorney announced to the court that he was dropping the prosecution.

The courtroom erupted in cheers. The Fenian president was a free man. Scores of his followers, however, remained behind bars, and behind enemy lines.

Irish Republican Army soldiers entered Montreal on June 11, but not in the way they envisioned. Rather than marching triumphantly through the city, the sixteen handcuffed prisoners encountered groans, hisses, and periodic cries of "Lynch them!" as they arrived at Bonaventure Station.

As the captives were escorted through the streets of Montreal by the Twenty-Fifth Regiment, their anxious eyes darted through the angry crowds lining the sidewalks. Fearing that Canadian justice might be delivered by the mob, the captives were relieved to finally arrive at the safety of the Montreal Prison.

As the Fenians' journey through the streets of Montreal demonstrated, the Canadian public was in no mood for mercy toward the sixteen men in custody in Quebec and the sixty-five fighters captured in Fort Erie, now in prison in Toronto. Residents of the Eastern Townships were still cleaning up broken furniture and fragments of glass from their ransacked homes. Soldiers killed at the Battle of Ridgeway still needed to be buried. Canadians were enraged that not only did the American government refuse to extradite the scoundrels who had attacked them, but it gave them a ride home.

The captured Irishmen had been lured to Canada with dreams of the adventure of their lives, and now they faced the nightmare of losing everything. The Canadian Parliament had approved the suspension of habeas corpus on June 8, and the prisoners faced indictment under legislation enacted during the 1837 rebellion that called for the death penalty for subjects of a foreign state convicted of entering Canada for the purpose of levying war.

The captives taken to the Montreal Prison—the majority of whom were from Massachusetts—worked as shoemakers, curriers, boot makers, tailors, clerks, and spoon makers. They included four Methodists, an Episcopalian, and the *New-York Tribune* reporter Joseph Kelly, a County Tipperary native who had left St. Albans on a horse belonging to a Welden House employee before being taken prisoner just north of the border.

Secretary of State William Seward expressed his hope to Britain's envoy to the United States, Sir Frederick Bruce, that "all of the misguided men" would be treated with leniency. But many Canadians believed the sacrifice of their young men at Ridgeway required a vigorous response, particularly toward those Irish-born fighters who could be tried as British subjects.

Thomas D'Arcy McGee, the former Young Irelander, wanted no quarter given to the Irish revolutionaries who followed in his footsteps. The fury of Canadian public opinion spilled from his pen in response to a request by Father T. F. Hendricken for clemency toward the prisoner Terence McDonnell of Waterbury, Connecticut. "This thing you ask can not be done," he wrote on June 14, "for this Fenian filibustering was murder, not war. What had Canada or Canadians done to deserve such an assault? . . .

"McDonnell and all the Fenians will have every justice done to them, publicly, in the broad light of day," McGee continued, "but to whatever punishment the law hands him over, no word of mine can ever be spoken in mitigation; not even, under these circumstances, if he were my own brother."

British authorities, however, feared that the execution of any Fenians, particularly American citizens, would result in diplomatic blowback from the United States and breathe new life into the Fenian movement. "The future relations of Canada [with the United States] and its deliverance from any chance of becoming a battlefield of Fenianism will depend in a great measure on the tact and temper with which this question of the prisoners is managed," Bruce wrote to Governor-General Lord Charles Monck.

The British government had learned from centuries of past experience that the execution of the leaders of Irish uprisings could do nothing to douse the fires of revolution. It could indeed feed the flames.

British and Canadian officials weren't the only ones celebrating the failure of the Fenian raids. Feeling validated by the defeat of the Roberts wing's forces, Stephens continued his money-raising tour of the United States. Stephens tried little to conceal his delight at the failure of the Irish rebels. He promised war in Ireland by the end of the year and a shift away from its Canadian diversion to a singular focus on the "men in the gap."

Seeing how Roberts and Sweeny had discredited themselves, Stephens expected them to be shunned and scorned. Instead, music stores hawked sheet music for patriotic Irish marches with the images of the Fenian leaders on the cover. A copy of the "Irish Marseillaise" bearing the likeness of Roberts sold for fifty cents, "General Sweeny's Grand March" for thirty. New Fenian circles that formed across the United States in the wake of the Canadian invasion were named in honor of Sweeny, Roberts, and John O'Neill, but not Stephens.

Again he misjudged the American affinity with men of action. No matter how foolhardy, the bold Fenian foray kindled imaginations.

In comparing Sweeny with Stephens, the *Hartford Courant* editorial-ized, "One has certainly done his best to make good his promises by his acts, while the others have done nothing. Of the two give us the soldier Sweeny."

The Fenian founder thought that the prodigal Irish sons would return to his flock; instead, the supporters of the Roberts wing hardened their opinions of him. Many still questioned his loyalties, believing that he was secretly a British spy. They harbored suspicions that he colluded with the White House to ensure their failure.

They reserved particular loathing, though, not for one of their own but for the wily Seward. "If the attempts of the Fenians to obtain a foothold in Canada have been temporarily postponed, thanks are due therefore less to the conduct of the English troops than to the treacherous attitude so suddenly taken by our Secretary of State," editorialized *The Irish-American*. Stephens did little, then, to heal internal divisions by meeting in person with the secretary of state.

※

Just days after walking out of a New York courtroom, Roberts strode up the steps of the U.S. Capitol, its massive dome finally completed after eleven years of construction. He still seethed at President Andrew Johnson and Seward, believing that the Irish Republican Army had failed "not through any efforts of English armed minions, but because the Administration of a great free country chose to exercise its fullest limits, and even beyond it the odious and tyrannic provisions of an obsolete law."

With the Roberts wing blaming the Democratic president for the fizzle of their Canadian invasion, the Radical Republicans who controlled Congress saw a political opportunity. Bitterly opposed to Johnson's approach to Reconstruction, which they believed to be too lenient, the Radical Republicans held a sizable majority on Capitol Hill, which they used months earlier to pass the Civil Rights Act of 1866 over Johnson's veto. Relations with the White House were so poor that talk of impeachment had already begun to rumble inside the capital city.

Prior to the Civil War, the Irish who had fled to America after the Great Hunger had been as Democratic as they were Catholic. The Irish saw the Republican Party as a haven for two groups that threatened their livelihood—Know-Nothings and abolitionists. With congressional elections approaching in the fall of 1866 and former Confederate states about to begin the process of being formally re-admitted to the Union, the Radicals saw in the Fenians a cudgel with which to break up Johnson and the long-standing party allegiance of the Irish.

In New York City, Republicans distributed handbills to the Irish that read, "Queen Victoria thanks President Johnson for his Inter-ference in your Patriotic Movements," and linked John Hoffman, the city's mayor and Democratic candidate for governor, with the president's proclamation. "A Fenian vote for Hoffman is an endorse-ment of Johnson's interference," read the campaign propaganda.

Roberts feared he might be shunned in Washington, D.C., as a criminal who violated the Neutrality Act. Instead, the Radical Repub-licans treated him as a guest of honor and lauded him as a freedom fighter. Only three days after his release from jail, the leader of the "men of action" received a reception worthy of a returning war hero. The Massachusetts senator and future vice president Henry Wilson introduced Roberts on the Senate floor, and he shook hands on the House floor with prominent Republicans including Representative Nathaniel Banks, a former nativist who had been no friend of the Irish in the past. That evening, Speaker of the House Schuyler Colfax introduced Roberts at a speech at the Orphans' Fair.

It was not only Republicans who rallied around the Roberts wing. Just forty-eight hours after Brigadier General Samuel Spear retreated from Quebec, the Democratic representative Sydenham E. Ancona of Pennsylvania, also a Johnson detractor, introduced a resolution in the U.S. House of Representatives to repeal or amend the Neutrality Act, which he said compelled the president to "discriminate most harshly" against the Fenians. Representative Robert C. Schenck, an Ohio Republican and former Union army general, also proposed a resolution of censure against the Johnson administration for its suppression of the Fenian raids.

Even though the Johnson administration had used the Fenians for its own leverage against Great Britain over the *Alabama* claims before betraying them, Roberts showed little reluctance about rushing into a relationship with new political bedfellows, whom he called "the only true and consistent party in the country."

Making his own visit to Washington, D.C., the chronically bitter Stephens resented the attention showered upon Roberts. When Stephens learned of Colfax's planned introduction of Roberts at the Orphans' Fair, he turned down the Speaker's offer to introduce him to the House as well. On the evening of June 19, he spoke before several hundred Fenian leaders at Odd Fellows Hall and repudiated any connection with the Canadian foray.

The audience escorted Stephens to the Metropolitan Hotel, where he appeared on a balcony and continued to fire barbs at Roberts. Stephens proclaimed his allegiance to the Democrats as the internal Fenian split now broke along party lines as well. The rhetorical firefight between Roberts and Stephens had grown so fierce that newspapers printed rumors that the two men had agreed to settle their dispute with pistols in a duel.

The Capitol Hill embrace of the Fenians who had attacked Canada angered not only Stephens but the British as well. "I fear it augurs badly for the termination of this Fenian agitation," Bruce wrote to Lord Clarendon after Colfax's introduction of Roberts in Washington. "It is a proof of the great influence the Irish vote will exercise in the elections, and I am much afraid that the wish to conciliate it may lead to some violent report, if not resolution on the Neutrality Laws as affecting this question."

※

The Fenians might not have held on to any of their territory, but they still thoroughly occupied the minds of Canadians as spring blossomed into summer. Canada had reason to feel on edge beyond just the attacks by the Irish Republican Army. Radical Republicans saw an opportunity to use the Fenians not only to erode political support for Johnson but also to fulfill the Manifest Destiny of the United States. American politicians who cast lustful eyes to the north believed that fears of another Fenian raid could drive up the cost of British defenses and Canadian taxes, producing a financial crisis that could lead to the success of annexationists within the country.

Many Americans believed it only a matter of time before the United States would swallow Canada, just as it had vast swaths of territory west of the Mississippi River throughout the century. The idea even had the imprimatur of God. "The United States should take Canada and incorporate it into the American Union," Pope Pius IX had told Rufus King, U.S. minister in Rome, in November 1865, "rather than allow the Fenians to possess themselves of it. Better that it should be done by a regularly constituted government than by a revolutionary, irresponsible government, subject to no control and liable to every excess."

There was nothing clandestine about American aspirations. In fact, on July 2, Representative Banks introduced a bill to the Committee on Foreign Affairs that put into writing the plan for the incorporation of Canada into the United States. The legislation called for the admission of four new states—Nova Scotia (including Prince Edward Island), New Brunswick, Canada East (Newfoundland and Quebec), and Canada West—and the territories of Selkirk, Saskatchewan, and Columbia.

The bill even assigned twelve congressmen to Canada West, eleven to Canada East, four to Nova Scotia, and two to New Brunswick. The legislation set aside $85.7 million to pay for the new northern states plus $10 million for the Hudson's Bay Company, as well as funds to build a transcontinental railroad across Canada and expand the canal system along the St. Lawrence River.

While Americans believed the Fenian raids might drive Canada into American arms, just the opposite was happening. The British provinces grew more united, more open to the idea of forming a confederation. The speaker of the Legislative Assembly told Lord Monck in August of "the gradual but decided change of public opinion in New Brunswick and Nova Scotia on behalf of a closer alliance with Canada" as a result of "the outrages which had been committed upon the soil of Canada by a lawless band of marauders."

As rumors of another Fenian raid continued to spread, a new Canadian nationalism began to sprout. "The covenant of our nationality has been sealed with blood," proclaimed the Toronto *Daily Telegraph*. As some Canadians wondered whether they could depend on Great Britain to defend them, the British statesman Benjamin Disraeli mused about whether to let its province go. "If the colonists can't, as a general rule, defend themselves against the Fenians, they can do nothing," he wrote. "What is the use of these colonial dead weights which we do not govern?"

Political Blarney

THE IRISH REPUBLICAN Army had the Queen's Own Rifles and the Tenth Royals on the run once again. A staccato of musket fire punctuated a sustained chorus of feral Fenian yells as General John O'Neill's men charged across the smoke-shrouded battlefield. Enduring withering fire, the Irish soldiers pushed the redcoats back at the points of their bayonets.

Fenian hands that weren't locked in combat with the enemy tore the Union Jack away from its standard-bearer, while Fenian boots trampled the hated emblem into the ground. Believing the cause to be lost, the Canadian forces broke into a panicked retreat as Lieutenant Colonel Alfred Booker failed once again to maintain the discipline of his men.

As soon as the Fenians drove the royal soldiers through a gate in a fence like sheep into a pen, thousands of spectators burst into applause. Lowering their firearms loaded with blank cartridges, the combatants exchanged friendly handshakes with their erstwhile foes. It was another successful reenactment of the Battle of Ridgeway.

The four hundred participants in the mock battle all had Fenian allegiances; some even had firsthand experience fighting at Limestone Ridge. Organizers of the reenactment might have had an easier time raising a private army to attack Canada once again than to recruit Irishmen to don red coats—even in jest—but the First Company of Veterans and members of the Emmet Guards agreed to assume the uncomfortable role of the enemy. The Corcoran Guards had the honor of playing the victorious Irish, with Captain John C. Nial portraying O'Neill as the general himself watched from the sidelines.

The sham battle was among the highlights during a day of Irish songs, dances, sports, and speeches at Clinton Grove outside Buffalo on August 21, 1866, which raised $10,000 for the cause of Irish freedom. Held on a Tuesday afternoon, the grand Fenian picnic drew upwards of twenty thousand people, including Irishmen from Cleveland to Boston and beyond.

From across the Niagara River at Fort Erie, the real soldiers of the Tenth Royals remained vigilant as they listened to the crackle of the faux musket fire. A British gunboat lurked along the international border, ports open and guns trained on Fenian excursion boats while watching every movement with unease.

Fenians might have chuckled at their paranoia, but the Canadians on the Niagara Peninsula had good reason to be on edge. O'Neill's victory at Ridgeway had ignited a Fenian fever throughout western New York. Cities with one Fenian circle now had three or four. "Localities where it was thought the old fire was dead, and nothing but the ashes left, have burst anew into flame," reported one Fenian in a letter to *The Irish-American*.

With the outpouring of Irish sentiment in upstate New York and the warm political embrace of the Fenians by the Radical Republicans, Canadians believed another invasion was imminent. The spymaster Gilbert McMicken's detectives reported in July and August that the Fenians were regrouping, and he worried that the Irish Republican Army would launch a "second and more serious invasion of Canada" in advance of that fall's congressional elections. As a precaution in the days leading up to the grand picnic in Buffalo, two thousand Canadian troops had been shifted east across Ontario from Stratford and Grimsby to Thorold, just miles from Niagara Falls.

The Roberts wing lacked the money and equipment necessary to launch yet another attack on Canada, but throughout the summer of 1866 the Fenian Brotherhood replenished its coffers with grand picnics similar to the one in Buffalo. Few speakers on the fundraising circuit proved to be as popular as O'Neill.

The unassuming general had emerged from the Battle of Ridgeway as the Fenians' rising star and the vessel for all their hopes, having delivered the first military victory by the Irish on British soil in 150 years. Blame for the retreat of his forces from the Niagara Peninsula never stained O'Neill. That blight fell on the White House, James Stephens, and, even in some corners, General Thomas Sweeny for devising the failed war plan.

O'Neill, however, would have sooner stared down bullets on the battlefield than an audience from behind a lectern. He had little use for words, believing the gift of gab an endemic fault of his people, who talked "too much and acted too little."

O'Neill proved a quick study, however. After posting bail at the end of June, following his indictment for violating the Neutrality Act, the general departed Buffalo to return home to Nashville. Stopping in Louisville, O'Neill was the featured speaker at the annual Fenian Brotherhood picnic on the Fourth of July. The Irishmen who paid their $1 admissions witnessed not only a grand display of fireworks but also a rhetorical flourish from O'Neill, who demonstrated a knack for oration that belied his own modest claims.

"The campaign has only commenced," the general shouted, and "though it may have received a temporary check it will ere long burst forth in all its fury." O'Neill pledged that "the green flag, so long trampled in the dust by a hated oppressor, will wave once again over our lovely little island home." He elicited cheers so loud that the crowd had difficulty hearing him above all the commotion.

Later that night, O'Neill arrived home in Nashville after more than a month away, returning to his wife and young child. Back at his Cedar Street claims agency, O'Neill resumed his work of challenging authority. He continued to fight the federal government for back pay, bounties, and pensions owed to soldiers and represented slave owners who he said were due $300 compensation for each of their slaves who enlisted in the U.S. Army. As a sign of O'Neill's growing fame, his newspaper advertisements now announced that while he could give references, "I take it that I am well enough known in this state."

Prior to the Battle of Ridgeway, he had little use for politics. But he began to have a political awakening after the White House inserted itself into the Fenian raids. "I never voted in all my life," he confessed to an audience in Nashville, "but henceforth my policy will be to adhere to that party which is in favor of Irish independence."

To O'Neill, the Republicans were that party. At an enormous Fenian picnic outside Chicago on August 15, the general appeared on the podium along with the Radical Republican Speaker of the House Schuyler Colfax and the Republican governor of Illinois, Richard Oglesby. They learned quickly that castigating President Andrew Johnson, linking him to Jefferson Davis and Queen Victoria, garnered surefire applause. Colfax played to the audience, saying he was "unutterably humiliated" by the president's proclamation.

O'Neill piled on Johnson for betraying the Irish and crushing their dream "when the freedom of their land was within their grasp." It was a defiant act to stand against a fellow son of Nashville. His friends pleaded with him not to assail the president; the man had been a forceful voice against the Know-Nothings in the 1850s, after all. O'Neill, however, was tiring of voices. He reiterated that he "intended hereafter to vote for the party and the men who by their deeds and not words had shown their sympathy for Irishmen."

The *Buffalo Commercial* denounced the "political blarney" on display by both the politicians and the Fenians. "Ambitious local politicians who have for years been constant in their abuse of Irishmen, and who have been pummeled by them at almost every poll in the city, now hang around Fenian meetings, and stultify themselves with pretended sympathy and friendship," the newspaper pronounced.

Still O'Neill's tour resumed. Even before he attended the grand Fenian picnic in Buffalo, August 21 had been a grand day for him. That morning inside the U.S. District Court, the assistant district attorney Charles O. Tappan, following orders handed down from Johnson, entered a nolle prosequi against O'Neill; his second-in-command, Colonel Owen Starr; and eleven other officers. Prosecution was abandoned. O'Neill would remain a free man. Under pressure from aspiring Democratic officeholders to make amends with Irish voters, Johnson halted the prosecutions of all Fenian leaders for violating the Neutrality Act and agreed to return the arms seized from the Fenians on the condition that they not be used again for violating the neutrality laws.

O'Neill exited the courthouse for the greener pastures of Clinton Grove. All of Buffalo, in fact, was awash in green. Irish flags fluttered beside the Stars and Stripes from the housetops of the city's prominent Fenian Brotherhood members. Rifle-toting Fenians wearing green shirts, green caps, and green bows of ribbon marched through the First Ward under the direction of Buffalo's head center, Patrick O'Day.

O'Neill could not be faulted if he flashed back to the night of May 31, when he marched with hundreds of other Fenians through the dark streets of Buffalo to launch the invasion of the Niagara Peninsula. This time, however, the Irish emerged in full daylight and by the thousands upon thousands.

With marching bands providing a soundtrack, a grand military parade of seven thousand people thronged Niagara Street and progressed the two miles to Clinton Grove. Fenian regiments marched alongside Civil War veterans and workers' associations from thirteen of Buffalo's grain elevator companies. The Irish enjoyed their big day out, in particular the Ridgeway reenactment. After the routing of the British, O'Neill ascended the speaker's platform. "I hope that all friends of Irish liberty will speak as we did at Limestone Ridge. We had our fight at Fort Erie and Ridgeway, but there was an enemy in our rear we did not anticipate," O'Neill bellowed. He told the Irish that the land across the river would have been theirs—if only Johnson and William Seward had not meddled.

The general had watched the Fenian Brotherhood fray over whether to participate in the Civil War and split once again over whether to target the British in Canada or Ireland. Much as he might have hoped that his success at Ridgeway might spur greater unification now, the Fenians faced yet another divide over party allegiance.

❦

As 150 Fenians convened in Troy, New York, for their Fifth National Congress on September 4, the Fenian president, William Roberts, hoped that the convention's venue, Harmony Hall, would prove aptly named as the leaders responsible for the Fenian raids gathered together for the first time since the attacks. In case the delegates required any more encouragement, banners mounted around the elegantly decorated hall were inscribed with inspirational quotations such as "Let us be friends to the men that are friends to us."

In order to discourage internal arguments, Roberts prohibited delegates from discussing the neutrality laws or debating politics, and to maintain operational secrecy, he also barred the press from reporting on its sessions. Unbeknownst to the Fenians, however, three British spies had infiltrated the convention from the inside and were reporting back to Ottawa—specifically on their covert military plans in the run-up to the November elections.

As the Roberts wing plotted its next incursion, Sweeny presented his official report on the Fenian raids to the convention. He blamed the failure of the attack on the U.S. government's seizure of their weapons and the inability of regimental colonels to accurately report and deliver their forces. The military committee, however, placed the blame for the performance of the colonels on the man who chose them in the first place, censuring Sweeny for appointing incompetent officers. Even Sweeny's supporters among the Fenian leadership acknowledged that while "Fightin' Tom" could command an army in the field, he was not as well suited to handle logistics.

The rebuke stung Sweeny, who couldn't help but remember that he had warned the Fenian political leaders of the pitfalls of pushing forward his desired timetable. While delegates reelected Roberts as president, Sweeny was forced to resign as Fenian secretary of war. When Roberts was unable to persuade General Philip Sheridan to become Sweeny's successor, he named General Samuel Spear, who had led the incursion into Quebec, as the new war secretary. Before the month was out, Sweeny had returned to service with the U.S. Army.

❧

Stepping into a packed Toronto courtroom on October 24, Robert Blosse Lynch was the first prisoner taken captive in Canada to stand trial. That he had found himself involved with the Fenian raids was perhaps no surprise. The County Galway native and Dublin University graduate had lived a life of adventure after emigrating from Ireland in 1842. Lynch had struck it rich in the California gold rush, divorced his wife after living together for one entire day, and narrowly escaped a lynching after being arrested for embezzlement as the city clerk in Milwaukee.

The Canadians accused Lynch of serving as a colonel in O'Neill's force. While residents of Fort Erie testified that they had seen Lynch commanding Fenian troops, the defendant argued that he was the victim of mistaken identity. He had been reporting for the *Louisville*

Courier and was, he claimed, being confused with Brigadier General William Francis Lynch, the no-show Illinois native whom Sweeny had tasked with attacking the Niagara Peninsula by boat from Cleveland. When testimony concluded on the trial's second day, the jury took barely more than an hour to decide on its verdict—guilty.

"By the statute the crime of which you have been found guilty is punishable with death, and I can exercise no discretion," the judge intoned. "You [will] be hanged by the neck till you are dead," John Wilson promised, "and may God have mercy on your soul!"

The next day, the most high profile of the Fenian prisoners entered the courtroom for his own trial. The incarceration of Father John McMahon had stirred controversy in the United States—even among those who decried the Fenians. The priest from Anderson, Indiana, said he was in Buffalo en route to Montreal to tie up the affairs of the estate of his brother, who had died four years earlier without a will, when the Fenians forced him to cross to Canada with them so that he could provide spiritual comfort to the wounded warriors on the battlefield.

"They took my traveling bag from me, my vestments and cloak, and I was waiting to get them back, when they compelled me to act as chaplain," he had told a reporter from the Toronto *Leader.* "When the battle was over, I was called upon to hear the confession of the dying men and administer the rites to them."

Although McMahon insisted that he, like most priests, had "always opposed and preached against" the Fenians, he was forced to stand trial. After hearing from numerous witnesses who placed him in Fort Erie with the Fenians, the jury deliberated for forty-five minutes before returning with their verdict. Before Wilson announced the sentence, McMahon's voice cracked as he told the judge, "I am innocent, my lord. I cannot plead guilty. I am innocent." The crier of the court asked for silence as the judge spoke.

"John McMahon, the jury have found you guilty on evidence, which, I think, admits of no doubt," Wilson said. "I have indeed a very painful duty to perform—one that I would gladly avoid if I could; but, I have no alternative, no discretion in the matter. The doom of the law is death for the crime of which you have been found guilty, and I but sit here humbly to carry out that law and to pronounce its penalties. . . .

"You will have time and opportunity also," the judge intoned, "before your sentence is carried out, to apply to your Maker for the forgiveness of your sins."

Outrage at McMahon's sentence intensified a few days later when the jury acquitted the Reverend David Lumsden—an Episcopal minister from Nunda, New York—on similar charges, although the evidence against him was stronger than that delivered against McMahon. Catholics on both sides of the border saw in the verdicts Protestant bias at work.

Seward ordered the American consul in Toronto to procure the trial records for examination as he lobbied the British for clemency for the Americans in custody. As the British took Seward's request under consideration, the court condemned to death five more Americans. The White House lobbied for leniency. Downing Street sought to avoid a diplomatic incident. Canadian authorities also faced internal pressure to make an example of the Fenian prisoners. In particular, the militias who had watched their comrades die wanted justice delivered with Irish blood.

Catholic French Canadians, however, were uneasy at the thought of a man of the cloth dangling from a noose. They feared that the executions could spark another raid. Newspapers reported, hyperbolically, that a twelve-thousand-man group that called itself the Fenian Avengers stood at the ready to storm Canada and prevent any of their comrades from being sent to the gallows. Many Canadians rightfully also worried that executions could transform the men into martyrs. "If the British Government dares to hang the Irish-Americans now in their power," O'Neill pledged to a standing-room-only crowd in Nashville, "the Fenians will, before the winter snows disappear from the hills of Canada, hang ten British subjects for each Fenian sacrificed."

For his part, O'Neill could only dream of a Fenian martyr—as long as it wasn't him. He castigated Lynch for being a coward—for continuing to protest that he was a newspaper reporter and not a soldier of war. (Lynch saw rank hypocrisy in this, considering O'Neill wasn't willing to risk arrest in Canada to testify in his defense.) The death sentences proved a propaganda boon, proof of the British "thirst for Irish blood," according to an advertisement for one Fenian rally. As Irishmen channeled their outrage into donations to the

Fenian Brotherhood, Roberts dreamed of the money that would pour into his coffers if a single Fenian was put to death.

❧

On November 24, the Earl of Carnarvon, British secretary of state for the colonies, informed the Canadian governor-general, Lord Charles Monck, from Downing Street of his intention to commute the sentences of Lynch and McMahon. Sir Frederick Bruce, British minister to the United States, told Seward that others who were subsequently condemned to death would be spared as well once all the Fenian trials were completed. "The sentence of death will certainly not be executed," Bruce wrote to Seward on December 8. "I need not add how desirable it is that nothing should take place on the Canadian frontier to interfere with the disposition to lenity which I know is entertained by Her Majesty's Government."

Bruce's communication came at a particularly sensitive time, just two days after the trials of the Fenians who attacked from Vermont began in Sweetsburg, Quebec. Fears ran high that the Fenians might attempt a raid on the small village in the Eastern Townships, just eighteen miles north of the American border. Special units of government police escorted the prisoners in and out of the courthouse.

The first trial was that of Thomas Madden for "feloniously joining himself to persons who had entered Lower Canada with intent to levy war against Her Majesty." A British subject by virtue of his birth in Ireland, Madden was "taken with arms in his hands" and accused of firing on the Canadian forces who were endeavoring to arrest him. The court found Madden guilty and condemned him to hang. The Fenians Thomas Smith and Michael Crowley, also recognized as British citizens, received the same sentence.

The last of the Toronto trials finished on January 29, and the following day eleven convicted prisoners who had not been sentenced were placed in the dock and sentenced to hang, with all appeals disallowed.

With the fate of twenty-one Fenians now in hand, Lieutenant General Sir John Michel, commander of the British troops in Canada, followed the orders of the British government and commuted their sentences to twenty years' imprisonment with hard labor.

Thomas D'Arcy McGee conceded that the commutation of the

sentences was the right decision, but he wasn't happy about it. "Those men deserve death," he said, "but, I will add, that the spirit of our times is opposed to the infliction of capital punishment where any other punishment can reach the case, and in these cases I hope it may be possible to temper justice with mercy."

Perhaps no one took the news of the commutations harder than Roberts, who had held out hope that the names of Lynch, McMahon, Madden, and the others would join the ranks of Irish martyrs to be remembered from generation to generation—and, importantly, spur the recruitment of soldiers and money.

"I regret to tell you that you are not going to be hanged," Roberts wrote to Lynch in one of the strangest letters of lament ever penned. "So great a crime upon a non-combatant like yourself would make every Irishman in America a Fenian, and furnish our exchequer with the necessary means to clear Canada of English authority in short order."

As one Ohio newspaper noted, the Fenian president's letter was "carrying patriotism to an excess." Roberts, though, knew that the men who stood up to the British and paid for it with their lives became the subjects of songs and verses. "A life that would otherwise pass away unknown, in a few years, at most, would become an honored portion of the history of our race and of the times," Roberts told Lynch. "It would be a glorious death for you."

Erin's Hope

WITH ONLY SIXTY-FIVE days remaining to honor his promise to lead an uprising in Ireland before the end of the year, James Stephens addressed his followers at New York City's Jones's Wood. "I speak to you now for the last time before returning to Ireland," Stephens bellowed. "I said that I would begin the fight in Ireland this year. I assure you, my countrymen, that I shall be there, and that our battle-flags shall be unfurled upon Irish soil before the New Year dawns." As he departed the stage on October 28, 1866, Stephens told the throng that the next time they would hear of him would be at the front leading troops against the Saxon aggressor.

Following the rally, Stephens disappeared from public view as rumors spread that he had sailed to France or Ireland. Fearing his imminent arrival to launch a revolution in Ireland, the British government stepped up its defenses, extended the suspension of habeas corpus in Ireland, and offered a £2,000 reward for his capture. Sir Frederick Bruce, British minister to the United States, instructed consuls in New York, Boston, Portland, and Philadelphia to monitor their ports for the departure of Stephens and immediately report the "name and nationality of the vessel in which he is embarked."

As the new year approached, Irish Americans opened their newspapers hoping to read about the launch of the long-promised uprising. Stephens, however, was still nowhere to be found. In early December, *The New York Times* reported that he was spotted in Paris.

Stephens, however, wasn't on the other side of the ocean. He wasn't even on the other side of Manhattan.

In reality, he had gone underground, just as he did after faking his death during the Young Irelander Rebellion. Using the alias William Scott, he was living fifty blocks south of where he was last seen in public in a modest room at 308 East Thirteenth Street. On December 15, he summoned a meeting of thirty top advisers. Looking haggard and ill after an attack of dyspepsia, Stephens grew angry at the pitiful state of military preparations when Colonel Thomas Kelly reported that the Fenians had less than one-quarter of the minimum thirty thousand rifles needed for the uprising. "I found that matters were even worse than my apprehensions," Stephens recalled.

Confronted with the harsh reality of the Fenians' lack of money and weapons, Stephens announced that he needed to break his promise. There would be no revolution in 1866. Ireland would have to wait—again. The decision infuriated his advisers, who had grown exhausted with his habitual hesitation and increasingly saw him solely as a speech maker and fund-raiser. At a subsequent meeting when Stephens refused to share his military plan for the invasion, Captain John McCafferty even pulled out a pistol and pointed it at the Fenian chief.

The military men effectively deposed Stephens. He had vowed to "either fight or dissolve the brotherhood in 1865," but 1867 had arrived with no action. He had opted again to not take the shot. Kelly now took charge of the plan for the uprising. To Fenian military men like Kelly, seven hundred years had been long enough to wait. They refused to spend yet another year under the British yoke. If Stephens refused to deliver on his promises, they would.

Kelly, McCafferty, and other Fenian military leaders set sail from New York on January 12, but Stephens missed the boat. The Fenian chief claimed that he had been a victim of a "deplorable trick" because the ship departed two hours earlier than he had been told, although a wounded ego and an empty wallet were more likely to blame. It took Stephens several weeks to raise the money to pay for passage to Paris, but he could not afford transit on to England or Ireland. So he remained in France.

Stephens would no longer play a central role in the Irish Republican Brotherhood. The grizzled patriot who had rekindled Irish nationalism and erected the transatlantic partnership with the diaspora had spent nearly a decade leading the Irish revolutionary movement. Such longevity in office testified to his leadership skills, but of course it also reflected his inability to achieve his goal of overthrowing British rule on the island of his birth. The IRB leader ultimately proved too cautious for his followers. They wanted a man of action. Stephens wasn't one of them.

❧

Kelly pressed ahead with plans from his new operational base in London, where he established the "Provisional Government of the Irish Republic" and assumed the role of chief executive. On March 5, 1867, he launched the long-awaited Fenian Rising. A messenger delivered the Fenians' proclamation of the Irish Republic, which had been drafted by Kelly and his fellow officers, to *The Times* in London. The manifesto was a radical, republican, and secular document that called for the separation of church and state, universal suffrage, and absolute liberty of conscience.

"We have suffered centuries of outrage, enforced poverty, and bitter misery," read the document. "Our rights and liberties have been trampled on by an alien aristocracy, who treating us as foes, usurped our lands, and drew away from our unfortunate country all material riches. The real owners of the soil were removed to make room for cattle, and driven across the ocean to seek the means of living, and the political rights denied to them at home, while our men of thought and action were condemned to loss of life and liberty."

That night, republicans sought to repossess what rightly belonged to them. The rebels launched scattered attacks on coast guard posts, police stations, and military barracks. In Cork, over one thousand Irishmen marched into the countryside to confront the British. The most serious fighting occurred in the village of Tallaght, southwest of Dublin, where a few hundred Fenians exchanged gunfire with a small force of constables, resulting in the deaths of two rebels.

It turned out to be a terrible night to schedule a revolution, because a winter storm unlike any seen in Ireland in half a century swept across the island. A tempest of snow fell for five straight days, leaving roads impassable. The Fenian Rising, which took twelve lives, proved a dismal military failure. Even without the meteorological hardship, the Irishmen lacked weapons, organization, and a cohesive military strategy. Spies and informers had infiltrated the operation, and the British were able, due to the suspension of habeas corpus, to detain ringleaders such as McCafferty in the days before the rebellion.

"It was as pitiful and silly a farce as ever ignorant fellows were seduced into," reported *Frank Leslie's Illustrated Newspaper.* "There appeared to be no plan, no organization, no head. Simply irregular bodies of poor, unarmed men, wandering about objectless." Stephens might have been too cautious for the liking of Kelly and other military leaders, but at least in this instance he had been correct: The Fenian Rising wasn't ready.

Sporadic skirmishes flared for several weeks after March 5. American Fenians grew discouraged at the newspaper reports from Ireland, but Kelly assured them the papers were filled with falsehoods. "Don't believe a tenth of the vile newspaper reports about complete suppression—utter routs—overwhelming defeats," wrote Kelly, who beseeched Irish Americans to keep sending money and supplies. "In heaven's name don't stop at anything until I proclaim hostilities ceased." It was not too late for the patriots to send help across the Atlantic, and he had a specific operation in mind: "A landing in Sligo at the present time would be of infinite service."

In packs of twos and threes, some forty Irishmen, most of them Civil War veterans, arrived at the foot of Manhattan's Canal Street on April 12 and boarded a small steamer for a pleasure cruise of New York Harbor. It seemed curious, though, that some of the men carried aboard luggage for the day trip.

The steamer returned to the dock devoid of passengers the following day, having deposited them aboard the *Jacmel Packet,* a two-masted brigantine that had plied the trade routes from the United States to Australia before it fell into the custody of New York City's customs collector in February 1867 and eventually became available to the Fenians two months later.

Captain John F. Kavanagh, a prominent Fenian who served as a naval lieutenant during the Civil War, took the wheel of the vessel on which he had never before set foot, and the *Jacmel Packet* spread its sails with an American flag flapping in the wind. Below deck, there was cargo marked as sewing machines and casks of wine consigned to merchants in Cuba. Their actual contents included five thousand stands of arms, three artillery batteries, one thousand sabers, and more than a million rounds of ammunition.

Kavanagh turned right out of New York Harbor toward the West Indies so as not to arouse suspicion, but after two days at sea he abruptly pointed the ship toward Ireland. Shortly before noon on April 21, Easter Sunday, the Fenians gathered on deck. Lowering the Stars and Stripes, the Irishmen raised a green flag with a sunburst into the sky while they unleashed a thirty-two-gun salute—one shot for each county in Ireland—before letting loose with wild cheers and handshakes. Kavanagh rechristened the ship *Erin's Hope* and read orders to land the guns in the northwest Irish city of Sligo with James Kerrigan, the former congressman who participated in the Eastport expedition, commanding the military expedition.

After thirty-three days at sea, the Irishmen caught their first glimpses of the homeland. Based on Kelly's reports, they expected to see green-and-gold flags waving over the wild Atlantic coast and boatloads of rebels rowing out to welcome them and their guns. For six days, however, *Erin's Hope* lurked along the shore, receiving no reply to their signal.

Finally, on May 25, Colonel Ricard O'Sullivan Burke approached in a cutter-rigged vessel on Sligo Bay and shouted the Fenian countersign from the deck. Posing as an English tourist, the County Cork native had managed to charm the locals in Sligo, who took him into their homes. One of Kelly's closest advisers, Burke had traveled the world before enlisting in the Fifteenth Regiment New York Volunteers at the outbreak of the Civil War and serving from Bull Run to Appomattox. A trained engineer, he worked as a Fenian agent purchasing arms in Great Britain and managed the Fenian Rising activities around Waterford.

Boarding *Erin's Hope*, Burke delivered unexpected news: The rebellion had petered out back in March. They were too late—two months too late. In truth, the time had been ripe two years earlier, when the IRB's power was at its peak, American anger toward the British at its height, and the Fenian Brotherhood unified. Thanks to dithering and division, the fruitful moment had spoiled.

With provisions running low on *Erin's Hope*, Kavanagh could not simply turn around and return to the United States. The guns could stay, but he needed to off-load some Fenians to ensure everyone's survival. Burke instructed Kavanagh to sail to the rebel stronghold of Cork in the southeast of Ireland in hopes of finding a safe harbor for the men to put ashore.

Dodging British cruisers, Kavanagh circled the southern half of Ireland. Under the cloak of a thick mist, on the morning of June 1, thirty-two Fenians led by Colonel William Nagle boarded a fishing boat and cruised into Dungarvan Bay on the coast of County Waterford, disregarding Kavanagh's warning not to land in daylight. Alerted by a member of the coast guard, police arrested the Fenians as they wandered country roads, their wet trousers from wading ashore betraying any possible alibis.

Erin's Hope returned to New York on August 1 after its nine-thousand-mile, one-hundred-day cruise. Meanwhile, three American citizens and expedition leaders—Nagle, Colonel John Warren, and Captain Augustine Costello—sat in Dublin's Kilmainham Jail. The British eventually released Nagle, who was born in the United States, along with most of the rebels who arrived aboard *Erin's Hope*. However, they tried the Irish-born Warren and Costello as British citizens in spite of their naturalized citizenship in the United States. The pair did not commit any actual crimes on British soil, had no weapons in their possession when arrested, and were American citizens, yet they were convicted of treason felony—in essence for words spoken in the United States that were heard by the arch informer John Joseph Corydon. Warren received a fifteen-year sentence, Costello twelve. The two Americans were sent to some of the most brutal of British prisons, where they were placed in solitary confinement, chained, and put to work picking apart strands of old tar ropes.

On top of the still-simmering tensions over the *Alabama* claims, the imprisonment of Warren and Costello flared as another flash point between the United States and Great Britain. The British government rejected the claim that anyone born in Great Britain had the right to renounce his or her British citizenship and pledge allegiance to another country. Once a subject of the Crown, forever a subject of the Crown. The idea particularly galled the majority of the Irish, who were born on British soil through no desire of their own.

The issue of citizenship had been a point of contention between the United States and Great Britain during the War of 1812, when the British pulled Irish sailors off American ships and treated them not as prisoners of war but as British deserters. More than half a century later, Irish Americans protesting the treatment of Warren and Costello lobbied President Andrew Johnson and his successor, Ulysses S. Grant, for their release.

Their efforts resulted in the congressional passage of the Expatriation Act of 1868, which rejected the principle of perpetual allegiance and asserted, "The right of expatriation is a natural and inherent right of all people." The United States began to renegotiate naturalization treaties with European countries that had the same policy as Great Britain.

Under international pressure, the British government released Warren and Costello in March 1869, and the following year the British Parliament passed legislation, dubbed the Warren and Costello Act, that acknowledged the right of a British citizen to renounce citizenship and become naturalized to a foreign country.

❈

Following the disappointment of the Fenian Rising, Kelly shifted his operational base from London to Manchester, a city where 15 percent of the population was born in Ireland. There, he blended into Manchester's Celtic enclaves and directed activities from a secondhand clothes shop that served as the IRB's secret headquarters. In August 1867, three hundred Fenians surreptitiously convened in Manchester and elected Kelly chief organizer of the Irish Republic, officially marking the end of Stephens's tenure.

In the early morning hours of September 11, Kelly loitered outside his secret headquarters with Timothy Deasy—an Irish-born Civil War veteran from Lawrence, Massachusetts—following a late-night meeting chaired by Burke. Given the hour, a Manchester policeman suspected the pair might be plotting a robbery. When the officer searched the two Irishmen, he discovered they were carrying loaded revolvers and arrested the pair for vagrancy. While Kelly told police he was a hatter named John White and Deasy claimed to be the bookbinder Martin Williams, Corydon informed the authorities of their true identities.

Immediately, Burke and other IRB members in Manchester plotted the rescue of the two Irishmen, who themselves had helped to spring Stephens from a Dublin prison two years earlier. Following a September 18 court appearance, police officers loaded Kelly and Deasy into a Black Maria for the three-mile journey to Belle Vue Jail.

Two miles from the courthouse, thirty to forty Irishmen who had been lying in wait ambushed the police van as it passed under a railway arch traversing Hyde Road. The twelve unarmed policemen guarding the Black Maria attempted to beat back the Irishmen with their clubs, but they were no match for the revolvers and axes wielded by the mob. Climbing atop the van, the Fenians attempted to smash a hole in the roof with boulders and large pieces of wood harvested from the roadside. When those attempts failed, one frustrated Fenian fired his revolver at the lock on the van's rear door. The bullet pierced the eye of a police sergeant who was unknowingly looking through the keyhole at the disturbance outside.

Finally able to open the door, the Fenians rushed into the van and freed Kelly and Deasy as the dead policeman's body fell to the

In what became known as the "Smashing of the Van," Fenians ambushed a police van traveling through the streets of Manchester, England, on September 18, 1867, and freed the Fenian leaders Thomas Kelly and Timothy Deasy.

ground. Still handcuffed, the prisoners fled out of sight. After being secreted away in the safe havens of the local Irish enclave, Kelly and Deasy arrived back in the United States at the end of October.

The news set off jubilation in Ireland. *The Irish People* praised the audacious rescue of "a well beloved and trusted Fenian chief from the very jaws of the British Lion." The English public, however, was so outraged at the violent murder of a police officer that it demanded a blood sacrifice of its own in return.

❧

In the wake of what became known as the "Smashing of the Van," an anti-Irish hysteria swept across Manchester. Police arrested sixty-two Irishmen they suspected of participating in the ambush, and twenty-three faced trials that began just weeks after the attack, leaving little time for heads to cool or defenses to be prepared.

Under the 1848 Treason Felony Act, anyone guilty of involvement in planning an offense was as guilty as those who executed it, which made it immaterial that the prosecution couldn't prove which man fired the shot that killed the police officer. After a sixteen-day trial, the jury returned guilty verdicts for five men, whom the court sentenced to die.

The condemned Irishmen included Michael Larkin, a thirty-two-year-old tailor and father of four; Thomas Maguire, a royal marine visiting his sister while on leave from a stint in India; and William Allen, a nineteen-year-old carpenter. The death row prisoners also included a pair of American citizens. Michael O'Brien, a thirty-one-year-old draper's assistant from County Cork who used the alias William Gould, served as a lieutenant with a New Jersey regiment during the Civil War. Edward O'Meagher Condon, also a native of County Cork, served as a sergeant in the Irish Legion and was wounded in the Battle of Nashville.

Following his sentencing, Condon delivered an inspiring address punctuated by three words that would become an enduring rallying cry for generations of Irish republicans. "You will soon send us before God, and I am perfectly prepared to go," he told the court. "I have nothing to regret, or to retract, or take back. I can only say, God Save Ireland!"

Days after the death sentences, British authorities discharged

Maguire, whose innocence was so clear that court reporters lobbied for his release. Condon's American citizenship saved him from
the gallows after the American minister to the United Kingdom,
Charles Francis Adams, lobbied the British government to commute his sentence. The U.S. secretary of state, William Seward, also
ordered Adams, whose father and grandfather (John Quincy and
John) served as American presidents, to seek clemency for the other
condemned American, O'Brien. The ambassador, however, disre-
garded the order because he had already asked the British to save
one American life, and two years earlier he had stepped in to spare
O'Brien after he was caught buying rifles in Liverpool with Burke.
"The charges brought of so purely a criminal nature, and sustained
by such strong evidence," Adams wrote to Seward, "did not seem to
me to be a proper case to attempt to interfere with the usual course
of law." The remaining three men would not be spared.

⚜

In the early morning hours of November 23, a yellow, murky fog
blanketed the gallows like a funeral shroud as thousands gathered
outside New Bailey Prison sang and shouted in anticipation of the
spectacle. Despite the early hour, nearby gin palaces did a brisk business lubricating spectators, while street vendors peddled coffee and
potatoes roasted on little stoves. With rumors that the Fenians would
try to shoot the hangman, William Calcraft, an assistant remained on
standby to ensure that the executions would continue, should the
executioner be gunned down.

Shortly after the prison clock struck 8:00 a.m., Calcraft placed the
three fatal cords dripping from the crossbar of the gallows around
the necks of Allen, Larkin, and O'Brien. He then pulled the bolt,
and the men plummeted from view.

"If you reflect on it, it is nothing, I am dying an honorable death,
I am dying for the fatherland, dying for the land that gave me birth,
dying for the island of Saints, and dying for liberty," the teenage
Allen wrote in a gallant missive to his aunt and uncle hours before
he mounted the scaffold clutching a crucifix. "It is sad to be parting
you all at my early age, but we must all die someday or another, a
few hours more and I will breathe my last on English soil. Oh, that
I could be buried in Ireland."

Prison officials, however, covered the bodies of the three Irishmen in quicklime to prevent a Catholic burial and interred them in unmarked graves inside the penitentiary. From that foggy morning on the gallows, the first political revolutionaries hanged in the United Kingdom since Robert Emmet in 1803 passed into the mists of Irish history. While the English considered the trio the "Manchester Murderers," Irish newspapers called them the "Manchester Martyrs."

The Irish revolted with anger at the "judicial murder" of Allen, Larkin, and O'Brien. They staged mass protests and mock funeral processions in Cork, Limerick, and Dublin that spread to the diaspora who filled streets from New Zealand to New York. American newspapers printed the martyrs' gallant final letters, and the images of Allen, Larkin, and O'Brien received places of honor in the homes of Irish Catholics. Annual commemorations of their executions became fixtures on the calendars of Irish nationalists.

The Irish also protested, as they always did, in song. Inspired by Condon's concluding words in the dock, "God Save Ireland" quickly became an unofficial anthem of Ireland sung in pubs and at the conclusion of nationalist meetings.

In a letter to Karl Marx, Friedrich Engels wrote that the hangings "accomplished the final act of separation between England and Ireland. The only thing the Fenians had lacked were martyrs. They have been provided with these." The Irish republican movement had lost three of its own but gained sympathy around the world. The popular support, however, wouldn't last long.

❧

On the eve of the executions of the Manchester Martyrs, more than fifteen thousand people had descended upon London's Clerkenwell Green for a torchlight rally to urge the Crown to have mercy on the three Irishmen. Just steps away at the Clerkenwell House of Detention, Burke sat inside a cell following his November 20 arrest for purchasing arms for the Fenians in England.

The man who had plotted the operation to free Kelly and Deasy now arranged for his own rescue. Burke smuggled out instructions to his fellow Fenians to blast the twenty-five-foot-high prison wall, which abutted a London city street, while he was in the exercise yard on the other side.

On the afternoon of December 12, a Fenian operative wheeled a thirty-six-gallon kerosene barrel brimming with gunpowder in a tarpaulin-covered barrow alongside the wall, but the flame on the fuse fizzled along with the rescue attempt. The next day, the fuse lit without a hitch and sparked an explosion so violent that it not only carved a sixty-foot-long inverted triangle in the prison wall but reduced two three-story tenement houses on the other side of the street to piles of rubble and badly damaged a dozen others. The Fenians had used nearly 550 pounds of gunpowder, far too much for the job that resulted in twelve deaths and more than 120 injuries.

Of the eight men arrested for the explosion, only twenty-seven-year-old Michael Barrett was found guilty. Calcraft, the hangman for the Manchester Martyrs, slipped the noose around Barrett's neck, too, as he swung from the gallows outside London's Newgate Prison on May 26, 1868, in the last public execution in Great Britain.

The "Clerkenwell Outrage" was the most alarming strike on London since the Gunpowder Plot of 1605. Londoners were understandably agitated at the Fenian threat. As blast victims continued to recover in London hospitals, rumors spread that the Irish planned to assassinate British leaders, burn down buildings with incendiaries, and attack the city's gasworks in order to plunge London into darkness. Detectives prowled every railway station, and Scotland Yard deployed soldiers and extra policemen to guard iconic landmarks, including the Bank of England, Buckingham Palace, the Tower of London, and the British Museum. Royal Navy boats guarded floating powder magazines on the Thames. Buckets of dirt stood ready in government offices to douse any firebomb attacks. More than fifty thousand citizens enrolled as special constables in London alone to help the authorities protect the city.

The heinous loss of life damaged the Fenian cause and blunted the momentum gained by the Irish republican movement following the hangings of the Manchester Martyrs. The turbulent year of 1867 ended with the IRB severely damaged. Stephens was again exiled in France, no longer the inciting force he once was. Another rebellion had been crushed by the British, and the Irish appeared no closer to freedom. Through it all, the Fenians had set out to inspire the birth of a new nation. Indirectly, they did just that.

13

The Call of Duty

C HURCH BELLS AND cannon fire echoed through the
Ottawa night. Patriotic revelers gathered around towering
bonfires that lit up the early morning hours of July 1, 1867,
to celebrate the advent of the Dominion of Canada—a confederation of the provinces of Ontario, Quebec, New Brunswick, and Nova
Scotia.

Dawn revealed a city that looked—and smelled—more like a
rough-edged frontier backwater than a cosmopolitan capital. Diplomats used to the refined metropolises of Europe kept their heads
down as they dodged a shotgun splatter of spittle and tobacco juice
staining the wooden plank sidewalks. Steps away from Parliament
Hill, pigs wallowing in mud and manure held their own congresses
in the middle of Ottawa's intersections.

Canada's creation was a civilized affair, negotiated over cigars and
brandy in dark-paneled conference rooms with British officials, who
supported a semiautonomous confederation as a way to reduce military commitments and expenses. Not all Canadians were happy with
the new confederation. While Ottawa celebrated, flags in Halifax,
Nova Scotia, sagged at half-mast and shopkeepers shuttered their
doors in mourning instead of celebration. Even in Canadian cities
that wholeheartedly supported the confederation, jubilation inter-
mingled with apprehension. Much as the new nation was inspired by
incursions from the south, angst about whether the newborn country

could survive to maturity lurked as its American neighbor was poised, ready to consume it whole.

Fear of the United States contributed to Queen Victoria's selection of the logging town perched above the Ottawa River as the nation's capital. Along with its location, straddling Canada's English-speaking and French-speaking regions, Ottawa was considered a safe enough distance inland to be protected from a possible invasion by the United States. Those with long memories in Ontario could recall that prior to the redcoats torching the White House, Americans had burned down the provincial assembly building in Toronto. Americans still possessed the province's parliamentary mace as a war trophy.

The United States continued to cast its land-hungry eyes north, ready to annex its neighbor. After all, Secretary of State William Seward had just months before signed a treaty to acquire Alaska from Russia for two cents an acre. Many Americans expected confederation to quickly end in failure, with Canada's eventual incorporation into the United States. "When the experiment of the 'Dominion' shall have failed, as fail it must, a process of peaceful absorption will give Canada her proper place in the Great North American republic," predicted *The New York Times.*

Thomas D'Arcy McGee recognized the American threat to his fledgling nation. He envisioned a country that stretched from the Atlantic to the Pacific, and he urged the incorporation of British Columbia into the union as quickly as possible in order to outflank the Americans on North America's geopolitical chessboard. As a further deterrent to the giant to the south, which had ten times Canada's population, he proposed that the entire population of Canada be armed. Most of all, he believed that Canadians needed to unify against the threat and that could be done only by rejecting sectarian ideologies, such as the Fenianism that sought to appeal to its Irish constituents.

Ironically, however, Canada might not have been a nation at all without the Fenians. Just as the Eastport fizzle had spurred pro-confederation forces to an electoral victory in New Brunswick a year earlier, the subsequent Fenian raids into Ontario and Quebec and the enduring threat of another attack alarmed many residents along the American border, convincing them that a union was necessary in order to protect their families and property.

McGee's escalating rhetoric against the Fenians eroded his support among the predominantly Irish Catholic constituents in Montreal, and his political star faded. Although McGee was considered one of the "Fathers of Confederation" who played a vital role in the early negotiations of the political union, he was excluded from the delegation sent to London to draft the British North America Act, which formally established the confederation. Then he was excluded from Prime Minister John A. Macdonald's inaugural cabinet, in order to allow greater religious and geographic balance in its composition.

Two days after the national celebration of the confederation, McGee returned to Montreal as campaigning began for Canada's first federal parliament. With the Irish turning even further against the perceived traitor, McGee faced the toughest campaign of his political career, which he won by fewer than three hundred votes.

❧

In shambles after the failure of the Fenian Rising in Ireland, the old Stephens-O'Mahony wing of the Fenian Brotherhood gathered in August 1867 and elected John Savage—a veteran of the 1848 rebellion, journalist, and author—as its leader. Meanwhile, the ascendant Roberts wing met in Cleveland the following month.

Although armed soldiers guarded the doors and delegates were sworn to secrecy, the details of the convention spilled onto the pages of the *Cleveland Herald,* which reported, with no apparent irony, that the Irishmen rejected a proposal to admit women into circles "because of their inability to keep a secret." William Roberts castigated Stephens and his followers for the failure of the Fenian Rising in Ireland and accused them of lavish spending on "fast horses and faster women."

In addition to electing General John O'Neill to the senate, convention delegates unanimously reelected Roberts, who agreed to serve only on the condition that the convention pledge $167,450 for another Canadian invasion. The Roberts wing would have to work hard, however, to amass that amount of money. It had raised more than $79,000 in the previous year but spent more than $87,000. Plus, the Irish Republic bonds were earning only $0.20 on the dollar. Roberts urged delegates to waste no more money on flags and other accoutrements. He wanted every dollar dedicated to arms and armaments.

General Samuel Spear, the acting secretary of war, had worked throughout 1867 to hone the Irish Republican Army into a sharper fighting force, organizing it into twenty-one regiments and even making sure it was better dressed with the development of regulation uniforms. The Fenian cavalry jacket, modeled after the U.S. Cavalry shell jacket, was bright green trimmed with yellow, while the infantry sported blue shell jackets with light blue or yellow trim. Brass buttons featured the raised letters "IRA" surrounded by a wreath of shamrocks, and brass belt plates bore the same three letters. Blue trousers with a green cord down the outside seam resembled those worn by the U.S. Army. Overcoats and blue kepis with green bands, which were sometimes worn with brass harp pins, completed the ensemble.

The Fenians also established regulations for commissioned officer uniforms that included a dark green frock coat, black trousers, a black hat, and a green silk sash. Major generals were permitted two silver sunbursts on their shoulder straps, brigadier generals one sunburst, colonels a silver phoenix, lieutenant colonels a silver shamrock, and majors a gold shamrock. The Irish Republican Army might have been able to compete sartorially with the redcoats, but it would never succeed if it couldn't match the modernity of the enemy's weapons.

In spite of his earlier pledge to return the guns seized from the Irish Republican Army during the prior year's raids, President Andrew Johnson had yet to fulfill his promise by September 1867, when the Fenian senators Frank Gallagher and James Gibbons traveled to Washington, D.C., to lobby for the return of the confiscated material. Johnson agreed as long as the Fenians vowed not to use them unlawfully. He directed Attorney General Henry Stanbery to oversee the return of approximately forty thousand weapons. The cache included hundreds upon hundreds of muskets, Smith carbines, bayonets, sabers, and even a pair of crutches and a bugle.

In just the short time since their manufacture, however, the Fenian stock of muzzle-loading Springfield rifles had become outdated by the advent of breech-loading rifles, which were being carried by American, British, and Canadian forces. Although breech-loading rifles still fired one shot at a time, soldiers could load their ammunition much more quickly by feeding a cartridge into a chamber in the rear of the barrel rather than having to pour the powder charge into the muzzle and ramrodding it into the barrel. An expert marksman could fire muzzle-loading rifles three times a minute, while breechloaders could shoot off twenty rounds in the same time.

The Fenian muzzle-loading Springfield rifles would be no match for the Snider conversions of the P1853 Enfield rifles carried by British troops. However, the Fenians were able to convert their muzzle-loaders into state-of-the-art breechloaders, thanks to a method in which a breech was cut into the original sealed chamber and the rifle stocks reused. By converting their rifles, the Fenians could also keep their pledge not to use the weapons given back to them against Canada. They were, technically speaking, no longer the same guns.

In order to keep pace in the arms race, the *Irish-American* editor Patrick J. Meehan, who served as the Fenian secretary of military affairs, visited the Springfield Armory and contacted the Colt's Manufacturing Company to explore options. Meehan ultimately decided to rent space in a former factory of the Trenton Locomotive Works and hire gunsmiths to perform the conversions on more than five thousand Springfield rifles. The Fenians, uncharacteristically, managed to maintain such secrecy around the Trenton, New Jersey, operation that few in the city had any idea that they had erected a makeshift armory. While new modern breech-loading Spencers cost $6 apiece and other gunsmiths quoted prices of $7 per rifle, the Fenian conversions cost $12 per gun, a decision that made financial sense for Meehan only because he had a personal stake in the Trenton operation.

With new uniforms and modernized weapons, the Irish Republican Army looked to the future with hopes of becoming a more professional fighting force. As a new year dawned, it turned to the leader of its greatest triumph to once again lead it into Canada.

❄

As New Yorkers prepared to flood Wall Street and the byways of lower Manhattan to listen to the bells of Trinity Church ring in the new year of 1868, Roberts convened the senate inside the Fenians' new headquarters, dubbed the Green House by the press, for an important New Year's Eve announcement. The Fenian president informed the senators gathered inside the Greenwich Village town house at 10 West Fourth Street that the closing moments of 1867 would also bring with them the end of his tenure.

Roberts, who had not drawn a single dollar in salary or expenses while serving as president, resigned not only to return to his lucrative dry-goods business but to clear the way for a reunion with the O'Mahony faction after two years of separation. Weeks earlier, Roberts and Savage had signed a tentative agreement to merge into the United Brotherhood, with the two factions nominating seven people each to serve on a governing council and both men resigning their positions in order, they said, to tender the reunified organization's presidency to John Mitchel.

The Irish nationalist firebrand had spent a year in Paris funneling money from the Fenian Brotherhood in the United States to Ireland. Although outspoken, Mitchel remained a respected figure among both Fenian Brotherhood and IRB leaders because he had little involvement in either organization, believing both to be engaging in foolhardy military schemes.

In the interim, the Fenians needed to replace Roberts. Meehan and his fellow senators sought someone vigorous and famous, and so, on New Year's Day, the fifteen-man senate unanimously elected the war hero O'Neill.

Meehan's *Irish-American* newspaper reveled in the ascension of a member of the rebellious O'Neill clan. "The Irish heart leaps fondly towards the historic name and the proud recollection of the days when Hugh and Owen stood for the rights of their people and native land, and dealt the assailants of both those sturdy blows."

O'Neill, who had resigned as inspector general a few months earlier to devote more time to his real estate and claims business, said he must answer the call of duty like a loyal soldier. There was one condition—that the senate unite behind him in preparing for another attack on Canada before the close of 1868.

O'Neill had fame, but he lacked a fortune like Roberts's. He had just paid a Washington, D.C., lawyer $6,000 to put the affairs of his lackluster business in order and would now have to forsake his enterprise once again. He did so only because he expected his tenure to be a short one.

But not long after O'Neill's ascension, word arrived from Paris that Mitchel, who thought a Canadian invasion and a transatlantic attack on Ireland during peacetime equally delusional, had no interest in returning to the United States to lead the revolutionary movement. Perhaps inevitably, the two rival clans returned to their sniping. The deal signed by Roberts and Savage fell apart. The Fenian movement remained, as ever, hopelessly divided.

With his presidential stint more than just an interim role, O'Neill threw his energy into fulfilling the pledge taken by the Fenian senate on New Year's Day "to go to work at once to put the national organization on a war footing." He attended state conventions from Maine to Minnesota and wrote as many as thirty letters a day to leaders of Fenian circles. The large, enthusiastic crowds that greeted O'Neill in city after city testified to his enduring popularity.

In a return to Buffalo, the launching point for O'Neill's greatest triumph, Colonel William Clingen led the Seventh Regiment of the Irish Republican Army as it escorted the Fenian president through the city to St. James Hall, where six thousand people squeezed inside to hear him speak. Hundreds more who could not gain admittance spilled onto the street outside.

"Your presence here in such vast numbers tonight will convince the most skeptical that the Fenian cause is not dead," O'Neill told his fellow Irishmen. "The men that crossed with me at Fort Erie are ready to fight again. You need no better proof of the fact than that they stand at my back here tonight." After the stirring oratory, more than one hundred men rushed the stage to enroll in the Irish Republican Army.

"The result of O'Neill's visit to Chicago has been to strengthen the Fenian cause fifty fold," one Canadian spy reported. "Many who were formerly adherents of the O'Mahony party, and had thrown up the cause as hopeless, are now its strongest supporters and are ready for any movement no matter how unlawful or rash it may be."

As O'Neill continued to energize Fenian audiences, he remained bitter toward the man he still blamed for thwarting his takeover of Canada two years earlier. With his power increasing, O'Neill traveled to Washington, D.C., to meet him in person—president to president.

❀

Washington, D.C., had truly become a federal city during the Civil War as the American government swelled to an unprecedented level. The newly constructed dome of the U.S. Capitol loomed over the cityscape, a powerful symbol of the Union, but the granite stump of the unfinished Washington Monument—its construction halted fourteen years earlier due to a lack of money—served as a reminder of the hard work that remained in building a more perfect union.

Seeking an audience with President Johnson, O'Neill stepped through the doors of the White House, which still bore burn marks on its walls from the British visit during the War of 1812, and joined the callers who flocked outside the president's office every day in search of a moment with the commander in chief to lobby for a patronage job or a pet project.

Accompanying the Fenian president on the trip was one of his closest confidants, Major Henri Le Caron. A slender, refined figure with a military mustache, Le Caron was described as having "one of the boniest faces in or out of the New World, a death's head with a tight skin of yellow parchment." A human chimney who consumed as many as sixteen cigars a day, Le Caron watched life through a haze of smoke. Beneath his lofty forehead and neatly combed black hair, his beady eyes remained on constant alert, continually darting around his surroundings.

In search of adventure, Le Caron had come to the United States from Paris at the outbreak of the Civil War. He served as a private and bugler with the Fifteenth Pennsylvania Cavalry before becoming a lieutenant in the Thirteenth U.S. Colored Cavalry. Fellow soldiers found something just a little odd about Le Caron but chalked it up to his being a Frenchman. Rumors circulated around the campfires that Le Caron was related to the princes of Orléans, although he had a strange tendency at times to slip into an English Cockney accent.

While stationed in Nashville, Le Caron became acquaintances with O'Neill, who was serving with the Seventeenth U.S. Colored Cavalry. O'Neill found himself drawn to the Parisian, who entertained him with tall tales and claimed Hibernian roots on his mother's side. It was in Nashville that Le Caron, like O'Neill, joined the Fenian Brotherhood.

Following the war, Le Caron moved to Illinois and pursued a career in medicine. He took classes at the Chicago Medical College and worked as a surgical assistant inside the Illinois State Penitentiary in Joliet until adventure beckoned once again a few months after O'Neill took leadership of the Fenians. "Come at once, you are needed for work," the Fenian president telegrammed Le Caron.

Summoned to Fenian headquarters in New York, Le Caron quit his job and left his family behind. O'Neill commissioned him a major and military organizer for the Irish Republican Army at a salary of $60 a month plus $7 a day for expenses. He tasked Le Caron with inspecting and reorganizing the organization's military units in the East, and now he brought him along to join in the audience with President Johnson, who had served as Tennessee's military governor at the same time both men were stationed in Nashville.

Johnson limped into 1868 as the lamest of lame ducks—even before his impeachment by the Republican-dominated House of Representatives and acquittal by a single vote following his trial by the Senate. The American president had heard the enduring criticism from Irish Americans about his actions during the Fenian raid of 1866 and thought it unjust. "They don't take into account that we can't do just what we want in these things," he told *The Cincinnati Commercial*. "As Andrew Johnson, I have always sympathized with this movement, but a man can't always do officially what he feels unofficially. We must obey certain laws of nations—we must obey the neutrality laws."

Johnson sat down with Le Caron and O'Neill, and he reiterated his support of the Fenian cause. "General, your people unfairly blame me a good deal for the part I took in stopping your first movement," the president said, according to Le Caron's account. "Now I want you to understand that my sympathies are entirely with you, and anything which lies in my power I am willing to do to assist you. But you must remember that I gave you five full days before issuing any proclamation stopping you. What, in God's name, more did you want? If you could not get there in five days, by God, you could never get there."

If Le Caron's report of the White House meeting was accurate, Johnson had once again signaled the support of the American government for the Fenian cause. The unresolved *Alabama* claims and cases of American citizens incarcerated in British prisons continued to divide the United States and Great Britain, and O'Neill intended to take full advantage of the split to strike Canada once again.

❧

Among O'Neill's first actions as president of the Fenian Brotherhood had been distancing the organization from the Clerkenwell prison explosion as well as from the reports arriving from overseas that Fenians had sent explosive letters addressed to prominent British officials in Dublin and thrown bottles of incendiary Greek fire, now being called "Fenian fire" by the British press, through the windows of London homes in hopes of setting them ablaze. The violent episodes caused Charles Dickens to feel uneasy about his safety as he embarked on a reading tour of the United States. "I have an opinion myself that the Irish element in New York is dangerous for the reason that the Fenians would be glad to damage a conspicuous Englishman," he wrote.

O'Neill had no interest in such an enterprise, however. Having become comfortable in his role as Fenian president and bolstered by the tacit support of the White House, O'Neill fixated on fulfilling the pledge that he had made to Canadian soldiers while departing Fort Erie in June 1866 to return soon with an even larger army. That Canada had cut some of its ties to Great Britain through confederation mattered not to the Fenian president. Any territory that was partly British was still British.

To its moral credit but military disadvantage, the Fenian Brotherhood clung to its dubious strategy of winning Ireland's freedom by challenging the British on the battlefield. For O'Neill, there was nothing gallant in bombing civilians, murdering political leaders, or perpetrating attacks through the postal service. An O'Neill could only find glory confronting the enemy soldier to soldier.

"The Fenian organization will not fight their battles by assassination of individuals," O'Neill told an audience in Buffalo in February 1868. Events in the coming weeks, however, would cause many to question the honesty of that pledge.

14

Blood in the Street

I N THE YEARS following the Civil War, people, money, information, and ideologies traveled faster than ever before. Steamships
delivered quicker trips across the oceans. Telegraphs slashed
the time it took for news to spread from days to hours. The unprecedented advances in communications and technology blurred
international borders and allowed for the globalization of Ireland's
political problems.

Leaders at the highest level of the British Empire worried about
the possibility of a transborder conspiracy among the Fenians and
the exportation of Irish political violence from nearby England to
faraway Australia. Their worst fears appeared to be realized when
an orderly room clerk to William Roberts reported to the Canadian
prime minister, John A. Macdonald, that a thirty-man Fenian assassination squad had departed the United States for England with
plans to kill Queen Victoria, the archbishop of Canterbury, and the
British prime minister.

Then, on March 9, 1868, a Canadian double agent reported
directly to Macdonald that Fenians in Chicago had plotted to dispatch three hired assassins to England to murder the Prince of Wales
by poison or dagger. Three days later, an Irishman indeed tried to
murder one of Queen Victoria's sons, but it was her second-eldest
son, Prince Alfred. The favorite son of the "Famine Queen" was
attending a picnic in a suburb north of Sydney, Australia, during the
first royal tour of Britain's antipodal colony when the Irish Catholic

immigrant Henry O'Farrell approached from behind and fired a pistol at close range into his back. "I'm a bloody Fenian and will die for my country!" yelled the Irishman. Fortuitously, the royal's India rubber braces slowed the velocity of the bullet, which miraculously missed his vital organs, allowing him to survive. O'Farrell was not in fact part of a conspiratorial network but a loner drawn to the Fenian ideology. In spite of a request from the prince himself to spare his shooter's life, the Irishman went to the gallows on April 21, 1868. By the time the news of Prince Alfred's shooting crossed from Australia to North America, another pro-British political figure had been shot by an Irishman—this time fatally.

❧

For most of the winter, illness exacerbated by chronic alcoholism had confined Thomas D'Arcy McGee to his house in Montreal, where many of his former Irish friends now shunned him. McGee's harsh words toward the Fenian cause had earned him an expulsion from the St. Patrick's Society of Montreal in November 1867, and he continued to antagonize the Irish by vilifying the Manchester Martyrs.

With his health at last improving, McGee returned to Ottawa. He took to the floor of the House of Commons in the early morning hours of April 7 during a late-night session where he stood by his principles, even if it came at a price. "I hope that in this House mere temporary or local popularity will never be made the test by which to measure the worth or efficiency of a public servant. He, sir, who builds upon popularity builds upon

A leader of the Young Irelander Rebellion in 1848, Thomas D'Arcy McGee earned the wrath of the Fenians when he became an outspoken supporter of the British Crown as a member of the Canadian Parliament.

a shifting sand," he said to applause. McGee told the chamber that a true leader was someone "ready to meet and stem the tide of temporary unpopularity, who is prepared, if needs be, to sacrifice himself in defense of the principles which he has adopted as those of truth—who shows us that he is ready not only to triumph with his principles, but even to suffer for his principles."

McGee closed his speech with a rhetorical flourish in which he declared himself "not as the representative of any race, or of any Province, but as thoroughly and emphatically a Canadian." It was one of the finest speeches he had ever delivered and well received by his fellow parliamentarians.

Buoyed by the address and his steadily improving health, McGee was in a celebratory mood once debate ended around 2:00 a.m. Sober for several months, he sidled up to the bar inside the House of Commons and purchased three cigars. He joined Prime Minister Macdonald for a smoke and then began to walk home.

Under the light of a full moon, he approached the Toronto House, where he had been boarding for nearly a month. Still suffering from an ulcerated leg, McGee limped and fumbled with his key as a figure approached from behind. Mary Ann Trotter, the boardinghouse's owner, sat awake within, awaiting not just McGee's return but that of her thirteen-year-old son, Willie, a page in the House of Commons.

That is my boy coming home, Trotter thought to herself as she heard the footsteps outside the dining room window, followed by the muffled tap on the door like the one she had instructed Willie to use when out late so as not to disturb any guests sleeping inside.

Trotter turned the knob and opened the door. A sudden flash blinded her, and a loud crack echoed through the empty street as she inhaled gunpowder. She saw a man in a white top hat slumped on the ground. Trotter closed the door. She grabbed a lamp, which illuminated the blood splattered on the foyer floor and on her night-gown. She opened the door again and found the figure slumped even further to the ground against the stone doorpost.

Trotter called for her other boarders, who approached the life-less body and identified it as McGee's. The parliamentarian had been shot in the back of the neck. The .32-caliber bullet that passed through his mouth was so powerful that it blasted his false teeth into the Toronto House foyer. McGee's glove and cigar lay in the street a few feet away as his blood pooled on the sidewalk and trickled into the gutter. The onetime Young Ireland member and fierce supporter of confederation was dead. The young Canadian nation now had its own martyr.*

❧

Even before the crime scene had been cleaned, Canadian leaders inside the House of Commons believed they knew the culprit: Fenianism. "If Thomas D'Arcy McGee had not taken the patriotic stand which he took before and during the Fenian invasion of this country," George-Étienne Cartier, minister of militia and defense, told a quiet chamber, "he would not be lying a corpse this morning."

The anguished prime minister rose to address the chamber. "He who was with us last night, no, this morning, is no more," Macdonald said as eyes naturally drifted to McGee's empty seat. "He has been slain, and I fear slain because he preferred the path of duty."

McGee's face had been so severely mutilated by the bullet that the traditional Victorian death mask was replaced by a plaster cast of his right hand, a more appropriate memorial of the poet, journalist, and man of words. Authorities plastered posters across Ottawa that offered a $2,000 reward for the apprehension of the killer. With habeas corpus still suspended in Canada, police rounded up forty Irishmen suspected of Fenian sympathies. Less than twenty-four hours after the assassination, police believed they had the murderer—Patrick James Whelan, who had been seen lurking about Parliament during McGee's final hours.

Born around 1840 in County Galway, the red-bearded Whelan had arrived in Canada a few years earlier. A tailor by trade, he had joined the Volunteer Cavalry in Quebec City, where he was arrested on suspicion of being a Fenian but released because of a lack of evidence. After marrying a woman thirty years his senior in Montreal, Whelan moved to Ottawa in November 1867 to work for the tailor Peter Eagleson, a Fenian supporter.

When the police entered Whelan's hotel room, they discovered several issues of *The Irish-American* and blank membership cards from Irish nationalist organizations, which suggested he had been a

---

* McGee remains the only Canadian federal politician ever assassinated.

Fenian recruiter. Although all six chambers of his Smith and Wesson revolver were loaded, the gun appeared to have been recently fired and its bullets matched that of the one fired at McGee. As detectives looked for proof of a larger Fenian conspiracy, Canada united in grief.

❦

An estimated 80,000 people—in a city of barely more than 100,000—lined the streets of Montreal on Easter Monday to honor one of the Fathers of Confederation and to send a defiant message to the gun-toting Fenians who threatened their country. While the organization's president, John O'Neill, condemned "the dastardly, cowardly assassination of McGee," other American Fenians were less forgiving, such as the one who told a New York *World* reporter, "McGee did as much as he could to disgrace our people by his double dealing and treachery, and we cannot feel very sorry for him. Some of us looked upon him as we would upon a poisonous rattlesnake."

Nearly eighty thousand people lined the streets of Montreal to pay their respects to Thomas D'Arcy McGee during his funeral procession.

On what would have been McGee's forty-third birthday, six gray horses draped in black velvet drew his hearse through the streets of Montreal. Spectators kept McGee close to their hearts, wearing black silk mourning badges that featured his photograph pinned to their chests. Fifteen thousand mourners joined in the massive procession accompanying the hearse. During the solemn funeral Mass in St. Patrick's Basilica, the vicar-general closed his eulogy with a denunciation of the Fenians that provoked a spontaneous burst of applause, the heartiest coming from many Irish hands, until the priest reminded the congregation they were in a house of God.

While Macdonald said he believed the shooting of his friend to be "a deliberate decision of the Fenian Organization" and "not the act of one individual only," investigators could find no evidence of conspiracy.

At Whelan's trial, the evidence against him was circumstantial at best. Still, his lack of an alibi, and the discovery of his boot prints in the snow opposite the Toronto House, were enough to seal his fate. They were bolstered by detectives who, hiding near Whelan's cell, testified that they heard him brag to a fellow inmate, "I shot that fellow like a dog."

After an eight-day trial, the jury delivered the verdict: guilty, sentenced to death. "I am here standing on the brink of my grave," Whelan told the court after the verdict, "and I wish to declare to you and to my God that I am innocent, that I never committed this deed, and that, I know in my heart and soul. In the next place I have been charged with being a Fenian. I assure you and every living soul that I never was so at any time—at home or abroad."

In his last hours on death row, Whelan penned a three-page letter to the prime minister in which he admitted to being present at the scene of the shooting and to knowing who pulled the trigger. If true, Whelan chose a trip to the gallows over being an informant. Whelan's execution the following year would be Canada's last public hanging.

❧

During the summer of 1868, the American government suspected that the Fenians might again be up to something closer to the border. Fearing that some Irish Catholic government agents were sympathetic to the Fenian cause, the U.S. War Department contracted with a private detective company newly founded by the Chicago police detective and native Scotsman Allan Pinkerton to investigate the Fenians in the Midwest. Pinkerton assured government officials that "the detectives detailed upon the operation were Protestant Irishmen" and "thoroughly to be relied upon."

Pinkerton's detectives unearthed little evidence of an imminent attack and discovered no weapons out of the ordinary around Chicago. What they did find, however, was growing discord among the Fenian leadership over the organization's treasury.

In spite of O'Neill's tireless fund-raising efforts, money problems derailed his hopes to have troops stationed in Canada by the end of 1868. Only one-third of the $167,450 pledged for the next Fenian raid at the Cleveland congress in September 1867 ever made its way into the organization's treasury over the ensuing nine months.

O'Neill and the senate began to clash over who was responsible for the depleted budget. Irishmen who had donated their hard-earned money criticized the organization's profligate spending, and some scrutinized the mounting expense account that accompanied O'Neill's frequent travels. "General O'Neill moves through the country with a staff larger than the King of Dahomy," groused *The Irish Republic.*

O'Neill conceded his expenses were high because of his considerable travel. "I have never believed, nor do I now, in what some are pleased to term 'economy,' in conducting the affairs of the Brotherhood, too much economy would kill it. Our people must have excitement and are willing to pay for it," he asserted to Senator Frank Gallagher.

The Fenian president knew that the real budget buster was Patrick J. Meehan's rifle conversion project, which nearly bankrupted the Fenian treasury and far exceeded the projected $25,000 cost. The final total climbed to $68,040. In order to cover the cost overrun, Meehan and other senators paid $7,500 out of their own pockets.

In April 1869, O'Neill and James Gibbons, who served as vice president and senate leader, announced that they were reducing the size of the headquarters staff and jettisoning its organizing corps in order to funnel as much money as possible into breechloaders and ammunition.

In fact, the only Fenian making hay in the spring of 1869 was eating it as well. On the opening day of the spring meeting at Jerome Park Racetrack outside New York City, a chestnut stallion named Fenian, bred by the investment banker August Belmont, ran away from an eight-horse field to capture the race named in honor of his owner—the Belmont Stakes. (The silver figure of Fenian still graces the top of the Tiffany trophy that has been given to subsequent winners of the Belmont Stakes.) After that one victorious burst of speed, however, Fenian never saw the winners' circle again.*

⚜

American and Canadian authorities detected little Fenian activity on either side of the border during the summer of 1869. "Were it not for the almost insane enthusiasm of O'Neill himself, I should consider the affair almost at an end," the new British minister to the United States, Edward Thornton, wrote to Secretary of State Hamilton Fish at the end of August.

The Fenian president, though, had become fed up with the ceaseless solicitation he needed to perform in order to stay solvent and the painfully slow progress of accumulating the war fund. "I am sick and tired of traveling from point to point, begging money, and will only continue as long as it is absolutely necessary," O'Neill wrote to Gallagher. Given his lineage, O'Neill wanted to shake the British Empire, not the money trees of America. Warriors, not fund-raisers, became Irish legends.

The Fenian president was determined to fight—no matter the size of the bankroll. He felt confident that the money would flow once he crossed the border and created a sensation. An impatient O'Neill told Gibbons that he could no longer delay the attack, but the senate president protested that given their lack of men and money another Canadian foray would be doomed to fail. Where Gibbons saw prudence, O'Neill saw cowardice.

The tensions between the Fenian president and senate grew increasingly bitter. O'Neill's critics accused him of embezzling money from the Fenian treasury and living comfortably on the donations of poor Irishmen. Flashing back to 1865, senators believed it a repeat

---

* Perhaps prompted by the news from the track, John O'Mahony filed a lawsuit against August Belmont & Co. days after the Belmont Stakes to recover $20,000 in gold that the Fenian Brotherhood had deposited with the investment firm in 1865 to bankroll the Irish Republican Brotherhood, which used money orders to withdraw funds in Dublin from the American account. After the raid on *The Irish People*, the Dublin Metropolitan Police discovered money orders traced back to the Fenian Fund account, which was then frozen. The case dragged on for seven years, but O'Mahony never received a dime.

of the extravagant spending by O'Mahony and his cronies inside Moffat Mansion.

In truth, the only people the Fenian president robbed were his wife and children—depriving them of family time and attention while he pursued his Canadian obsession—and his personal debts continued to mount, forcing him to even borrow $364.41 from his underling Henri Le Caron. As O'Neill and Meehan pointed fingers at each other for the budget-busting armory project, their friend-ship fell apart. The pages of *The Irish-American* began to direct their editorial barbs at the Fenian president.

❧

Even without the backing of the senate, O'Neill proceeded with his preparations for a Canadian invasion. The Fenian president knew firsthand that a lack of weapons and supplies, more than a dearth of manpower, crippled his invasion in 1866 and hastened his withdrawal from the Niagara Peninsula. As a result, he vowed that every soldier who participated in the next Fenian raid would have a gun in his hands and all the provisions necessary.

The Fenians had accumulated a sizable arsenal under O'Neill's leadership. According to the Canadian spymaster Gilbert McMicken, by the end of 1869 they had amassed more than five thousand breech-loading rifles, eighteen thousand muzzle-loading rifles, twenty thousand uniforms, four hundred saddles, and more than seven hundred sabers. All that O'Neill believed the Irish Republican Army still required to complete its preparations was breech-loading ammu-nition. "It should not be forgotten that an arm which discharges twenty shots per minute is an extravagant weapon and that the supply of ammunition to meet its requirements must be proportionately great," O'Neill wrote in a circular to members.

In early November, O'Neill began to deploy the Fenian war stores to secret locations along the Canadian border. He summoned Le Caron, whom he had promoted to lieutenant colonel and acting adjutant general of the Irish Republican Army, to New York. The Pari-sian left behind his family and medical practice in Illinois, which was more lucrative than the $100-per-month salary that O'Neill offered, to direct the movement of arms and supplies to towns in upstate New York and Vermont that hugged the Canadian frontier. The Fenian president then traveled to Buffalo and recruited Colonel William Clingen to oversee the movement of arms hidden in Pittsburgh to cities on the Great Lakes, including Buffalo, Cleveland, and Detroit.

Le Caron and Clingen relied on a network of Fenian agents along the border—such as railroad company employees, hardware merchants, and grocers—who would not arouse suspicions by receiving large volumes of crates and barrels. Once shipped to border towns, the guns and supplies were hidden in the sprawling barns and outbuildings of Irish farmers in the countryside.

In spite of their efforts at subterfuge, the British and Canadian governments still had considerable intelligence about where Le Caron and Clingen stashed arms along the international boundary. Edward Archibald, the British consul in New York, had received such detailed information from his country's spies that he was even able to hand sketch maps of the country roads around St. Albans, Vermont, and Potsdam, New York, with the locations of the stashes. Although the British and Canadians might have known where the arms were, Archibald believed there was little they could do about it. He estimated that one thousand troops would be required to seize the vast arsenal, and he doubted, given the number of Irishmen in the U.S. Army, that the secrecy of such a vast operation could be maintained.

�֍

The Fenian president never wavered in his belief that Ireland could be freed only by the rifle and saber, and he remained more determined than ever to wash away the wrongs of Ireland in the blood of its enemy. It was the Roberts wing's strategy of freeing Ireland by attacking Canada that had originally drawn him to the Fenian Brotherhood four years earlier, and his victory at Ridgeway only solidified his opinion that the only practical way to liberate his homeland was to invade America's northern neighbor.

Like the newly elected president of the United States, Ulysses S. Grant, O'Neill was a soldier at heart, which made him exasperated at the senate's slavish devotion to deliberation at the price of actually getting something done. Didn't the senators remember they had broken away from John O'Mahony in 1865 because of his excessive passivity and refusal to strike Canada? They were supposed to be the "men of action," but nearly four years had slipped away since the last Fenian raid as the senate held meeting after meeting. O'Neill knew that Fenianism, like any revolutionary movement, required action to justify its existence and keep money flowing into its coffers. He saw inaction as the root cause of the Fenian Brotherhood's declining membership and financial difficulties.

"I was painfully aware that the longer we waited, the less confidence would the Organization and the Irish people generally have in our ability to succeed," the Fenian president recalled. "And besides, the thousands of our countrymen who participated in the late war were fast settling down in life, and if we deferred matters much longer, it would be almost impossible to secure a sufficient number of veteran soldiers for the proper inauguration of the movement." While O'Neill hoped to repeat his military triumph at Ridgeway, he also knew from Irish history that choosing to fight the British could be enough in itself to declare victory. A respectable effort could reenergize the Fenian Brotherhood and flood its coffers.

O'Neill ignored the report from Senator Richard McCloud, who served as treasury secretary, that the Fenians lacked enough money to pay their clerks, let alone attack a sovereign nation. He believed himself destined to lead an Irish army to a battlefield victory over the British, and he was no longer willing to let the senate dictate whether or not he could fulfill his life's mission. "The right to fight for Ireland I ask of no man living," O'Neill wrote. "I inherit that right from my fathers, it being the only legacy left me, and I will exercise it, I trust, before England becomes much older in crime, or Ireland more decrepit in her misfortune."

One Ridgeway Would
Never Be Enough

WHILE PRIESTS IN Ireland and the United States regularly castigated the Fenians from their pulpits, Ireland's first-ever cardinal, Paul Cullen of Dublin, wanted the condemnation in writing as well. Although the pontiff had issued a papal bull on October 29, 1868, excommunicating "those who become members of the Masonic sect, of the Carbonari, or of other similar sects that plot either openly or secretly against the Church or legitimate authorities," there had been debate in rectories and pews about whether or not the decree included the Fenian Brotherhood. Anyone with a rudimentary awareness of the Fenians knew, of course, that secrecy was not exactly their forte. What actually made Cullen and other clergy members nervous was that the Fenians represented a threat to the status quo.

All but two Irish bishops joined Cullen and British bishops in appealing to Pope Pius IX, who eliminated any ambiguity when, on January 12, 1870, he "decreed and declared that the American or Irish society called Fenian is comprised among the societies forbidden and condemned." According to the church, it was incompatible for Fenians to also be Catholics, and now they faced the penalty of excommunication for their patriotism.

Fenians couldn't help but wonder why the Holy Father denounced them while staying silent about their oppressor—a Protestant one at that. It also seemed duplicitous that a pope who didn't want the Irish to take up arms to liberate their island had no qualms about their doing so when it came to his territory. They remembered how the call for money and soldiers had emanated from Ireland's pulpits in 1860 as the forces of Victor Emmanuel threatened the Papal States. Upwards of one thousand men joined the Irish Papal Brigade, and many of those battle-hardened mercenaries subsequently became Fenians.

Catholic Fenians questioned why fighting for country, but not for God, was a sin so venal that they must be banished. Thanks to Cullen, who crafted the dogma of papal infallibility that was adopted by the First Vatican Council, they couldn't even question the wisdom of the pope's decision.

The Irish viewed the edict as another backroom deal between the English government and the Holy See—just like the blessing Pope Adrian IV supposedly bestowed upon his fellow Englishman King Henry II that began the seven-century occupation of their island. "What England failed to accomplish through the agency of pliant judges, packed juries, [and] paid informers, she now seeks to effect by the cunning diplomacy of a few English and some Irish bishops of British proclivities," *The Irish People* editorialized.

When a New York City priest read the papal bull from his pulpit, half of his congregation stood up and abruptly left Mass. "The Irish people, thanks to the Fenian Brotherhood, have learned to discriminate between matters spiritual and temporal," commented *The Irish People* in an editorial likely written by John O'Mahony. "If love of country be such a heinous sin, the bulk of Irish Catholics have been outside the pale of the Church for the last seven hundred years."

❦

John O'Neill wasn't about to let anyone—even the pope—deter him from his singular goal. Colonels Henri Le Caron and William Clingen continued the work they had started in the fall of 1869 to ship several tons of arms, munitions, and uniforms to northern Vermont and upstate New York in cases marked "Bristol brick" and "Blacksmiths' coal."

Unlike most generals, O'Neill needed to worry about not just one national government but two, which meant that he needed to move a vast arsenal to the border without the knowledge of the American government. "It was as much our object to evade the United States authorities as it was to battle with the Canadians," he later recounted.

Registering in hotels under the code name McClelland, the Fenian president traveled incognito with Le Caron, who used the alias G. R. Smith, to supervise the attack preparations. Wherever they traveled along the border, Fenian leaders remained vigilant for any spies in their midst. On a visit to Malone, New York, they noticed a man named John C. Rose who stayed in the same hotel as Le Caron and constantly followed him from place to place. A Fenian sympathizer in town from Ottawa recognized Rose and told Edward J. Mannix, the Fenian head center in Malone, that he suspected the man shadowing Le Caron was a Canadian police agent. Administering their own justice, the Fenians beat Rose up so badly that he was laid up for months. The Irishmen had their own informers, too, feeding them information. When New York's governor, John Hoffman, learned that Generals George Meade and William Tecumseh Sherman knew the whereabouts of the stockpiled Fenian weapons, he tipped off the Fenians, and Le Caron moved the materials to new locations.

By February 1870, the relationship between the cocksure O'Neill and the cautious senate became so frayed that the Fenian Brotherhood, already broken in two, split once more into the senate and O'Neill wings. In 1865, the senate broke with O'Mahony because it thought his pace too slow. Now it severed ties with O'Neill because it thought his pace too fast.

The withering attacks on the Fenian president proved too much for James Keenan, O'Neill's newly appointed secretary of civil affairs. A trained physician who had arrived from Ireland six months earlier, Keenan wrote occasional pieces for *The Irish-American,* and in a February 21 letter he directed his pen at the newspaper's publisher, Senator Patrick J. Meehan, who increasingly sided with his fellow senators against the Fenian president. A painful rift had opened between O'Neill and Meehan, who had been so close to the Fenian president that he was the godfather of his daughter, Mary Ella.

In a staunch defense of the Fenian president's war plan, Keenan castigated senators who questioned whether the organization had enough money in the treasury or sufficient weaponry to launch an attack. The mistrust between O'Neill's men and the senate only grew when they met on February 27 inside the Fenian Brotherhood's

Manhattan headquarters. The treasury secretary, Richard McCloud, removed the organization's financial records to his apartment for an examination, and the following night's meeting proved a stormy affair. Senators made plans to hold their own convention in the Midwest, where they had a greater base of support, and they rejected Keenan's appointment to the Fenian leadership, believing him too much of an O'Neill crony.

Listening from another room, Keenan heard the biting words directed at him by Meehan. When the contentious meeting adjourned a little before 11:00 p.m., he watched closely as Meehan and a pack of his fellow senators descended the staircase to West Fourth Street and stopped on the sidewalk on Broadway. The Irishman crept up behind Meehan, pulling his hand out of his inner coat pocket. Pointing a five-barrel Colt revolver at the back of the publisher's neck, Keenan fired a single shot and watched as Meehan crumpled to the sidewalk.

A policeman who heard the gunshot chased Keenan down, while the senators carried Meehan to a nearby drugstore for medical assistance, summoning a priest to perform the last rites. According to *The Irish-American* (which might have embellished the scene for the benefit of its publisher), Meehan made a dying plea for Fenian unity to his fellow senator Frank Gallagher, saying, "Frank, I hope this will be a warning to the General not to surround himself with such men. Let the General retrace his steps and work with the Senate who are his best friends. If my death will unite all I will not have called in vain, and the cause will triumph in the end."

Although Keenan's shot had come at such close range that powder scorched and blackened Meehan's neck, the *Irish-American* publisher not only survived but was even able to identify his assailant when the police hauled him into the drugstore shortly after the shooting. Doctors were never able to retrieve the bullet lodged in Meehan's neck, but he recovered and, perhaps more miraculously, eventually lobbied for Keenan's release from prison. After serving two years of a ten-year sentence, Keenan received a pardon from New York's governor, Hoffman, in 1872 and returned to Ireland.

Due to Keenan's "insane" actions, O'Neill found himself, as he wrote, "in an extremely embarrassing position." In light of Meehan's plea for Fenian unity in the moments after his shooting and amid whispers that the Fenian president had ordered Keenan to pull the trigger, O'Neill announced the day after the shooting that "in view of the lamented catastrophe" he would move the Eighth National Convention from New York to Chicago, as the senate had wished to do. Two weeks later, after renewed accusations, he took back his olive branch, reverting to his original plan to stage the annual congress in New York on April 19. Reconciliation was no longer possible.

"One Ridgeway is enough in this generation," James Gibbons told his fellow Fenians. "Ridgeway served a glorious purpose, but a second Ridgeway would be ruin." For O'Neill and his vastly expanding ego, however, one Ridgeway would never be enough.

❦

The now-annual rumors that the Fenians were emerging from hibernation in America to plan another raid over the border signaled the arrival of spring in Canada. The Fenian scare that arrived in 1870 came just after St. Patrick's Day when a Canadian spy who had infiltrated the Fenian Brotherhood reported that an attack was certain to occur by April 15.

With the British government having begun to reduce its garrison the prior year, the self-governing dominion bore a greater responsibility for its defense. Based on the intelligence reports, the Canadian minister of militia and defense deployed six thousand militia to guard the border between Quebec and the United States while gunboats patrolled the liquid boundary with America.

On April 14, the Canadian prime minister, John A. Macdonald, reported to Parliament that based on reliable information, "the peace of the country was again in danger from the invasion of lawless men from the United States belonging to the Fenian organization." Believing his country faced a greater danger than it had four years earlier because greater secrecy shrouded the operation, the prime minister called on lawmakers to suspend habeas corpus, as during the Fenian raids of 1866. Macdonald told his fellow citizens that these annual alarms about foreign attacks had unfortunately become Canada's new reality, and he predicted "a continuance of these attempts for many years."

Canadian authorities cast wary eyes at any Irishmen in their midst. In some instances, Irishmen arriving from the United States were arrested under the suspicion of being Fenian, and *The New York Herald* reported that in Montreal "detectives and spies haunt the hotels, depots, and drinking saloons in search of Fenians in disguise." The Canadian public, however, was growing fatigued after five consecutive springtime alarms. Frustration mounted at the inability of the Canadian government to properly address the threat and at the United States for giving safe haven to these foreigners who continued to terrorize them.

April 15 passed, however, without Irish soldiers marauding through Canada or even lurking in border towns in the United States. The Canadian government said its preemptive deployment of troops had deterred the foreigners, and the minister of militia and defense reported that an immediate Fenian invasion was no longer likely.

Canada had once again cried wolf, with the Fenian menace failing to materialize. With America's northern neighbor jaded by yet another false alarm, the Irish wolf decided that it was the perfect time to pounce.

Secrets and Lies

H ENRI LE CARON became a familiar face in the hotels of border cities such as Burlington, Vermont, and Ogdensburg, New York, during the winter and spring of 1870 as he squirreled away Fenian supplies along the frontier. Le Caron knew more than anyone else about the location of every rifle, every uniform, and every hardtack barrel procured by the Irishmen for the upcoming invasion. What the Fenian colonel didn't know, however, was just how imminent that attack would be when John O'Neill summoned him to meet in Buffalo on May 21.

Shortly after O'Neill welcomed Le Caron, he informed his aide of his promotion to adjutant general with a rank of brigadier general. Then O'Neill broke the news: The next attack on Canada would begin in seventy-two hours, and "no power on earth could stop it." The choice of date was deliberate: May 24 would be Queen Victoria's fifty-first birthday, a public holiday in Canada.

Le Caron was surprised to hear it. Only $2,000 of the $30,000 sought for the invasion had trickled into Fenian headquarters, but O'Neill was hardly concerned. "I did not deem it necessary to wait the collection of the full amount, as I was satisfied, as soon as we advanced across the border and took up a position there, all the money needed for breech-loading ammunition, the principal deficiency, would be forthcoming," he recalled.

The Fenian leader told Le Caron that he had already sent letters to

Fenian commanders instructing them to depart on May 23 to either Malone, New York, or St. Albans, Vermont. Fearing that any early movements could jeopardize the secrecy of his operation, O'Neill directed all Fenians to leave for the front on the same day—no matter whether they were coming from New York or New Orleans.

"Take no man who is a loafer or a habitual drunkard," the hero of Ridgeway instructed his commanders. In order to keep the mission covert, he directed his men to "avoid the use of uniforms or any insignia that would distinguish them" when traveling to the border as well as to refrain from speaking of any Fenian matters en route.

O'Neill's careful preparations ensured that the Fenians were much better equipped for this raid than they had been four years earlier. While many of the Irish Republican Army soldiers who followed General Samuel Spear into Quebec in 1866 lacked weapons, Le Caron reported that the Fenians had accumulated enough war matériel to arm a force of at least twelve thousand men.

Unlike General Thomas Sweeny's 1866 war plan for the invasion of Quebec and Ontario's Niagara Peninsula, which was broadcast in newspapers for days and weeks in advance, O'Neill had succeeded in keeping the press guessing. The front pages buzzed with rumors of Fenian troop movements from Maine to Minnesota, but they were nothing more than gossip. While the *Buffalo Evening Post* announced O'Neill's imminent arrival in Chicago, the newspaper had no idea that the Fenian general was around the corner ensconced in the Mansion House.

Le Caron's stay in Buffalo, though, lasted mere hours; both he and O'Neill boarded a train to the front in northern Vermont. Happy to be back in the more comfortable role of general, O'Neill felt self-satisfied with the apparent success of his ruse. "Every precaution had been taken to impose secrecy, and though the country is flooded with a sea of British spies, not one detail of the plans was divulged," he boasted.

As their train sped eastward across upstate New York, a buoyant O'Neill bragged to Le Caron "that the Canadians would be taken entirely by surprise." The Fenian general's most trusted adviser knew better.

O'Neill had ordered his underlings to be on a constant lookout for British spies, yet he was blind to the secret agent who had penetrated his inner circle. Henri Le Caron was neither Fenian nor French, neither Gaelic nor Gallic. In fact, he was the furthest thing from it. O'Neill's right-hand man was as English as tea and crumpets.

Henri Le Caron's true identity was Thomas Billis Beach—a British spy serving queen and country.

The second of thirteen children, Beach was born in Colchester, England, in 1841. He craved adventure from his earliest days and confessed to having a "wild mad thirst for change and excitement." Beach told tall tales to escape the confines of reality, and as a twelve-year-old boy he packed up his marbles, trophies, and toys one morning in search of thrills—and perhaps some personal space in such a crowded house—in London. His parents retrieved him before he had gone too far on his sixty-mile walk, but having tasted adventure, he made another attempt. This time he was gone for two weeks.

Like a wild horse determined to run free, the young boy could not be tamed. His desperate parents sent him to a strict Quaker curtain maker for a seven-year apprenticeship, but that lasted all of eleven months before the master returned the apprentice to his family. At age fifteen, Beach finally fulfilled his wish and snuck off to London for good. His employment as a clerk in a drapery firm came to a quick end, though, when he accidentally set the premises ablaze.

Seeking excitement in a foreign land, Beach moved to Paris in 1859, though he spoke not a word of French. Then a new adventure on a new continent beckoned when the Confederate shots fired at Fort Sumter reverberated across the Atlantic. Answering the call for Union army recruits at the outbreak of the Civil War, the teenager sailed to the United States in 1861 and enlisted for three months, posing as a Frenchman and using an alias—Henri Le Caron—in order, he claimed, to save his worrying parents from learning that their boy was fighting in a foreign war.

Three months turned into five years, and after the war Le Caron settled in Nashville. There he became acquainted with his fellow Union army veteran O'Neill, who told him of the Fenian plan to attack Canada. Le Caron dropped a mention of his discussion with O'Neill in a letter to his father, who took it to his local member of Parliament, who passed it along to the British home secretary.

When Le Caron returned to England at the end of 1867 in the wake of the Clerkenwell prison explosion, he found a country terrified by the threat of Fenian violence. Seeing his country thrown into such panic by the Irish menace, Le Caron needed little persuasion from British officials to become a spy. "I never sought Fenianism," he wrote in his memoir. "Fenianism rather came to me."

The Fenian colonel Henri Le Caron, who claimed to be a Frenchman with an Irish mother, was actually a British spy named Thomas Billis Beach who betrayed Fenian secrets to the Crown.

Upon his return to the United States, Le Caron offered his services to O'Neill, who gladly accepted the overture from a man with his military experience. By the end of 1868, Le Caron was drawing checks from both the Fenian Brotherhood and the British government. He worked closely with the Dublin-born Robert Anderson, one of Scotland Yard's first spymasters, and as the Fenian threat to Canada increased, he had direct contact with Gilbert McMicken, the Canadian intelligence officer who oversaw the espionage of the Irish.

As the head center of the Fenian circle he founded in Lockport, Illinois, Le Caron received reports and financial accounts from Fenian Brotherhood headquarters in New York—which he duly forwarded to London and Ottawa. Although he wasn't Catholic, he played the part, attending Mass and singing with the choir at St. Rose of Lima Catholic Church in Wilmington, Illinois.

Le Caron spilled Fenian secrets to McMicken in letters and cipher telegrams that employed a fairly simple code, using a displacement of letters, which could be cracked by knowing which letter was *A*. Le Caron used a variety of monikers—such as LeC, Beach, and R. G. Sayer—and referred to O'Neill by his code name, Brady. McMicken and other Canadian agents traveled to American border towns to meet Le Caron in person and smuggle his communications out of the United States. In fact, John C. Rose (the man who had been badly assaulted by the Fenians in Malone, New York) was spying not *on* Le Caron but *with* him.

A risk taker and a supremely talented liar, Le Caron proved so adept at his job that Canadian detectives, unaware of his employment by the Crown, kept him in their crosshairs, believing him to be one of the Fenians' most accomplished leaders. O'Neill would never learn Le Caron's true identity.

He couldn't say he hadn't been forewarned. The chain-smoking Frenchman had never been fully trusted by many Fenians. Some suspected, as *The Irish-American* reported, that he "would not hesitate a moment to sell the cause of Ireland for a trifling consideration." In 1868, he was formally charged with carelessness, dangerous conduct, and suspicious acts for writing down names of Fenians in a notebook. An investigating committee found no basis to the accusation. Feigning indignation, the spy told O'Neill he would resign after having his character so impugned, but the Fenian general insisted that he wanted him to stay. In so doing, he wrote his own fate.

❀

Some of O'Neill's confidants had pushed for an attack on Canada's sparsely populated western frontier, where the border was lightly defended. "Prominent leaders say that no foolish raid will be made upon the eastern frontier, where every man's hand being against the invaders their defeat would be insured," *The New York Times* reported in April 1870. O'Neill, however, never cared much for conventional wisdom.

O'Neill thought that Sweeny's original war plan had been so sound, in fact, that he planned to once again use St. Albans, Vermont, and Malone, New York, as the staging points for his border incursions. His soldiers would march on the same roads of Vermont and upstate New York that had been trodden by Fenian boots four years earlier.

O'Neill hoped to storm across the border before the American and Canadian governments could interfere with them and entrench a small force on Canadian soil for at least two or three days. He expected that thousands of Irish on both sides of the border, upon hearing the news of the invasion, would then rush to join the cause and form a much larger army.

O'Neill's plan called for the Irish Republican Army to launch a two-pronged attack on St. John's, a city along Quebec's Richelieu River halfway between Montreal and the American border. At least thirteen hundred men would march north from Franklin, Vermont, and cross the border at Eccles Hill, where General Samuel Spear had made his camp in 1866. Meanwhile, a contingent of five hundred men armed with breechloaders would seize a train in Rouses Point, New York, and run it into St. John's to capture the city, where they would meet a detachment sweeping eastward from Malone, New York. Farther to the east, two hundred Irishmen from Rhode Island would march to capture the town of Richmond, where a Grand Trunk Railway branch from Portland, Maine, connected with the main road.

With St. John's and Richmond in their hands, the Irish Republican Army would sabotage the railroad tracks to make it difficult for the Canadian militia to organize and concentrate a force to drive them back as O'Neill awaited the thousands of Irishmen he thought would rush to their aid and allow them to threaten Montreal. He expected to encounter little resistance until the Fenians advanced within sight of Montreal, where he believed the city's sizable Irish and French populations would naturally arise to assist them against the Anglo-Saxon order (an inflated assumption given the way the assassination of Thomas D'Arcy McGee had dampened Fenian support in Canada). O'Neill told *The Daily Phoenix* that once he planted a permanent foothold in Canada, he expected "100,000 Fenians will rush to the front."

As the Fenians had done in 1866, O'Neill put a great deal of faith in the power of good news to persuade his fellow Irishmen on both sides of the border to rush to the cause. Fenians had flocked to Buffalo for days on end after having heard the news of his triumph at Ridgeway, only to be prevented by American authorities from crossing the border to join him. O'Neill didn't expect similar interference this time.

❧

When O'Neill told Le Caron about the May 24 date for the planned invasion, the alarmed spy immediately telegraphed his contacts in Ottawa. The secret agent had already forwarded full details of the Fenian war plan; now McMicken knew the timing as well.

On May 22, a disguised O'Neill disembarked from his sleeping car in the small farming community of Georgia, Vermont, twenty-five miles south of the Canadian border, and climbed aboard a buggy that whisked him away to the countryside. Only a few scattered Fenians knew his whereabouts. O'Neill holed up for the next forty-eight hours in a friend's house as Fenians mobilized across the country on May 23.

Fenian circles opened recruiting stations in cities across America and called upon Irishmen to fight for their country. The Irish, however, had heard all this before. There had been so many broken promises, so many false alarms in the past five years, that they hesitated. In the mill city of Lawrence, Massachusetts, Colonel Hugh McGinnis ordered his men to proceed to Vermont on the afternoon of May 23. Instead, Colonel McGinnis departed to St. Albans as an army of one; he would report on the state of affairs and send for his men if he found out that there was indeed going to be a fight.

In cities such as Boston where the Fenians could find willing volunteers, they lacked the money to pay for their railroad fares. In Bridgeport, Connecticut, Major Daniel Murphy gathered thirty men whom he described as "ready and anxious to be the first in the field." Murphy and his men had to spend the entire day raising $300 to pay for their train tickets north.

The delayed departure meant that Murphy's men were sleeping on "the soft side of a plank board" in Springfield, Massachusetts, more than two hundred miles south of the international border when O'Neill emerged from his hiding spot two hours after midnight on the scheduled date of the attack, ready to lead his Fenian army into Canada.

❈

A drenching rainstorm greeted O'Neill as he took his seat for the buggy ride to St. Albans. In spite of the time, the Fenian general found plenty of company on the muddy country roads of northern Vermont during the wee hours of May 24. The Fenians had hired 125 teams that worked through the pitch-black night to haul wagonloads of supplies and arms that had been stashed away in the largely Irish farming community of Fairfield and surrounding towns to the Canadian border in Franklin.

Nearly every team in St. Albans and Burlington had been engaged by the Fenians for the night. The Fenians paid farmers and livery stables for a night's work or offered promises that they could share in the plunder expected to be seized in Quebec.

Dawn had broken by the time O'Neill's buggy slogged into St. Albans, where he planned to deliver his final instructions to his close friend and chief of staff, General John J. Donnelly, before taking the train to Malone. There he would rally the other half of his troops. Donnelly assured O'Neill that he would have between one thousand and twelve hundred men from Rhode Island and Massachusetts ready to fight on May 24, with an equal number trailing right behind them. Colonel E. C. Lewis reported that an additional six hundred men from Vermont and northeast New York would also be present for the attack, with another six hundred arriving the following day. That would give O'Neill a four-thousand-man army by the end of the invasion's second day.

O'Neill watched as the 6:00 a.m. train pulled in to the depot at St. Albans. He expected hundreds of Irishmen to pour out of the train. However, there were only twenty-five, maybe thirty men from Massachusetts and eighty or ninety from Vermont and northeastern New York.

Unlike four years earlier, O'Neill had secured the guns and the supplies. But where were his bloody men? He had only about one-tenth of the soldiers he had expected. He saw no choice but to delay the attack by twenty-four hours in the hopes that the sixteen hundred men promised by Donnelly and Lewis would materialize. "Even if 800 arrived, I foresaw that they would be ample to take a position, and this was all we wanted at the outset," he said. O'Neill canceled his plan to travel to Malone and ordered Donnelly to divert all Fenians going to upstate New York to the border town of Franklin, fourteen miles northeast of St. Albans, where he proceeded to spend the night.

The Fenian general knew, however, that any postponement could be fatal to the operation. It would not only give Canadian and American authorities time to gather forces to stop him but give his own men an opportunity to have second thoughts. "Every hour's delay," Le Caron recalled, "added to the danger of failure and collapse."

❧

Rain fell on St. Albans during the forenoon of May 24 as the U.S. marshal George Perkins Foster and his deputies kept watch. The boys with the brogues had returned to northern Vermont. From his lodgings at the Welden House, the marshal sent regular dispatches to Washington, D.C., where President Ulysses S. Grant stood ready to take action.

At a cabinet meeting, the commander in chief listened as Secretary of State Hamilton Fish shared the telegrams he had received from army officers and federal marshals who were monitoring the border between Buffalo and Vermont. Once confronted with reports that the Fenians were on the move, the president didn't dither as his predecessor Andrew Johnson had four years earlier.

Within hours of the cabinet meeting, a proclamation signed by Grant began to cross the telegraph wires, warning American citizens against any violations of the country's neutrality laws. The president ordered federal marshals to arrest any offenders, and he directed Attorney General Ebenezer Hoar, if at all possible, to prosecute the railroads that were transporting Fenian units to the Canadian border. General William Tecumseh Sherman, Grant's fiery Civil War colleague who had succeeded him as commanding general of the army, warned the president, however, that his options for preventing a raid were more limited than he might have thought. "We cannot prevent unarmed men from entering Canada, unless it is proven that they are marauders bent upon mischief," he said.

O'Neill was certainly determined to make mischief, but every passing hour that he spent waiting in Vermont jeopardized all the effort he had made to keep the attack a secret. The White House now knew of the movement of the Fenian troops, and thanks to Le Caron the secret was out on the other side of the border as well.

⚜

The persistent downpours that drenched Montreal on Queen Victoria's birthday foiled plans for a military parade through the city streets. Outside the city's newspaper offices, Montreal residents read the reports that an Irish threat loomed only fifty miles away. Wild rumors circulated, and while many believed the reports a simple ploy to sell more newspapers or yet another false alarm by the authorities, the militias and regulars who had congregated for the parade knew something was afoot when they were forced to spend hour after hour in their drill shed awaiting further orders from Ottawa. That afternoon, the Canadian troops were told that one company from each battalion would be sent to the American border.

Soldiers who had expected to spend the day parading through Montreal now marched off to the war front. Accompanied by the music of two military bands and cheering crowds lining the sidewalks, the soldiers sang lively choruses on their two-mile walk to the Grand Trunk Railway Station. As the first train departed for St. John's filled with troops to repel the attack from Vermont, residents of houses that flanked the track leaned out of their windows to cheer and wave handkerchiefs. Hours later, another train left the station with soldiers bound for Huntingdon, Quebec, to confront the Irishmen who, according to Le Caron, would be invading from Malone, New York.

That night, Queen Victoria's seventh child held a large dinner party at his temporary quarters in Montreal before attending a military ball in his mother's honor. Twenty-year-old Prince Arthur, who was in Canada to serve with the Queen's Rifle Brigade, was enjoying an evening of dancing when the music suddenly stopped and an announcement came that the prince and his fellow officers had been ordered to the front.

Leaving the ballroom for the battlefield, Prince Arthur reported for duty. More than fifty years earlier, the prince's godfather, the Duke of Wellington, had been torn away from a ball in Brussels to confront Napoleon on the plains of Belgium. The British prince could only hope that this Fenian raid would end with O'Neill meeting his Waterloo.

A Burlesque of a War

O N THE MORNING of May 25, General John O'Neill conveyed only confidence as he buckled his spurs, telling a reporter for the *Boston Advertiser* that he anticipated "no serious resistance in Canada." He only hoped "there will be enough to amuse his men."

For all his bluster, the general's army remained woefully short-handed. His plans called for an army of three thousand but instead had three or four hundred. All the twenty-four-hour delay had achieved was to diminish his element of surprise. But he held out hope in the reports that four hundred soldiers from New York were on the march from St. Albans and soon to arrive.

O'Neill departed the Franklin Hotel with his close friend and chief of staff, General John J. Donnelly. Five years his junior, the reserved Donnelly had left behind a lucrative law practice and his newlywed wife to join the Union army. Twice wounded in battle, he served as a staff officer and aide-de-camp in the Army of the Cumberland and joined General William Tecumseh Sherman as he stormed through the South on his March to the Sea. After his young wife passed away, just months after he returned home, Donnelly threw himself into the Fenian cause, acting as a recruiting agent in Massachusetts and Rhode Island.

O'Neill and Donnelly rode to the Fenian camp at Hubbard's Corner, halfway between the town of Franklin and the Canadian border, where they were the unwanted guests of one J. H. Hubbard. As the generals arrived, the soldiers were unloading dozens of wagons laden with weapons, equipment, and supplies. O'Neill had provided boxes of hardtack, crates of ham, and barrels of crackers, ensuring that his army had a proper commissariat and that they would have no need to loot the residents of Quebec, as Samuel Spear's men had done four years earlier.

Fenian soldiers also pried open dozens of boxes packed with ammunition and rifles that had been taken apart lock, stock, and barrel to be shipped in ordinary crates without arousing the suspicion of authorities. While some members of the Irish Republican Army preferred to carry into battle their own trusted weapons—Spencer rifles, Bridesburg muskets, converted Sharps carbines, and even muzzle-loading Springfields—others received the breech-loading Springfield rifles that had been converted in the Fenian armory in Trenton, New Jersey. As a reminder of the cause, the soldiers found the left side of their stock flats engraved with shamrocks and the letters "IR," the two-letter abbreviation for the Irish Republic. To load their guns, the Fenians distributed black leather shot pouches and an allotment of forty rounds of ball cartridges. They even prepared to engage the enemy with a secret weapon—a three-pound, breech-loading field gun mounted on a caisson that was camouflaged underneath a haystack.

The Irish Republican Army was not only better armed but also better dressed than it had been on its last visit to Vermont in 1866, when the soldiers sported a mishmash of Union and Confederate uniforms. Many now cloaked themselves in the regulation blue-and-green Fenian uniforms. Reflecting their dual allegiances, some Fenians wore cross and waist belts with the letters "U.S.," others the image of a harp.

O'Neill's army differed from its predecessor in more than just uniform. Many of those experienced Civil War veterans who had mobilized in 1866 had become disillusioned by the split in the Fenian Brotherhood or else had resumed civilian life and were unwilling to disrupt it for another Canadian foray. The army that answered O'Neill's latest call to arms included young boys, some no older than fifteen and a significant number under the age of twenty, donning military uniforms for the first time.

One anxious boy already feared the worst. "I tell you, there'll be hard work today and a good many hurt," Daniel Ahern of Winooski, Vermont, told a reporter. "And I know I'll be one of them. No use to contradict me. I know I'll be hurt."

Some of the lads had been just seven years old when the first shots were fired at Fort Sumter, and their knowledge of the Great Hunger came only from the stories they'd heard from their parents and grandparents. O'Neill couldn't help but wonder whether these first-generation Americans would really be ready to die for the cause of a faraway island they had never known.

❧

As O'Neill's men drilled on a makeshift parade ground, he contemplated the road ahead to Canada. He had received reports that the enemy was waiting, but he didn't know exactly where they were hiding and how many of them there were.

Around 11:00 a.m., a carriage from St. Albans containing the U.S. marshal George Perkins Foster; his deputy, Thomas Failey; a local surgeon; and a *Boston Traveller* correspondent rolled up to a barricade erected by the Fenians, across the road leading to the border. A sentinel ordered it to stop.

An irate Foster immediately demanded that the Fenians dismantle their roadblock and reopen the public road. The impatient marshal then sped ahead to the Fenian camp, where he ordered O'Neill to end the "unlawful proceeding." Sitting on a stone wall, the marshal read the presidential proclamation to the Fenian general, who then, according to one account, "expressed his contempt for the president in language more forcible and profane than polite." Foster told O'Neill that he had the authority but lacked the manpower to prevent him from violating the law before leaving to apprise the Canadians of the situation.

O'Neill was squeezed between two countries. Before him, enemy territory and armed soldiers. Behind him, U.S. authorities and armed law enforcement. Though he was severely shorthanded, O'Neill decided he had but one course of action.

The general spoke a few quiet words to Donnelly, who stepped forward and barked out his order: "Fall in!"

❧

O'Neill rode at the head of the Irish Republican Army as it marched with disciplined precision in columns of four down the same road as Spear's men had in 1866. The general ordered Colonel Henri Le Caron to stay back, locate the four hundred troops from New York he heard were en route from St. Albans, and rush them to the front. Le Caron agreed, but of course he intended to do no such thing.

Before they could confront the enemy, the Fenians encountered an unexpected traffic jam, the country road clogged with curious spectators as well as local teamsters awaiting payback. Having hauled Fenian supplies for the previous three nights, they drove their empty wagons to the border to await the Canadian plunder they had been promised as payment for their services.

The Fenians rounded a bend in the road, and the border finally came into view. The ribbon of road in front of them descended into a small valley, and through its crease bubbled the fordable Chickabiddy Creek, nearly parallel to the dividing line thirty yards to the south. Huddled together on the American side of the line was a cluster of barns, outbuildings, and the houses of Alvah and Chauncey Richard. A tannery, mill, and several farmhouses sat on the Canadian side.

If war hadn't been on the afternoon's agenda, the soldiers might have better appreciated the beauty. "The soft sweet breezes of the spring morning played upon our faces while the brilliant sunlight sent its rays flashing upon our bayonets and dancing on the waters underneath," Le Caron recalled. "On the other side there rose in graceful outlines the monarchs of a Canadian forest, overtopped by a rocky cliff standing out in bold and picturesque relief."

That rocky cliff was Eccles Hill, which rose steeply on the west side of the road between Franklin and Frelighsburg, Quebec. On its steep slopes, approximately fifty Canadian defenders hid behind bushes and in rifle pits that were concealed by time-scarred boulders. The approaching Fenians recognized the Sixtieth Battalion Volunteer Militia in their ornate crimson jackets with gold trim.

As Lieutenant Colonel Brown Chamberlin, the battalion's commander and a member of the inaugural Canadian Parliament, prepared his men for the advancing Irishmen, he found himself interrupted by Marshal Foster, who had by then crossed over the border from the Fenian camp. The marshal assured Chamberlin that the U.S. government was doing everything possible to prevent the Fenian raid but admitted that he lacked sufficient troops to do so.

The marshal then delivered a personal pledge from O'Neill that unlike the Fenians four years earlier the men under his command would not be permitted to harm women or children or plunder peaceful citizens. Chamberlin was in no mood to receive consolation from the enemy. The lieutenant colonel pointed out that a message from "men who were mere pirates and marauders" was "scarcely satisfactory to those whom they intended to murder."

The head of the Fenian column was soon visible, marching around the bend to the border. "I thought they intended to attack you soon," Foster told Chamberlin, "but not so soon as this."

❦

With the Irish Republican Army approaching, Chamberlin returned to the Sixtieth Battalion, who were joined atop Eccles Hill by a band of local farmers determined to prevent history from repeating itself. Four years earlier, they had watched helplessly as the Fenians crossed unimpeded into the Eastern Townships, leaving their homes, farms, and property "entirely at the mercy of the lawless marauders who entered the country unmolested," according to Asa Westover. The fifty-two-year-old, who had a salt-and-pepper beard and the weather-beaten face of a farmer who had spent decades in the sun, certainly remembered what had happened in 1866. He never forgot the humiliation of the Irish Republican Army knocking on his farmhouse door demanding food. After helping themselves to a hot meal, the Fenians helped themselves to the family's valuables.

After confederation in 1867, Canadians took greater ownership of their defense, and the following summer Westover persuaded thirty men from Dunham, Frelighsburg, St. Armand, Stanbridge East, and surrounding towns to take matters—and guns—into their own hands. They signed an agreement to organize a small band of sharpshooters, called the Home Guards, who planned to be ready at a moment's notice should any invaders seek to enter Canada.

The Home Guards paid for their weapons out of their own pockets. Westover, whose grandfather was a Loyalist who'd fled Massachusetts during the American Revolution, returned to that state to purchase approximately fifty breech-loading, single-shot Ballard sporting rifles.

Through frequent rifle practice, he converted his band of farmers into a company of able riflemen. Even when the fierce winter snow piled outside, the Home Guards took target practice in barns and drilled in members' homes. Locals mocked the homegrown militia for preparing for a threat they thought would never be repeated; now the men found their efforts vindicated.

Inspired by the crimson sashes worn by British army officers, Westover's men donned red scarves draped over the right shoulder and fastened under the left arm. Having received word of the Irish Republican Army's arrival in northern Vermont, Chamberlin ordered Westover to station his Red Sashes on Eccles Hill along the road leading north from Hubbard's Corner and above the site where the Irish Republican Army camped during its 1866 raid.

Thirty-seven Red Sashes occupied the promontory on the afternoon of May 24 and spent a restless night keeping watch. The next morning, they were joined by the Montreal Regiment of the Victoria Rifles, commanded by Colonel William Osborne Smith, along with the Sixtieth Battalion carrying their Snider-Enfield rifles. Chamberlin stationed ten men and an officer in the right rear as well as two officers and thirty-six men strung along Eccles Hill to supplement the local farmers.

Exhausted from lack of sleep, Westover and seventeen of his Red Sashes descended Eccles Hill in the late morning of May 25 to eat at a local farm when a cry came: "They're coming! They're coming!" The Canadian farmers fled their meal, hoping it wouldn't be their last.

❧

Poor Alvah Richard couldn't seem to shake those Irishmen who he said displayed "more courage 'n sense." For the second time in four years, the Fenians had landed at the doorstep of his dairy farm. They could have chosen any route along the four-thousand-mile border with Canada, and they had chosen the very same road.

Given that the sixty-two-year-old Richard sold cattle in Montreal and conducted most of his business north of the border, the farmer's sympathies rested wholeheartedly with the Canadians. In fact, when Richard purchased his farm abutting the frontier, he believed it to be in Canada.

The families who lived along this stretch of the international boundary routinely crossed the border as they moved from house to house and job to job. Through marriages and friendships, they had loyalties among themselves that trumped national allegiances. Richard's brother Stephen, for instance, had married Mary Ann Eccles, of the eponymous hill. Her aunt was Margaret Vincent, the nearly deaf woman killed accidentally by the Seventh Royal Fusiliers during the last Fenian raid. There were even Richards among the roll of the Red Sashes.

When he heard the news of the Fenians' return, Richard sent his wife, daughter, and domestic to a neighbor's home where it was safer while he guarded the house with his son, Albert. When the Irish Republican Army arrived outside their two-story brick farmhouse, one hundred yards from the border, O'Neill asked the farmer whether he could survey the battlefield from his north-facing bedroom. Richard refused. He didn't want "them ruffians up in the best chamber puttin' their dirty boots on Grandma's handmade quilts," he said.

Outside Richard's farmhouse, O'Neill addressed his men for a final time before meeting the enemy: "Soldiers, this is the advance guard of the Irish American Army for the liberation of Ireland from the yoke of the oppressor. For your own country you now enter that of the enemy. The eyes of your countrymen are upon you. Forward, MARCH!"

Before they could obey, though, Captain William Cronan of Burlington, Vermont—whose men had asked to be given the front— stepped forward to say his piece. "General," he intoned, doffing his hat, "I am proud that Vermont has the honor of leading this advance. Ireland may depend upon us to do our duty." Not to be outdone, Colonel John H. Brown told the troops he was honored to command the skirmish line and that "all he asked of them was to keep cool and obey orders."

The speechmaking concluded, Cronan's advance guard departed the Richard farmhouse and led the charge to capture Canada.

❀

Positioned at the front of the Irish Republican Army, Private John Rowe reached into his bag of Boston crackers for some last-minute sustenance as Cronan signaled the attack with a wave of his sword.

A recent Fenian convert and a sergeant in Burlington's Boxer Fire Company, Rowe and the rest of the Vermont Fenians cheered as they charged past the iron post marking the border. The valley crackled with energy as Captain John Lonergan, a hero at the Battle of Gettysburg and head center of the Fenian Brotherhood in Vermont, rode near the vanguard of the attack with a green silk battle flag waving in the breeze. Sparked by the adrenaline and Irish pride coursing through his body, the twenty-five-year-old Rowe sprinted to the front of the pack, approaching the short wooden bridge spanning Chickabiddy Creek.

Up on Eccles Hill, the Sixtieth Battalion occupied the left side of the line; the Red Sashes were posted to the right, from the crest of the hill along a line of rocks extending down toward the creek at its base. From their perch, the Red Sashes had clear views as the Fenians ran exposed through the valley. They held their fire until the enemy drew within range of their guns.

Crouching behind a boulder, James Pell of Dunham, Quebec, squinted down the thirty-inch barrel of his Ballard rifle. He remembered well how Irishmen had ransacked his house and smashed his piano on their previous visit to the Eastern Townships. As he held his rifle's heavy hexagonal barrel and peered through its graduated sight, Pell focused on the first green figure rushing toward the bridge.

Pell's finger squeezed the trigger, and the butt of his rifle bit into his shoulder. A sharp crack reverberated around the dale. Rowe collapsed to his knees, his hands still clutching his rifle. Pell's shot pierced an artery on the Fenian's left arm and tore through his lungs, leaving him to suffocate in his own blood on the bridge where he lay.

The Fenians were greeted with a further downpour of Canadian bullets after Pell's opening salvo. The younger soldiers were struck with panic at the sight of their fallen comrade and their first taste of combat. They jumped off the bridge and crawled underneath it for cover. Others scattered, harboring themselves behind stone walls, outhouses, and chicken coops. William O'Brien of Moriah, New York, was shot dead. Others fell wounded while seeking shelter.

When a Canadian shot brushed the high felt hat off the head of the *St. Albans Messenger* correspondent Albert Clarke, who had commanded a company of the Thirteenth Vermont Infantry at Gettysburg, he beat a hasty retreat from the lumber pile on which he

Canadian forces fire at Fenian invaders during the Battle of Eccles Hill.

stood, under "no disposition," he said, "to satisfy his curiosity further at the risk of his life." Many of the other spectators who had come to Richard's farm for an afternoon of entertainment suddenly found that the war was not as enjoyable as they had envisioned. So many Fenians had taken flight that the rounds of ammunition rattling around inside the tin interiors of their swaying black leather shot pouches, according to one eyewitness, "could be distinctly heard even above the din of the civilians who were still scampering in both directions from the field."

In total, as many as fifty Fenians—and a dozen war correspondents and spectators who hadn't counted on being quite so close to the action—fled for cover in Richard's brick farmhouse. The farmer was furious, for not only had the throng stomped through his kitchen in their muddy boots, but they had taken shelter in his cellar, where he stored his precious foodstuffs. O'Neill managed to dash up the stairs to survey the battlefield, such as it was, from an attic window. He could see that the main body of the Irish Republican Army had finally regrouped on the wooded summit of a hill fifty yards to the west of Richard's farmhouse. Flame and smoke belched forth from Eccles Hill and Richard's farm, but the return fire was "very ill directed," Chamberlin reported, "sometimes more resembling a *feu de joie* than anything else." The stray shots that reached Eccles Hill either whistled through its underbrush or pinged off its boulders.

Although the Fenians outnumbered the Canadians nearly six to one, the Red Sashes and the Sixtieth Battalion had the advantage of a nearly impregnable position. Thousands of years earlier, the retreating glaciers had sculpted the perfect fortress "behind which twenty men could have defied a thousand," one newspaperman reported.

The Richard farmhouse found itself pockmarked with bullets as Canadians took aim at O'Neill's perch. When Richard heard a noise in the attic, the indignant farmer stormed up his stairs, discovered O'Neill, and forcibly evicted him. The Fenian general emerged into the light and examined the battlefield through his looking glass. *Where is Le Caron with his reinforcements from New York? Why is their field gun not yet deployed?*

Le Caron had proven ruthlessly effective in his campaign of disruption. Back at the Fenian camp, between smokes, the British spy delayed the deployment of the New Yorkers. He rendered the field gun inoperable by removing its breech piece and hiding it where it couldn't be found for several hours. Matters didn't improve for the Irish Republican Army when a loud cheer erupted from Eccles Hill: A battalion of the Royal Victoria Rifles and cavalry troops from Montreal had arrived as reinforcements.

Frustrated, O'Neill gathered those troops within shouting distance in a protected area behind Richard's house. He castigated his men in green for their timidity. "Men of Ireland, I am ashamed of you! You have acted disgracefully today; but you will have another chance of showing whether you are cravens or not. Comrades, we must not, we *dare* not go back with the stain of cowardice on us. Comrades, I will lead you again, and if you will not follow me, I will go with my officers and die in your front!" He then ascended a hillside orchard to rally his soldiers next to the Richard farm.

Returning, the general stopped to check on a wounded Fenian lying on the side of the road when Marshal Foster suddenly appeared at his side. O'Neill was under arrest, Foster declared, by no less an authority than President Grant himself.

O'Neill didn't give himself over so easily. "You must not do so," he warned, "I am armed."

Undeterred, Foster grabbed O'Neill before he could escape and

The cover of *Frank Leslie's Illustrated Newspaper* depicts John O'Neill's arrest during the Battle of Eccles Hill.

threw him into the backseat of his waiting carriage. With a crack of the driver's whip, the horses darted from the battlefield, beginning the fifteen-mile return journey to St. Albans. As they passed through the rear of the Irish Republican Army, Foster warned O'Neill that any attempt to cry for help might cost him his life. The marshal kept his hand close to O'Neill's mouth to prevent any shouts for assistance, but the cocked Colt revolver pressed against the general's temple proved the more effective silencer.

"Clear the way! Clear the way!" shouted Foster and his deputy, and the green sea of soldiers—unaware of the coach's occupants— obliged. One man, however, caught sight of the detainee as he sped by: Le Caron, and he could only smile. "To have given the command to shoot the horses as they turned an adjacent corner would have been the work of an instant," he recalled, "but it was no part of my purpose to restore O'Neill to his command."

O'Neill had been considered the Fenians' best military mind. Now the hero of Ridgeway was being escorted off the battlefield by his own government, without so much as a bullet fired in defense. His detractors could only have gloated.

※

When Donnelly, the next in command, heard news of O'Neill's arrest, he walked away from his men, dropped his head into his hands, and wept for several minutes. Once recomposed, Donnelly convened an impromptu war council. Given the arrest of their commander and the increasing desertion of soldiers back to St. Albans, the officers were left with no choice but to abandon their attack and hold position until they could escape under the cover of darkness.

Around 3:00 p.m., Donnelly ordered a truce flag to be raised in the hopes of removing the bodies of Rowe, O'Brien, and the wounded. The gunshots ceased. Colonel Smith, however, sent a message to the Fenians by way of an envoy of Red Sashes, letting it be known that he refused to negotiate with the marauders. Donnelly traded sharp words with the contingent of Red Sashes, and bullets were exchanged soon again, which left him among the upwards of thirty Fenians trapped inside buildings on Richard's farm, unable to leave without risking their lives. In an attempt to divert Canadian fire, the Fenians managed at last to pull the caisson with their three-pounder field gun to the brow of the hill adjacent to Richard's farmhouse. After they trained it on their enemy and loaded the shot into the breech-loading cannon, however, it refused to fire. Under the command of Colonel Hugh McGinnis, they finally coaxed it to launch—first with an ax, then with a hammer, and finally with a crowbar. The shots landed in the swamp at the base of Eccles Hill, harmless to the opposing troops but enough to draw their attention away, as Fenians vacated their sanctuaries and beat a hasty retreat.

Colonel Smith responded with orders to attack. A bugle sounded, and the Canadians cheered as they advanced toward the border and peppered the Irishmen with gunfire. Donnelly was struck in the hip as he tried to scale a stone wall to return to his men. When a loud cry of "double quick" rang out on the American side of the border, the Fenians, according to the *St. Albans Messenger,* "converted their retreat into a regular skedaddle." They fled into the woods to the east and ran south down the dirt road toward the camp at Hubbard's Corner. Canadian officers chased them no farther than the borderline. The body of Rowe lay on the bridge as a marker of their deepest advance into the British Empire.

The demoralized Fenians cast off their green uniforms like snakes shedding their skins. They tossed their ammunition pouches and knapsacks to the side of the road in order to lighten their loads. Straggling back to camp, some nursed cups of coffee and gnawed on pieces of ham, while others kicked off their shoes and peeled off their stockings.

Their resignation was complete: Irishmen sold their rifles to local farmers for $2 apiece. Le Caron could not resist an opportunity to stealthily twist the knife. He urged townspeople to "help themselves" to thousands of their weapons—an offer freely accepted. *The Irish-American* estimated that as a result "before daylight the next day, war material sufficient to equip between three and four thousand men disappeared."

One retreating soldier whipped off his green jacket and turned it inside out because, as he told a *Burlington Free Press* reporter, he felt betrayed by the Fenian leaders. "It's all up; and damn the men that got us up here. I come from Massachusetts. They told us it'd be a glorious business, and a good job, and all that; and then got us into Canada and sent us down there to be shot at for two hours," he said. "I've got enough of this Fenian business; and I'm going home."

❧

The Battle of Eccles Hill, or what some newspapers called the Battle of Richard's Farm, had ended with two Fenians dead and nine injured. For their part, the Canadians suffered not a single casualty.

A reporter for the *Boston Advertiser* saw the young Daniel Ahern being treated for a ball in the hip. "What did I tell you?" the boy shouted. "I told you I'd be shot; and here I am." Ahern cursed his officers, except Captain Cronan, as traitors or cowards.

According to the *Burlington Free Press,* O'Neill was the target of the "most profane and abusive epithets" and denounced by his men "as not only a traitor, but an arbitrary ignoramus." His arrest had been so humiliating that many Fenians whispered it had been deliberate on his part, as a ploy to avoid gunfire.

Though the charge was unfair, O'Neill's crimes of leadership were numerous enough. The *Burlington Free Press* thought it such a "curious and crazy piece of generalship" to attack the well-entrenched enemy that it demonstrated either an expectation of the Canadians fleeing "at the first show of an advance" or an absence of common sense. It was also a curious choice, given all the roads O'Neill could have selected, to attempt an entry into Canada directly below a natural fortress.

The general's greatest failure, however, might have been his decision not to scout the Canadian position in advance to know just how strong it was. Perhaps he relied too much on history as a guide, recalling how he and Spear had crossed effortlessly into Canada four years earlier, encountering not a single soldier at the border.

Le Caron did the Fenian general no favors, delaying the arrival of the New York reinforcements and the deployment of the fieldpiece. All the same, O'Neill failed to take advantage of his considerable edge in manpower and attempt a flank movement around Eccles Hill by advancing on Pigeon Hill, a village about two miles to the west. He refrained perhaps because of a concern that his army was too young and inexperienced. (O'Neill would claim he was plotting just such a flank movement when he was arrested.)

After the Fenians departed the battleground, curiosity seekers harvested Richard's farm for souvenirs such as bayonets, swords, powder horns, belts, water bottles, and IRA coat jacket buttons left behind by the Irishmen. Soldiers posed next to the body of Rowe, whose right-handed grasp on his weapon became only tighter in death. According to the *St. Albans Messenger*, the Canadians ripped the IRA buttons and pieces of braid from his uniform jacket, rifled through his pockets, and carried off his belt. The Fenian evoked no pity; the treatment, the Canadians said, "served him right."

As the sun faded, Canadians planted their spades into the rocky soil of Eccles Hill and excavated a shallow grave into which they placed Rowe's body facedown without prayers, last rites, or fanfare. Using scattered blocks of granite, they erected a two-foot-high cairn over his burial plot so, as they told one reporter, "that Fenian shouldn't rise again."

As a final insult, one farmer from Cook's Corner, Quebec, rode across the border and hitched his horses to the caisson that carried the Fenian field gun. Under the cover of night, he hauled it back to his barn before presenting it to Westover as a trophy of war the following afternoon. A testament to the diminutive "farmer force" that repelled the much larger Irish Republican Army, the cannon sits today next to a historical marker on the crest of Eccles Hill.

❧

As it did four years earlier, St. Albans became a refuge of broken dreams and shattered hearts. General Samuel Spear could still well remember the day in 1866 when he was forced to retreat back to the town after his brief foray into Quebec. He arrived yet again in the Vermont town the day after the Battle of Eccles Hill to consult with his fellow officers, who promptly elected him their commander in chief in a war council.

While Spear claimed, unconvincingly, to be nothing more than a "sightseer" in northern Vermont, in truth the general had come to resuscitate the attack. But his efforts had been undermined. Because the Springfield rifles that had been sent to the front had been either sold, tossed aside, or seized by authorities, Spear needed to access those reserves of weapons that remained hidden in the countryside. And with General O'Neill detained, the only Fenian who knew their whereabouts was Colonel Le Caron.

Spear appealed to Le Caron to supply him with five hundred stands of arms and ammunition within twenty-four hours. The spy insisted that the task would be impossible given the authorities who were watching their every move. Despite the general's pleas, Le Caron wouldn't budge. (He would earn every penny of the $2,000 bonus he was eventually paid above his regular retainer.)

With no help forthcoming, Spear marched four hundred Fenians out to the countryside to where he suspected the surplus weapons had been hidden—to no avail. Spear fumed that they "had to march back like a pack of god-damn fools."

The episode drained Spear of any remaining enthusiasm for war. He ceased operations. Still in a disagreeable mood, Spear tore into O'Neill, telling the *Rutland Herald* that the Fenian president "got up this movement on his own responsibility against the better judgment of the leading officers of the Brotherhood." He complained that O'Neill had kept too much information to himself, so that not even his secretary of war knew the location of their weapons. "Instead of that here I am unable to do nothing after a cost of thirty-seven thousand dollars to the Brotherhood, all lost."

O'Neill, meanwhile, stewed in a jail cell in Burlington, Vermont.

Eccles Hill was no Ridgeway, and O'Neill refused paternity for the debacle. He blamed the men who both did and didn't show up in Vermont. If the three thousand men he had counted on had materialized, he would have been on his way to Montreal already. "I never was in a battle before that I was so utterly ashamed of," the Fenian general confided to a *Rutland Herald* reporter, before laying into the soldiers he'd had at his disposal.

The only consolation for O'Neill was that a much larger force had descended upon Malone, New York. They couldn't have any worse a day than the one the Fenians just faced.

Another Fight, Another Flight

A S THE REPORTER John Boyle O'Reilly wandered around the Irish Republican Army's encampment the day after the Battle of Eccles Hill, he saw little trace of the bustling bivouac he had encountered twenty-four hours earlier. The soldiers were gone, and their wagonloads of supplies had vanished. Not even "empty boxes or broken cartridge tins" remained, he wrote in *The Pilot,* America's leading Irish Catholic newspaper.

Down the road at the Canadian border, there was more activity. Alvah Richard toiled to repair dozens of bullet holes on his property. Curiosity seekers from both sides of the border gawked at the farmer's homestead and scoured his fields for relics. Redcoats and Red Sashes kept periodic vigil from across the boundary, when they weren't posing for photographs with each other and the captured Fenian cannon.

A devout Irish patriot and a Fenian himself, O'Reilly had traveled to upstate Vermont from Boston to chronicle a tale of Irish warriors bravely striking the British Empire. What he witnessed instead was a farce. Dispirited, he wandered through the remains of the Irish Republican Army, treading carefully around the border lest he wander into Queen Victoria's domain, where a price still lay on his head.

It was a tortuous path that led O'Reilly to New England that day, his Celtic pride a constant across decades of hardship on three continents. Born in 1844 along the banks of Ireland's River Boyne, he had, as a lad, roamed among ancient megaliths, sacred Druid sites, and the ruined castles of high kings and chieftains. From Dowth Castle— his twelfth-century ancestral home in County Meath—O'Reilly could look across the river to the spot where William of Orange defeated the Catholic forces of King James II at the Battle of the Boyne in 1690, consigning Ireland to Protestant rule. He could dip his fishing line into the same legendary waterway in which Finn McCool captured the Salmon of Knowledge.

O'Reilly imbibed the history that flowed through the Boyne valley, as well as poems, stories, and songs about Irish patriots—many of them O'Reilly chieftains and princes themselves—passed on from his parents. Like John O'Neill, O'Reilly knew that a member of his clan had the choice to either silently accept British oppression or fight for his freedom.

For a boy bred to rebel against British tyranny, this was no choice at all. O'Reilly joined the Irish Republican Brotherhood as a teen-ager in 1863 and worked as a secret recruiter inside the British army's Tenth Hussars to ensure that the military would back the Irish people when the next rising occurred.

When an informer blew O'Reilly's cover in 1866, he was court-martialed for treason, found guilty, and condemned to twenty years of penal servitude. Chained, subsisting on bread and water, and sentenced to hard labor, O'Reilly toured the worst prisons England had to offer, from Chatham to Dartmoor. Behind the iron-barred door of cell 32 in London's Millbank Prison on the banks of the Thames, O'Reilly spent eight months in solitary confinement and enforced silence, the chimes of Big Ben every quarter hour his only companion.

After several unsuccessful escape attempts, O'Reilly was exiled to the far side of the world in the fall of 1867. Arriving on board the last convict ship to Australia just weeks before the policy of transporta-tion was due to come to an end, he was dumped at the Fremantle penal colony in Western Australia in January 1868, along with more than sixty other Fenians.

A year later, O'Reilly staged a dramatic escape, hiding for seven-teen days in the bush—sleeping on a bed of leaves, striking possums against trees for food—until he rowed out to a waiting American whaler in the Indian Ocean. He arrived in Philadelphia in November

1869 with $30 and a bag of whales' teeth as his only possessions. The evidence of his hardship at the hands of the British was confined to a scar on his left arm from a failed suicide attempt and his skin still bronzed from the fierce Australian sun.

Bringing to his new home his long-standing belief that Ireland could be freed only by military action, O'Reilly quickly joined the Fenian Brotherhood. A budding journalist—he published a newspaper on his voyage from England to Australia—the Irishman made his way to Boston in January 1870, where he earned a temporary assignment with *The Pilot*.

Assigned to cover the Fenian convention in New York that April, O'Reilly was the only reporter allowed inside the proceedings. The twenty-five-year-old writer had started to sour on the Fenian Brotherhood after witnessing the infighting among the organization's leaders, but he felt new hope when he was dispatched to the front to cover O'Neill's latest Canadian venture.

The newspapers that O'Reilly browsed on the ride from Boston described "thousands of men and trains of war material" arriving in St. Albans. The reality turned out to be quite different. Stepping off the train, O'Reilly found few of the men and little of the excitement that he'd anticipated.

Still, all was not lost. With a greater force gathering in upstate New York, the Canadian governor-general, Sir John Young, wrote to the Colonial Office on May 26 that he anticipated a "more serious" attack than at Eccles Hill to take place near Huntingdon, Quebec. While some disheartened Irishmen just wanted to return home, others were determined to continue the fight. Even though President Ulysses S. Grant had issued his proclamation against the Fenians, the federal authorities took no action to prevent the Irishmen from riding the rails from St. Albans to Malone, New York. O'Reilly joined the Irish Republican Army as they boarded trains heading west.

❧

When the *Pilot* reporter stepped off the train in Malone on May 26, he discovered that, just as at St. Albans, the "thousands" of Fenian soldiers reported by the press numbered only in the hundreds. Still, with its fresh troops and reinforcements arriving on every train, the

Irish Republican Army found itself in a stronger position in New York than it had been in Vermont.

O'Reilly also noted another difference in these soldiers, revealed in the wisps of gray underneath their hats. "They were older and steadier soldiers than the men who had been engaged at Richard's farm," O'Reilly reported. They weren't the "raw boys who were frightened at the whizz of a bullet."

Most of the Fenians descending upon Malone hailed from three Irish Republican Army regiments. Colonel William L. Thompson, a thirty-four-year-old postal worker and native of Scotland, commanded the Sixth Regiment from Albany. Colonel William B. Smith arrived with the Seventh Regiment from Buffalo. And Colonel Edward Campbell led the Eighth Regiment from western Pennsylvania. They were aided by Captain Edward J. Mannix, the thirty-eight-year-old head center in Malone who had attempted to organize the raid from the town in 1866.

Among those who arrived on the day after the Battle of Eccles Hill was a new commander, Owen Starr. Upon arriving in Malone, the thirty-year-old Louisville merchant who had fought at O'Neill's side at Fort Erie and Ridgeway ventured twelve miles north to the Fenians' forward encampment in a small settlement near the Trout River. For three days straight, wagons had been arriving at the camp tucked behind a church, delivering barrels of pork and hardtack and boxes of breech-loading Springfield rifles, bayonets, and ammunition—enough to equip several thousand men—that had been squirreled away in the barns and cellars of sympathetic farmers throughout the North Country. They also hauled spades, picks, and other entrenching tools bought from Malone shopkeepers. The Irish Republican Army named the base located half a mile south of the border Camp O'Neill, in honor of the Fenian president.

The Canadian frontier remained undefended, allowing the Fenians to launch raiding parties into foreign territory. One group of raiders led by Colonel Thompson rode nearly two miles across the border and, wielding hatchets, chopped up the telegraph station at a store at Holbrook's Corners. Following strict orders, they didn't touch any of the establishment's liquor selection (though that didn't stop them from absconding with forty pounds of tobacco). Another band of raiders was at work on an entrenchment on the road to Holbrook's Corners when Starr recalled all his men back to American territory.

By late on May 26, news had arrived at Camp O'Neill that enemy troops were en route from Montreal. After midnight, Starr convened a war council and, to little surprise, favored action. The general naturally gravitated toward a fight, and especially in the wake of the Battle of Eccles Hill he felt that the Fenian cause needed some good news—however small it might be—in order to keep the money flowing and the men volunteering. Starr proposed to make a small inroad into the flat, undefended Canadian territory, build an entrenchment, and hope for the arrival of reinforcements in time to salvage at least a part of his operation—to, at the very least, cause some mischief and headaches for the enemy.

The war council could not reach a consensus. Some thought it a mad enterprise. But the general decided to move on his own, taking however many Fenians were willing to join him. Starr distributed general orders from Camp O'Neill, instructing his army not "to war against peaceful citizens." He pledged to arrest and punish any soldier who entered a private house without orders.

As the dark morning sky began to brighten, three hundred soldiers grabbed their Springfield rifles. Starr offered rousing words to his soldiers, but they belied his own hesitation. He left his carriage at the ready on the American side of the border. Even the general, apparently, had doubts about the length of their stay.

❧

After marching half a mile into Canada, the Fenians rounded a bend that gave them a clear view ahead to Holbrook's Corners. Starr ordered his men to resume work on the barricade started by the raiding party the previous day in order to establish a defensive bulwark.

The Irishmen's experience with manual labor came in handy. They dismantled fences from the hop fields flanking the road and piled the logs and rails to form a four-foot-high barrier across their entire front—their left flank abutting the woods and their right flank against the Trout River. To increase their cover, the soldiers dug a one-foot-deep trench along their right flank.

The Fenians were still constructing their breastwork when the glint of bayonets could be seen on the hill at Holbrook's Corners. A stream of redcoats approached. Because Starr and the other generals had done no reconnaissance, the arrival of the Canadian militia and British regular forces caught them by surprise.

The general was no less surprised by their number. It quickly became apparent to the 300 soldiers in green that unlike their brethren at Eccles Hill they were significantly outmatched. Led by Lieutenant Colonel George Bagot, who had spent nearly a quarter century in a British uniform, the Canadian army marched onto the scene with more than 1,000 soldiers, nearly half of whom belonged to the Sixty-Ninth Regiment of Foot, a venerable British infantry unit that dated back to the Seven Years' War and fought Napoleon at Waterloo. They were joined by 225 members of the Fiftieth Battalion Huntingdon Borderers, 275 members of the Montreal Garrison Artillery, and 80 members of the Montreal Engineers.

It had taken eighteen hours for the men of the Sixty-Ninth Regiment—already exhausted from fighting a massive blaze in Quebec City three days earlier—to arrive at the border from Montreal. They had managed to catch two hours of sleep on the parade ground in Huntingdon, twelve miles to the north, before the bugle blare awoke them at 3:00 a.m. Milk and cold water handed out by farmers offered them encouragement as they marched to the border. They were ready for whatever the Fenians had to offer.

❖

Colonel Bagot ordered the Montreal Garrison Artillery and Engineers on horseback to cross a bridge over the Trout River, north of the barricade, and to advance on the east side of the river, with the notion of fording it and striking the barricade from the rear. The rest of his force advanced in three columns.

Bagot assigned the local Huntingdon Borderers militia, who were defending their homes and families, the post of honor—a chance to be the first to engage the enemy. Shortly after 8:00 a.m., they were given the order to attack. The Borderers on the right of the Canadian line raised their Snider-Enfield rifles and fired gunshots into the hop field about five hundred yards in front of them, occupied by the Irish Republican Army's advance picket. The Fenian picket returned fire in kind, but they quickly retreated one hundred yards to the barricade.

The Canadian volunteers charged across a plowed field, vaulting fences and unleashing an unceasing barrage. When they closed to within four hundred yards of the barricade, the panicked Fenians began to show their nerves. They opened fire prematurely, their wayward shots whizzing high and wide over the heads of the volunteers, whose return fire riddled the Fenian barricade, sending splinters exploding through the air.

Meanwhile, Bagot's flankers had established excellent cover behind a forest of poles holding up the vines in the hop fields. The wild gunshots from the Fenians' breech-loading Springfields could do nothing to stop the redcoats from continuing to close in.

The Fenians' resolve fled. The general gave the order to retreat. Some defiant soldiers begged their commander to change his mind. "Let us die rather than go back!" one soldier implored. Starr, however, couldn't be dissuaded. He told his army to run for the border.

With Irishmen disappearing, Bagot's forces breached the hastily constructed barricade. They charged with fixed bayonets, the Fenians running and firing indiscriminately until they reached the cast-iron post that marked the 45th parallel and the sanctuary of American territory. Although Lieutenant Colonel Archibald McEachern of the

Canadian forces fire as the Irish Republican Army flees toward the sanctuary of the American border during the Battle of Trout River.

Huntingdon Borderers wanted to chase the Fenians all the way back to Camp O'Neill, Bagot refused to allow his men to cross. However, their discretion didn't prevent the Fenians from running until their enemies were no longer in sight.

Starr's jaunt to Canada was over ninety minutes after it began, but it was not without its casualties. One of the skirmishers in front of the barricade, Dennis Duggan of Troy, New York, was killed. Three Fenians were wounded, including thirty-five-year-old James Moore, who was rendered unable to walk and was captured by a pair of militia, who found him hiding in the bush. The Canadian volunteers clamored to bayonet or shoot their prisoner, but they were restrained by the British regulars. The sole Canadian injury was a Huntingdon Borderer who was grazed on the forehead by a splinter sent flying by a bullet.

Starr's decision to order a quick retreat was debated immediately by his men and in the days to come by the press. "Had they stood their ground they might have mowed down our men," the *Montreal Witness* postulated, given the Fenians' strong defensive position. *The New York Herald* was less sanguine about their prospects, pointing to their three-to-one disadvantage. "Had the Fenians remained upon the ground ten minutes longer," declared the newspaper, "not one of them would have been left to tell the tale."

❧

In the wake of what newspapers derided as "Starr's Stampede" over the border, many of the Irishmen retreated past Camp O'Neill and continued twelve miles south to Malone. Along the way, crestfallen soldiers crouched at streams to take sips of water from their cupped hands and doze underneath the canopies of sprawling trees.

At their encampment, the Fenians reverted to finger-pointing. Officers claimed that they tried desperately to get their men to regroup and form a line, while privates complained that they were thwarted in their desires to charge. Some Irishmen even threatened to lynch Starr for his cowardice. The general, though, was nowhere to be found. After rushing away from the border in his waiting carriage, he ensconced himself in a Malone hotel before skipping town the same evening on a train to Buffalo.

While the shattered Fenians lumbered back to Malone, three

hundred reinforcements at last arrived in the upstate New York town, looking to join the fight. Among those pulling in to the train station was Pittsburgh's Fenian leader, Dr. Edward Donnelly. When Donnelly asked where the commanding officer was, he received an unexpected reply: "He is lying drunk in the hotel."

General John Gleason, a thirty-two-year-old County Tipperary native who liked "a battle better than his breakfast," according to one reporter, stepped into the void left by Starr. He tried to rally his reluctant troops to launch a second attack. The arrival of the reinforcements had brought the size of the Irish Republican Army in the vicinity to upwards of thirteen hundred men. The math, he argued, was on their side.

The general found support in Dr. Donnelly, as well as Father John McMahon, the Indiana priest who had recently been released after spending more than three years in a Canadian prison after the Battle of Ridgeway. The two civilians made for an unlikely pair of war hawks as they attempted to whip up the troops that had encamped at the fairground in Malone.

With their speechifying complete, a color-bearer unfurled an Irish flag and called on the men to fall in. Only thirty did so. The disheartened Fenians might have hungered for Ireland's independence, but after the previous day's humiliations they couldn't stomach another raid.

This latest attempt on Canada was officially put to rest that night when a familiar face, General George Meade, arrived by train from St. Albans along with General Irvin McDowell, the onetime commander of the Army of the Potomac, and upwards of five hundred U.S. soldiers. Meade once again arrived to snuff out the last chance of any Fenian raid. His forces seized twenty-three boxes of weapons and arrested Gleason, Donnelly, Mannix, and four other Fenian leaders on Sunday morning, before sending them to Canandaigua, where they would be tried for violating the Neutrality Act. The rest of the Irish Republican Army, however, remained stranded in Malone.

When President Grant received news of the Battle of Eccles Hill, he muttered that it was "one of the most ludicrous things he ever knew." He was in no mood for charity; Meade received orders not to pay for transportation home for the Fenians remaining in Malone and St. Albans. So, broke and disappointed, hundreds of Fenians loitered on Malone's street corners and inside its hotel barrooms until the authorities prohibited the sale of liquor of any sort to the Irishmen. With stomachs rumbling, they banged on doors in search of food. The overtaxed residents of Malone wanted the Fenians to go home just as badly as the Irishmen did.

Grant was no more generous toward the citizens of Malone. "The people along the frontier have been sympathizing with these movements and aiding these people," he groused, "and if it is annoying to them both, it is well that they should sweat a while." If the local and state authorities "wished to rid themselves of the invaders," they could foot the bill.

On May 30, the railway company stepped in, agreeing to transport the Fenians at half price. A member of New York governor John Hoffman's office came with offers from both the state's chief executive and Tammany Hall's William "Boss" Tweed to cover the remainder, and at last the six hundred Fenians still stranded in Malone finally departed, a week after the ignominious Battle of Trout River.

❧

Six days after the Fenians spoiled his mother's birthday party in Montreal, Prince Arthur came to Eccles Hill to personally thank the Canadian volunteers and Red Sashes who had repelled the Irish Republican Army. Queen Victoria's third son was presented with a Fenian uniform and cap—a trophy of war that according to some newspaper accounts had been stripped from the corpse of John Rowe, still buried in a shallow grave on the promontory.

The day following the royal visit, Lieutenant Colonel William Osborne Smith gave his assent for Rowe's body to be removed by his brethren—as long as no Fenian crossed the border in the process. The task fell to a St. Albans undertaker, who exhumed Rowe's body and placed it in a coffin to be escorted back to his hometown of Burlington, Vermont, by his commander, Captain William Cronan.

On June 2, a merciful priest, ignoring the Roman Catholic Church's condemnation of the Fenian Brotherhood, held a joint funeral inside Burlington's St. Mary's Cathedral for the two fallen privates from the Battle of Eccles Hill, Rowe and William O'Brien. The decomposed state of the Fenians' bodies, coupled with a heat wave that sent temperatures scraping one hundred degrees, required that their bodies be kept across the street on the porch of St. Mary's Hall while the mourners celebrated the requiem Mass.

As their bodies were laid to rest, many silently delivered last rites for the Fenian Brotherhood as well. "The entire Fenian movement is now practically at an end, for the failures at St. Albans and here, kill the whole thing," *The New York Times* reported from Malone. Most of America's newspapers echoed these sentiments, castigating the Irish immigrants who seemed to remain more preoccupied with the land of their birth than with their adopted home. The most severe lashing, however, would come from one of their own.

⚜

O'Reilly had arrived at the Canadian border ready to pen an ode to a new generation of Celtic warriors. Instead, he scripted its obituary. The journalist told the readers of *The Pilot* that the Fenian soldiers, confronted with proof of their failure, returned "sadder and wiser men." That included O'Reilly.

He recounted that Fenians he interviewed at Trout River "burst into tears at what they termed their disgrace." The *Pilot* reporter blamed their leadership. "Judging from the military physique of the greater number, there can be no doubt that, with qualified officers, these men would prove that they did not merit the name they now feared—cowards."

The Pilot was only more critical in its next edition, criticizing the "mad foray" by "criminally incompetent" Fenian leaders. "Fenianism, so far as relates to the invasion of Canada, ceases to exist, but it has done all the evil it could do. It has torn thousands of men away from their homes and their employment in a wild and futile enterprise. It has caused the deaths of several brave men and the imprisonment, perhaps death, of many others, and it has given occasion to the enemies of the Irish people to renew the slurs which such enterprises have given birth to before now."

Eccles Hill and Trout River did something to O'Reilly that not even solitary confinement in Millbank Prison or banishment to Australia could do: It tempered his patriotic fervor. It stripped some of the romantic veneer off those poems and songs he had heard as a boy that first compelled him to join the Irish Republican Brotherhood.

Disillusioned, O'Reilly doubted that the Fenian Brotherhood would ever be able to deliver independence for Ireland.

During O'Reilly's short time in the United States, he had come to see the way many Irish had remained stubbornly separated from mainstream American life. But the Fenian raids of 1870 marked a turning point. He would become an impassioned advocate not for Irish independence but rather for assimilation into American society—for the Irish to break out of their enclaves, reach beyond their clans, and stop undertaking these forays that caused the rest of America to question their true allegiance.

The debacle at Trout River marked the end of the Second Fenian War, as it was known. It could be viewed as nothing more than a complete failure. This time there were no Ridgeways, no moral victories to claim. Unlike 1866, the Fenians couldn't fault their preparation. The failure of 1870 was that of execution. One could question O'Neill's wisdom in recycling much of General Thomas Sweeny's plan of attack—down to the use of the same gateways from St. Albans and Malone—but O'Neill managed to both secure sufficient weapons and supplies and transport them to the front without alerting federal authorities to their presence.

While newspapers in the past had "laughed at the Fenians as an army without a commissariat," the Huntingdon *Gleaner* noted, "the truth is, it was a splendid commissariat without an army worthy of it." O'Neill simply didn't have the men to engineer a victory. This was in part a result of the division that had torn the Fenian Brotherhood apart in the previous five years.

And while O'Neill might have managed to organize the raid without his plans spilling onto the front pages of newspapers, he failed to notice the enormous breach that stood by his side. In Le Caron, Canadian and British authorities had an incalculably valuable asset. Faced with the inherent difficulty of having to launch a sneak attack, with forces mobilized from hundreds of miles away, and having to surprise not one but two governments, O'Neill was always up against long odds.

Complicating matters for the Fenians, the political landscape had turned against them in the intervening four years. Feelings toward

Great Britain were not nearly as raw as they were in the aftermath of the Civil War, and Canada was no longer a British colony but a fledgling country. British troops might have been lackluster in their response in 1866, but the homegrown militias that confronted the Fenians proved fierce and quick in defense of their homes and farms.

The Irishmen who had picked up their rifles at Eccles Hill and Trout River longed to be bathed in glory. Instead, they departed from the Canadian border in a shower of ridicule. Newspapers giddily printed the joke that the "I.R.A." emblazoned on the buttons of the Fenians' green jackets stood, not for the "Irish Republican Army," but for their new motto—"I Ran Away."

19

The Fenians Behind Bars

T HE THICK STONE walls of the Burlington, Vermont, jail that kept the summer heat at bay did little to shield John O'Neill from the scorn fired in his direction after the debacles at Eccles Hill and Trout River. The Fenian general graced the cover of *Frank Leslie's Illustrated Newspaper,* but unfortunately for him the illustration depicted his battlefield arrest. The *Canadian Illustrated News* also printed a drawing of Marshal George Perkins Foster loading the Fenian general into a waiting coach, but added further insult by portraying O'Neill as a short, winking Irishman with simian features, a ridiculously ostentatious uniform, and a jug of liquor at his feet. He was part leprechaun, part gorilla.

Instead of leading an Irish army into glory like his forebears, O'Neill had become an object of derision. Deprived of nearly everything but free time, the stubborn Irishman had plenty of idle moments to reflect on the fiasco and ultimately concluded that he wasn't to blame. In a rebuttal to his critics, O'Neill wrote, in a lengthy jailhouse missive, that he "had the arms and war material in the proper place at the proper time" and the hundreds of Fenians who failed to report for duty as he ordered "were the chief authors of disaster by their criminal inactivity." The repeated delays and false alarms, he said, had conditioned the Fenian soldiers to disbelieve the call to arms when it came. "The people, so often deceived and disappointed in the past, could not believe that we were in earnest, and thousands of good men who were anxious to be with us, kept indulging their doubts and fears until too late to be of service," O'Neill wrote.

After being abandoned by his men on the battlefield, O'Neill felt the Fenians were deserting him now in jail. Even after the court reduced the general's bail from $20,000 to $15,000, none of his friends or colleagues arrived with the money. It wasn't just antipathy toward him, though. Fenian coffers were so empty that the secretary of war couldn't even scrape together enough spare change to pay for a telegram from Vermont, let alone post his leader's bail.

❧

The Irish-American predictably criticized O'Neill's "unauthorized and unjustifiable" raid as "a crime against the cause of Ireland and liberty" and "one of the most idiotic on record." The resentment toward the Fenian general ran so high that Vice President James Gibbons wrote to the Fenian senator Frank Gallagher, "O'Neill would not be safe anywhere, what a mercy it was for him that the government took *him* in charge."

In Philadelphia, Gibbons made sure to distance himself and the senate wing from O'Neill's actions, which he denounced to the press as "merely a personal enterprise by irresponsible persons" that wasted "valuable war material" and "years of patient toil and preparation." American newspapers were confounded as to what would provoke O'Neill to launch such an apparently absurd enterprise. Perhaps underestimating the trauma inflicted by the Great Hunger and generations of British rule, they decided the motive must have been monetary, a publicity stunt to keep the contributions that paid O'Neill's presidential salary flowing.

Newspapers once again portrayed the Fenians who donated money not as Irish patriots but as poor, ignorant dupes fleeced by the smooth-talking charlatans. "Even if they were able to conquer Canada, nobody believes it would produce the liberation of Ireland from British rule," editorialized *The New York Times*. "It would be just as sensible to expect Russia to liberate Poland if she heard that our Polish fellow-citizens had overpowered the garrison of Alaska."

For weeks following the attacks, O'Neill and his officers were vilified in the press and condemned by their fellow Fenians. Until now they had avoided the judgment of the U.S. government. Their time of impunity was now up.

❧

Every July, the easy breezes and cool waters of the Finger Lakes lured city dwellers to Canandaigua, New York. Owen Starr, however, had no desire to spend another summer in the small town between Buffalo and Syracuse.

Four years earlier, the Fenian general sat inside a Canandaigua courtroom to face charges of violating the Neutrality Act of 1818 after the Battles of Ridgeway and Fort Erie. Now Starr returned to the hamlet perched on the northern tip of Lake Canandaigua to face the same charges for his role in the Battle of Trout River. He walked away a free man in 1866; federal authorities felt less forgiving when he stood before the U.S. Circuit Court on July 12, 1870.

Following the latest Fenian raids, President Ulysses S. Grant expressed his frustration at the dual allegiances proclaimed by Irish Americans. "This thing of being a citizen of the U.S. for the purpose of voting, and being protected by this government and then claiming to be citizens of another government must be stopped," he thundered to his cabinet. Fenians needed to choose: Were they Irishmen or Americans? Hoping to deter any further attacks on Canada, the president ordered the Fenian officers prosecuted.

In addition to raising the president's ire, Starr and the other Fenian officers arrested in upstate New York had the misfortune of standing trial on the same day that centuries-old animosities imported by the Irish brought even more violence to America. To commemorate the anniversary of William of Orange's 1690 victory at the Battle of the Boyne, which ensured Protestant rule of Ireland for centuries to come, three thousand Protestant Orangemen paraded through Manhattan on July 12 chanting, "To hell with the pope," and singing provocative anti-Catholic tunes such as "Croppies Lie Down," which celebrated the brutal repression of the United Irishmen in the 1798 rebellion.

With animosities as raw as the day "King Billy" triumphed nearly two centuries earlier, the Protestants proved to be bad winners, and the Catholics even worse losers. Orangemen marching up Broadway taunted Catholic laborers digging ditches for the Croton Aqueduct and carving Central Park out of the heart of the island. Wielding picks and shovels as well as pistols and knives, the outraged workmen attacked anyone wearing an orange scarf, sash, or bow as a bloody factional fight erupted on the streets of New York around Elm Park. Eight Irishmen died* in the religious feud.

The New York Times and other newspapers blamed Fenians for firing the first shots in the Orange Riot, though they offered no proof that those involved were members of the Fenian Brotherhood. "Events have at intervals occurred in the history of this country which have justly called up a blush of shame on the faces of patriotic Irishmen; but we doubt if they ever have received so great a reason for deep humiliation," wrote John Boyle O'Reilly, who castigated both sides in *The Pilot.* "What are we today in the eyes of Americans? Aliens from a petty island in the Atlantic, boasting of our patriotism and fraternity, and showing at the same moment the deadly hatred that rankles against our brethren and fellow countrymen. Why must we carry, wherever we go, those accursed and contemptible island feuds?" To many Americans, the Orange Riot was one more bloody example of the violence brought to their country by these hordes of impoverished foreigners who practiced a strange religion.

After the selection of a mostly Anglo-Saxon jury, Starr knew the news couldn't possibly help his fate.

❧

Just as he had done four years earlier when he took on Starr and his fellow Fenians as pro bono clients following their arrests in the wake of the Battle of Ridgeway, the noted Buffalo attorney Grover Cleveland came to the aid of the Irishmen. Although work on a case forced the future president to remain in Buffalo, Cleveland arranged for a friend to defend the Fenian raiders at no charge.

The prosecution called the raid a criminal act, and the jury agreed, finding Starr and two of his compatriots guilty. The U.S. Circuit Court judge Lewis B. Woodruff sentenced Starr and William Thompson to two years in prison and fined them $10. Edward J. Mannix received a

* More than sixty would die in a reprisal of the violence during the following year's July 12 march by the Orangemen in New York.

one-year prison sentence and a $10 fine. The trio were transported to the state prison in Auburn, where, unlike other felons, the political prisoners were spared not only hard labor but the barber's shears, allowing them to maintain their flowing hair and fashionable facial whiskers.

After sending the three Trout River raiders to their relatively comfortable quarters, Judge Woodruff continued on his circuit to Windsor, Vermont, to preside over the trials of O'Neill and his fellow Fenians arrested at the Battle of Eccles Hill. The courtroom in the small central Vermont town was filled to capacity on July 29 as O'Neill stood before the bench and was asked whether he was guilty or not guilty. The Fenian general smiled as he delivered his pronouncement: "Guilty!"

Eager to rehabilitate his wounded image, O'Neill knew he would have an opportunity to address the court prior to his sentencing, and the following day he seized his chance to star in a bit of Irish political theater. Carrying on a hallowed tradition of patriotic courtroom rhetoric, O'Neill rose to his feet and delivered an impassioned speech from the dock.

The general told the court that he had learned a lesson from the latest raid—that defeating the British lion in its Canadian lair was impossible. "There is not the remotest chance of success," O'Neill proclaimed. "If there were, though I might go to the gallows tomorrow, I would tell my countrymen to go on; but I now believe that there is not, and I shall therefore advise them to desist; and so far as my influence will go, I will use it to convince the Irish people in America that any farther attempt in that direction would be futile."

O'Neill then continued, "I cannot, and I never shall forget the land of my birth. I could not, while fighting in the armies of the United States, when face to face with those who would haul down and trample beneath their feet the flag of freedom, and baring my bosom to their bullets—I could not forget that I was born in another land—a land oppressed and tyrannized over. I cannot now forget it; I never shall forget it. No matter what may be my fate here—I am still an Irishman, and while I have tried to be a faithful citizen of America, I am still an Irishman, with all the instincts of an Irishman."

O'Neill's oration moved many Irish eyes in the courtroom to tears, but it engendered little sympathy from Woodruff, who noted that the general was a repeat offender who expressed regret only for the failure of his fruitless enterprise, not his violation of American law. "Any real or supposed wrong of your country or your countrymen furnishes no just vindication, though it may in a sort explain the insane folly and wickedness of making that the occasion of suffering and wrong to a people who are innocent of any share in the infliction of which you suppose that you and your people had cause to complain," reprimanded the judge.

Woodruff rejected O'Neill's appeal for a lighter punishment due to his Civil War service and sentenced him to two years in prison and, in light of his destitution, a nominal $10 fine. The Fenian general greeted his fate with a calm smile.

As soon as court adjourned, local Fenians took up a subscription for the benefit of O'Neill's wife and children. William Maxwell Evarts, the former attorney general under President Andrew Johnson and a future secretary of state who was in Windsor on court business, led the contributions with a $50 gift. Donations arrived from quarters ranging from employees of the Vermont Central Railroad to the U.S. representative Benjamin Butler, the Civil War major general and friend of the Irish. Contributions even came from as far away as the Wyoming Territory, where the Allen, Larkin & O'Brien circle contributed $26.

The four Fenians sentenced to the Windsor State Prison along with O'Neill received similar penal accommodations to their counterparts in New York. They were given their own rooms, their own meal table, and the same fare as the superintendent and his family. They were not required to labor or wear prison clothes and could receive callers whenever they pleased. One of those calling on O'Neill in Windsor would turn out to be a quite unexpected visitor, a longtime foe who hoped unity might save the organization he founded.

❧

Believing that the failure of the latest Canadian raid presented a chance for reconciliation, the senate wing gathered inside Cincinnati's Mozart Hall on August 24. The object of their convention, they declared, "was to give effect to the desire of the Irish people for an united National Organization for Ireland's independence."

Seeking a fresh start and a way to cleanse the Irish republican movement of the memory of O'Neill's latest foray, the convention abandoned the name of the Fenian Brotherhood and, tapping into the spirit of Theobald Wolfe Tone and the 1798 rebellion, rechristened themselves the United Irishmen. The changes made by the senate wing were more than cosmetic, though. They abolished the presidency held by O'Neill along with all paid officials and a central treasury, relying instead on numerous district treasuries.

The Cincinnati convention voted to act in concert with the Irish National Brotherhood, a new organization based in St. Louis that sought to supplant the Fenian Brotherhood. The United Irishmen proposed the creation of a seven-person directory—three members of the United Irishmen, three members of the old O'Mahony wing led by John Savage, and one member of the Irish National Brotherhood—to guide the Irish republican movement in the United States.

The dream of a United Irishmen, however lofty the thought, never came to fruition. When the Savage wing communed for its convention in New York on August 30, it summarily rejected the overture.

Savage, though, was interested in a much more surprising merger, given his renunciation of any further Canadian raids—one with O'Neill. The New York convention tasked three members, including the Fenian Brotherhood founder John O'Mahony, with visiting O'Neill in prison and consulting "on the feasibility of a Union of all Irish nationalists claiming the name of Fenians."

O'Mahony had seen his organization broken in two by men such as O'Neill who had taken what he saw as an ill-decided path. Only months earlier, he had written in *The Irish People* that O'Neill and the other ringleaders of the latest Canadian raid "had no more right to use the word Fenian, as properly applied to them than the inhabitants of Timbuctoo would have to proclaim themselves Yankees." The old Fenian, however, was willing to put aside his prior differences if it might revive the brotherhood.

O'Neill remained so upset at what he perceived as a betrayal by the senate wing that he was willing to join forces with Savage's organization, even though it had always opposed the ventures into Canada that he had led. He affixed his signature to a three-point, hand-scrawled agreement in which he pledged to accept "the constitution of the Fenian Brotherhood as presided over by Chief Executive John Savage, as the constitution of the United Fenian Brotherhood."

❦

The Fenian prisoners had barely settled into their new quarters when a groundswell movement calling for their clemency gained momentum. In addition to the Irish who were sympathetic to the Fenian cause—if not their methods—Republican politicians who craved their votes to maintain their majority in Congress lent their voices to the cause. With a fellow Republican in the White House, prominent party members called on Grant to release the Irishmen. After all, if the Union could pardon those Confederates who took up arms against their own countrymen, why lock up these men who had an adventure that took no lives but their own?

Although he had pressed for the prosecution of the Fenians, Grant remained cognizant of the Democratic Party's choke hold on the Irish vote as the midterm elections approached. With several corruption scandals beginning to plague his administration, the Republican president felt the temptation to release the Fenians from prison and ingratiate his party with the Irish.

When the commander in chief informed Hamilton Fish in August 1870 that he was considering a pardon of the Fenian prisoners, the secretary of state sympathized with the president's plight. "Purely political prisoners are the worst kind of birds to keep caged," he wrote to the president. However, Fish persuaded Grant to delay his decision for at least a few weeks until the end of the fishing season because he feared Canada might retaliate by closing its fisheries to American ships. "It will do no great harm to O'Neill to spend a few weeks in the cool climate of Vermont," he told Grant.

The lure of the Irish vote ultimately proved too powerful for Grant. With midterm elections already under way in several states, the president on October 12 issued unconditional pardons for nine Fenians and remitted their fines.

The Canadians protested the clemency, but Fish defended the action. He told Edward Thornton, the British minister to the United States, that as long as the Fenians remained incarcerated, a large segment of the Irish population would maintain a constant agitation. "Their prolonged imprisonment would give them the honors of martyrs," Fish said.

Although Grant also issued a proclamation promising that future violators of neutrality laws would be "rigorously prosecuted" and exempt from clemency, the pardon and the president's eagerness to appease the Fenians reflected the political clout that had been achieved by the Irish two decades after the Great Hunger drove them into exile in the United States. In the midterm election of 1870, William Roberts, the former president of the Fenian Brotherhood who had embraced the Republicans in previous campaigns, won election to Congress from New York as part of the Tammany Hall Democratic machine. The Fenians helped to establish Irish Americans as power players in the political system that would see them rise from city halls to the White House over the ensuing century.

⚜

As winter descended in Vermont, O'Neill left Windsor State Prison a free man. Struggling to scratch out a living now that his claims agency was in tatters and he no longer drew an income as president of the Fenian Brotherhood, O'Neill published a pamphlet, which sold for thirty cents, that detailed his latest attempt to invade Canada and included a brief reminiscence of the Battle of Ridgeway for those Irishmen seeking a happier ending.

As part of his pardon agreement, the Fenian general pledged to Grant that his days of attacking Canada were over, and he didn't hesitate to put it into writing. The only policy for the Fenian Brotherhood going forward, he insisted, was to fight for Ireland on Irish soil. O'Neill wrote that his experience had proven that it was logistically impossible to get enough men and arms across the border while eluding both the American and the Canadian authorities.

"That we have been a source of trouble and expense to you for nearly five years I need not tell you," he wrote in a message to all Canadians, "but your trouble is now at an end." In spite of his pledge, O'Neill continued to face recurring questions about whether he would ever invade Canada again. Didn't they know he was a reformed man? His answer was clear: "No! Emphatically no."

Perhaps he actually believed it.

Losing Their Lifeblood

ILLIAM GLADSTONE TOOK off his coat to better wield his ax. As he awaited the results of the recent parliamentary election, the leader of the United Kingdom's Liberal Party passed the time on the first day of December 1868 felling trees on his country estate in the north of Wales. The chaos of 1867—with the Fenian Rising, the Manchester Martyrs, and the Clerkenwell prison explosion—had shaken the country, and Gladstone promised he would deliver answers to the "Irish question."

The cadence of Gladstone's repeated hatchet blows ceased when a messenger arrived and handed him a telegram. The fifty-eight-year-old politician read the missive and coolly muttered, "Very significant." Infused with the knowledge that he had been elected prime minister, Gladstone resumed his grounds-keeping work for a few minutes before resting on his ax handle. "My mission is to pacify Ireland," he declared to a colleague. The newly elected prime minister then resumed his strenuous task in silence and didn't loosen his grip on the hatchet until the tree smashed to the ground. A more arduous task awaited.

Years of pressure from Fenians on both sides of the Atlantic had finally persuaded the British government to implement structural reforms in Ireland, and Gladstone made good on his campaign promises. In the summer of 1870, the British Parliament passed a historical land reform law that prevented the eviction of tenants who paid their rent on time and required landlords to compensate tenants for property improvements at the end of their leases.

As the calendar passed into 1871, the Irish Church Act disestablished the Protestant Church of Ireland and repealed the law requiring the Irish to pay tithes to it. "One of the triumphs conceded to your power has been the demolition of her State Church in Ireland, and this triumph alone is worth *one thousand* defeats," James Gibbons declared to his fellow Fenians.

Emboldened by their progress in the halls of Westminster, the Irish grew more outspoken in their calls for Gladstone to pardon the Fenian political prisoners still held in British jails, especially after the United States had freed O'Neill and his fellow officers.

The conditions endured by the Fenians held in British jails were far more brutal than anything experienced by their counterparts in America or Canada. The British had condemned the Fenians to their harshest prisons, hoping to crush the spirits of the men they believed to be terrorists. They stuffed nine men into cells fourteen by seven feet in size. They cut them off from all communication with their families. They censored their letters to remove any mention of their poor health. Guards with swords and heavy clubs escorted the Fenians to Communion inside prison chapels.

The Irish rebels naturally resisted their captors. Their people had been doing that for seven centuries, after all. British wardens coped with many defiant Fenians, but then there was Jeremiah O'Donovan Rossa.

❦

Few Fenians were as unrepentant or suffered more for the cause of Ireland's freedom than Rossa. Born into an Irish-speaking household in 1831, the County Cork native learned English as a second language. Even before he could read, the young boy listened as his father told tales of English soldiers ripping open Irish women with their bayonets and smashing Irish infants against walls. He had just become a teenager when the Great Hunger descended upon County Cork, tearing his family apart. He watched friends die and witnessed the living do unthinkable things to survive, such as the family taken in by his father who killed their donkey in order to have something to eat. He buried a friend's dead mother in a shallow grave, placing a pillow under her head and an apron over her face so the dirt would not touch it.

When Black '47 arrived, Rossa's potato crop died, and then so did his father. Creditors seized the family's furniture from the widowed mother of four. Their landlords evicted them from their home. The family scattered, and Rossa's mother and siblings sailed for the United States in hopes of anything better, leaving him alone in Ireland. The loss of his father and his family, by death and exile, radicalized Rossa. While other Irishmen claimed the Great Hunger was an act of God, Rossa blamed the British for starving Ireland and taking away his family.

"There was no 'famine' in Ireland," he wrote. "There is no famine in any country that will produce in any one year as much food as will feed the people who live in that country during that year."

Rossa's childhood experiences transformed the Irish lad into a Fenian rebel. "If the operation of English rule in Ireland abases the nature of the Irishman," he wrote, "the Irishman ought to fight the harder and fight the longer, and fight every way and every time, and fight all the time to destroy that rule."

One of the Irish Republican Brotherhood's earliest recruits, Rossa founded the secret Phoenix National and Literary Society after meeting with James Stephens. He was arrested in 1858 and again after the 1865 raid on *The Irish People,* where Rossa worked as the business manager. A British court sentenced him to penal servitude for life. He disobeyed his British wardens and guards at every turn. Hoping to tame the unruly Fenian, British authorities sent him to the dreaded Millbank Prison. They didn't realize, however, that there was no taming Rossa.

❦

In his virtual dungeon at Millbank, Rossa slept in a hammock bed that he compared to a coffin. He bathed every two weeks in a trough along with three other prisoners. Forbidden to speak with his fellow inmates, he tapped out prayers to his fellow Fenian John Devoy on Christmas Eve. He wasn't even allowed to walk because of the noise it would make—not that there was much room to maneuver in a cell seven feet by four feet.

Rossa spent his days sitting on a bucket and tediously "picking oakum," tearing apart and unraveling old tar ropes into flossy strands with his blistered fingers. Failure to pick his daily quota of three pounds was punished with a twenty-four-hour diet of one pound of dry bread and two pints of water. It was a diet he was quite familiar with. By his own estimation, Rossa spent nearly an entire year punished with just bread and water.

After flinging his filled chamber pot at a prison governor, he spent thirty-five consecutive days in solitary confinement with his hands bound behind his back, even during meals (prison laws permitted such a penalty for a maximum of three days). For more than five years, Rossa did not experience a full stomach or a restful night of sleep.

Still he refused to let the British extinguish his patriotic fire. In fact, the confinement only intensified it. Many Fenian political prisoners were held in similar conditions in British jails, and Irish voices around the world protested their treatment and called for their release. More than one million people took to the streets in demonstrations organized by the Amnesty Association in the first months of 1869, and when that failed to persuade British authorities, voters in Tipperary elected Rossa to the House of Commons in a true protest vote.

The Amnesty movement gained strength in 1870 as more revelations surfaced about the poor treatment of the Fenian inmates. Prime Minister Gladstone, who had condemned the treatment of political prisoners by the Kingdom of Italy, found the moral high ground quickly crumbling beneath him. After an official commission led by Lord Devon released a damning report on the torture of the Fenian prisoners on December 16, 1870, a notice conveyed by the lord mayor of Dublin arrived for Rossa from 10 Downing Street.

❧

Faced with the awful truths of the Devon Commission report, Prime Minister Gladstone granted Rossa and forty other political prisoners held in British jails and Western Australia a "royal clemency." Fenians who had been arrested while serving in the British military, however, were exempt from the decree.

Rossa and the other political prisoners were granted their release on one condition: They would have to stay out of the United Kingdom for the duration of their sentences, a geographic banishment that included Ireland. If they set foot on Irish soil, they could be rearrested. In the case of Rossa, who had his sentence commuted, it meant a twenty-year exile. For prisoners such as the Civil War veteran Thomas F. Bourke, it meant banishment for life.

The Fenians might have been liberated from prison, but they weren't truly free. What the British called a "conditional pardon," the old Fenian firebrand John Mitchel called a "sham amnesty." Many Irish viewed the pardons as just another forced exile, little different from those endured by the refugees who fled the Great Hunger or the convicts transported to Australia. The Fenian prisoners "were not released to freedom," John Savage said, "but forced into banishment."

Rossa emerged from Chatham Prison, to which he had been transferred, on January 7, 1871. After taking a train to London and then Liverpool, he, Devoy, and three other Fenians boarded the transatlantic Cunard steamship *Cuba*. Before braving the ocean crossing, the *Cuba* slipped into Cork Harbor to pick up mail and family members of the Fenians. Rossa could remember his youthful days when this port was called Cobh, but the British had even taken that away from the Irish, rechristening it Queenstown when the monarch visited in 1849.

Rossa stared out at his beloved homeland, his cherished County Cork, for the first time in nearly six years. "There she lay before us, with her hopes and the high hopes of our youth blasted," he recalled. He wanted to embrace Ireland and tread its soil once again, but as a stipulation of his release he could only gaze at Erin. It proved one final cruel torture administered by the British.

Rossa had at first considered Australia a new home, to "evade the factions of Fenianism in the United States." However, in Australia he would still be living under a British flag, which would not be a good career move for an aspiring Fenian leader bent on rebellion.

There really was only one natural place for Rossa and his fellow Fenians to go.

❦

Shortly after the sun set on January 19, the *Antelope* shoved away from Manhattan's Castle Garden, where so many exiles from Ireland had first entered the United States, and crept into the frigid waters of New York Harbor. Huddled in their great coats to protect from the chill, some of Irish America's foremost leaders, such as Mitchel and William Roberts, stood on the deck of the steamboat and swept the dark horizon with an eyeglass in search of salvation. For so long Ireland had looked west to its exiled children in America to save them from the British. Now the Fenians looked east for the arrival of leaders who could save them from themselves.

The release of the British prisoners had engendered greater excitement than the freeing of O'Neill and his Fenian raiders three months earlier, and Irish Americans hoped that the arrival of the Fenians aboard the *Cuba*, nicknamed the Cuba Five, would spark a burst of Irish pride that could unify their numerous factions.

The passengers aboard the *Antelope* were eager to greet the Cuba Five on behalf of Tammany Hall, which had raised more than $20,000 for a welcome reception. Not long after their departure, the Irishmen heard a cacophony of gunshots and cheers from other boats in the harbor as a blazing blue light emerged from the darkness and the *Cuba* entered view. The band aboard the *Antelope* struck up "The Star-Spangled Banner" as the crew launched fireworks into the sky. The steamship's big paddle wheel furiously churned through the harbor's murky waters as the Tammany Hall reception committee charged toward the light to welcome the exiles to their new home.

Aboard the *Cuba*, Rossa peered out at the shoreline where Celtic hands held blazing torches aloft. Thundering cannons and Irish airs serenaded the Fenians as they arrived in a city so Irish that it was nicknamed New Cork.

Having pocketed £7 playing poker with his fellow exiles, Rossa felt that good fortune had accompanied him on the transatlantic voyage. When he scanned the latest New York newspapers, brought aboard the steamer by the pilot who would coax it into port, he began to question his luck.

❦

Across the chop of New York Harbor, the race was on. Along with the *Antelope,* the U.S. Treasury Department cutter *Bronx* and the New York Board of Health steamer *Andrew Fletcher,* carrying the city's health officer and members of the Knights of St. Patrick, rushed to be the first to greet the *Cuba* as it halted off the coast of Staten Island awaiting quarantine inspection.

The *Bronx* arrived first, and Thomas Murphy, the Republican collector of the port of New York, lugged his heavy frame up the ladder of the *Cuba*. Still trying to catch his breath, Murphy offered an official welcome from the U.S. government. He informed Rossa that the exiles could board his government ship to be taken to the quarters he had arranged for them at the plush Astor House.

Murphy's reception, however, was interrupted by the Irishmen who had just arrived from the *Antelope* and the *Andrew Fletcher*. Rossa was swept away into the steamship's saloon, where the Young Irelander Richard O'Gorman delivered a competing welcome on behalf of the Democratic leaders of New York City. O'Gorman informed the Cuba Five that Tammany Hall had secured rooms for them at the Metropolitan Hotel on Broadway and planned a grand procession in their honor at which time they would receive the money that had been donated for their benefit. Rossa's heart sank. "I saw immediately that the question of our reception had grown into a party fight," he recalled.

After O'Gorman concluded his speech, the indignant general Francis Frederick Millen, who had accompanied Murphy, jumped onto a chair and began to shout. "Are you the United States, sir?" the city's health commissioner barked at Millen, the leader of the Legion of St. Patrick, the United Irishmen's military adjunct. "No, but I desire to save the men from being made the tools of Tammany tricksters," retorted the general.

The parties traded vulgarities. Shouting turned to shoving, and a brawl nearly ensued. Rossa was seldom ruffled, but the political circus being performed before his eyes left even him shaken.

Murphy apologized to Rossa for the behavior of the Tammany men. "I am pained at what you have witnessed here tonight," he said. "The national government come to receive you, and a faction that has been for years degrading the character of our race steps in to create disturbance. The Irish people are glad of your release; they are honest, but they have got into the hands of a party of thieves and swindlers, who on every important occasion strive to use them against the interests of the country, and, as you see here tonight, to our common disgrace."

When Dr. John Carnochan, a city health officer and cog in the Tammany Hall machine, attempted to keep the *Cuba* in quarantine to prevent the exiles from leaving with Murphy on the federal revenue cutter, the Cuba Five had had enough.

"Gentlemen," Rossa told the greeters, "my companions think as I do, that the matter of this public reception requires some consideration, and we would like to consult about it." The exiles retired to an inner cabin where a purser stood guard to keep the Americans out. When the Cuba Five emerged, Rossa read a hastily crafted address to both factions.

"We desire that all Irishmen should be united. It is painful to us tonight to see so much disunion amongst yourselves," he said. "For what your reception concerns us as individuals we care little compared to what we feel about it in connection with the interest of Irish independence, and as you have not united cordially to receive us, we will not decide on anything until the arrival of our brothers." The Cuba Five announced they would stay on board the ship for the night and go to their own private hotel the following day, delaying any public welcome until their comrades traveling aboard the *Russia* arrived in New York City a few days hence.

American Fenians had hoped that the Cuba Five might be able to unify them, but their partisan and factional divisions were laid bare before the exiles could even set foot on American soil. They had managed to turn a triumphal moment into a fiasco. Fenians were left wondering whether there was anything the Cuba Five would be able to do to heal them. Perhaps they were beyond saving.

❧

After quarantine officials released the steamship the following afternoon, the Cuba Five boarded a tender to Jersey City and ferried into New York City. A throng of well-wishers waiting at the foot of Cortlandt Street enveloped the exiles, who were ushered into a coach and escorted through the streets of Manhattan by General Millen and the Legion of St. Patrick, who were bedecked in green coats, blue trousers, and black hats topped with plumes.

Having declined the posh quarters procured by the federal government and Tammany Hall, the Cuba Five lodged in more modest accommodations at Sweeney's Hotel near the Five Points neighborhood. Atop the hotel, a grand green banner with an Irish harp waved from the highest flagstaff beckoning the city's Irish.

Three thousand callers clogged the lobby, barroom, and parlors of the hotel. The United Irishmen treasurer, Richard McCloud, presented Rossa with a $1,000 donation and read a lengthy address. "You have set a noble example, and one which will not fail to be imitated until the white slavery of Ireland will be as dead as the black slavery of America," McCloud told the exiles.

Day after day, reception after reception, delegations from across the East—some bearing money, but more often delivering wordy addresses—flowed through Sweeney's Hotel. Even the Sabbath brought no rest for the weary, who were still weakened from their imprisonment. Rossa's calloused hands, already resembling a "Pittston miner" from his years of captivity, according to *The New York Herald,* grew swollen and sore from all the shaking. To the Cuba Five, it must have appeared that Irish America was doing its best to literally fulfill the traditional Gaelic greeting of "céad míle fáilte"—meaning "a hundred thousand welcomes."

Although they sought to avoid being drawn into American party politics, the exiles feared they could not decline Tammany Hall's offer to stage a parade in their honor without appearing ungracious. A reluctant Rossa accepted, although he told city aldermen, "We do not wish by our presence here to seem to be favoring one political party as opposed to another. This I wish to have clearly understood."

St. Patrick's Day arrived five weeks early; New York transformed into an emerald city on February 9. Men wearing green neckties and shamrocks in their lapels walked arm in arm with young ladies in green dresses. "God Save Ireland" banners waved from building windows. Even the horses hauling streetcars laden with passengers wore Irish flags fastened to their heads.

An estimated 300,000 people stood on the sidewalks of New York to honor the Cuba Five and the nine exiles who had arrived subsequently on the *Russia.* The Sixty-Ninth Regiment, Ancient Order of Hibernians, Emmet Guards, United Irishmen, and Fenian Brotherhood all marched south from Tammany Hall on Fourteenth Street, past Mayor Abraham Oakey Hall at the City Hall reviewing stand, and back uptown to Madison Square.

Near the head of the procession, a horse with buckling legs struggled to bear the weight of the Tammany Hall boss, William Tweed, who had proclaimed himself grand marshal. (By the end of the year, Rossa would be so disgusted with Tweed that he ran unsuccessfully against him on the Republican ticket for the New York Senate.)

For at least a few hours, the Irish had come together as one. Serenaded by a band playing "The Wearing of the Green," the Irish exiles managed to keep their shoes clean as they rode in carriages over the mucky parade route. There would be plenty of mudslinging to follow.

⚜

Several weeks after the grand parade through Manhattan, the celebration of the Fenian exiles continued in the nation's capital, much to the consternation of the British, who did not approve of the open arms given to men they still considered criminals. After a welcome resolution introduced by Congressman Benjamin Butler passed the House by a wide 172-to-21 margin, the exiles called on the White House on February 22.

President Ulysses S. Grant stood on the steps of the executive mansion and greeted thirteen of the exiled prisoners as they were introduced by Thomas F. Bourke, who had become a spokesman for the group. The president, a man of few words, only shook their hands, saying, "Glad to see you."

The outpouring that greeted the Fenian exiles energized the Irish nationalists in the United States, and even after experiencing the discord among Irish Americans firsthand, Rossa still thought it possible to create a union. However, he knew enough that persuading the existing organizations to surrender their autonomy under a single executive would be impossible.

Instead, Rossa and his fellow prisoners proposed the creation of an Irish confederation, which would serve as an overarching umbrella organization on top of the existing groups. In an address released from Sweeney's Hotel on March 13, the exiles assured existing nationalist organizations that they would remain autonomous in their own affairs but would be required to send a quarter of their revenue to the confederation's central treasury, which would be controlled by a central council with representation from each member organization. Ultimate authority would rest with a five-person directory picked from among the recently released Fenian prisoners, with Rossa as its inaugural chairman.

The United Irishmen enthusiastically embraced the idea and immediately agreed to transfer their power and authority to the exiles. Calls arose for the Fenian Brotherhood to join the confederation and give up its name to become part of the United Irishmen. "A bright hope is better than a sad memory. Fenian, to strange ears, is a word of mean sound," editorialized *The Pilot*, "which the Irish revolutionists will do well to bury with all the honors due to its venerable antiquity."

For all its supporters, there was at least one Fenian in the United States who would never consent to any such plan.

Although still without an official position, John O'Mahony had slowly regained power inside the organization he founded thirteen years earlier, and he wasn't about to see the Fenian Brotherhood usurped by the Irish Confederation and the next generation of revolutionaries. O'Mahony remained skeptical of the exiles' stated intention of cooperating with the Fenian Brotherhood. He believed they wanted to swallow it whole.

O'Mahony would not be a party to the extermination of his brainchild, let alone the eradication of the Fenian name that had become synonymous with Irish republicans around the world. When the Fenian Brotherhood leaders convened in New York on March 21 to consider the proposal to join the Irish Confederation, O'Mahony called the special convention to order and then delivered an impassioned plea. "Some may think that there is but little in a name—that an organization, like the rose, would smell as sweet under any other designation," he said. "After all the concessions we have offered, I believe that to surrender the name at this crisis would be to surrender the cause of Ireland. . . .

"We would be unworthy of the holy cause in which we are engaged were we to consent to have the brand of infamy affixed upon the glorious name of Fenianism, which, however reviled by enemies today, will be revered by future generations of Irishmen," O'Mahony said.

John Savage also voiced his opposition to the plan, berating

Rossa and his fellow exiles as undemocratic for seeking to lead an organization without an election. "The exiles have not been elected by anybody, but have assumed to themselves the management of Irish revolutionary affairs in the United States," the Fenian chief executive groused.

The Irish Confederation unity plan had the unintended consequence of cementing the union between the Savage wing and John O'Neill. Summoned from Boston to speak at the convention, the former president of the Fenian Brotherhood received a warm ovation as he told the delegates that he hoped they would never change their name.

"I am tonight, gentlemen, a Fenian," O'Neill told the convention. "Why should the men who were Fenians here, who went to Ireland as Fenians, who boasted of being Fenians, who were convicted as Fenians, liberated as Fenians, and received and *feted* and feasted in this country as Fenians, and nothing else, why should these men repudiate Fenianism?" The Fenian Brotherhood soundly rejected the proposal to join the Irish Confederation. Additionally, they adopted a measure to replace its chief executive with a twenty-one-member elected executive council, to which O'Neill was nominated.

Rossa and his fellow exiles discovered that the fractures in Irish America were just too cavernous to bridge. The same infighting that plagued the Fenian Brotherhood dragged down the Irish Confederation, before its eventual collapse in 1873. Rather than elevating the Irish in America, the exiles became engulfed in their chaos.

⚜

As the Irish nationalists continued to bicker, the United States and Great Britain entered a new phase of cooperation, marking the beginning of a special relationship that would make the two countries the closest of allies in the following century and beyond.

At the beginning of 1871, powerful voices still backed a simple solution to the problem of the Fenians raiding the Canadian border: Get rid of the border. Nearly four years after the confederation of Canada, the Massachusetts senator Charles Sumner continued to call for annexation as a way to solve the deadlock on the *Alabama* claims—the reparations the Union had demanded for damages incurred from Confederate warships built in English ports. "The greatest trouble, if not peril, being a constant source of anxiety and disturbance, is from Fenianism, which is excited by the British flag in Canada," he wrote in January 1871. "Therefore, the withdrawal of the British flag cannot be abandoned as a condition or preliminary of such a settlement as is now proposed."

While Sumner sought to keep the *Alabama* claims open for as long as it took until Great Britain ceded Canada or granted its independence, Grant eventually sided with Secretary of State Hamilton Fish, who thought the idea unrealistic. Convinced by Fish of the importance of restoring peaceful relations with Great Britain, Grant called for the reopening of negotiations on the *Alabama* claims at the same time that Gladstone's government also expressed its willingness to settle the diplomatic dispute.

On February 27, 1871, a ten-man joint high commission that included the Canadian prime minister, John A. Macdonald, met for the first time inside a library at the U.S. State Department. Grant became a regular presence strolling through Lafayette Square and leaving a trail of cigar smoke in his wake as he visited Fish's house to receive updates on the negotiations, although he bothered to meet with Macdonald only twice—once to say hello, once to say good-bye. While the *Alabama* claims were the overriding concern, the commissioners devoted two-thirds of their meetings to issues between Canada and the United States such as Atlantic fisheries, trade, and disputed boundaries.

On May 8, in the city torched by the British nearly sixty years earlier, the members of the joint high commission scrawled their signatures on the Treaty of Washington. Among its forty-three articles, Great Britain declared remorse "for the escape, under whatever circumstance, of the *Alabama* and other vessels from British ports, for the depredations committed by those vessels." The treaty renewed the reciprocity of fisheries as Canada deeply desired, and the two nations were permitted to ship fish and fish products to each other duty-free. The Canadians granted access to the St. Lawrence River in perpetuity and gained the right to travel freely on rivers flowing through Alaska.

The United States and Great Britain agreed to submit outstanding questions to arbitration. The emperor William I of the newly united German Empire agreed to arbitrate the disputed boundary for the

San Juan Islands in the Pacific Northwest. The treaty called for a five-person tribunal—with one member each appointed by Grant, Queen Victoria, the emperor of Brazil, the king of Italy, and the president of the Swiss Confederation—to meet in Geneva and determine the specific damage amount due to the United States for the *Alabama* claims. (In September 1872, the tribunal ordered Great Britain to pay the United States compensation of $15.5 million.)

To the fury of some Canadians, already outraged at the toleration of Fenian activities by the American government, the commissioners agreed to drop claims for damages from the Fenian raids. The Gladstone government, instead, assumed the burden of compensating Canadians for the attacks.

The Fenians weren't pleased with the treaty either. No longer would the U.S. government turn a blind eye to their Canadian forays, as leverage to get Great Britain to settle the *Alabama* claims. No longer was the Fenian Brotherhood a useful pawn on the diplomatic chessboard.

Anglophobia provided the lifeblood of Fenianism. It was inbred in the Irish. But the Treaty of Washington reflected its waning in the United States. With the conditional pardon of the political prisoners from British custody and the passage of Gladstone's reforms, the Fenian movement lost some of the grievances that fueled its militancy.

For one militant Fenian, however, hatred of Great Britain could never be diluted. He would make one more last-gasp attempt to strike Canada.

The Invasion That Wasn't

EMBERS DANCED LIKE fireflies and ash fell like snow upon the Fenian wagon train as it rattled north through an American cauldron. An extreme drought in the summer of 1871 had turned the Great Plains into a tinderbox. A red sea of flames washed over the middle of the North American continent from Kansas to Manitoba. Tongues of fire six to twelve feet high fed on the prairie grass and devoured freshly reaped harvests of wheat, oats, and corn, torching months of toil in an instant. Ordinary fire blocks proved impotent. Blazes hurdled over roads and leaped over rivers. The fires were so ferocious that they appeared to ignite spontaneously.

The first days of autumn brought little relief to a land so parched that even the soil burned. Driven east by scalding winds, the wildfires roared across the prairie like a buffalo stampede.* The inferno bestowed a perpetual twilight upon the middle of America. Great billowing smoke clouds dimmed the sun during the day, while an otherworldly orange glow floating above the horizon brightened the night.

The black soot of the charred prairie begrimed the faces and

---

* A week after John O'Neill's journey to the Dakota Territory, fires sparked by the drought and high winds in the Midwest would incinerate Chicago and on the same night cause the deadliest forest fire in American history that killed as many as twenty-five hundred people near Peshtigo, Wisconsin.

darkened the clothing of John O'Neill and a force of twenty-seven Fenians in the last days of September as they tracked the meandering path of the Red River dividing Minnesota from the Dakota Territory as it flowed north.

In spite of his previous pledges to the White House and his fellow Fenians that he would forever resist such temptations, O'Neill had been seduced yet again by a plan to attack Canada. The chance to cleanse himself of the shame of Eccles Hill and redeem his family name was irresistible. Hugh O'Neill might never have kicked the British out of Ireland as he'd hoped, but at least he had never suffered the shame of having been arrested on the battlefield by a local marshal.

As he looked out the window of his stagecoach, O'Neill saw the glimmer of the encircling blazes. The fires illuminated the way forward to Canada. Sometimes, though, those inextinguishable flames burned with such ferocity that the acrid smoke prevented the Fenian general from seeing what lay ahead.

❦

This time, the plan to invade Canada wasn't O'Neill's but that of another son of Ireland—William Bernard O'Donoghue. When the Fenian general first met O'Donoghue several months earlier, he had seen in the twenty-eight-year-old something he liked—himself. The pair of Great Hunger refugees both favored action over oratory and harbored a smoldering hatred of the British, one that raged behind seemingly placid facades.

Born in Ireland's County Sligo, O'Donoghue had already learned to despise the British by the time his family fled to New York City around 1848. Two decades later, the devout Irishman joined the western missions of the Roman Catholic Church in Canada's Red River Colony, which lay north of Minnesota and the Dakota Territory. O'Donoghue taught mathematics at the College of St.-Boniface and studied for the priesthood, until he found a higher calling in taking up arms against the Crown.

O'Donoghue joined the Red River Rebellion launched in 1869 by the colony's dominant ethnic group, the Métis, who drew their lineage from two centuries of intermarriage between French fur traders and Native American women. Fearing the loss of their rights as an ethnic, linguistic, and religious minority, the predominantly French-speaking Catholics launched an uprising to protest the transfer of their land from the Hudson's Bay Company to Canada and the appointment of an English-speaking governor. Led by Louis Riel, the descendant of an immigrant to Canada from Limerick in the early eighteenth century, they seized Fort Garry, present-day Winnipeg, and formed their own provisional government with O'Donoghue serving as treasurer. The Canadian government put down the rebellion in August 1870 and carved the confederation's fifth province, Manitoba, out of the Red River Colony, but harsh feelings endured.

Forced into exile in the United States, O'Donoghue wasn't willing to cede the fight. Rebuffed by President Ulysses S. Grant in a White House visit, the Irishman lobbied the Fenian Brotherhood to come to the aid of the Métis. He argued that because of their collective grievances at the hands of the British Empire there was a natural alliance between the Métis and the Irish. O'Donoghue also assured councilors that they would be supported and welcomed as liberators by the Métis, who accounted for approximately 9,800 of Manitoba's 11,960 residents, although he had received no such pledge from Riel.

With no stomach for another venture into Canada, particularly because there was still hope of uniting Irish American nationalists in the wake of the arrival of the Cuba Five, the Fenian council told O'Donoghue they would give him no aid except for their prayers. O'Neill, however, was so driven by redemption and vengeance toward the British

The Canadian government issued service medals such as this one emblazoned with the image of Queen Victoria to Fenian raid veterans.

Empire that he resigned from the Fenian Brotherhood in order to participate in the raid. In a concession to their former president, the Fenian council agreed to his request to not oppose or condemn the attack so long as he didn't try to enlist any members of the brotherhood into his scheme. That would be the limit of their support.

Going it alone, O'Neill traveled across the Midwest, recalling his past glories in a lecture titled "Ireland, Past, Present, and Future" and secretly trying to raise men, money, and munitions. It was an unlikely scene: By night, O'Neill assured audiences that he had sworn off any interest in Canada. By day, he recruited former Fenian comrades to join his latest venture.

Most of his overtures, though, were met with rejections, except for the one toward General John J. Donnelly, his chief of staff, who had been among the wounded at Eccles Hill. Having managed to recruit an army of barely more than two dozen men, the persistent O'Neill traveled west to take Canada once again.

❧

As O'Neill's posse traveled through the incinerated grasslands of the Dakota Territory, the Canadian spymaster Gilbert McMicken trailed just behind them on the road north to Fort Garry to begin his new assignment. When rumors of a Fenian raid reached Manitoba in late August, a panicked lieutenant governor, Adams G. Archibald, beseeched the Canadian prime minister, John A. Macdonald, to send help. In need of a trusted set of eyes to keep watch over the internal and external threats in Manitoba, Macdonald appointed McMicken agent of dominion lands for Manitoba and dispatched him to Fort Garry.

Passing through Chicago, McMicken had met with Colonel Henri Le Caron, who informed him that an attack was imminent. After the disasters at the Battles of Eccles Hill and Trout River and O'Neill's imprisonment, Le Caron had concluded that the Fenian threat to Canada had finally dissolved. "I had no thought of its ever reviving again," he recalled. The spy thus put his career in espionage to rest, returning to his medical studies before opening up a practice in Wilmington, Illinois, where he lived with his wife and three children.

That life took a turn when he was handed a telegram written by O'Neill, summoning him to a meeting in Chicago on June 15. More than a year had passed since their last encounter, when Le Caron watched with a wry smile as O'Neill was arrested behind Alvah Richard's farm and forcibly removed from the battlefield. The secret agent, his confidence undiminished, assumed the former Fenian general had come to pay him back the hundreds of dollars he had borrowed. He was surprised, then, when O'Neill produced letters from O'Donoghue detailing the Red River plot.

O'Neill told his confidant that he needed the weapons from the Fenians' cache that had remained hidden after the prior year's raids. Only Le Caron knew their location. Would he help O'Neill recover the four hundred surplus Springfield rifles and ammunition? Le Caron obliged. He accompanied O'Neill to a hidden repository in Port Huron, Michigan, containing the rifles that had been contracted by the Fenians the year previous.

In the Fenians' wake, along the Red River, McMicken collected scraps of information about their plan, like bread crumbs left behind on the trail. He transmitted them in coded messages back to Prime Minister Macdonald in Ottawa. From an Irish stagecoach driver who groused that the Fenians had made a "damned mistake" not waiting until November, when the frozen rivers would have impeded the arrival of Canadian reinforcements, McMicken learned that the raiders' plan was to meet in Pembina, a village just south of the Canadian border in the Dakota Territory, and start the march for Fort Garry on the morning of October 5.

❧

Like giant wooden guideposts, a string of newly planted telegraph poles that awaited the draping of wires shepherded the Irishmen into Pembina, the only permanent white settlement in the Dakota Territory north of the 45th parallel. After passing ramshackle cabins cobbled together by impoverished squatters, the expedition arrived in the town huddled on the west bank of the Red River two miles south of Canada. With a population of only 250 residents, Pembina was still the most populous town in the Dakota Territory. Twice every year, the Métis gathered in the border town for their traditional buffalo hunts. Now O'Donoghue used the village as the rendezvous point for an army stalking a more elusive prey.

As the days until the raid dwindled, the Fenians continued their recruitment efforts among the discontented Métis who had fled to Pembina after the Red River Rebellion. When O'Donoghue finally reached out to the Métis leaders in Manitoba, two nights before the attack, however, they made it clear to their former treasurer that they had no interest in his scheme.

The refusal dealt a terrible blow to O'Donoghue's plans. His army of three dozen men, mostly Fenians, was absurdly small for a force intending to take over a vast province. Still, he knew that the charge of a light brigade such as theirs might work. After all, the provincial militia wasn't much bigger. Archibald had a garrison of only eighty men to defend Fort Garry and much of Manitoba, and the makeshift force called out by the lieutenant governor still hadn't left Fort Garry. They remained a two-day march from the border. And O'Donoghue held out hope that once he crossed the border, Riel would change his mind and mobilize the Métis to join the rebellion.

In Washington, D.C., Secretary of War William W. Belknap told Secretary of State Hamilton Fish that he entertained "little apprehension of any organized invasion of Manitoba from the territory of the United States." O'Neill and O'Donoghue were about to prove him wrong.

❧

O'Neill, O'Donoghue, and their men slunk out of Pembina on the morning of October 5 while the village slumbered. By dawn's early light, three dozen men had gathered their rifles and set off for Canada. Around 7:30 a.m., the raiders marched across the international boundary that had been surveyed by the U.S. Army major Stephen Long in 1823, five years after a treaty between the United States and Great Britain established the 49th parallel as the international boundary.

Unlike at Eccles Hill sixteen months earlier, there were no Canadian forces waiting to ambush O'Neill and his men once they set foot on foreign soil. The men carried Fenian guns, but O'Neill maintained his pledge to disassociate the attack from the brotherhood. No green flag led the charge into Canada; none of the soldiers wore green uniforms or brass IRA buttons. As the force approached its first target, the Dominion Customs House, the men hid in a ravine until receiving the all-clear signal from Louison "Oiseau" Letendre, one of the Métis from Pembina who had joined the mostly Irish ranks.

Stirred from his sleep by a report of an armed force approaching, the assistant customhouse officer A. B. Douglass might have thought he was still dreaming when he looked out of his window. On constant guard against Native American raids, Douglass instead saw the Irish O'Neill carrying his sword at his side, leading a Lilliputian force armed with breech-loading Springfield rifles, bayonets, and sidearms. O'Donoghue trotted alongside on horseback. Lest their intention be in doubt, rolling behind them were three carts full of arms and ammunition, as well as an empty double wagon waiting to haul the supplies they planned to seize from a nearby Hudson's Bay Company trading post.

After awakening George W. Webster, a courier en route to St. Paul with a dispatch from Archibald, Douglass sprinted from the customhouse to warn the Hudson's Bay Company post. However, O'Donoghue tracked him down on horseback and pointed a revolver at his head, and the Canadian official thought better of his plan.

The raiders advanced to the Hudson's Bay Company trading post—a complex that included a store, a warehouse, and several outbuildings hidden behind a rough-hewn log stockade eight to ten feet high, with bastions at all four corners. They burst through the gates so quickly that William H. Watt, the one-armed trading post manager from the Orkney Islands, couldn't lock the doors in time. O'Neill's men faced no resistance either from the other occupants of the post—Watt's clerk and an older married couple.

For their first order of business, the invaders took breakfast. Then, rifling through the post's provisions, the Fenians plundered food and supplies, which they loaded onto their wagon and a boat they planned to launch down the Red River to Fort Garry, seventy-five miles away.

As the morning sun brightened, the marauders captured unsuspecting passersby on the road to Pembina. By 9:00 a.m., at least twenty were roaming inside the trading post's stockade. One Métis prisoner from the American side of the border pleaded with his captors for his release by virtue of his citizenship. The raiders agreed to liberate the American. Unbeknownst to them, he carried a secret plea for help penned by the Canadian occupants of the customhouse, Douglass and Webster.

While O'Neill held a war council with his fellow ringleaders around noontime, a breathless Fenian sentinel burst in with the startling news.

"The American troops are coming!"

❧

O'Neill looked out to see the U.S. Army captain Loyd Wheaton, the commanding officer at Fort Pembina, riding a four-mule wagon. He was accompanied by a line of about thirty armed soldiers advancing on the "double quick" with an army ambulance. Apparently, the American prisoner who had been released did not seek help from Canadian authorities but instead ran three miles south to deliver his note to Wheaton inside the U.S. Army's Fort Pembina.

Wheaton had been stationed at the citadel, which had been completed the year before, to enforce the 1868 Treaty of Fort Laramie signed by the Dakota Territory's white settlers and the Lakota. He never expected to be drawn into a confrontation on the prairie between Irish exiles and the British Empire. But when the loose lips of a Fenian sympathizer in Fort Garry revealed the entire plot to the U.S. consul James Wickes Taylor after one, two, three pours from a decanter of gin, Wheaton received orders to prepare the Twentieth Infantry to respond to a possible attack. Archibald also informed Taylor that the Manitoba and Canadian governments would not object if the United States sent troops across the boundary to suppress a Fenian attack.

Although the invaders had a slight numerical advantage and a superior defensive position behind the trading post's stockade, panic spread among O'Neill's men at news of the arrival of American troops. Colonel Thomas Curley ordered the wagons laden with plunder to move immediately. But the Irishmen scattered in every direction—through the trading post gates and into the woods or the brush along the Red River. With his one arm, Watt failed to grab O'Donoghue before he fled on horseback. O'Neill scurried so abruptly that he left behind his trusty sword.

Wheaton ordered his men to fire a volley over the heads of the Fenians, but when that failed to stop the escape, the thirty-three-year-old captain drew his pistol and galloped in pursuit of the raiders. The Fort Pembina commandant would not have to worry about return fire; even for the cause of Ireland, a former Union soldier like O'Neill would never sanction firing at another man in blue. "I had fought too long under the Stars and Stripes to want to fight United

States troops, whether they had crossed the line legally or illegally," he later recounted to the St. Paul *Pioneer*.

The captain arrested O'Neill, Curley, Donnelly, and ten of the rank and file without resistance. Like children, the Fenians were made to unload their wagons before their punishment was inflicted. The federal troops seized seventy-seven breech-loading Springfield rifles, seventeen muzzle-loading rifle muskets, five carbines, eleven sabers, and twelve thousand ammunition cartridges.

When O'Donoghue was in the clear, he traded in his horse for a canoe. He paddled five miles north on the Red River toward the Métis settlements, where he expected to be given safe haven. Instead, he found himself captured by two of Riel's scouts, who tied him up with ropes and brought him back over the border to Wheaton that evening.

The raid passed without any injuries or damage, and the Fenians were thwarted with nothing to show for their efforts, newspapers noted, outside "a hearty breakfast." O'Neill was in a familiar place— American custody. He was loaded into an army ambulance for the ride back to Fort Pembina. It was the American government that had cut his supply lines after the Battle of Ridgeway. It was the same that dragged him off the battlefield at Eccles Hill. And once again, it was the United States, not Canada or Great Britain, that thwarted his plans.

"I believe the action of Colonel Wheaton to be entirely unauthorized, in crossing into British territory and arresting anyone," O'Neill later groused to the St. Paul *Pioneer*. He was wrong in more ways than he knew.

❀

Surveyors in the nineteenth century knew it was far easier to draw a border on a map than to mark it on the ground. In the decades after Major Long surveyed the international boundary using the heavens as his guide, both the American and the British governments eventually concluded that his dividing line was actually south of the 49th parallel, although exactly where the formal divide actually lay was in dispute.

In May 1870, U.S. Army Corps of Engineers surveyors, under the direction of Captain D. P. Heap, resurveyed the border and concluded that Long's frontier was 4,763 feet—nearly an entire mile—south of the 49th parallel. That meant that, according to Heap's redrawn border, the Dominion Customs House and the Hudson's Bay Company trading post seized by O'Neill's men were not a quarter mile north inside Canadian territory as they believed, but actually three-quarters of a mile south of the border, on American soil.

While the U.S. State Department was willing to honor the long-established dividing line for commercial purposes, pending an official joint boundary survey, that wasn't the case for military jurisdiction. Although Wheaton had been granted permission by both the Canadian and the Manitoba governments to cross the border with the Twentieth Infantry, the U.S. Army captain believed it irrelevant when it came to the Dominion Customs House and the Hudson's Bay Company trading post outside Pembina, because they sat on what he considered American land, south of Heap's border.

O'Neill was unaware of Heap's survey. That meant that not only had he failed to invade Canada, he had failed to *enter* Canada—at least in the eyes of the U.S. government. What that also meant, however, was that O'Neill and his fellow raiders could not be prosecuted for violating the Neutrality Act. Technically speaking, they had never in fact attacked Canada.

Citing a lack of evidence and "want of jurisdiction," the U.S. commissioner George I. Foster of the Dakota Territory dismissed the case against O'Neill and his fellow marauders on October 9 after two full days of proceedings. O'Neill was a free man. But in a sense, this was a fate worse than conviction. It was the ultimate humiliation for the hero of Ridgeway. Not only couldn't he capture Canada, but he couldn't find it.

In the days following the attempted invasion of Canada, newspapers ridiculed "the Fenian fiasco," calling it "another reckless and ridiculous Fenian raid." O'Neill's former friends and followers were hardly kinder in their assessments. "This time the attempt was even more farcical than his performance of St. Albans," groused *The Irish-American,* which made it clear that "O'Neill's folly" was his and his alone. "The application of the term 'Fenians' in the narrative is a misnomer, as O'Neill has been repudiated by all sections of that organization, and his movement was in no sense a Fenian affair."

The "Garibaldi of the Green Isle" no longer inspired respect; now only laughter and pity. After the Red River disaster, Ridgeway—and not Eccles Hill—appeared to be the fluke in the general's record. O'Neill blamed the expedition's failure on "a mere accident" of geography. But his ignorance of the resurveyed boundary was more gross negligence than mishap.

In addition, just as he had done with the French Canadians in Quebec in previous raids, O'Neill had again miscalculated the extent to which the enemy of his enemy would be his friend. O'Donoghue's sales job had convinced O'Neill that they could count on support from the Métis. The Irishman's stature among Riel and the Red River Colony was much weaker than he advertised. Not only did Riel refuse to aid O'Donoghue's venture, but he pledged the allegiance of the Métis to the Manitoba government, providing scouts to guard the frontier from further raids from the United States.

While the press depicted the Red River raid as a comic opera, it also revealed a tragedy worthy of Shakespeare. O'Neill's hasty insistence, his default to action, obliterated his ability to see any distinction between courage and recklessness. O'Neill had become so consumed by the sense of his own abilities and his hatred of the British that it blinded him to reality—that Le Caron was a spy, that O'Donoghue lacked the support of the Métis, that the borderline was off, that he and O'Donoghue were by then a pair of quixotic romantics tilting at windmills. The Fenian fire that burned so hot inside O'Neill's zealous heart no longer lit the way. It clouded his vision.

The Next Best Thing

FTER DISCUSSING THE disastrous Red River raid with Fenians in Chicago, Henri Le Caron was certain John O'Neill would never threaten Canada again. "All denounce O'Neill in strong terms," he reported to Gilbert McMicken. "He is a dead duck for ever." By now, though, the British spy should have known better. Given his family pedigree, O'Neill could no sooner abandon the fight against the British than he could renounce his name. And anyone with Celtic blood coursing through his veins, as Le Caron claimed, would have known that seven centuries of defiance made the Irish a tenacious—others might say stubborn—people.

O'Neill still believed it was his calling to be at the head of an Irish army, but the time had come to change tactics. While O'Neill bided his time until the day he would liberate Ireland, he decided instead to emancipate the Irish from America's noisy factories, filthy mines, and wretched tenements and deliver them to the fresh air and virgin prairie of the Great Plains.

Fenian leaders had long talked about the idea of establishing their own colonies in North America. O'Neill was determined to turn that talk into action. "Absolute possession of the soil is the only true independence for a laboring man," wrote O'Neill, who believed the underlying cause for the Great Hunger was that absentee British landlords—not the Irish—owned the land.

A quarter century earlier, the Irish had migrated west to flee starvation. Now O'Neill thought they should follow the sun once again to escape poverty. While some claimed that Irish immigrants needed to break out of their insular enclaves and integrate themselves into American culture, O'Neill took the opposite tack. He wanted to remove his fellow Irish Catholics altogether.

꧁

The American West offered the Irish the prospect of cheap land. Under the Homestead Act of 1862, both native-born Americans and immigrants who applied for citizenship could take ownership of up to 160 acres of public land for an $18 filing fee as long as they lived on the parcel for five years, farmed it, and built a dwelling. Civil War veterans and other soldiers received added incentives. Irish American newspapers frequently printed advertisements such as one from the Union Pacific Railroad that promised "Cheap Farms! Free Homes!" in the "Garden of the West."

As early as December 1870, *The New York Times* reported that O'Neill had embarked on a lecture tour to promote a scheme "for providing homes for his countrymen in the West." At the time, his enterprise had been little more than a cover for his recruitment of men for the Red River raid. After the failed attack, O'Neill pursued it in earnest. He spent parts of 1872 and 1873 scouting locations in Minnesota, Wisconsin, Illinois, and Missouri before deciding upon a plot of land in the Elkhorn valley of northern Nebraska as a suitable place for planting his Irish colony. The general signed an agreement with the land agents Patrick Fahy and S. M. Boyd to colonize a settlement with twenty-five families in return for $600 and seventy lots.

Throughout the winter of 1873 and 1874, O'Neill toured traditional Irish strongholds—from the mill cities of New England to the copper mines of Michigan's Upper Peninsula. After regaling audiences with tales from his three raids on Canada, he delivered a sales pitch for his new business venture: "Why are you content to work on the public projects and at coal mining when you might in a few years own farms of your own and become wealthy and influential people?"

With the panic of 1873 triggering a severe economic downturn, O'Neill's promise of a fresh start was especially appealing to those who were out of work. Using the same powers of persuasion that led hundreds of Irishmen to attack Canada, O'Neill persuaded an initial colony of thirteen men, two women, and five children to transplant themselves to Nebraska by giving them what he always gave his fellow Irishmen—hope for better lives.

❈

Adrift on an ocean of tall prairie grass bending in the wind, O'Neill made the second exodus of his life in the spring of 1874. The general who had fled the Great Hunger had high hopes for his new venture. "We could build up a young Ireland on the virgin prairies of Nebraska and there rear a monument more lasting than granite or marble to the Irish race in America," he wrote to Bishop James O'Connor of Omaha.

As the sun reached its zenith on May 12, 1874, the settlers finally arrived at their new home, originally called Holt City but quickly changed by Colonel James H. Noteware, immigration agent for the state of Nebraska, to O'Neill, in honor of the colony's leader (to say nothing of his distinguished forebears).

The Irish had always lived off the land, but not land like that they found in Nebraska. The flat, desolate prairie and barren sand hills sported few trees to offer shade from the blazing sun, let alone timber for building and burning. The colonists who had lived shoulder to shoulder in the tenements of Brooklyn, Philadelphia, and St. Louis now found deer, antelope, coyotes, and wolves to be their only neighbors.

Shelter was the first order of business for the colonists. With the nearest timber six miles away, O'Neill and his followers built a sod house thirty-six feet long and eighteen feet wide to house the entire colony. The settlers jokingly dubbed their rude, crowded quarters the "Grand Central Hotel."

It was a hard existence, but nothing ever came easy to the Irish. Unlike their ancestors in Ireland, many of the settlers who followed O'Neill were city dwellers with no farming experience. Already off to a late start in Nebraska's short growing season, the settlers attempted to tear into the tough, knotted prairie sod and plant potatoes, corn, and other crops in the black, sandy loam. The blazing summer sun, however, brought drought and heat so suffocating that one pioneer reported that as he peered into the mirages shimmering on the horizon, he could see towns one hundred miles away "so plainly mirrored on the nearby prairie that one could see between the buildings."

The pioneers had expected a land of milk and honey, only to discover that their Irish Moses had led them into the desert—devoid of trees, water, and comfort. And that was even before the arrival of a plague straight out of the Old Testament.

On a mid-July day, the skies above the Irish prairie colony blackened as a dark cloud dimmed the sun and emptied its contents. The storm that swept in from the northwest didn't deluge the settlers with badly needed raindrops, however, but a shower of grasshoppers. The pioneers found themselves ankle-deep in "Rocky Mountain locusts" that crunched like snow underfoot.

While the wheat, rye, and barley crops were too ripe for the grasshoppers' palates, they swarmed every stalk of corn, devouring them down to their cobs, and then ate those, too. The swarm stayed in O'Neill for a day, no more than two, before flying east to continue its destruction, leaving behind only the stubble of cornstalks.

The great "grasshopper raid" devastated the newly planted crops that the nascent colony relied upon for subsistence. The harvest of 1874 did not come close to approaching the 250 to 300 bushels per acre that O'Neill had promised.

Although newcomers had trickled in throughout the summer, by October 1, 1874, all but five of the original colonists had abandoned the settlement. As the first settlement prepared for the onset of winter, O'Neill returned to the East to begin recruiting his next colony.

Encouraged by a report from the land agent Fahy promising a large hotel and several businesses in a "thickly settled" colony, a second group of pioneers ventured to Nebraska in the spring of 1875, eager to settle in what they heard was a bustling hamlet.

The colonists arrived in a colony with no stores, no buildings. The town was just a motley collection of sod houses and dugouts. The settlers had visions of lazy afternoons rocking in chairs on the veranda of the Grand Central Hotel. They discovered it was a sarcastic moniker for the most rudimentary of shelters. They didn't appreciate the humor.

Believing they had been swindled to come to a godforsaken land, many of the new arrivals blamed O'Neill. After all, his name was on the place. They thought the general who had led the Irish into a folly in Canada had now done the same in the American heartland.

Desperate to salvage his reputation from another tarnishing, O'Neill denounced Fahy in *The Irish World* and gave every man who purchased lots in O'Neill an equal number in a new eighty-acre addition to the town. The offer renewed public confidence in his embryonic Irish American colony.

The arrival of O'Neill's wife, children, and two oldest nephews also buoyed his spirits. A pregnant Mary Ann had traveled west with the original colony the prior year but remained with the children in Omaha, 180 miles away, to give birth. Once O'Neill's white clapboard residence was completed in 1875, baby Katherine, six-year-old Mary Ella, and eight-year-old John made their new house a home.

That was quickly followed by the construction of the town's first general store, church, and school. After the discovery of gold in the nearby Black Hills, the merchants of O'Neill made the real fortune by selling supplies to the prospectors. Although the colonists continued to duel with the dreaded grasshoppers, relations with the native Pawnees remained friendly.

In the spring of 1876, O'Neill led a third colony of 102 men, women, and children to Nebraska and followed that the next year with a migration of 71 men. With plans to plant as many as one hundred settlements on the prairie, he established a Philadelphia headquarters for "O'Neill's Irish American Colonies" and hired an experienced Fenian recruiter, Colonel William MacWilliams, to assist him.

By all outward appearances, O'Neill was fixated on his future in Nebraska. In actuality, though, he remained consumed by his obsession from the past.

❀

The general called his colonization work "the next best thing to fighting for Ireland," and while he thought it noble work, it wasn't his true calling. "I shall continue at it despite every obstacle until called upon for sterner work when I will be found where an O'Neill properly belongs," he wrote, "which is not so much in talking about Ireland's wrongs, as in fighting for Ireland's rights."

O'Neill cryptically mandated that one-eighth of the land for each of his colonies be "devoted to the cause of Ireland," and by the end of 1876 the general viewed his burgeoning colonies as bases of operation from which he could amass an army to rise against the British and possibly return to Canada. The profile of the typical pioneer—young, male, and daring—made for an ideal soldier. Plus, his secluded towns were away from the prying eyes of federal authorities and British spies.

"I had a double object in encouraging our people to emigrate from the overcrowded cities and states of the east to settle upon the cheap and free lands of the west," O'Neill admitted. "The first was that they might better their own condition and that of their families and the second that they might be in a position, from their improved circumstances and their nearness to the contemplated field of future operations, to assist the cause of Irish liberty. I think I can safely promise from the colonies which I have already established at least some of the young men to assist on the battle field while the older ones are raising corn, flour, potatoes to help sustain them."

The general received a report from the Black Hills that the Irishmen there were ready to follow his command to the battlefield whenever ordered. Until O'Neill was ready to move, they would bide their time and hone their skills.*

"The prairies are wide, and there is plenty of room for drill and instruction," O'Neill wrote, "and there is no law against shooting deer and antelope, in season which will be very good practice— until we can find other game." There was little doubt that the game O'Neill coveted roamed north of the border and across the ocean.

❀

The movement that O'Neill had helped give rise to fed off the fervor of its participants. But without Anglophobia, fresh memories of the Great Hunger, and nativism to fuel it, the Fenian Brotherhood had become a spent force by the time O'Neill settled in Nebraska. Forever mired in its foibles, it had become eclipsed, in the repub-

---

* Decades later, the Nebraska newspaperman John G. Maher, a purveyor of tall tales, printed stories that the British sought revenge for attacks on Canada and planned to dispatch warships up the Mississippi, Missouri, and Niobrara Rivers to capture the city bearing O'Neill's name.

lican movement, by Clan na Gael (Irish for "Family of the Gaels"), which had been launched in 1867 as a haven for Fenians who had had enough of the organization's dysfunction and lack of secrecy. The upstart organization raised funds and procured arms to free Ireland by physical force. But it forswore any raids on Canada. In 1876, Clan na Gael* staged the most electrifying moment for the Irish republican movement in America since the Battle of Ridgeway when it purchased the whaling bark *Catalpa,* sailed it halfway around the world, and rescued six Fenians held captive in the British penal colony of Western Australia.

The Fenian Brotherhood was a shadow of its former self. So was John O'Mahony, who had returned to lead the organization he founded after being elected head center in 1872. The Young Irelander was now anything but young. Years of stress and poverty had aged him beyond his years. The luster had evaporated from his deep-sunken eyes, leaving him "the mere framework of a mighty man," according to John Boyle O'Reilly.

The Fenian Brotherhood survived until 1887, but O'Mahony wouldn't last that long. With Bernard Doran Killian, who had directed the first Fenian raid from Eastport, at his side, the "Father of Fenianism" died inside a spartan fourth-floor garret atop a dingy New York tenement house on February 6, 1877, at the age of sixty-two.

"He was not merely the guide or fabricator of Fenianism. He, more than any man alive or dead, was the spirit and subtending principle of the movement," O'Reilly wrote. "His whole life and aspirations were bound up in one word—Fenianism."

The Fenian Brotherhood decided to honor O'Mahony by re-creating one of his greatest triumphs, the transatlantic farewell for his fellow Young Irelander Terence Bellew MacManus in 1861. The Fenians embalmed O'Mahony's body in preparation for a send-off worthy of a head of state. After a solemn requiem funeral Mass celebrated by three Jesuit priests who ignored the Vatican decrees

---

* Dispatched once again in service of his native Great Britain, the secret agent Henri Le Caron infiltrated Clan na Gael as he did the Fenian Brotherhood. Le Caron managed to maintain his alias—and his secret—for more than a quarter century until he revealed his true identity in 1889 before a special parliamentary committee investigating the connections between the Irish constitutional nationalist Charles Stewart Parnell and Clan na Gael.

about the Fenian Brotherhood, thousands of Irishmen accompanied a plate-glass hearse that bore O'Mahony's body up Fifth Avenue and down Broadway to a waiting steamship that bore the child of Erin back to mother Ireland.

Following torchlight processions through the streets of Queenstown and Cork, O'Mahony's coffin arrived in Dublin, where Cardinal Paul Cullen shuttered the doors of the city's churches to the Fenian founder. Cullen's decision only strengthened the resolve of the Fenians to turn O'Mahony's funeral into a political protest. On Sunday, March 4, 250,000 people participated in one of the biggest public demonstrations seen in Dublin since the mock funeral for the Manchester Martyrs as O'Mahony's funeral cortege rolled through the city's muddy lanes to Glasnevin Cemetery.

Fenian hands lowered O'Mahony into the same grave containing the bones of MacManus. After mourners showered flowers on the lid of his casket, they shoveled the Irish earth on its native son. "Outlaws and felons according to English law but true soldiers of Irish liberty," read the inscription on the monument eventually erected over the grave of O'Mahony, MacManus, and four other Fenians. "Their lives thus prove that every generation produces patriots who were willing to face the gibbet, the cell, and exile to procure the liberty of their nation and afford perpetual proof that in the Irish heart faith in Irish nationality is indestructible."

❧

Back in the United States, O'Neill continued his fight. He split his time between growing his colonies in Nebraska and touring the country in search of more recruits who might eventually join his next army. The workload took a toll on his health, and when the general returned home after delivering a lecture in Little Rock, Arkansas, in November 1877, Mary Ann O'Neill could see that her husband was not well.

A cold he had developed on the five-day journey home exacerbated his chronic asthma. Then, on his first night home, he suffered a slight stroke. After he recovered for a few weeks at home, Mary Ann, pregnant once again with their daughter Genevieve, took him on the long trip to St. Joseph Hospital in Omaha for further treatment. As her husband's condition improved, Mary Ann felt confident enough that he was on the road to recovery to return home to their three children. Following Mary Ann's departure, however, O'Neill contracted pneumonia after falling and spending hours on a cold floor before anyone discovered him there.

He passed away during the final hour of January 7, four thousand miles from home.

Unlike O'Mahony, the forty-three-year-old O'Neill was buried in American soil, but not in the town that bore his name. Too many of the Irish colonists there remained bitter toward the general, believing him a swindler who had falsely represented Nebraska as an Eden for the Irish. The hard feelings remained even a decade after his death, when a proposal was made to rebury O'Neill in the town. "Leave him in Omaha," said a town spokesman. "He led the Irish astray, and was the cause of their suffering tragic hardships."

He might have had detractors, but the Irish would remember O'Neill as the dashing hero of Ridgeway, a soldier who defeated the British on their own soil. Some wished that the climactic moment of his life had come at the end, rather than at the beginning, of his Fenian career. "In our short-sighted human judgement we cannot help wishing rather that, ere errors of head, not of heart, diverted him from the path of true patriotism, he had fallen, in the flush of victory, at Ridgeway, like so many of his race with the old flag over head, and the charging cry of Ireland ringing in his ear," declared *The Irish-American*.

Perhaps the Fenian general felt the same way. John O'Neill had been born to fight the British and die on the battlefield for Ireland. He managed to fulfill half of his destiny.

EPILOGUE

J AMES STEPHENS WAS dead again.

For the second time in fifty-three years, the ink-stained fingers of Kilkenny's pressmen laid the type for the obituary of their native son. Unlike the death notice from 1848, the words printed in the spring of 1901 conveyed the truth.

With the Union Jack still flying over Ireland, the British government had finally permitted Stephens to return to his homeland in 1891 under one condition—no public demonstrations against the Crown. A quarter century after the Irish Republican Brotherhood founder struck terror in British hearts and escaped Ireland as the most wanted man in the empire, Stephens returned to Dublin an impoverished old man, more pitied than feared.

On Palm Sunday, two days after his death, the Fenian chief's oak and mahogany coffin—draped in the Irish republican tricolor of green, white, and orange—was lifted into a hearse and drawn by six horses on a five-hour procession through Dublin.

In fading daylight, the cortege squeezed through the gates of Glasnevin Cemetery and rolled through a dense forest of Celtic crosses to the hallowed "republican plot," which housed Ireland's most precious relics—the bones of its heroic patriots who fought British tyranny. The hearse stopped just steps away from the final resting place of John O'Mahony. The two Fenian giants who had fought the British—and each other—were now reunited in death.

For decades, Stephens had carried the republican movement on his shoulders. Now it was time for those he inspired to return the favor. Veterans of the 1867 Fenian Rising placed the coffin of the Fenian chief on their shoulders and lowered it into the ground next to his wife.

Critics said Stephens failed in his life's work because free Irish soil was not shoveled on his grave, but what they didn't understand was that true failure would have been to do nothing at all.

"If we ever hope to see Ireland free, we must honor the attempt as well as the triumph," Dr. Denis Dowling Mulcahy said after O'Mahony's funeral. The leading IRB member knew the island would be forever British if fear of failure deterred Ireland's patriots from attempting the fight. The Irish might have been subjugated, but they couldn't be conquered as long as they resisted, just as Stephens had.

The arrogance, insecurity, and dictatorial tendencies of Stephens undeniably infected the IRB and its relationship with the Fenian Brotherhood in the United States. Yet Stephens had awakened Ireland from its national stupor after the trauma of the Great Hunger and the failure of the 1848 rebellion. With his death, he joined the legends in the mists of Irish history. The Irish placed his picture on their walls next to those of Theobald Wolfe Tone, Robert Emmet, and the other rebels whom the IRB founder had heard about as a child.

A fresh crop of curious Irish children who gathered around fireplaces heard their parents tell the tales of the ghost of a man thought to be dead who walked the length of Ireland and prophesied that one day they would be free. They heard the stories of the old days when young men and martyrs rose up against the British in 1848 and 1867. This new generation weaned on the legends of Stephens and his fellow Fenians would ultimately seize the opportunity to evict the British after centuries of tyrannical rule.

❧

"Ireland's opportunity will come when England is engaged in a desperate struggle with some great European power or European combination," the Fenian John Devoy predicted in 1881. That time finally came more than thirty years later when a gunshot on a Sarajevo street tore through the jugular of Archduke Franz Ferdinand and launched World War I.

With Great Britain consumed by the horror of the grinding trench warfare on the western front, a fresh crop of IRB leaders such as Tom Clarke, who had worked as an assistant editor on Devoy's newspaper during a nearly ten-year stint in the United States, believed their moment had arrived. While the IRB's military council continued its secret planning for another rising, Clarke received a telegram from his old friend Devoy on June 29, 1915: "Rossa dead. What shall we do?" Devoy's fellow member of the Cuba Five Jeremiah O'Donovan Rossa had passed away earlier that day at the age of eighty-three. Eager to repeat the transatlantic funerals of O'Mahony and Terence Bellew MacManus and stage a Fenian pageant that would greatly assist with recruitment, Clarke wasted little time in sending his response.

"Send his body home at once."

On the first day of August in 1915, hundreds of thousands of people lined the streets of Dublin to honor the Fenian firebrand who took the violent fight for Ireland's independence to the very heart of the country he believed responsible for the suffering he had witnessed during the Great Hunger. After assuming the leadership of the Fenian Brotherhood, Rossa employed a relatively new technology capable of inflicting mass casualties—dynamite.

Following the blueprint established by O'Mahony and Stephens of using the United States as his base of operations, he oversaw the building of explosives in Brooklyn and dispatched operatives to Great Britain throughout the first half of the 1880s to carry out a terrifying bombing campaign that struck not only British military and commercial targets, such as arsenals and gasworks, but also iconic London landmarks including Victoria Station and the Tower of London. The Fenians bombed a pub next to Scotland Yard, which resulted in the destruction of police records on them, and even the inner sanctum of the British government, the chamber of the House of Commons.

The Fenian whom the newspapers began to call "O'Dynamite Rossa" even took credit for mayhem with which he had no connection. When Queen Victoria injured herself slipping on a step at Windsor Castle, Rossa said it was his agents who applied the lard to grease the stairs.

Rossa's "dynamite campaign" came to an end in 1885, the same year an Englishwoman shot him in the back on a Manhattan street in a failed assassination attempt. He endured for another three decades before his death on Staten Island and the return of his body to Ireland.

The Fenian's funeral procession took hours to pass spots along the route to Dublin's Glasnevin Cemetery, where Rossa's grave awaited inside the republican plot. The political theater orchestrated by the IRB had a stirring finale, as Padraig Pearse, a little-known school headmaster and member of the IRB's secret military council, stepped forward in his Irish Volunteer uniform to deliver the graveside oration, which he said was "on behalf of a new generation that has been re-baptized in the Fenian faith. . . .

"The seeds sown by the young men of '65 and '67 are coming to their miraculous ripening today," Pearse said in homage to the previous generation. "They think that they have pacified Ireland. They think that they have purchased half of us and intimidated the other half. They think that they have foreseen everything, think that they have provided against everything; but the fools, the fools, the fools! They have left us our Fenian dead, and, while Ireland holds these graves, Ireland unfree shall never be at peace."

The speech was followed by three volleys over the grave of Rossa. In hindsight they had the ring of revolution.

The day after commemorating Christ's resurrection in the pews of Ireland, the IRB rose anew on Easter Monday 1916. Nearly fifty years after John O'Neill led the Irish Republican Army charging across the Niagara Peninsula to strike a blow for Ireland, another group of young Irishmen grabbed their guns to undertake what most of their countrymen thought to be a folly.

Less than a year after delivering the oration over Rossa's grave, Pearse and more than one thousand latter-day Fenians seized buildings in downtown Dublin and launched an armed insurrection. At four minutes past noon on April 24, 1916, as the final peals of the Angelus bells dissolved over Dublin, Pearse stood under the massive pillars of the General Post Office with Clarke and other IRB members to read a formal proclamation declaring the establishment of the Irish Republic.

"In the name of God and of the dead generations from which she receives her old tradition of nationhood, Ireland, through us, summons her children to her flag and strikes for her freedom," shouted Pearse. "She now seizes that moment, and, supported by her exiled children in America and by gallant allies in Europe, but relying in the first on her own strength, she strikes in full confidence of victory."

Her exiled children in America. The prominent place given to the diaspora in the United States in the foundation document of the Irish Republic acknowledged that the Easter Rising would not have been possible without the transatlantic partnership first established by Stephens and O'Mahony. Devoy estimated that Clan na Gael supplied the IRB with nearly $100,000 in the years preceding the Easter Rising. In addition, five of the seven signatories of the Irish Proclamation had spent considerable time in the United States. Clarke had even become a naturalized American citizen.

Fierce street fighting between the rebels and the British army turned the heart of Dublin into smoldering rubble for six days before Pearse offered an unconditional surrender. The last man out of the General Post Office before it was consumed by flames was a naturalized American citizen as well, the IRB supreme council member Diarmuid Lynch.

The Easter Rising claimed nearly five hundred lives, more than half of them civilians caught in the cross fire. The British responded by arresting more than thirty-five hundred suspected IRB sympathizers.

Like the Fenians who raided Canada, the leaders of the Easter Rising were political radicals who lacked the mantle of a popular mandate. Their rebellion might have ended in futility like so many Irish insurrections before them had the British not forgotten the lessons from the time of Stephens and O'Mahony.

Rather than grant clemency to the leaders of the Easter Rising as they had for the Fenian raids and the 1848 and 1867 rebellions, the British executed by firing squad the seven Irish Proclamation signatories—including Pearse and Clarke—and seven other rebel leaders just weeks after the rebellion.

Outrage followed the judicial murders, just as it had after the execution of the Manchester Martyrs. By killing the Easter Rising leaders, the British had transformed another Irish military failure into a political success. Pearse and his fellow patriots became the latest blood sacrifice on the altar of Irish freedom.

As W. B. Yeats wrote in his poem "Easter, 1916," "All changed, changed utterly."

❦

By creating a fresh set of martyrs, the British fueled a revolution that would eventually lead to the fulfillment of most of the Fenians' dreams. Irish republicans formed their own breakaway parliament, which declared independence from Great Britain and proclaimed itself the legislature of the new Irish Republic in 1919. They gained their own country in 1922 with the establishment of the semi-autonomous Irish Free State after the two-and-a-half-year Irish War of Independence, although Ireland remained a British dominion similar to Canada.

However, freedom did not come with peace. Irish republicans cleaved once again, this time over the treaty with the British, which ceded only twenty-six of the island's thirty-two counties to the Irish Free State. The remaining six counties in the north of Ireland remained British territory. An ensuing civil war might have killed even more Irishmen than the British had in the battle for their freedom. Not until 1949 were the last strings with the British Crown severed with the formal establishment of the Republic of Ireland.

Present through all the turmoil was an Easter Rising commandant who was born in the United States and spared the firing squad—Éamon de Valera. The most seminal figure of Irish history in the twentieth century, de Valera served for more than thirty years as either Ireland's head of government or its head of state. The rebel carrying a gun through Dublin in 1916 was the same man to offer official welcome to America's first Irish Catholic president, John F. Kennedy, when he visited Ireland in 1963.

Like the Irish republican movement itself, de Valera had strong ties to the United States. Born in New York City on October 14, 1882, he was brought to Ireland in 1885 after his father's death. When de Valera became one of two Easter Rising leaders to receive clemency from their death sentences, some suspected that his American birth had saved him. The real reason, however, was likely the luck of being one of the last scheduled to be killed. By the time of his planned execution date, the British had relented in the wake of the backlash.

Following his clemency, de Valera led the IRB's political wing,

Sinn Féin, and was elected president of the Irish Volunteers, which would come to be known as the Irish Republican Army during the War of Independence. The British sent him back to prison for plotting against them, but he managed to stage a prison break with a culinary twist. De Valera made a waxed impression of a master key taken from the prison chaplain while he celebrated Mass, and IRB accomplices baked the duplicate key inside a cake delivered to him in England's Lincoln Prison. While Irish girls flirted with the prison guards as a distraction, de Valera used the key to escape the jail.

On the lam, de Valera became president of Ireland's breakaway parliament and stowed away on a ship in June 1919 to return to the country of his birth in order to raise money and support for the establishment of an Irish Republic. There he would give thanks to the leader of the "men of action" who had preceded him in the fight for freedom.

❀

Much as Stephens had done several times half a century earlier, de Valera toured the United States in hopes of raising badly needed funds, speaking before thousands of people in Boston, Chicago, and San Francisco. When he arrived in Omaha at the end of October 1919, he passed through the gates of Holy Sepulchre Cemetery and joined the congregation around the fifteen-foot-high granite column that had been christened by locals the "shrine of the Fenians." Adorned with swords, shamrocks, an Irish harp, and an American eagle, the memorial had been erected by the Emmet Monument Association over the grave of John O'Neill on the crest of the cemetery's hill.

Incredibly, the idea of an Irish invasion of Canada did not die with O'Neill. While an Irish brigade took up arms against the British during the Boer War in the south of Africa, newspapers printed reports of Fenians amassing in Dunkirk, New York, on the day after Christmas in 1899 to prepare for an invasion of America's northern neighbor. The report turned out to be baseless, but in April 1900 three Clan na Gael members did dynamite a lock of the Welland Canal in Ontario, causing some damage but not the hoped-for catastrophic flood.

De Valera's attendance at the monument's official dedication reflected the important role played by O'Neill and the Fenian

Brotherhood in advancing the cause of Irish independence. The Fenian Brotherhood was the first to organize the Irish diaspora into financial and material support that flowed from America to Ireland. It made the United States a player in Anglo-Irish relations, a role that would continue in Northern Ireland, and demonstrated that America could provide Irish republicans with a base of operations beyond the legal reach of the British government.

While O'Neill and his fellow "men of action" could have simply talked about the liberation of Ireland as they luxuriated in their freedom three thousand miles away from the suffering, they instead offered their blood. They left a legacy of freedom on two continents. Many of them had taken up arms in the Union army that liberated African Americans from slavery. They were incidentally responsible for the creation of a new nation; in no small part due to the Fenian raids, Canada gained the right to self-government in 1867, pointing it toward its ultimate independence. Although plagued by naïveté, disunity, and indiscretion, the Fenian Brotherhood was a link in the chain of history that led Irish republicans to ultimately topple the British lion.

De Valera stepped forward in the Holy Sepulchre Cemetery and spoke of O'Neill's connection to Irish independence. "The Fenian Brotherhood for which General O'Neill fought is the backbone of the Irish republic," de Valera intoned. "We have vindicated O'Neill by establishing the republic."

De Valera bent down to place a wreath of roses at the base of the great granite shaft below the words inscribed on O'Neill's grave marker:

> By nature a brave man. By principle a soldier of liberty. He fought with distinction for his adopted country and was ever ready to draw his sword for his native land.
> God Save Ireland.

Acknowledgments

While writing can be a solitary endeavor, writing this book would not have been possible without the support of a small army of contributors.

For seven centuries, the Irish people defied attempts to exterminate their culture in part by keeping alive the tales of those who dared to resist. In that vein, I owe a debt of gratitude to previous generations of authors, historians, and scholars who chronicled and preserved the story of the Fenian Brotherhood. Their diligent efforts served as the foundation upon which this book was constructed.

I owe particular thanks to scores of archivists and librarians. They are the unsung guardians of the knowledge and facts that enlighten our world. Seldom has their work been as vital as it is at this moment in time.

My humble library card served as a remarkable passport to the past. The ability to have books and documents delivered to me from repositories across the United States greatly aided my research. Thank you to Tricia Donnelly and the staff at Memorial Hall Library in my hometown of Andover, Massachusetts, who assisted in fulfilling my numerous interlibrary loan requests. I am also indebted to the volunteers of the Lawrence, Massachusetts, division of the Ancient Order of Hibernians and the staff of the South Lawrence Branch Library who maintain a voluminous collection of books on Irish and Irish American history just down the road.

Thank you as well to the librarians, curators, and archivists of the Allen County Library, Anderson Public Library, Archdiocese of Omaha, Boston Athenaeum, John J. Burns Library at Boston College, Bytown Museum, Catholic University of America, Clogher Historical Society, Diocese of Burlington, Filson Historical Society, Fort Erie Historical Museum, Franklin County (N.Y.) Historical and Museum Society, Franklin (Vt.) Historical Society, Haverhill Public Library, Library and Archives Canada, Library of Congress, Madison County Historical Society, McCord Museum, Minnesota Historical Society, Missouri Historical Society Library and Research Center, Monaghan County Library Services, National Library of Ireland, New York Public Library, Ogdensburg Public Library, Omaha Public Library, St. Albans Free Library, Saint Albans Museum, Santa Clara University, SUNY Plattsburgh, Swem Library at the College of William & Mary, University of Notre Dame, Western Reserve Historical Society, and Wilson's Creek National Battlefield.

Particular thanks go to Julie Madlin; Tom Fox; Arlene Royea Ayotte of the Brome County Historical Society; Ellen Gressling and Alexandra Mills from Concordia University's Special Collections; Kathy Flynn and Amita Kiley of the Lawrence History Center; Rolande Laduke of the Missisquoi Historical Society; Tiffany Link and the staff of the Maine Historical Society; and Fiona Anthes, Eric Fernberg, and the staff of the Canadian War Museum.

I'm grateful to Bob Bateman for sharing information on his ancestor Timothy Deasy and to Sheridan Vincent, who provided information on Margaret Vincent and her family. Mary Lynn Rakebrand Sedivec shared ancestral information on John O'Neill. From Ireland, John Makem offered valuable insight into General O'Neill, the O'Neill clan, and the impact of the Great Hunger in County Monaghan and Clontibret.

Natalie Butterfield shared her knowledge about O'Neill, Nebraska, and demonstrated that the Fenian spirit endures in the Cornhusker State. Jeannie Mejstrik was a tremendous help in supplying photographs and archival materials from the O'Neill Public Library. Thanks to both for their sanity checks on my writings about the history of their town. Fellow authors Ellen Alden, Steve Jungmann, and J. M. Erickson also offered their feedback on chapter drafts as well as welcome words of support.

Thanks to the members of the Fenian Brotherhood Emmet Circle of NY & NJ who took the time to answer my questions. In particular, Jim Madden proved a valuable font of knowledge about Fenian firearms and uniforms.

One of the highlights of my research was visiting with Carole Richard on the family's ancestral farmland along the U.S.-Canada border in Franklin, Vermont. Carole kindly welcomed me into her home to show me artifacts left behind by the retreating Irish Republican Army and gave me a glimpse at the farmhouse from which Alvah Richard twice watched the Fenians invade Canada.

Ireland's story has always been told in song, and another highlight was attending a concert by Derek Warfield & the Young Wolfe Tones that brought Ireland's patriotic tunes and revolutionary spirit to life. Derek was very gracious with his time and willingness to share his research on John O'Neill and the Fenian movement.

Thanks to my agent, Katherine Flynn, whose enthusiasm for the idea of a book on the Fenian raids on Canada was a source of great encouragement. Part cheerleader, part therapist, Katherine served as a welcome source of inspiration and calm at my most frenzied moments.

I am deeply indebted to the extraordinarily talented team at Doubleday. Foremost thanks to Yaniv Soha, my editor, for believing in me and in the potential of this project. His patience and steady hand were of great comfort and value. Yaniv's editorial direction, along with that of Cara Reilly, sharpened my prose and distilled a supersized manuscript to a more manageable narrative without losing any of the vital elements of the story.

Production editor Nora Reichard and the copyediting staff polished the narrative with a careful eye. Any mistakes that remain are mine alone. Kudos to enormously talented designer Michael J. Windsor for his dramatic and colorful jacket, and thanks to the production and marketing teams at Doubleday.

Of course this book would not have been possible without the love, patience, and unwavering support of my family. My children, Drew and Sydney, have been boundless sources of encouragement and flashed their potential as future editors by asking me on a regular basis if I had finally finished the book. The act of writing might not be an easy undertaking but neither is being married to a writer. I had the luck of the Irish in marrying my wife, Erin. She bore the burden without complaint when I was traveling to archives or simply time traveling in my writer's bunker.

Finally, to generations of Milmoes, Whalens, Turners, and all my ancestors from Ireland who endured famine and hardship before starting a new life in a new country, thank you for your persistence.

Notes

Abbreviations

ACHS: American Catholic Historical Society and maintained at the Catholic Historical Research Center of the Archdiocese of Philadelphia

BCHS: Brome County Historical Society

CUA: Catholic University of America, American Catholic History Research Center and University Archives, Fenian Brotherhood Collection

LAC: Sir John A. Macdonald Fonds, Library and Archives Canada

MHS: Missouri Historical Society, Fenian Brotherhood Papers

NYPL: Thomas William Sweeny Papers, Manuscripts and Archives Division, New York Public Library

PIT: Allen Family Papers, University of Pittsburgh, ULS Archives and Special Collections

Prologue

2 Wearing green ribbons: Kohler, "For I Never Would Have Surrendered," 12–13; *Buffalo Express*, June 1, 1866.

2 nine wagons laden with secretly stockpiled rifles: *Fenian Raid at Fort Erie*, 30.

2 "The governing passion of my life": Noonan, "General John O'Neill," 318.

2 "Canada is a province": *Official Report of Gen. John O'Neill*, 3–4.

Chapter 1: The Young Irelanders

7 An outlaw in his own land: Doheny, *Felon's Track*, 138.

7 The *Kilkenny Moderator: Times* (London), Aug. 21, 1848.

7 To further the ruse: *James Stephens, Chief Organizer of the Irish Republic,* 34.

7 They laid the casket: Ryan, *Fenian Chief,* 41–42.

8 A voracious reader: Ibid., 340.

8 Covering as many as forty miles a day: Doheny, *Felon's Track,* 123–38.

8 Along his trek: Ibid., 132–43.

9 Under the Penal Laws: MacManus, *Story of the Irish Race,* 458–59.

9 They were permitted to own a knife: Ó Dufaigh, *Book of Clontibret,* 358.

9 An eldest son: Plemmons, *Fianna,* 35.

9 Even in death: Stern, "How Dagger John Saved New York's Irish."

10 The average adult workingman: Callahan, *Emerging Biological Threats,* 169.

10 Because they required less space: Kelly, *Graves Are Walking,* 8.

11 When the horror reappeared in 1846: Smith, "Ghosts in Green," 39.

11 Frantic farmers sprinkled: Crowley, *Atlas of the Great Irish Famine,* 30.

11 Emaciated figures, tired of a diet: Kelly, *Graves Are Walking,* 1–2.

11 Ireland's damp conditions: Lee, *Making the Irish American,* 90.

11 Jail populations in Ireland exploded: Kelly, *Graves Are Walking,* 336.

12 "Irish property must": Lee, *Making the Irish American,* 90–91.

12 The resulting spike in taxes: Kelly, *Graves Are Walking,* 335.

12 "Relief ought to be": *Edinburgh Review,* Jan. 1848, 314.

12 "The judgement of God": Coogan, *Famine Plot,* 63–64.

12 Although far more food was imported: Kelly, *Graves Are Walking,* 310.

13 "holy war to sweep": Webb, *Compendium of Irish Biography,* 341.

14 After seeing famished children: Mitchel, *Last Conquest of Ireland (Perhaps),* 148.

14 By the light of the summertime moon: Ryan, *Fenian Chief,* 6–8.

15 On the evening of July 25: Ibid., 7–11.

15 After the meeting: Ramón, *Provisional Dictator,* 31.

15 Although descended from the medieval: Kee, *Ireland,* 104.

15 His appeal to O'Brien's sense: Gwynn, *Young Ireland and 1848,* 250–51.

16 Sure enough, as soon as the rebels: Ryan, *Fenian Chief,* 19.

16 "General, in the name of Jesus": Ibid., 23–26.

16 Stephens and Terence Bellew MacManus: Ryan, *Phoenix Flame,* 32.

17 "We are all Irishmen": *Report of the Trial of W. S. O'Brien for High Treason,* 432.

17 "An O'Brien never": Duffy, "Four Years of Irish History," 88.

18 Stephens directed the remaining rebels: Ramón, *Provisional Dictator,* 36–42.

18 Stephens crumpled to the ground: *James Stephens, Chief Organizer of the Irish Republic,* 32.

18 He was descended from the chieftain: Devoy, *Recollections of an Irish Rebel,* 266.

18 Following the example of his grandfather: Sayers, "John O'Mahony," 52.

18 "I kept away from any public adhesion": Cavanagh, *Memoirs of Gen. Thomas Francis Meagher,* 265.
18 The pair spent the night: Sayers, "John O'Mahony," 91.
19 It would take years: *James Stephens, Chief Organizer of the Irish Republic,* 36.
19 The pair left O'Mahony: Ramón, *Provisional Dictator,* 46–47.
19 Stephens rejected a notion: Doheny, *Felon's Track,* 141.
19 In addition, two weeks earlier: Kinealy, *Repeal and Revolution,* 203.
20 "All the time that I appeared": Ramón, *Provisional Dictator,* 46–47.
20 After traveling across England: Ibid., 48.
20 Paris became a home in exile: Ryan, *Fenian Chief,* 43.
20 In August 1849: Ramón, *Provisional Dictator,* 57.
20 Inside their derelict room: Ryan, *Fenian Chief,* 46–47.
20 "Once I resolved that armed insurrection": Delany, *The Green and the Red,* 43.
20 Whether or not the Irishmen: Sayers, "John O'Mahony," 159–62.
21 For his portion: *National Labor Tribune,* March 17, 1877.
21 Four years of a Parisian exile: Sayers, "John O'Mahony," 164–67.

Chapter 2: Bold Fenian Men

22 John O'Mahony followed in the wake: Libby, "Maine and the Fenian Invasion of Canada," 216.
22 Some emigrants reported: Bartoletti, *Black Potatoes,* 128.
23 By the 1850s, more than a quarter: Strausbaugh, *City of Sedition,* 55.
23 Breathing putrid air: Stern, "How Dagger John Saved New York's Irish."
23 "America for Americans!": *Christian Register,* Aug. 19, 1854.
23 Know-Nothings advocated an increase: Davis, *Nation Rising,* 212.
24 According to some scholars: Bayor, *New York Irish,* 253, 634.
24 Rumors even spread: Davis, *Nation Rising,* 201.
24 In March 1854, Know-Nothings seized: Klein, "When Washington, D.C., Gave the Pope a Truly Rocky Reception."
24 They mandated the reading: *Irish Times,* March 21, 2016.
24 They disbanded Irish American militia units: Samito, *Becoming American Under Fire,* 17–24.
25 O'Mahony could encounter signs: *New York Times,* Sept. 25, 1854; *New York Herald,* May 13, 1853.
25 "This is an English colony": Dolan, *Irish Americans,* 187.
26 Mitchel's broadsides against hypocritical abolitionists: Weiss, *Life and Correspondence of Theodore Parker,* 397.
26 "When my country": Kee, *Green Flag,* 168.
26 Members drilled weekly: Stephens, *Birth of the Fenian Movement,* 83–84.

26 Their activities in New York: Brundage, *Irish Nationalists in America*, 96–97.
27 "There can be no such thing": Lawson, *Defences to Crime*, 671.
27 "There seems to me no more hope": Ramón, *Provisional Dictator*, 77.
27 Out of touch with his family: Ryan, *Fenian Chief*, 59.
28 With its people still processing: Ibid., 323.
28 To get a better sense: *James Stephens, Chief Organizer of the Irish Republic*, 41.
28 "The cause is not dead": Ryan, *Fenian Chief*, 80–81.
28 He wrote to Stephens: Golway, *For the Cause of Liberty*, 128.
28 At the close of December 1857: *Boston Post*, May 17, 1866.
29 In addition to £80 to £100 per month: Denieffe, *Personal Narrative of the Irish Revolutionary Brotherhood*, 159–60.
29 Stephens couldn't take it as anything: D'Arcy, *Fenian Movement*, 11–12.
29 As Ireland commemorated: Stephens, *Birth of the Fenian Movement*, 76.
29 To maintain secrecy: Evans, *Fanatic Heart*, 25–26.
30 "He seemed to have me": Ryan, *Fenian Chief*, 90–99.
30 Stephens again dispatched Denieffe: Stephens, *Birth of the Fenian Movement*, xxv.
30 "The Irish-Americans will not subscribe": Ryan, *Fenian Chief*, 110.
30 In his diary, Stephens described: Delany, *The Green and the Red*, 66–67; Stephens, *Birth of the Fenian Movement*, 8–26.
31 In early 1859, O'Mahony would: D'Arcy, *Fenian Movement*, 12–13.
31 The group started with: *Proceedings of the First National Convention*, 8.
31 Stephens returned to Ireland: Stephens, *Birth of the Fenian Movement*, 56–77.
32 "Those who denounce us": D'Arcy, *Fenian Movement*, 15.
33 "It was necessary to get the people": *Boston Post*, May 17, 1866.
33 By November 1859, O'Mahony had organized: D'Arcy, *Fenian Movement*, 16.
33 "reproached him in words": Denieffe, *Personal Narrative of the Irish Revolutionary Brotherhood*, 60.

Chapter 3: The Civil War

34 Irish natives not only accounted: Shiels, " 'Lives of Her Exiled Children Will Be Offered in Thousands.' "
34 "Ireland will be more deeply": *Moore's Rural New Yorker*, Aug. 3, 1861.
34 Feeling a kinship with fellow rebels: Gleeson, *The Green and the Gray*, 41; Damian Shiels, "How Many Irish Fought in the American Civil War?," *Irish in the American Civil War*, Jan. 18, 2015, irishamericancivilwar.com; Shiels, "Time to Move Beyond the Irish Brigade?"
35 The Irish still struggled: Strausbaugh, *City of Sedition*, 176.
35 The County Kilkenny native John O'Keeffe: Donlon, "John O'Keeffe and the Fenian Brotherhood in the American West and Midwest," 86–87.

35 "It is a moral certainty": Cavanagh, *Memoirs of Gen. Thomas Francis Meagher,* 369.

36 Following a funeral Mass: Ibid., 13.

36 On September 16, Archbishop John Joseph Hughes: D'Arcy, *Fenian Movement,* 18.

36 According to Stephens, 150,000 people: *James Stephens, Chief Organizer of the Irish Republic,* 54.

36 "The facecloth is removed": Denieffe, *Personal Narrative of the Irish Revolutionary Brotherhood,* 168.

37 "*One hundred and thirteen pounds*": Stephens to O'Mahony, April 7, 1862, CUA.

37 "No other living man": J. Hamilton (Stephens) to his nephew, Jan. 18, 1865, CUA.

37 "The establishment of the paper": J. Hamilton (Stephens) to O'Mahony, Dec. 11, 1864, CUA.

37 *The Irish People* debuted: *James Stephens, Chief Organizer of the Irish Republic,* 59.

37 On November 11, he got married: Ryan, *Fenian Chief,* 181.

38 Marriage proved an easier go: *James Stephens, Chief Organizer of the Irish Republic,* 60.

38 Although Stephens had stayed true: Golway, *For the Cause of Liberty,* 139.

38 Unwilling to submit: O'Mahony to Charles Joseph Kickham, Oct. 19, 1863, CUA.

38 On October 19, 1863: O'Mahony to James Kelly (Stephens), Oct. 19, 1863, CUA.

38 "I am sick—almost to death": *Inter Ocean,* Dec. 27, 1865.

38 "standing drag-chain and stumbling-block": Ryan, *Fenian Chief,* 194.

38 A group of impatient Fenians: D'Arcy, *Fenian Movement,* 39.

38 On November 3, 1863, eighty-two delegates: *Proceedings of the First National Convention,* 17; Sayers, "John O'Mahony," 255.

39 The head center would now be: D'Arcy, *Fenian Movement,* 35–39.

39 O'Mahony hoped the decision: O'Mahony to Charles Joseph Kickham, Oct. 19, 1863, CUA.

39 Archbishop Peter Richard Kenrick: Rafferty, *The Church, the State, and the Fenian Threat,* 68.

39 The two-week fair: Griffin, " 'Scallions, Pikes, and Bog Oak Ornaments,' " 90–97.

39 "Next year will be": Ryan, *Fenian Chief,* 205.

39 Fenian circles arose: *Proceedings of the Second National Congress,* 22.

40 While the Army of the Potomac: Galwey, *Valiant Hours,* 244–45.

41 O'Mahony and the Fenian Brotherhood's: D'Arcy, *Fenian Movement,* 52.

41	"the deadliest blow": Stephens to the Head Center and Central Council, Fenian Brotherhood, June 24, 1865, CUA.

41	British crews sporting fake: Burnell, "American Civil War Surrender on the Mersey."

42	When Queen Victoria sat down: Victoria, Queen of Great Britain, *Letters of Queen Victoria,* 250.

Chapter 4: Torn Between Brothers

43	As James Stephens continued to promise: Campbell, *Fenian Fire,* 58–59.

43	In a drawer of Luby's nightstand: Devoy, *Devoy's Post Bag,* 165.

43	In addition to decapitating: William G. Halpin to John O'Mahony, Oct. 6, 1865, CUA.

44	"Had we been prepared": J. Daly (Stephens) to O'Mahony, Sept. 16, 1865, CUA.

44	With a £2,300 reward: *Times* (London), March 30, 1901.

44	"Once you hear of my arrest": J. Daly (Stephens) to O'Mahony, Sept. 16, 1865, CUA.

44	General Thomas William Sweeny: Morgan, *Through American and Irish Wars,* 104.

44	Few Americans embodied the spirit: Ibid., 10–11.

45	He wrote that his military service: Jentz and Schneirov, "Chicago's Fenian Fair of 1864," 7.

45	In addition to approving: *Proceedings of the Fourth National Congress of the Fenian Brotherhood,* 30.

46	His Crystal Palace Emporium: *Irish-American,* Jan. 30, 1864.

46	As he filled out his cabinet: Morgan, *Through American and Irish Wars,* 108.

46	Sweeny asserted his belief: Denieffe, *Personal Narrative of the Irish Revolutionary Brotherhood,* 266–68.

46	The lightly defended border: Miller, *Borderline Crime,* 40–42.

47	The patriots erroneously expected: Klein, "7 Times the U.S.-Canada Border Wasn't So Peaceful."

49	While the British governor of Vancouver Island: Ibid.

49	"If we could march into Canada": Stewart, *Reminiscences of Senator William M. Stewart of Nevada,* 177–79.

50	The news, however, could not dampen: Millett, *The Rebel and the Rose,* 213.

50	According to Killian's account: Libby, "Maine and the Fenian Invasion of Canada," 216.

50	The Fenians would hang their expectation: D'Arcy, *Fenian Movement,* 84.

51	A suspicious neighbor had noticed: *Times* (London), March 30, 1901; *Irish Times,* Nov. 13, 1865.

51	"You cannot visit me": *James Stephens, Chief Organizer of the Irish Republic,* 72.

51 He remained with the general population: Dorney, *Griffith College Dublin,* 17.

51 Over the course of a monotonous: Arnold, "Treadmill Originated in Prisons."

51 Two weeks after his arrest: "Statement by Colonel Eamon Broy," 3.

51 Along with the prison turnkey: *Irish-American,* March 30, 1901; "Statement by Colonel Eamon Broy," 10.

52 Fleeing through the prison yard: *Morning News* (Belfast), July 9, 1884.

52 It was in that moment: "Statement by Colonel Eamon Broy," 3–4.

52 The news of Stephens's escape: Rowe, "The Rescue of James Stephens, from Richmond Jail," 63–66.

52 "I do not know him to be a liar": Devoy, *Devoy's Post Bag,* 160.

53 Tasked by the Fenian senate: *New York Herald,* Nov. 18, 1865.

53 They leased the "Fenian White House": To the Members of the Fenian Brotherhood, Circular, Dec. 7, 1865, ACHS.

53 On top of the rent: *Brooklyn Daily Eagle,* Dec. 11, 1865.

53 For a man comfortable wearing: Sayer, "John O'Mahony," 298.

54 The Fenians even issued: D'Arcy, *Fenian Movement,* 112–13.

55 "traitorous diversion from the right path": Denieffe, *Personal Narrative of the Irish Revolutionary Brotherhood,* 207–8.

55 After O'Mahony ordered Killian: Sayers, "John O'Mahony," 300–1.

55 Believing the situation in Ireland: *James Stephens, Chief Organizer of the Irish Republic,* 84.

55 The senate drew up articles: Morgan, *Through American and Irish Wars,* 112.

56 Meeting in special session: D'Arcy, *Fenian Movement,* 104.

56 He retaliated by expelling Roberts: Devoy, *Devoy's Post Bag,* 8.

56 F. B. McNamee reported: McNamee to My Dear Christian, March 26, 1866, NYPL.

56 "It seems to me": Samito, *Becoming American Under Fire,* 179.

56 The British protest might have been: Sweeny to Rawlings, Dec. 9, 1865, NYPL.

57 This meant that O'Mahony: Libby, "Maine and the Fenian Invasion of Canada," 218.

57 Many Irish Americans agreed: *Nashville Daily Union,* Feb. 16, 1866.

57 The measure was overwhelmingly: *Waterford News,* March 16, 1866.

57 "We promise that before the summer": D'Arcy, *Fenian Movement,* 114.

58 The Fenian Brotherhood held: Donlon, "John O'Keeffe and the Fenian Brotherhood in the American West and Midwest," 87.

58 "Father O'Keefe spoke": S. W. McDonald to O'Mahony, March 9, 1865, CUA.

58 The following morning: *Frank Leslie's Illustrated Newspaper,* April 7, 1866.

58   Colonel John W. Byron: Campbell, *Fenian Fire*, 64.

59   In Dublin alone: Samito, *Becoming American Under Fire*, 180.

59   Similar scenes occurred: *Frank Leslie's Illustrated Newspaper,* April 7, 1866.

59   "a profanation of the": Rafferty, *The Church, the State, and the Fenian Threat*, 66.

59   "When the priests descend": Ibid., 81.

59   Now the spymaster had been directed: Neidhardt, " 'We've Nothing Else to Do,' " 5.

60   Rumors flew that the Fenians: Steward and McGovern, *Fenians*, 108.

60   President Johnson had been: Stahr, *Seward*, 467.

60   Secretary of War Edwin Stanton: Welles, *Diary of Gideon Welles*, 2:450–51.

60   "use all vigilance to prevent": *Papers of Ulysses S. Grant*, 16:107–9.

61   "I do not think Sweeny": Neidhardt, "American Government and the Fenian Brotherhood," 34.

61   The first St. Patrick's Day: *Irish-American*, March 24, 1866.

Chapter 5: The Eastport Fizzle

62   Just the day before: *New York Herald*, March 17, 1866.

62   In no mood to parade: *Baltimore Sun*, March 19, 1866.

63   Killian argued that the Fenians: *New York Herald*, April 12, 1866; Nowlan, *Campobello*, 84.

63   Killian reportedly assured: *Chicago Tribune*, May 10, 1866.

63   Having spent months concocting his plan: Steward and McGovern, *Fenians*, 107.

63   Many of them had fled: McCarron, "Ireland Along the Passamaquoddy," 101.

63   The Fenian Brotherhood had just paid: Steward and McGovern, *Fenians*, 166.

64   "the men who propose": Steward and McGovern, *Fenians*, 115.

64   "In my opinion, the real reputation": *Official Report of the Investigating Committee of the Department of Manhattan*, 15.

64   According to O'Mahony, he reluctantly approved: *Chicago Tribune*, May 10, 1866.

64   General Bernard F. Mullen: *Official Report of the Investigating Committee*, 1.

64   "A target for artillery practice": Ibid., 34.

64   He sealed the sailing papers: *Army and Navy Journal*, May 12, 1866; *Official Report of the Investigating Committee*, 3.

65   Fed wild counterintelligence: *New York Herald*, April 5, 1866.

65   In other newspapers, the Fenians planted: *Spirit of Jefferson*, April 17, 1866.

65   The New York *World*, however: New York *World*, April 5, 1866.

65 On April 6, "General" Killian: Vroom, "Fenians on the St. Croix," 411.

65 Rumors of a possible Fenian raid: Davis, "Fenian Raid on New Brunswick," 317–18.

66 "armed and equipped": Libby, "Maine and the Fenian Invasion of Canada," 225.

66 O'Mahony suspected that Killian: *New York World,* April 5, 1866.

66 "Thomas D'Arcy McGee": Harmon, *Fenians and Fenianism,* 80.

66 During the Great Hunger, he accused: Sim, *Union Forever,* 71; Brundage, *Irish Nationalists in America,* 94.

67 He called Fenianism: Neidhardt, " 'We've Nothing Else to Do,' " 5.

67 They were, he said: Senior, "Quebec and the Fenians," 36.

67 The head center ordered Downing: *Army and Navy Journal,* May 12, 1866.

67 "a handsome fellow, glib-tongued": Devoy, *Recollections of an Irish Rebel,* 269.

67 "I notice *you seem*": Downing to O'Mahony, April 20, 1864, CUA.

68 McDermott was selling Fenian secrets: Senior, *Last Invasion of Canada,* 49.

68 "Wherever there are three Fenians": *New York Times,* Jan. 7, 1868.

68 "He was constantly fomenting": Devoy, *Recollections of an Irish Rebel,* 269.

68 One editor of a St. Stephen newspaper: Davis, "Fenian Raid on New Brunswick," 323.

68 "No news travels so freely": Twain, "Unburlesquable Things," 138.

68 When it became clear: Steward and McGovern, *Fenians,* 114.

68 Left without a portion: *Official Report of the Investigating Committee,* 42.

69 *The St. Croix Courier* reported: Libby, "Maine and the Fenian Invasion of Canada," 228.

69 Killian and his officers: *New York Herald,* April 15, 1866.

69 As Killian waited for his cases: Davis, "Fenian Raid on New Brunswick," 322–23.

69 "The Provincials are": Ibid., 323.

69 However, many in Eastport: *Quoddy Tides,* May 13, 1983.

69 The St. John *Telegraph* reported: Davis, "Fenian Raid on New Brunswick," 323.

70 On April 9, eighty Fenians left Portland: *Daily Eastern Argus,* April 10, 1866.

70 By April 11, two British warships: Jenkins, *Fenians and Anglo-American Relations,* 136.

70 In the spirit of Paul Revere: Dallison, *Turning Back the Fenians,* 92.

70 "Arm yourselves! The Fenians": Vesey, "When New Brunswick Suffered Invasion," 199–200.

70 Doyle caused further mischief: Davis, "Fenian Raid on New Brunswick," 330.

71 "We want that English flag!": Lormier, *History of the Islands and Islets in the Bay of Fundy,* 83–84.

71 He vowed that the "convention": Davis, "Fenian Raid on New Brunswick," 328–29.

71 "If the people of the Provinces": Vesey, "When New Brunswick Suffered Invasion," 202.

72 On April 16, Meade received a telegram: Meade, *Life and Letters,* 2:285.

72 Aboard were 129 cases: *Boston Journal,* April 25, 1866.

72 "urging that the arms": Welles, *Diary of Gideon Welles,* 2:486.

73 Although dressed in civilian clothes: *Papers of Ulysses S. Grant,* 16:109–10.

73 The general immediately ordered: Davis, "Fenian Raid on New Brunswick," 327.

73 He also told the leaders: Meade, *Life and Letters,* 2:284–85.

73 The explanation was laughable: *Papers of Ulysses S. Grant,* 16:109–10.

73 "Requisition cannot be filled": *Official Report of the Investigating Committee,* 42.

74 The fire destroyed: *Correspondence Relating to the Fenian Invasion and the Rebellion of the Southern States,* 167–70.

74 After rounding one of the islands: Davis, "Fenian Raid on New Brunswick," 331.

74 They then sank: *Official Report of the Investigating Committee,* 56–57.

74 In spite of his political: *Maine Farmer,* April 26, 1866.

74 Meade reported to Grant: *Papers of Ulysses S. Grant,* 16:110–13.

75 Upset that they could only: *Daily Eastern Argus,* April 28, 1866.

75 General Meade, who had caught: Meade, *Life and Letters,* 2:285.

75 "Moffat Mansion farce": *New York Herald,* May 7, 1866.

75 members of the Roberts wing chortled: *Irish-American,* April 28, 1866.

75 It caused some Canadians: *Chronicle Herald,* July 2, 2017.

75 "The failure of this project": McLean, "Competing Fenianisms," 135.

76 Many of the disappointed: *Morning Freeman,* May 1, 1866.

76 "Let us unite": *Army and Navy Journal,* May 12, 1866.

76 When the head center refused: *New York World,* May 1, 1866.

76 The tribunal discovered: *Official Report of the Investigating Committee,* 47–51.

77 In addition, even without proof: Libby, "Maine and the Fenian Invasion of Canada," 244–45.

77 Before he could be expelled: *New York World,* May 1, 1866.

Chapter 6: Erin's Boys

78 Donations to Moffat Mansion: *Baltimore Daily Commercial,* May 2, 1866.

78 The sullen O'Mahony exchanged: *New York World,* May 11, 1866.

78 Stephens appeared on the hotel's balcony: *James Stephens, Chief Organizer of the Irish Republic,* 97.

78 In a brief address: *Buffalo Commercial,* May 11, 1866.

78 "In consenting to": *James Stephens, Chief Organizer, the Irish Republic,* 98.

78 "In sanctioning this divergence": *New York Herald,* May 12, 1866.

79 "mad and most inglorious fiasco": Pender, "Fenian Papers," *Journal of the Cork Historical and Archaeological Society* 81 (1976): 124.

79 Reunification prospects further dimmed: Sayers, "John O'Mahony," 307.

79 For his part, Roberts accused: *Nashville Daily Union,* May 26, 1866.

79 The twenty-eight clerks: *Buffalo Express,* May 5, 1866.

79 Layers of dust: *Louisville Courier Journal,* Jan. 3, 1866.

79 With circles no longer: *Baltimore Sun,* May 16, 1866.

80 Stephens moved the Fenian headquarters: *Brooklyn Daily Eagle,* May 25, 1866.

80 After hearing news of: Denieffe, *Personal Narrative of the Irish Revolutionary Brotherhood,* 255–56.

80 So, with the burden: Sim, *Union Forever,* 90.

80 To the west: Hunt, *Brevet Brigadier Generals in Blue,* 607.

81 Samuel Perkins Spear: Ibid., 575.

81 Following the well-trodden path: Denieffe, *Personal Narrative of the Irish Revolutionary Brotherhood,* 266–72.

81 "With the revenues": Ibid., 272.

82 When the guns finally fell silent: McCollum, "Needham Musket Conversion."

82 Fenian operatives could purchase: *Buffalo Commercial,* April 27, 1866.

82 While many of the Fenian Brotherhood: Taylor, "In Queen Victoria's Secret Service," 58.

82 Sweeny also dispatched Tevis: Bilby, "Black Powder, White Smoke," 6.

82 The Fenians ultimately acquired: Denieffe, *Personal Narrative of the Irish Revolutionary Brotherhood,* 233.

82 The Fenian war secretary: Vronsky, "Combat, Memory, and Remembrance in Confederation Era Canada," 68.

83 According to one account: "Untold Story of the Intelligent Whale."

83 His original plan called for: D'Arcy, *Fenian Movement,* 145–46.

83 "I wept over": *An Phoblacht,* Jan. 27, 2000.

84 "The man dies": Emmet, *Life, Trial, and Conversations,* 111.

84 At least thirteen thousand people: Department of Culture, Heritage, and the Gaeltacht, "National Famine Commemoration."

84 Clontibret lost over 17 percent: John Makem interview.

85 He had a horse shot out: John O'Neill pension file, 575.926, National Archives and Records Administration.

86 "If resolutions could give liberty": *Official Report of Gen. John O'Neill,* 3–4, 32.

86 "There is no spot of earth": Noonan, "General John O'Neill," 315.

86 So militant had O'Neill: *Official Report of Gen. John O'Neill,* 31.

86 Similar scenes played out: Denieffe, *Personal Narrative of the Irish Revolutionary Brotherhood*, 240–41.

86 "Come at once": Donlon, "John O'Keeffe and the Fenian Brotherhood in the American West and Midwest," 90–91.

86 The second lieutenant: Recollections of John O'Keeffe, MHS.

87 Born in Clontibret: Fredericks, "Growth of the Catholic Church in Anderson, Indiana," 25.

87 Knowing their pastor had limited means: *Index to Reports of Committee of the House of Representatives*, 40th Cong., 2nd Sess., 2.

87 As O'Neill rode north: *Official Report of Gen. John O'Neill*, 37.

87 "Everything in connection with them": *New York World*, May 31, 1866.

87 In response, Sweeny ordered: Denieffe, *Personal Narrative of the Irish Revolutionary Brotherhood*, 242.

88 To the Seventh Regiment: *Irish-American*, Dec. 13, 1902.

88 Fenian sympathizers who worked: Denieffe, *Personal Narrative of the Irish Revolutionary Brotherhood*, 238.

88 Many of the crates: Finerty, "Thirty Years of Ireland's Battle—V," 279.

89 "ignorant little Irishman": D'Arcy, *Fenian Movement*, 148–49.

89 "We don't wish them": *Buffalo Courier*, June 1, 1866.

89 "This town is full": Senior, *Last Invasion of Canada*, 61.

90 "I cannot conceive it": D'Arcy, *Fenian Movement*, 157.

90 The U.S. attorney William A. Dart: Ibid., 158.

90 Hynes held in his hands: *Hartford Courant*, June 2, 1866.

90 Hynes looked at O'Neill: *Official Report of Gen. John O'Neill*, 37.

91 "good and true to the cause": Denieffe, *Personal Narrative of the Irish Revolutionary Brotherhood*, 217–18.

91 While the Irish Republican Army mobilized: Damian Shiels, "Medal of Honor: Boatswain's Mate Patrick Murphy, U.S.S. Metacomet," *Irish in the American Civil War*, Feb. 22, 2015, irishamericancivilwar.com.

92 To a chorus of cheers: Vronsky, *Ridgeway*, 48.

Chapter 7: A Lawless and Piratical Band

93 On the night of May 31, 1866: Junor, "Taken Prisoner by the Fenians," 86–87.

93 Although many militiamen: Vronsky, *Ridgeway*, 66–76.

94 The new commander of the Queen's Own Rifles: Radforth, "Highly Promising Youths," 21.

94 Not until 2:00 p.m.: *Niagara Falls Review*, Nov. 5, 2016.

94 "The soil of Canada": Macdonald, *Troublous Times in Canada*, 37.

95 Above the moss-grown rubble: *Official Report of Gen. John O'Neill*, 38.

95 Using axes stolen: Vronsky, *Ridgeway*, 54.

95 "I prevailed on the mayor": Recollections of John O'Keeffe, MHS.

95 "We have no issue": *Buffalo Daily Courier,* June 5, 1866.

95 O'Neill pledged that his men: Keneally, *Great Shame,* 440.

95 However, they didn't take any saddles: Vronsky, *Ridgeway,* 54.

95 They offered Fenian bonds: *Index to the Executive Documents of the Senate of the United States,* 40th Cong., 2nd Sess., 40.

96 The Fenian-contracted tugs: Vronsky, *Ridgeway,* 38.

96 Scores of soldiers who thought: Donlon, "John O'Keeffe and the Fenian Brotherhood in the American West and Midwest," 90–91; Finerty, "Thirty Years of Ireland's Battle—VI," 431.

96 The Irishmen burned their extra rifles: *Official Report of Gen. John O'Neill,* 39; *Correspondence Respecting the Recent Fenian Aggression,* 41.

96 The more grizzled soldiers: Recollections of John O'Keeffe, MHS.

97 The university student: Ellis, "Adventures of a Prisoner of War," 199.

97 Without Peacocke's approval: Ibid., 203.

97 Booker had no battle experience: Vronsky, *Ridgeway,* 72–73.

97 As the Canadian volunteers disembarked: *Correspondence Respecting the Recent Fenian Aggression,* 12.

97 Junor and his fellow students: Junor, "Taken Prisoner by the Fenians," 87.

97 O'Neill made his headquarters: Vronsky, "Combat, Memory, and Remembrance in Confederation Era Canada," 133.

98 The Fenians saw the familiar: Finerty, "Thirty Years of Ireland's Battle—VI," 433.

98 Junor heard the command: Junor, "Taken Prisoner by the Fenians," 87.

98 "To most of us": Recollections of John O'Keeffe, MHS.

98 The Canadian skirmishers: Radforth, "Highly Promising Youths," 21.

99 They dashed from stump to stump: Martin, "Green Terror," 52.

99 Once the Fenians had emptied: Ellis, "Adventures of a Prisoner of War," 200.

99 As they progressed: *Fenian Raid at Fort Erie,* 43.

99 Not only did the terrain: *Correspondence Respecting the Recent Fenian Aggression,* 12.

99 With their center uncovered: *Official Report of Gen. John O'Neill,* 39.

99 They sounded a chorus: *Irish-American,* Dec. 13, 1902.

99 "The cavalry are coming!": *Fenian Raid at Fort Erie,* 44.

99 Bugles ordered the Canadian: Junor, "Taken Prisoner by the Fenians," 90.

100 "We were all called to form": *Fenian Raid at Fort Erie,* 44.

100 Once Booker realized: Keneally, *Great Shame,* 441.

100 After nearly two hours of fighting: *Fenian Raid at Fort Erie,* 44; Finerty, "Thirty Years of Ireland's Battle—VI," 433.

100 Junor ran along the crossroad: Vronsky, *Ridgeway*, 62–63.

100 The bullet pierced: Ellis and King, "Fenian Casualties and Prisoners," 274.

101 Three more succumbed: Vronsky, "Combat, Memory, and Remembrance in Confederation Era Canada," 222.

101 Toronto newspapers issued: *Hartford Courant*, June 2, 1866; King, *King's Handbook of Boston*, 288.

101 *The Nation* in Dublin: Wilson, *Thomas D'Arcy McGee*, 2:279.

102 "It is difficult to believe": *Detroit Free Press*, June 2, 1866.

102 The Fenians had expected Canadians: Junor, "Taken Prisoner by the Fenians," 89.

102 Plus, the Irishmen in Canada: *Buffalo Daily Courier*, June 5, 1866.

102 "I decided that my best policy": *Official Report of Gen. John O'Neill*, 39.

102 The Irishmen shared pipes: Ellis, "Adventures of a Prisoner of War," 203.

102 The Irishmen arrived back: *Correspondence Respecting the Recent Fenian Aggression*, 18.

103 The twenty-five village blocks: Vronsky, *Ridgeway*, 49.

103 Gathered on the banks: *Trial of American Citizens in Great Britain*, 37.

103 "Give it to them": "Fenians Hide n' Go Seek."

103 With his men pushed back: *Correspondence Respecting the Recent Fenian Aggression*, 15–18.

103 The only escape route: Recollections of John O'Keeffe, MHS.

103 O'Neill emerged victorious: *Official Report of Gen. John O'Neill*, 40.

104 They danced to keep warm: Junor, "Taken Prisoner by the Fenians," 89.

104 O'Neill approached O'Keeffe: Recollections of John O'Keeffe, MHS.

104 Thirteen were killed: Ellis and King, "Fenian Casualties and Prisoners," 271.

104 After the last of his able-bodied men: Ellis, "Adventures of a Prisoner of War," 203.

105 "We would have as readily surrendered": *Official Report of Gen. John O'Neill*, 40.

105 The thirteen Fenian officers: *Army and Navy Journal*, Jan. 12, 1867.

105 When daylight arrived: Walker, *Fenian Movement*, 96.

105 When the British troops: King, "John McMahon, Fenian Priest," 9.

105 Inside his carpetbag, the troops: *Charleston Daily News*, Nov. 18, 1869.

105 However, the British found: Macdonald, *Troublous Times in Canada*, 82.

105 In all, the British captured: *Courier-Journal*, June 16, 1866.

105 They then took a tug: *Inter Ocean*, June 23, 1889.

106 With his recommendation to impose: Meade, *Life and Letters*, 285–88.

106 With reports arriving: *Papers of Ulysses S. Grant*, 16:216.

106 Satisfied that O'Neill's brief invasion: Report of Major General George G. Meade to Secretary of War, Oct. 12, 1866, in *House Executive Document No. 3*, 39th Cong., 2nd Sess., 42–44.

106 "This is a war on the Irish": Welles, *Diary of Gideon Welles*, 2:518.

106 Inside the undergraduate lounge: Radforth, "Highly Promising Youths," 22.

107 Sorrow turned to anger: *Baltimore Sun,* June 7, 1866.

107 Eventually, sixty-five Fenian prisoners: *Correspondence Relating to the Fenian Invasion,* 141.

107 "The autonomy of British America": Boyko, *Blood and Daring,* 274.

107 With barely enough room: *Official Report of Gen. John O'Neill,* 41.

107 After visiting the prisoners: *Boston Journal,* June 8, 1866.

107 The situation grew so desperate: *Buffalo Evening Post,* June 5, 1866.

107 Some prisoners cussed out Sweeny: Finerty, "Thirty Years of Ireland's Battle—VII," 540.

107 The Irish Republican Army believed: *Buffalo Evening Post,* June 8, 1866.

108 Three companies of U.S. artillery troops: *Inter Ocean,* June 23, 1889.

108 The officers lacked money: Brodsky, *Grover Cleveland,* 6, 29–30.

108 "Gentlemen, you may not be aware": *Fenian Raid of '66,* 278.

108 While detained on the USS *Michigan: Hartford Courant,* June 6, 1866.

108 "I saw at that time": *Burlington Free Press,* June 10, 1870.

109 O'Keeffe saw the change: Recollections of John O'Keeffe, MHS.

Chapter 8: Iron Wills and Brave Hearts

110 "I take possession": Andrews, "How 'Unpreparedness' Undid St. Albans," 677–78.

110 They even shot poor Elinus Morrison: Haynes, *St. Albans,* 45.

110 The outrage even drove: Busseau, *"Fenians Are Coming . . . ,"* 3–5.

111 "Vairmont Yankee Scare Party": Prince, *Burn the Town and Sack the Banks,* 136.

111 The village's most illustrious resident: Rick Beard, "When the Rebels Invaded Vermont," *New York Times,* Oct. 17, 2014, www.nytimes.com.

111 The seat of Franklin County: *Burlington Free Press,* June 1, 1866.

111 Speaking in low voices: *Boston Journal,* June 4, 1866.

111 When a delegation of town authorities: Ibid.

111 With it clear that the village: *Vermont Transcript,* June 8, 1866.

112 "the excitement among the Irish": Wilson, *Thomas D'Arcy McGee,* 2:279.

112 A green flag waved: *Boston Journal,* June 7, 1866.

112 Women showed their solidarity: *Irish-American,* June 16, 1866.

112 Even a group: *St. Johnsbury Caledonian,* June 15, 1866.

112 *The New York Times* devoted: *New York Times,* June 2, 1866; *New York Herald,* June 2, 1866.

112 "The whole border": *Irish-American,* June 9, 1866.

112 "startling but most intensely": Ibid.

112 The Fenian secretary of war: Denieffe, *Personal Narrative of the Irish Revolutionary Brotherhood,* 260.

113 An officer insisted: *St. Albans Messenger,* June 11, 1866.

113 Two weeks earlier: *Ogdensburg Journal,* Sept. 26, 1911.

113 Customs agents found: *Vermont Transcript,* June 1, 1866.

113 The general was outraged: Bushnell, *It Happened in Vermont,* 72.

114 The tidy village's weekly: Denieffe, *Personal Narrative of the Irish Revolutionary Brotherhood,* 244–45.

114 Shortly after Spear: *Burlington Free Press,* May 31, 1866.

114 "The President approves": *Burlington Free Press,* June 2, 1866.

115 The Fenians grew wise: McKone, *Vermont's Irish Rebel,* 421–24.

115 "We Irishmen are determined": *Vermont Transcript,* June 8, 1866.

115 Some found open arms: *Boston Journal,* June 4, 1866.

115 Others camped in the woods: *Burlington Free Press,* June 5 and 4, 1866.

115 Hundreds of government troops: *Buffalo Evening Post,* June 7, 1866.

115 Sweeny convened a war council: Morgan, *Through American and Irish Wars,* 122.

115 The general's handpicked man: Busseau, *"Fenians Are Coming . . . ,"* 13.

115 Spear reported to Sweeny: Denieffe, *Personal Narrative of the Irish Revolutionary Brotherhood,* 250.

116 "beg, borrow, or take": Ibid.

116 "Never has there been": *Vermont Transcript,* June 8, 1866.

116 "think of calling out the militia": *Burlington Free Press,* June 7, 1866.

116 St. Albans had refused to enforce: Haynes, *St. Albans,* 30.

116 The town's old-timers: Bryan, *Real Democracy,* 6.

116 "ninety-nine out of every": *Columbian,* June 9, 1866.

117 "Good luck to you!": *Boston Journal,* June 5, 1866.

117 It was no small irony: Boyko, *Blood and Daring,* 241–89.

117 Not fully convinced of the loyalty: Dafoe, "Fenian Invasion of Quebec," 342.

117 Montreal's mayor, Henry Starnes: *Burlington Free Press,* June 8, 1866.

117 "Whoever is not with us": *Boston Journal,* June 5, 1866.

118 "You must allow me": D'Arcy, *Fenian Movement,* 163.

118 "all judges, magistrates, marshals": Macdonald, *Troublous Times in Canada,* 117.

118 When Major A. A. Gibson: *Boston Journal,* June 8, 1866.

118 The general had turned in: Senior, *Last Invasion of Canada,* 121.

119 Offering no resistance: *Burlington Free Press,* June 7, 1866.

119 The following morning: *Boston Journal,* June 9, 1866.

119 Sweeny waived his examination: Macdonald, *Troublous Times in Canada,* 121.

119 He had received word: *Boston Journal,* June 8, 1866.

119 Spear found his rank and file: *Correspondence Respecting the Recent Fenian Aggression,* 68.

119 The lucky ones: *Boston Journal,* June 8, 1866.

119 The local Fenians: *Burlington Free Press,* June 7, 1866.

119 Mahan, a major: Denieffe, *Personal Narrative of the Irish Revolutionary Brotherhood,* 251.

Chapter 9: The Fenians Are Coming!

121 The defense of Quebec's Missisquoi County: Senior, *Last Invasion of Canada,* 116–17.

121 Carter, a British army officer: Darch, "For the Sake of Ireland."

121 Many of them had been forced: Somerville, *Narrative of the Fenian Invasion of Canada,* 127.

121 Inside the Eastern Townships: *Vermont Transcript,* June 8, 1866; Dafoe, "Fenian Invasion of Quebec," 345.

122 It was common for members: Farfan, *Vermont-Quebec Border,* 8.

122 As they marched: *St. Albans Messenger,* June 8, 1866.

122 By one estimate: *Burlington Free Press,* Feb. 16, 1866.

122 Just after 10:00 a.m.: *Correspondence Respecting the Recent Fenian Aggression,* 33.

122 His cavalry hugged: *St. Albans Messenger,* June 8, 1866.

123 "You are now on British soil": *Louisville Daily Courier,* June 9, 1866.

123 Spear proclaimed the establishment: *Correspondence Respecting the Recent Fenian Aggression,* 67–68.

123 Colonel Contri stepped forward: *Boston Journal,* June 8, 1866.

123 Spear then announced: *St. Albans Messenger,* June 8, 1866.

123 "The Fenians are coming!": Darch, "For the Sake of Ireland."

123 "The cry was still": Denieffe, *Personal Narrative of the Irish Revolutionary Brotherhood,* 251.

123 "were not robbers": *Correspondence Respecting the Recent Fenian Aggression,* 67–69.

124 At one farm: *St. Albans Messenger,* June 8, 1866.

124 Sentries armed with muskets: *Correspondence Respecting the Recent Fenian Aggression,* 68–69.

124 They confiscated the British ensign: Busseau, *"Fenians Are Coming . . . ,"* 12–13.

124 "Give me men": Denieffe, *Personal Narrative of the Irish Revolutionary Brotherhood,* 252–53.

125 While only $6,000 of losses: Somerville, *Narrative of the Fenian Invasion of Canada,* 128.

125 Spear placed three of his men: *St. Albans Messenger,* June 8, 1866.

125 Not only were individual men: Macdonald, *Troublous Times in Canada,* 112.

125 Fearful that the Fenians: Senior, *Last Invasion of Canada,* 123.

126 On the morning of June 9: Dafoe, "Fenian Invasion of Quebec," 345.

126 Fenian scouts brought news: Busseau, *"Fenians Are Coming . . . ,"* 12–13.

126 A few even directed: Finerty, "Thirty Years of Ireland's Battle—VII," 540.

126 Many Fenians tossed aside: Senior, *Last Invasion of Canada,* 124.

126 While the Irish continued to straggle: Busseau, *"Fenians Are Coming . . . ,"* 19.

127 "little scamps such as one": Dafoe, "Fenian Invasion of Quebec," 345.

127 So exuberant were four: D. L. McDougall to Brigade-Major, in *Correspondence Respecting the Recent Fenian Aggression,* 33.

127 Having given his word: *Vermont Journal,* June 12, 1866.

127 Spear wept as he rode: *St. Albans Messenger,* June 11, 1866.

127 "that he would rather": Macdonald, *Troublous Times in Canada,* 113.

127 They milked the enemy ensign: Senior, *Last Invasion of Canada,* 122.

127 It was dragged through: *Brooklyn Daily Eagle,* June 18, 1866.

128 The lone fatality: Darch, "For the Sake of Ireland."

128 "My God, it is a woman": Busseau, *"Fenians Are Coming . . . ,"* 26.

128 Her gravestone at Pigeon Hill: Darch, "For the Sake of Ireland."

128 "We will show the world": *Vermont Transcript,* June 15, 1866; *St. Albans Messenger,* June 11, 1866.

128 "abandon our expedition against Canada": Macdonald, *Troublous Times in Canada,* 92-93.

129 "these liberal offers will have": Ibid., 120.

129 "Let no Fenian disgrace": *Rock Island Argus,* June 14, 1866.

129 Spear and the officers: Macdonald, *Troublous Times in Canada,* 113.

129 Similar scenes played out: D'Arcy, *Fenian Movement,* 165.

129 They fled by the hundreds: Macdonald, *Troublous Times in Canada,* 93.

129 In all, the War Department: Walker, *Fenian Movement,* 103.

129 "It grieves me to part": Macdonald, *Troublous Times in Canada,* 93.

Chapter 10: Hail the Vanquished Hero

131 Instead, his dominion comprised: *New York Times,* June 10, 1866.

131 Hours after Sweeny: *New York Times,* June 8, 1866.

131 Far from offering resistance: *New York Times,* June 9, 1866.

131 As news of the arrest: *New York World,* June 8, 1866.

131 No fewer than a dozen Fenians: *New York Times,* June 9, 1866.

131 "I will not give bail": *Irish-American,* June 16, 1866.

132 "He's making a damned ass": *New York Times,* June 9, 1866.

132 The government-furnished accommodations: D'Arcy, *Fenian Movement,* 167.

132 The proprietors of New York's first luxury hotel: *New York Times,* June 9, 1866.

132 "He got himself in there": *New York Times,* June 10, 1866.

132 Prolonged cheering greeted Roberts: *New York Times,* June 13, 1866.

132 George Weishart as the "wretched informer": *New York Times,* June 16, 1866.

132 James Gibbons refused to answer: *New York Times,* June 12, 1866.

133 William Cole told the court: *Irish-American,* June 16, 1866.

133 The *New York Herald* reporter John Gallagher: *New York Times,* June 13, 1866.

133 "failed to connect": *New York Times,* June 12, 1866.

133 Those concerns were not unfounded: *New York Times,* June 16, 1866.

133 "the utter impossibility": *New York World,* June 16, 1866.

133 In light of that: *New York Times,* June 16, 1866.

133 As the captives were escorted: *Philadelphia Inquirer,* June 13, 1866.

134 The captives taken: Borthwick, *History of the Montréal Prison,* 266.

134 They included four Methodists: *St. Albans Messenger,* June 11, 1866.

134 "all of the misguided men": *Papers Relating to the Foreign Affairs,* 241.

134 "This thing you ask": *Semi-weekly Wisconsin,* June 27, 1866.

135 "The future relations of Canada": Boyko, *Blood and Daring,* 274.

135 New Fenian circles: *Irish-American,* July 28, 1866.

136 "One has certainly done": *Hartford Courant,* June 9, 1866.

136 Many still questioned: *Philadelphia Inquirer,* June 14, 1866.

136 "If the attempts": *Irish-American,* June 23, 1866.

136 "not through any efforts": *Philadelphia Evening Telegraph,* June 15, 1866.

137 "Queen Victoria thanks": D'Arcy, *Fenian Movement,* 202.

137 "discriminate most harshly": *Harrisburg Telegraph,* June 11, 1866.

137 "the only true": *New York Times,* June 10, 1866.

138 The audience escorted: *Pittsburgh Daily Commercial,* June 21, 1866.

138 "I fear it augurs": D'Arcy, *Fenian Movement,* 178.

138 "The United States should": Ibid., 223.

139 There was nothing clandestine: Macdonald, *Troublous Times in Canada,* 146–48.

139 "the gradual but decided": *American Annual Cyclopaedia,* 76.

139 "The covenant of our nationality": Neidhardt, *Fenianism in North America,* 73.

Chapter 11: Political Blarney

140 A staccato of musket fire: *New-York Tribune,* Aug. 22, 1866.

140 Organizers of the reenactment: *Irish-American,* July 28, 1866.

140 The Corcoran Guards: *Buffalo Commercial,* Aug. 22, 1866.

141 The sham battle: *Cincinnati Enquirer,* Aug. 22, 1866.

141 Held on a Tuesday: *Tennessean,* Aug. 22, 1866.

141 From across the Niagara River: *Philadelphia Evening Telegraph,* Aug. 18, 1866.

141 A British gunboat: *Irish-American*, Sept. 1, 1866.

141 "Localities where it was thought": *Irish-American*, Aug. 4, 1866.

141 The spymaster Gilbert McMicken's detectives: Wilson, *Thomas D'Arcy McGee*, 2:291–92.

141 As a precaution: *New York World*, Aug. 22, 1866.

142 "too much and acted too little": "Speeches of Hon. Schuyler Colfax and General J. O'Neill."

142 "The campaign has only commenced": *Louisville Daily Courier*, July 6, 1866.

142 "I take it that": *Tennessean*, Dec. 29, 1866.

142 "I never voted in all my life": *Chicago Tribune*, July 17, 1866.

143 he was "unutterably humiliated": *Ottawa Citizen*, Aug. 21, 1866.

143 "when the freedom of their land": "Speeches of Hon. Schuyler Colfax and General J. O'Neill."

143 denounced the "political blarney": *Buffalo Commercial*, Aug. 22, 1866.

143 That morning inside: *Irish-American*, Sept. 1, 1866.

143 All of Buffalo: *Buffalo Evening Post*, Aug. 22, 1866; *New-York Tribune*, Aug. 22, 1866.

144 "Let us be friends": *Buffalo Commercial*, Sept. 5, 1866.

144 In order to discourage internal arguments: Walker, *Fenian Movement*, 112.

145 The rebuke stung Sweeny: Morgan, *Through American and Irish Wars*, 149.

145 The County Galway native: *Inter Ocean*, Jan. 14, 1884.

145 While residents of Fort Erie: Macdonald, *Troublous Times in Canada*, 126–27.

146 "By the statute": *Trials of the Fenian Prisoners in Toronto*, 83.

146 "They took my traveling bag": *Buffalo Commercial*, June 15, 1866.

146 Before Wilson announced the sentence: *Trials of the Fenian Prisoners in Toronto*, 135–38.

147 Newspapers reported, hyperbolically: *Nashville Union and American*, Nov. 17, 1866.

147 "If the British Government": *Nashville Union and American*, Nov. 7, 1866.

147 "thirst for Irish blood": *Tri-weekly Union and American*, Nov. 6, 1866.

148 "The sentence of death": *Papers Relating to Foreign Affairs*, 181.

148 Special units of government police: *Irish-American*, Dec. 7, 1866.

148 "feloniously joining himself": Busseau, *Correspondence Respecting the Recent Fenian Aggression*, 65.

149 "Those men deserve death": Wilson, *Thomas D'Arcy McGee*, 2:283.

149 "I regret to tell you": *Nashville Union and Dispatch*, Dec. 18, 1866.

149 "carrying patriotism to an excess": *Vinton Record*, Dec. 20, 1866.

149 "A life that would otherwise": *Nashville Union and Dispatch*, Dec. 18, 1866.

Chapter 12: *Erin's Hope*

150 "I speak to you now": *New York Times,* Oct. 29, 1866; *Freeman's Journal,* Nov. 12, 1866.

150 "name and nationality": D'Arcy, *Fenian Movement,* 214–15.

150 In early December: *New York Times,* Dec. 2, 1866.

151 Using the alias William Scott: *New-York Tribune,* Jan. 1, 1867.

151 Looking haggard and ill: Ryan, *Fenian Chief,* 247.

151 "I found that matters": D'Arcy, *Fenian Movement,* 219–20.

151 "either fight or dissolve": Rutherford, *Secret History of the Fenian Conspiracy,* 2:40.

151 The Fenian chief claimed: Ramón, *Provisional Dictator,* 224–26.

152 Kelly pressed ahead: Busteed, *Irish in Manchester,* 211.

152 "We have suffered centuries": *Times* (London), March 8, 1867.

152 A tempest of snow: Mullane, *Cruise of the "Erin's Hope,"* 5.

153 "It was as pitiful": *Frank Leslie's Illustrated Newspaper,* May 25, 1867.

153 "Don't believe a tenth": D'Arcy, *Fenian Movement,* 241–43.

153 In packs of twos and threes: U.S. Congress, *House Executive Documents,* 40th Cong., 2nd Sess., 236–37.

153 The steamer returned: D'Arcy, *Fenian Movement,* 244.

153 Captain John F. Kavanagh: Mullane, *Cruise of the "Erin's Hope,"* 6–11.

154 Posing as an English tourist: Burleigh, *Blood and Rage,* 7.

154 A trained engineer: Devoy, *Devoy's Post Bag,* 35–36.

155 Burke instructed Kavanagh: *Dublin Evening Post,* Oct. 31, 1867.

155 Dodging British cruisers: Mullane, *Cruise of the "Erin's Hope,"* 25–32.

156 Following the disappointment: Joye, "Stone That 'Smashed the Van,'" 27.

156 While Kelly told police: Busteed, *Irish in Manchester,* 211–12.

157 Climbing atop the van: Denvir, *"God Save Ireland!,"* 9–10.

158 "a well beloved": D'Arcy, *Fenian Movement,* 269.

158 Under the 1848 Treason Felony Act: Busteed, *Irish in Manchester,* 215.

158 "You will soon send us": Denvir, *"God Save Ireland!,"* 22.

158 Days after the death sentences: *Irish Times,* Nov. 23, 2014.

159 The ambassador, however: U.S. Congress, *House Executive Documents,* 40th Cong., 2nd Sess., 1867–68, 171–76.

159 In the early morning hours: *Observer,* Nov. 24, 1867.

159 while street vendors: *Irish Times,* Nov. 20, 2017.

159 With rumors that the Fenians: *Observer,* Nov. 24, 1867.

159 "If you reflect on it": Allen to Uncle and Aunt Hogan, Nov. 22, 1867, PIT.

160 Prison officials, however: *Southern Star,* Dec. 10, 2017.

160 American newspapers printed: *Daily Ohio Statesman,* Dec. 18, 1867.

160 "accomplished the final act": *Irish Times,* Nov. 23, 2014.

160 On the eve: *Newcastle Daily Journal,* Nov. 22, 1867.

160 The man who had plotted: *Manchester Guardian,* Dec. 14, 1867.

161 On the afternoon of December 12: Burleigh, *Blood and Rage,* 7–8.

161 The Fenians had used: Devoy, *Devoy's Post Bag,* 36.

161 Detectives prowled every railway station: *Sydney Morning Herald,* Feb. 15, 1868.

161 Royal Navy boats: *Frank Leslie's Illustrated Newspaper,* Feb. 15, 1868.

161 Buckets of dirt: Rafferty, *The Church, the State, and the Fenian Threat,* 102.

161 More than fifty thousand citizens: Anderson, *Lighter Side of My Official Life,* 22–23.

Chapter 13: The Call of Duty

162 Church bells and cannon fire: *New York Herald,* July 2, 1867.

162 Steps away from Parliament Hill: Gwyn, *Nation Maker,* 14–15.

162 Canada's creation was a civilized affair: *Chronicle Herald,* July 2, 2017.

162 While Ottawa celebrated: *New York Herald,* July 2, 1867.

163 "When the experiment": Lippert, *War Plan Red,* 46–47.

163 Thomas D'Arcy McGee recognized: Wilson, *Thomas D'Arcy McGee,* 2:301.

164 Two days after the national celebration: Ibid., 2:308–26.

164 "because of their inability": *Cincinnati Enquirer,* Sept. 11, 1867.

164 Plus, the Irish Republic bonds: *Albany Evening Journal,* Sept. 12, 1867.

165 The Fenian cavalry jacket: "Fenian Brotherhood I.R.A. Belt Buckle."

165 Blue trousers with a green cord: *New York Herald,* March 19, 1867.

165 Overcoats and blue kepis: D'Arcy, *Fenian Movement,* 228–30.

165 In spite of his earlier pledge: *Baltimore Sun,* Sept. 27, 1867.

165 Johnson agreed as long as: Cole, *Prince of Spies,* 32–33.

165 He directed Attorney General: *Pulaski Citizen,* Nov. 22, 1867.

165 The cache included: Geo. G. Munger to General W. F. Barry, Feb. 20, 1867, ACHS.

166 An expert marksman: Cole, *Prince of Spies,* 46.

166 The Fenian muzzle-loading: McCollum, "Needham Musket Conversion."

166 By converting their rifles: Bilby, "Black Powder, White Smoke," 6.

166 Meehan ultimately decided: Ibid.; McCollum, "Needham Musket Conversion."

166 The Fenians, uncharacteristically: *New York Times,* May 25, 1870.

167 dubbed the Green House: *Philadelphia Inquirer,* April 19, 1870.

167 Weeks earlier, Roberts and Savage: *Charleston Daily News,* Dec. 21, 1867.

167 "The Irish heart leaps": *Irish-American,* Feb. 15, 1868.

167 O'Neill, who had resigned: *Nashville Union and American,* Oct. 8, 1867.

167 He had just paid: *Official Report of Gen. John O'Neill,* 32.

168 "to go to work": Ibid., 11.

168 He attended state conventions: O'Neill to "Dear Sir & Bro," Nov. 12, 1868, ACHS.

168 In a return to Buffalo: *Buffalo Daily Courier,* Feb. 1, 1868.

168 "Your presence here": Ibid., Feb. 3, 1868.

168 "The result of O'Neill's visit": D'Arcy, *Fenian Movement,* 294.

169 "one of the boniest faces": Macdonald, *Diary of the Parnell Commission,* 120.

169 A human chimney: Le Caron, *Twenty-Five Years in the Secret Service,* 94.

169 Rumors circulated around: Kirk, *History of the Fifteenth Pennsylvania Volunteer Cavalry,* 328.

169 While stationed in Nashville: Clark, "Spy Who Came in from the Coalfields," 93.

169 O'Neill found himself: Edwards, *Infiltrator,* 35.

169 It was in Nashville: Kirk, *History of the Fifteenth Pennsylvania Cavalry,* 330.

170 Following the war: Clark, "Spy Who Came in from the Coalfields," 93.

170 "Come at once, you are needed for work": Le Caron, *Twenty-Five Years in the Secret Service,* 53–54.

170 "They don't take into account": Bergeron, *Papers of Andrew Johnson,* 13:546.

170 "General, your people": Le Caron, *Twenty-Five Years in the Secret Service,* 59.

171 Among O'Neill's first actions: *Philadelphia Evening Telegraph,* Dec. 31, 1867; *Manchester Guardian,* Dec. 17, 1867.

171 "I have an opinion": Forster, *Life of Charles Dickens,* 324.

171 "The Fenian organization": *Buffalo Daily Courier,* Feb. 3, 1868.

Chapter 14: Blood in the Street

172 Then, on March 9, 1868: Donald Mackay to Macdonald, March 9, 1868, LAC.

173 "I'm a bloody Fenian": *Age,* July 7, 2017.

173 Fortuitously, the royal's India rubber braces: *Irish Times,* Oct. 13, 2017.

173 O'Farrell was not in fact: *Australian,* Aug. 5, 2017.

173 By the time the news: *Buffalo Express,* April 25, 1868.

173 "I hope that in this House": Taylor, *Hon. Thos. D'Arcy McGee,* 40–43.

174 Under the light of a full moon: *Trial of Patrick J. Whelan,* 1–12.

174 The .32-caliber bullet: Bytown Museum exhibit.

174 McGee's glove and cigar: *Trial of Patrick J. Whelan,* 11.

175 "If Thomas D'Arcy McGee": Taylor, *Hon. Thos. D'Arcy McGee,* 47.

175 "He who was with us": Slattery, *Assassination of Thomas D'Arcy McGee,* 474.

175 "He has been slain": Taylor, *Hon. Thos. D'Arcy McGee,* 44–45.

175 Born around 1840: Boyko, "Patrick James Whelan."

176 An estimated 80,000 people: *Globe and Mail,* April 13, 2013.

176 "the dastardly, cowardly": Wilson, *Thomas D'Arcy McGee,* 2:347.

176 "McGee did as much": *New York World,* April 8, 1868.

176 During the solemn funeral Mass: *New York Herald,* April 14, 1868.

177 "a deliberate decision": Wilson, *Thomas D'Arcy McGee,* 2:346–47.

177 "I shot that fellow": *Trial of Patrick J. Whelan,* 39, 86.

177 In his last hours on death row: Boyko, "Patrick James Whelan."

177 Fearing that some Irish Catholic: D'Arcy, *Fenian Movement,* 317–18.

177 "the detectives detailed": U.S. Congress, *House Executive Documents,* 40th Cong., 2nd sess., 288–91.

178 Only one-third of the $167,450: *Proceedings of the Senate and House of Representatives of the Fenian Brotherhood in Joint Convention at Philadelphia, Pa.,* 15–17.

178 "General O'Neill moves": *Vermont Daily Transcript,* Feb. 5, 1869.

178 O'Neill conceded his expenses: *Official Report of Gen. John O'Neill,* 36.

178 "I have never believed": O'Neill to Gallagher, Jan. 4, 1870, ACHS.

178 In order to cover: James Gibbons to the Officers and Members of the F.B., April 7, 1870, ACHS.

178 In April 1869: Gibbons to the Officers and Members of the F.B., April 8, 1869, ACHS.

178 On the opening day: *New York Times,* June 6, 1869.

179 "Were it not for the almost insane": D'Arcy, *Fenian Movement,* 318.

179 "I am sick and tired": O'Neill to Gallagher, Dec. 16, 1869.

180 In truth, the only people: Le Caron, *Twenty-Five Years in the Secret Service,* 77.

180 As O'Neill and Meehan: *Official Report of Gen. John O'Neill,* 7.

180 According to the Canadian spymaster: D'Arcy, *Fenian Movement,* 326.

180 "It should not be forgotten": O'Neill to the Officers and Members of the Fenian Brotherhood, and the Friends of Irish Liberty Generally, Oct. 27, 1869, MHS.

180 He summoned Le Caron: Cole, *Prince of Spies,* 48.

180 The Fenian president then traveled: *Irish-American,* July 30, 1870.

181 In spite of their efforts: Archibald to Thornton, Dec. 13, 1869, LAC.

182 "I was painfully aware": *Official Report of Gen. John O'Neill,* 5.

182 "The right to fight": O'Neill to the Officers and Members of the Fenian Brotherhood, Jan. 21, 1870, MHS.

Chapter 15: One Ridgeway Would Never Be Enough

183 "those who become members": *Catholic Encyclopedia,* 5:689.

183 "decreed and declared": *Belfast News-Letter,* Feb. 8, 1870.

184 Upwards of one thousand men: Rafferty, *The Church, the State, and the Fenian Threat,* 11.

184 "What England failed to accomplish": D'Arcy, *Fenian Movement,* 332.

184 When a New York City priest: *Commercial Appeal,* March 25, 1870.

184 "The Irish people": Sayers, "John O'Mahony," 348.

184 Colonels Henri Le Caron and William Clingen: *Burlington Free Press,* April 25, 1870.

184 "It was as much our object": *Daily Phoenix,* June 4, 1870.

185 Registering in hotels: Cole, *Prince of Spies,* 53.

185 On a visit to Malone: Le Caron, *Twenty-Five Years in the Secret Service,* 75–76.

185 Administering their own justice: Cole, *Prince of Spies,* 52.

185 When New York's governor, John Hoffman: D'Arcy, *Fenian Movement,* 334–36.

185 A trained physician: *New York Herald,* March 1, 1870.

185 A painful rift: John O'Neill pension file, 575.926.

186 McCloud, removed the organization's: *Official Report of Gen. John O'Neill,* 6–7.

186 Listening from another room: D'Arcy, *Fenian Movement,* 342.

186 A policeman who heard: *New York Herald,* March 1, 1870.

186 "Frank, I hope this": *Irish-American,* March 19, 1870.

186 Although Keenan's shot: *New York Herald,* March 2, 1870.

186 After serving two years: *Public Papers of John T. Hoffman,* 489.

186 Due to Keenan's "insane" actions: *Official Report of Gen. John O'Neill,* 7.

187 "in view of the lamented catastrophe": O'Neill to the Officers and Members of the Fenian Brotherhood, March 1, 1870, MHS.

187 "One Ridgeway is enough": Gibbons to the Officers and Members of the Fenian Brotherhood, March 23, 1870, ACHS.

187 The Fenian scare: Borthwick, *History of the Montréal Prison,* 221–22.

187 With the British government: Nevins, *Hamilton Fish,* 1:388–89.

187 Based on the intelligence reports: *Papers Relating to the Foreign Relations of the United States,* 258.

187 "the peace of the country": *Chicago Tribune,* April 15, 1870.

188 "detectives and spies": *New York Herald,* April 23, 1870.

188 The Canadian government said: McGee, *Fenian Raids on the Huntingdon Frontier,* 27.

Chapter 16: Secrets and Lies

189 Henri Le Caron became a familiar face: Cole, *Prince of Spies,* 50–59.

189 "no power on earth": Le Caron, *Twenty-Five Years in the Secret Service,* 81–83.

189 Only $2,000 of the $30,000: *Official Report of Gen. John O'Neill,* 44.

189 "I did not deem it": Ibid., 9.

190 "Take no man who": Le Caron, *Twenty-Five Years in the Secret Service,* 79–83.

190 While the *Buffalo Evening Post* announced: *Buffalo Evening Post,* May 22, 1870; Cole, *Prince of Spies,* 58–59.

190 Le Caron's stay in Buffalo: *Official Report of Gen. John O'Neill,* 15.

190 "Every precaution had been taken": *Daily Phoenix,* June 4, 1870.

190 "that the Canadians": Le Caron, *Twenty-Five Years in the Secret Service*, 82.

191 The second of thirteen children: Edwards, *Infiltrator*, 26.

191 "wild mad thirst": Le Caron, *Twenty-Five Years in the Secret Service*, 8.

191 Beach told tall tales: Edwards, *Infiltrator*, 55; Le Caron, *Twenty-Five Years in the Secret Service*, 2–10.

192 When Le Caron returned: Edwards, *Infiltrator*, 53–54.

192 "I never sought Fenianism": Le Caron, *Twenty-Five Years in the Secret Service*, 25.

192 He worked closely: O'Brien, *Blood Runs Green*, 68.

192 As the head center: Cole, *Prince of Spies*, 30.

192 Although he wasn't Catholic: Clark, "Spy Who Came in from the Coalfields," 95.

192 Le Caron spilled Fenian secrets: Cole, *Prince of Spies*, 45–57.

192 In fact, John C. Rose: Le Caron, *Twenty-Five Years in the Secret Service*, 76.

193 "would not hesitate": *Irish-American*, June 18, 1870.

193 Feigning indignation, the spy: Cole, *Prince of Spies*, 40–45.

193 "Prominent leaders say": *New York Times*, April 25, 1870.

193 He expected that thousands: Tuttle, "Fenian Campaign," 208–9.

193 O'Neill's plan called for: *Official Report of Gen. John O'Neill*, 16–17.

194 He expected to encounter: *Fenian Raid of 1870*, 53.

194 O'Neill told *The Daily Phoenix*: *Daily Phoenix*, June 4, 1870.

194 The secret agent had: Le Caron, *Twenty-Five Years in the Secret Service*, 81–83.

195 On May 22, a disguised O'Neill: *Official Report of Gen. John O'Neill*, 15.

195 In the mill city: Ibid., 44–51.

195 O'Neill emerged from his hiding spot: Ibid., 15.

195 The Fenians had hired: *New-York Tribune*, May 25, 1870.

196 Nearly every team: *New-York Tribune*, May 24, 1870.

196 The Fenians paid farmers: *St. Albans Messenger*, May 27, 1870.

196 Donnelly assured O'Neill: *Official Report of Gen. John O'Neill*, 54.

196 Colonel E. C. Lewis reported: Ibid., 15.

196 O'Neill watched as the 6:00 a.m. train: Ibid., 6–9.

196 "Even if 800 arrived": *Daily Phoenix*, June 4, 1870.

196 "Every hour's delay": Le Caron, *Twenty-Five Years in the Secret Service*, 84.

197 Rain fell on St. Albans: *Burlington Free Press*, May 25, 1870.

197 From his lodgings: *St. Albans Messenger*, March 22, 1879.

197 At a cabinet meeting: Nevins, *Hamilton Fish*, 1:393–95.

197 "We cannot prevent": *Burlington Free Press*, May 28, 1870.

197 The persistent downpours: *Fenian Raid of 1870*, 39–40.

198 Soldiers who had expected: Ibid., 6–7.

198 That night, Queen Victoria's seventh child: *Boston Daily Advertiser*, May 28, 1870.

Chapter 17: A Burlesque of a War

199 "no serious resistance": *Boston Daily Advertiser,* May 26, 1870.

199 His plans called for an army: *Daily Phoenix,* June 4, 1870.

199 Five years his junior: Tuttle, "Fenian Campaign," 210–11.

199 After his young wife passed away: Howard, *Strange Empire,* 226, 353.

199 O'Neill and Donnelly rode: Richard family scrapbook.

200 As a reminder of the cause: Burnside, "Fenian Musket," 30.

200 To load their guns: Campbell, *Fenian Invasions of Canada of 1866 and 1870,* 39.

200 They even prepared: Richard family scrapbook.

200 Many now cloaked themselves: Joye, "Wearing of the Green," 51.

200 Reflecting their dual allegiances: Campbell, *Fenian Invasions of Canada of 1866 and 1870,* 39.

200 Many of those experienced: Tuttle, "Fenian Campaign," 211–12.

201 Around 11:00 a.m., a carriage: *St. Albans Messenger,* March 22, 1879.

201 end the "unlawful proceeding": Roche, *Life of John Boyle O'Reilly,* 109.

201 "expressed his contempt": Macdonald, *Troublous Times in Canada,* 160.

201 Foster told O'Neill: *Irish-American,* June 18, 1870.

201 The general spoke a few quiet words: Roche, *Life of John Boyle O'Reilly,* 109.

202 The general ordered: Le Caron, *Twenty-Five Years in the Secret Service,* 85.

202 Before they could confront: *Fenian Raid of 1870,* 28.

202 "The soft sweet breezes": Le Caron, *Twenty-Five Years in the Secret Service,* 85–86.

202 On its steep slopes: Sowles, "History of Fenianism and Fenian Raids in Vermont," 30–31.

202 The marshal assured Chamberlin: *St. Albans Messenger,* June 3, 1870.

203 "men who were mere pirates": Macdonald, *Troublous Times in Canada,* 166–67.

203 "entirely at the mercy": Westover to John Dougall & Son, March 6, 1866, BCHS.

203 After helping themselves: Busseau, *"Fenians Are Coming . . . ,"* 30.

203 After confederation in 1867: Westover to John Dougall & Son, March 6, 1866, BCHS.

203 Westover, whose grandfather: Smith, "War at the Border," 19.

204 Through frequent rifle practice: Reid, *Diary of a Country Clergyman,* 233–36.

204 Even when the fierce winter snow: Busseau, *"Fenians Are Coming . . . ,"* 30.

204 Locals mocked the homegrown militia: *Brief Account of the Fenian Raids,* 9.

204 Inspired by the crimson sashes: Westover to John Dougall & Son, March 6, 1866, BCHS.

204 Having received word: Busseau, *"Fenians Are Coming . . . ,"* 30–31.

204 "They're coming! They're coming!": *Brief Account of the Fenian Raids*, 21.

204 "more courage 'n sense": "Finian Raid Stories," Missisquoi Historical Society, 51.

204 Given that the sixty-two-year-old: Richard family scrapbook.

204 In fact, when Richard purchased: Carole Richard interview.

204 The families who lived: Busseau, *"Fenians Are Coming . . . ,"* 30.

205 Richard's brother Stephen: Richard family genealogy.

205 When the Irish Republican Army arrived: *Burlington Free Press*, July 23, 1958.

205 "them ruffians up": "Finian Raid Stories," Missisquoi Historical Society, 51.

205 "Soldiers, this is the advance guard": *St. Albans Messenger*, May 27, 1870.

205 Positioned at the front: Missisquoi County Historical Society, *Fenian Raids, 1866–1870*, 21.

206 The valley crackled: *Burlington Free Press*, May 27, 1870.

206 Up on Eccles Hill: Missisquoi County Historical Society, *Fenian Raids, 1866–1870*, 13.

206 He remembered well: *Burlington Free Press*, June 4, 1870.

206 Pell's finger squeezed: Richard family scrapbook.

206 The Fenians were greeted: *Burlington Free Press*, May 30, 1870.

206 William O'Brien of Moriah, New York: Roche, *Life of John Boyle O'Reilly*, 110.

206 When a Canadian shot: *Burlington Free Press*, May 27, 1870.

207 Many of the other spectators: Aldrich, *History of Franklin and Grand Isle Counties*, 346.

207 "could be distinctly heard": Richard family scrapbook.

207 In total, as many as fifty Fenians: Tuttle, "Fenian Campaign," 213.

207 The farmer was furious: *Rutland Weekly Herald*, June 2, 1870.

207 O'Neill managed to dash: Missisquoi County Historical Society, *Fenian Raids, 1866–1870*, 13.

207 "very ill directed": Report of Brown Chamberlin, May 28, 1870, in *Sessional Papers*, vol. 4, no. 7, 70–72.

208 "behind which twenty men": *Frank Leslie's Illustrated Newspaper*, June 18, 1870.

208 When Richard heard a noise: *Burlington Free Press*, July 23, 1958.

208 Le Caron had proven: Edwards, *Infiltrator*, 87; McMicken to Macdonald, July 1, 1870, LAC.

208 "Men of Ireland": *Official Report of Gen. John O'Neill*, 20–21.

208 "You must not do so": *Irish-American*, June 18, 1870.

209 As they passed through: *St. Albans Messenger*, May 27, 1870.

209 The marshal kept his hand: *St. Albans Messenger*, May 1, 1893.

209 "Clear the way!": Ibid.

209   "To have given the command": Le Caron, *Twenty-Five Years in the Secret Service,* 88.

210   Given the arrest: Roche, *Life of John Boyle O'Reilly,* 111.

210   Around 3:00 p.m.: Senior, *Last Invasion of Canada,* 163.

210   Donnelly traded sharp words: *Brief Account of the Fenian Raids,* 24–25.

210   Under the command: *Columbian Register,* June 4, 1870.

210   The shots landed: Busseau, *"Fenians Are Coming . . . ,"* 38.

210   Colonel Smith responded: Richard family scrapbook.

210   Donnelly was struck: *Burlington Free Press,* May 26, 1870.

210   "converted their retreat": *St. Albans Messenger,* June 3, 1870.

210   The body of Rowe: McKone, *Vermont's Irish Rebel,* 496.

211   Their resignation was complete: *St. Albans Messenger,* June 3, 1870.

211   He urged townspeople to: *Irish-American,* June 18, 1870.

211   "It's all up": *Burlington Free Press,* May 27, 1870.

211   "What did I tell you?": Tuttle, "Fenian Campaign," 211–12.

211   Ahern cursed his officers: *Irish-American,* June 18, 1870.

211   "most profane and abusive epithets": *Burlington Free Press,* May 30, 1870.

211   His arrest had been so humiliating: *Burlington Free Press,* May 27, 1870.

212   O'Neill would claim: *Burlington Free Press,* May 30, 1870.

212   After the Fenians departed: *St. Albans Messenger,* June 3, 1870.

212   Soldiers posed next to the body: Tuttle, "Fenian Campaign," 214.

212   According to the *St. Albans Messenger: St. Albans Messenger,* June 3, 1870.

212   As the sun faded: *Burlington Free Press,* May 30, 1870; Campbell, *Fenian Invasions of Canada of 1866 and 1870,* 43.

212   "that Fenian shouldn't rise again": *New-York Tribune,* May 27, 1870.

212   As a final insult: Missisquoi County Historical Society, *Fenian Raids, 1866–1870,* 76.

213   While Spear claimed: *Burlington Free Press,* May 26, 1870.

213   Spear appealed to Le Caron: Le Caron, *Twenty-Five Years in the Secret Service,* 89.

213   He would earn: *Vermont Life,* Summer 1961, 40.

213   "had to march back": *Burlington Free Press,* June 3, 1870.

213   "got up this movement": *Rutland Weekly Herald,* June 2, 1870.

Chapter 18: Another Fight, Another Flight

215   As the reporter John Boyle O'Reilly: Roche, *Life of John Boyle O'Reilly,* 112.

215   Down the road: *Burlington Free Press,* May 30, 1870.

215   Born in 1844: Roche, *Life of John Boyle O'Reilly,* 3–4.

216   O'Reilly imbibed the history: Schofield, *Seek for a Hero,* 6.

216 O'Reilly joined the Irish Republican Brotherhood: Kenneally, *From the Earth, a Cry*, 19.

216 Behind the iron-barred door: Roche, *Life of John Boyle O'Reilly*, 53–65; Evans, *Fanatic Heart*, 43–50.

216 A year later, O'Reilly: Roche, *Life of John Boyle O'Reilly*, 80.

216 He arrived in Philadelphia: Kenneally, *From the Earth, a Cry*, 138–56.

217 Bringing to his new home: Evans, *Fanatic Heart*, 174.

217 A budding journalist: MacManus, *Story of the Irish in Boston*, 207–9.

217 "thousands of men": Roche, *Life of John Boyle O'Reilly*, 108.

217 Stepping off the train: Evans, *Fanatic Heart*, 180.

217 "more serious" attack: McGee, *Fenian Raids on the Huntingdon Frontier*, 34.

218 "They were older": Roche, *Life of John Boyle O'Reilly*, 113.

218 "raw boys who were frightened": Evans, *Fanatic Heart*, 180.

218 Colonel William L. Thompson: *Daily Alta California*, July 28, 1870.

218 They were aided: Brown, "Fenian Raids, 1866 and 1870," 41.

218 For three days straight: *New-York Tribune*, May 28, 1870.

218 They also hauled: *Malone Palladium*, May 26, 1870.

218 The Irish Republican Army named: *Malone Palladium*, Feb. 6, 1908.

218 Following strict orders: *Fenian Raid of 1870*, 42–43.

218 Another band of raiders: *Malone Palladium*, June 2, 1870.

219 Starr proposed to make: *Harrisburg Telegraph*, June 9, 1870.

219 "to war against peaceful citizens": *New York Herald*, June 1, 1870.

219 He left his carriage: Roche, *Life of John Boyle O'Reilly*, 113.

219 After marching half a mile: Campbell, *Fenian Invasions of Canada*, 47.

219 Starr ordered his men: Hill, *Voice of the Vanishing Minority*, 67.

219 They dismantled fences: *Fenian Raid of 1870*, 44–46.

219 The Fenians were still: McGee, *Fenian Raids on the Huntingdon Frontier*, 41.

220 Led by Lieutenant Colonel George Bagot: Hart, *The New Annual Army List, Militia List, and Indian Civil Service List*, 315.

220 They were joined by 225 members: *Fenian Raid of 1870*, 43–44.

220 It had taken eighteen hours: Smyth, *Records of the Sixty-Ninth*, 18.

220 They had managed to catch: McGee, *Fenian Raids on the Huntingdon Frontier*, 38.

220 Milk and cold water: *Fenian Raid of 1870*, 44.

220 Colonel Bagot ordered: *St. Albans Messenger*, June 3, 1870.

220 Bagot assigned the local: Campbell, *Fenian Invasions of Canada of 1866 and 1870*, 48.

220 The Borderers on the right: Senior, *Last Invasion of Canada*, 170.

221 Meanwhile, Bagot's flankers: Butler, *Sir William Butler*, 117.

221 "Let us die": *New-York Tribune*, May 28, 1870.

221 They charged with fixed bayonets: *Fenian Raid of 1870*, 48.

221 Although Lieutenant Colonel Archibald McEachern: *St. Albans Messenger,* June 3, 1870.

222 One of the skirmishers: McGee, *Fenian Raids on the Huntingdon Frontier,* 42.

222 The Canadian volunteers: *St. Albans Messenger,* June 3, 1870.

222 The sole Canadian injury: Campbell, *Fenian Invasions of Canada of 1866 and 1870,* 50.

222 "Had they stood their ground": *Burlington Free Press,* May 30, 1870.

222 "Had the Fenians remained": *New York Herald,* May 28, 1870.

222 In the wake of what newspapers: *Harrisburg Telegraph,* June 9, 1870.

222 Along the way: *Burlington Free Press,* May 28, 1870.

222 After rushing away: *Pittsburgh Daily Commercial,* June 11, 1870.

223 "a battle better than his breakfast": *Daily Missouri Democrat,* June 2, 1870.

223 The arrival of the reinforcements: Senior, *Last Invasion of Canada,* 171.

223 The general found support: *Burlington Free Press,* May 28, 1870.

223 This latest attempt on Canada: *Malone Palladium,* June 2, 1870.

223 His forces seized: *Fenian Raid of 1870,* 58.

223 "one of the most ludicrous things": *Proceedings of the Vermont Historical Society,* 35–36.

223 So, broke and disappointed: *Fenian Raid of 1870,* 61–62.

224 With stomachs rumbling: *Washington Post,* March 22, 1908.

224 "The people along the frontier": D'Arcy, *Fenian Movement,* 356.

224 "wished to rid themselves": *Burlington Free Press,* May 30, 1870.

224 A member of New York governor: *Fenian Raid of 1870,* 64–65.

224 Queen Victoria's third son: *Burlington Free Press,* March 15, 1981.

224 On June 2, a merciful priest: McKone, *Vermont's Irish Rebel,* 508–9.

224 The decomposed state: *Burlington Free Press,* June 3, 1870.

225 "The entire Fenian movement": *New York Times,* May 29, 1870.

225 "sadder and wiser men": Roche, *Life of John Boyle O'Reilly,* 115.

225 "burst into tears": Ibid., 112–15.

225 "mad foray" by "criminally incompetent": *Tralee Chronicle and Killarney Echo,* June 24, 1870.

225 "Fenianism, so far as relates": Kenneally, *From the Earth, a Cry,* 149.

226 The debacle at Trout River: *Burlington Free Press,* May 28, 1870.

226 "laughed at the Fenians": Hill, *Voice of the Vanishing Minority,* 69.

227 "I Ran Away": *Boston Daily Advertiser,* May 31, 1870.

Chapter 19: The Fenians Behind Bars

228 The thick stone walls: *Burlington Free Press,* July 22, 1870.

228 The Fenian general: *Frank Leslie's Illustrated Newspaper,* June 11, 1870.

228 The *Canadian Illustrated News: Canadian Illustrated News,* June 4, 1870.

228 "had the arms and war material": *Official Report of Gen. John O'Neill,* 3–4.

228 "The people, so often deceived": Ibid., 27.

229 Even after the court: *Burlington Free Press,* June 8, 1870.

229 Fenian coffers were so empty: Nevins, *Hamilton Fish,* 1:394.

229 "unauthorized and unjustifiable": *Irish-American,* June 4, 1870.

229 "O'Neill would not be safe": Gibbons to Gallagher, July 5, 1870, ACHS.

229 "merely a personal enterprise": *New-York Tribune,* May 26, 1870.

229 "valuable war material": Gibbons to the Officers and Members of the Fenian Brotherhood, May 28, 1870, ACHS.

229 "Even if they were able": *New York Times,* May 29, 1870.

230 "This thing of being a citizen": D'Arcy, *Fenian Movement,* 359.

230 Orangemen marching up Broadway: Gordon, *Orange Riots,* 27–51.

231 *The New York Times* and other newspapers: *New York Times,* July 13, 1870.

231 "Events have at intervals": Roche, *John Boyle O'Reilly,* 116–17.

231 Just as he had done: Brodsky, *Grover Cleveland,* 30.

232 The trio were transported: *Daily Alta California,* July 28, 1870.

232 The courtroom in the small central Vermont town: *Lawrence American,* Aug. 5, 1870.

232 The Fenian general smiled: *Philadelphia Evening Telegraph,* July 29, 1870.

232 The general told the court: *Official Report of Gen. John O'Neill,* 57–60.

232 O'Neill's oration moved many: *Chicago Tribune,* Aug. 6, 1870.

233 "Any real or supposed wrong": *Official Report of Gen. John O'Neill,* 61–62.

233 The Fenian general greeted: *Lawrence American,* Aug. 5, 1870.

233 William Maxwell Evarts: *New York Times,* Aug. 4, 1870.

233 Donations arrived from quarters: *Official Report of Gen. John O'Neill,* 55.

233 They were given their own rooms: *Chicago Tribune,* Aug. 6, 1870.

233 "was to give effect": *Irish-American,* Sept. 3, 1870.

234 The Cincinnati convention: *New York Herald,* Aug. 24, 1870.

234 The United Irishmen proposed: *Irish-American,* Sept. 3, 1870.

234 Savage, though, was interested: *Address of the Council of the Fenian Brotherhood,* 1.

234 "had no more right": *Tralee Chronicle and Killarney Echo,* June 24, 1870.

235 "Purely political prisoners": *Papers of Ulysses S. Grant,* 20:222–27.

235 With midterm elections already under way: McGee, *Fenian Raids on the Huntingdon Frontier,* 54.

235 "Their prolonged imprisonment": D'Arcy, *Fenian Movement,* 365–66.

236 "That we have been a source": *Official Report of Gen. John O'Neill,* 28–30.

Chapter 20: Losing Their Lifeblood

237 William Gladstone took off his coat: Morley, *Life of William Ewart Gladstone,* 252.

238 "One of the triumphs": Gibbons to the Officers and Members of the Fenian Brotherhood, July 1, 1870, ACHS.

238 The conditions endured: Savage, *American Citizens Prisoners in Great Britain*, 8–11.

238 Born into an Irish-speaking: Devoy, *Devoy's Post Bag*, 10.

238 Even before he could read: Rossa, *Rossa's Recollections*, 115–17.

238 He buried a friend's dead mother: Kenna, *Jeremiah O'Donovan Rossa*, 11–12.

239 "There was no 'famine' ": Rossa, *Rossa's Recollections*, 35.

239 "If the operation of English rule": Ibid., 119.

239 In his virtual dungeon: Golway, *Irish Rebel*, 65–69.

239 He wasn't even allowed: Rossa, *Irish Rebels in English Prisons*, 178.

239 Rossa spent his days: *Philadelphia Inquirer*, Feb. 23, 1871.

240 After flinging his filled chamber pot: *Papers of Ulysses S. Grant*, 21:224.

240 For more than five years: Golway, *Irish Rebel*, 65.

240 More than one million people: Devoy, *Devoy's Post Bag*, 1.

240 After an official commission: Rossa, *Irish Rebels in English Prisons*, 416–17.

241 called a "sham amnesty": Devoy, *Devoy's Post Bag*, 1.

241 "were not released to freedom": *Proceedings of the Tenth General Convention*, 9.

241 Rossa stared: Rossa, *Irish Rebels in English Prisons*, 416–24.

241 Shortly after the sun set: *New York World*, Jan. 21, 1871.

242 The passengers aboard: D'Arcy, *Fenian Movement*, 369.

242 Not long after their departure: *New York World*, Jan. 21, 1871.

242 Thundering cannons and Irish airs: Golway, *Irish Rebel*, 4.

242 Having pocketed £7 playing poker: Devoy, *Recollections of an Irish Rebel*, 329–30.

243 The *Bronx* arrived first: Rossa, *Irish Rebels in English Prisons*, 424–27.

243 O'Gorman informed the Cuba Five: *New York Sun*, Jan. 21, 1871.

243 "I saw immediately": Rossa, *Irish Rebels in English Prisons*, 424–27.

243 After O'Gorman concluded: *New York World*, Jan. 21, 1871.

243 The parties traded vulgarities: Rossa, *Irish Rebels in English Prisons*, 424–27.

243 When Dr. John Carnochan: *New York World*, Jan. 21, 1871.

244 "We desire that all Irishmen": Rossa, *Irish Rebels in English Prisons*, 426–27.

244 After quarantine officials: *New York Herald*, Jan. 21, 1871.

244 Atop the hotel: Buckley, *Diary of a Tour of America*, 211.

245 Three thousand callers: *New York World*, Jan. 21, 1871.

245 The United Irishmen treasurer: *New York Herald*, Jan. 21, 1871.

245 resembling a "Pittston miner": *New York Herald*, Jan. 23, 1871.

245 Although they sought to avoid: Rossa, *Irish Rebels in English Prisons*, 424–27.

245 "We do not wish": *New-York Tribune*, Jan. 31, 1871.

245 Men wearing green neckties: Buckley, *Diary of a Tour in America*, 215.

245 Even the horses hauling streetcars: *New York Herald,* Feb. 10, 1871.

245 An estimated 300,000 people: *New York Times,* Feb. 10, 1871.

245 The Sixty-Ninth Regiment: *New York Herald,* Feb. 10, 1871.

246 After a welcome resolution: *New York Times,* Feb. 23, 1871.

246 President Ulysses S. Grant stood: *Tennessean,* Feb. 23, 1871.

246 "Glad to see you": Rossa, *Recollections of an Irish Rebel,* 362.

246 In an address released: *New-York Tribune,* March 14, 1871.

247 The United Irishmen enthusiastically: Devoy, *Devoy's Post Bag,* 33.

247 "A bright hope is better": D'Arcy, *Fenian Movement,* 379.

247 "Some may think that": *Proceedings of the Tenth General Convention,* 3–24.

248 The same infighting: D'Arcy, *Fenian Movement,* 386.

248 "The greatest trouble": Corning, *Hamilton Fish,* 77.

249 Convinced by Fish: Smith, *Grant,* 508–12.

249 Grant became a regular presence: Martin, *The Presidents and the Prime Ministers,* 26–32.

249 While the *Alabama* claims: Smith, *Grant,* 512–13.

250 To the fury of some Canadians: Nevins, *Hamilton Fish,* 1:470.

Chapter 21: The Invasion That Wasn't

251 Tongues of fire: McMicken, *Abortive Fenian Raid on Manitoba,* 1–7.

251 The fires were so ferocious: Kingsbury, *History of Dakota Territory,* 589.

251 The first days of autumn: *New York Herald,* Oct. 5, 1871.

251 The inferno bestowed: *Manhattan Nationalist,* Sept. 22, 1871.

251 The black soot of the charred prairie: McMicken, *Abortive Fenian Raid on Manitoba,* 1–7.

253 Led by Louis Riel: Rogers, "Louis Riel's Rebellion," 153.

253 O'Donoghue also assured: De Trémaudan, "Louis Riel and the Fenian Raid of 1871," 137; Frémont, "Archbishop Taché and the Beginnings of Manitoba," 135.

253 With no stomach: Pritchett, "Origin of the So-Called Fenian Raid on Manitoba in 1871," 38–39.

254 Going it alone: *Buffalo Commercial,* May 31, 1871.

254 When rumors of a Fenian raid: Archibald to Macdonald, Aug. 31, 1871, LAC.

254 Passing through Chicago: Edwards, *Infiltrator,* 95.

254 "I had no thought": Le Caron, *Twenty-Five Years in the Secret Service,* 97.

254 The secret agent: D'Arcy, *Fenian Movement,* 377.

255 In the Fenians' wake: McMicken, *Abortive Fenian Raid on Manitoba,* 6.

255 Like giant wooden guideposts: Kingsbury, *History of Dakota Territory,* 583.

255 After passing ramshackle cabins: "Fenians in Dakota," 122.

255 When O'Donoghue finally reached out: De Trémaudan, "Louis Riel and the Fenian Raid of 1871," 138.

256 Archibald had a garrison: *Report of the Select Committee on the Causes of the Difficulties in the North-West Territory in 1869–70*, 140.

256 "little apprehension of any organized": "Canadian-American Defence Relations," 7.

256 Around 7:30 a.m., the raiders: Adams G. Archibald memorandum, Oct. 9, 1871, in *Sessional Papers*, vol. 7, no. 26, 6–8.

256 As the force approached: Swan and Jerome, "Unequal Justice," 24–38.

256 Stirred from his sleep: Adams G. Archibald memorandum, Oct. 27, 1871, in *Sessional Papers*, vol. 7, no. 26, 4–5.

257 After awakening George W. Webster: *Sydney Morning Herald*, Dec. 26, 1871.

257 They burst through the gates: Cowie, *Company of Adventurers*, 175.

257 O'Neill's men faced no resistance: "Fenians in Dakota," 118–20.

257 For their first order: Young, *Manitoba Memories*, 214–16.

257 Then, rifling through the post's provisions: Walker, *Fenian Movement*, 191.

257 As the morning sun: *Sydney Morning Herald*, Dec. 26, 1871.

257 Unbeknownst to them: Webster to John A. Macdonald, Oct. 12, 1871, LAC.

257 While O'Neill held a war council: *Sydney Morning Herald*, Dec. 26, 1871.

258 Apparently, the American prisoner: Webster to Macdonald, Oct. 12, 1871, LAC.

258 Wheaton had been stationed: Guttman, "No Country for Lost Irishmen," 62.

258 But when the loose lips: Chipman, "How Gin Saved Manitoba," 518–19.

258 Archibald also informed Taylor: Blegen, "James Wickes Taylor," 200.

258 Colonel Thomas Curley ordered: Young, *Manitoba Memories*, 214–16.

258 With his one arm: Webster to Macdonald, Oct. 12, 1871, LAC.

258 O'Neill scurried so abruptly: *Times-Picayune*, Oct. 22, 1871; *New York Herald*, Oct. 21, 1871.

259 Like children, the Fenians: Archibald memorandum, Oct. 27, 1871, 4–5.

259 The federal troops seized: "Fenians in Dakota," 118–20.

259 When O'Donoghue was in the clear: Archibald memorandum, Oct. 27, 1871, 4–5.

259 "a hearty breakfast": *Times-Picayune*, Oct. 22, 1871.

259 "I believe the action": Johnson, "Fenian 'Invasion' of 1871."

259 In May 1870: Lass, *Minnesota's Boundary with Canada*, 79.

260 That meant that: "Fenians in Dakota," 118–20.

260 While the U.S. State Department: Archibald memorandum, Oct. 9, 1871, 6–8.

260 O'Neill was unaware: Noonan, "General John O'Neill," 316.

260 "want of jurisdiction": "Fenians in Dakota," 127.

260 "the Fenian fiasco": *Spirit of Democracy*, Oct. 24, 1871.

260   "another reckless and ridiculous": *New York Times*, Oct. 13, 1871.

260   "This time the attempt": *Irish-American*, Oct. 21, 1871.

260   "O'Neill's folly" was his and his alone: *Tennessean*, Oct. 18, 1871.

260   "The application of the term": *Irish-American*, Oct. 21, 1871.

261   "a mere accident": Noonan, "General John O'Neill," 315.

Chapter 22: The Next Best Thing

262   "All denounce O'Neill": RGS (Le Caron) to J. Bell (McMicken), Oct. 22,
      1871, LAC.

262   Fenian leaders had long talked: O'Neill, *Northern Nebraska as a Home for
      Immigrants*, 4–6.

263   "Cheap Farms! Free Homes!": *Irish-American*, June 22, 1872.

263   "for providing homes": *New York Times*, Dec. 11, 1870.

263   He spent parts of 1872: O'Neill, *Northern Nebraska as a Home for Immigrants*, 77.

263   The general signed an agreement: Passewitz, "O'Neill, Nebraska," 12.

263   "Why are you content": McCulloh, *Piece of Emerald*, 6.

263   Using the same powers: Yost, *Before Today*, 5.

264   "We could build up": O'Neill to O'Connor, Dec. 27, 1876, Archdiocese of
      Omaha.

264   As the sun reached its zenith: Passewitz, "O'Neill, Nebraska," 15.

264   The flat, desolate prairie: Yost, *Before Today*, 185.

264   The colonists who had lived: O'Neill, *Northern Nebraska as a Home for
      Immigrants*, 81.

264   "so plainly mirrored": Yost, *Before Today*, 185.

265   On a mid-July day: Ibid., 7.

265   While the wheat, rye, and barley: *Irish-American*, Feb. 20, 1875.

266   Desperate to salvage his reputation: Yost, *Before Today*, 7.

266   The offer renewed: McCulloh, *Piece of Emerald*, 9–14.

266   With plans to plant: O'Neill, *Northern Nebraska as a Home for Immigrants*, 4;
      Noonan, "General John O'Neill," 304.

266   "the next best thing": Noonan, "General John O'Neill," 283.

266   "I shall continue at it": *Frontier*, July 24, 1924.

267   "devoted to the cause": O'Neill, *Northern Nebraska as a Home for
      Immigrants*, 4.

267   "I had a double object": Noonan, "General John O'Neill," 317–18.

267   "The prairies are wide": *Frontier*, July 24, 1924.

268   "the mere framework": Roche, *Life of John Boyle O'Reilly*, 175.

268   With Bernard Doran Killian: *New York Herald*, Feb. 7, 1877; *Irish-American*,
      Feb. 17, 1877.

268   "He was not merely": Roche, *Life of John Boyle O'Reilly*, 175.

269   Fenian hands lowered: *Irish-American*, March 24, 1877.

269 The workload took a toll: *Omaha Daily Herald,* Jan. 9, 1878.

270 Following Mary Ann's departure: McCulloh, *Piece of Emerald,* 6.

270 He passed away: *Omaha Daily Herald,* Jan. 8, 1878.

270 "Leave him in Omaha": Noonan, "Characterization of General John O'Neill," iii.

270 "In our short-sighted human judgement": *Irish-American,* Jan. 19, 1878.

Epilogue

271 On Palm Sunday: Ramón, *Provisional Dictator,* 246.

271 In fading daylight: *Times* (London), April 1, 1901.

272 "If we ever hope": *Nation,* March 3, 1877.

272 "Ireland's opportunity will come": Schmuhl, *Ireland's Exiled Children,* 19.

273 "Rossa dead. What shall we do?": Golway, *Irish Rebel,* 207.

273 The Fenians bombed a pub: Burleigh, *Blood and Rage,* 17.

273 began to call "O'Dynamite Rossa": *St. Louis Post-Dispatch,* Oct. 25, 1877.

273 When Queen Victoria injured herself: *Idaho Semi-weekly World,* May 4, 1883.

274 "on behalf of a new generation": McIntire, *Speeches in World History,* 299–300.

274 "In the name of God": Golway, *Irish Rebel,* 228.

275 Devoy estimated that Clan na Gael: Devoy, *Recollections of an Irish Rebel,* 392–93.

275 In addition, five of the seven signatories: Schmuhl, *Ireland's Exiled Children,* 20.

275 The last man out: Ibid., 149.

275 The Easter Rising claimed: Ibid., 5–6.

276 "All changed, changed utterly": Yeats, *"Easter, 1916," and Other Poems,* 53.

276 When de Valera became: Kostick, *Easter Rising,* 69.

277 De Valera made a waxed impression: Santos, "Greatest Escape from Lincoln Prison."

277 On the lam, de Valera became: Schmuhl, *Ireland's Exiled Children,* 129.

277 Much as Stephens had done: Coogan, *Eamon de Valera,* 148–49.

277 When he arrived in Omaha: *Omaha Daily Bee,* Aug. 12, 1895.

277 "shrine of the Fenians": *Omaha World Herald,* Jan. 14, 1900.

277 Adorned with swords: *Omaha Daily Bee,* Feb. 19, 1911.

277 The report turned out to be: *Inter Ocean,* May 13, 1900; Williams, *Call in Pinkerton's,* 57.

278 De Valera stepped forward: *Omaha Daily Bee,* Oct. 29, 1919.

278 "The Fenian Brotherhood": *Omaha World Herald,* Oct. 29, 1919.

Bibliography

Selected Bibliography

Address of the Council of the Fenian Brotherhood. Sept. 29, 1870.

Aldrich, Lewis Cass, ed. *History of Franklin and Grand Isle Counties, Vermont.* Syracuse, N.Y.: D. Mason, 1891.

The American Annual Cyclopaedia and Register of Important Events of the Year 1866. New York: D. Appleton, 1867.

Anbinder, Tyler. *City of Dreams: The 400-Year Epic History of Immigrant New York.* Boston: Houghton Mifflin Harcourt, 2016.

———. *Five Points: The 19th-Century New York City Neighborhood That Invented Tap Dance, Stole Elections, and Became the World's Most Notorious Slum.* New York: Free Press, 2001.

Anderson, Sir Robert. *The Lighter Side of My Official Life.* London: Hodder and Stoughton, 1910.

Andrews, Roland Franklyn. "How 'Unpreparedness' Undid St. Albans." *Outlook,* Nov. 22, 1916, 673–84.

Annual Report of the Adjutant General of Missouri for 1864. Jefferson City, Mo.: W. A. Curry, 1865.

Arnold, Cassie. "The Treadmill Originated in Prisons." *Mental Floss,* Jan. 10, 2014. www.mentalfloss.com.

"Asa Westover, Esq." *New Dominion Monthly,* July 1870, 63.

Bartoletti, Susan Campbell. *Black Potatoes: The Story of the Great Irish Famine, 1845–1850.* Boston: Houghton Mifflin, 2001.

Bayliss, Mary Lynn. *The Dooleys of Richmond: An Irish Immigrant Family in the Old and New South.* Charlottesville: University of Virginia Press, 2017.

Bayor, Ronald H., and Timothy J. Meagher. *The New York Irish.* Baltimore: Johns Hopkins University Press, 1996.

Bergeron, Paul H. *The Papers of Andrew Johnson.* Vol. 13, *September 1867–March 1868.* Knoxville: University of Tennessee Press, 1966.

Bilby, Joseph G. "Black Powder, White Smoke." *Civil War News,* Oct. 2017.

———. *The Irish Brigade in the Civil War: The 69th New York and Other Irish Regiments of the Army of the Potomac.* Conshohocken, Penn.: Combined, 2000.

Blegen, Theodore C. "James Wickes Taylor: A Biographical Sketch." *Minnesota History Bulletin* 1 (Nov. 1915): 153–219.

Borthwick, J. Douglas. *History of the Montréal Prison, from a.d. 1784 to a.d. 1886.* Montreal: A. Periard, 1886.

Bothwell, Robert. *Your Country, My Country: A Unified History of the United States and Canada.* New York: Oxford University Press, 2015.

Boyko, John. *Blood and Daring: How Canada Fought the American Civil War and Forged a Nation.* Toronto: Vintage Canada, 2014.

———. "Patrick James Whelan." *Canadian Encyclopedia,* Jan. 29, 2008. www .thecanadianencyclopedia.ca.

A Brief Account of the Fenian Raids on the Missisquoi Frontier in 1866 and 1870. Montreal: "Witness" Steam Printing House, 1871.

Brodsky, Alyn. *Grover Cleveland: A Study in Character.* New York: St. Martin's Press, 2000.

Brown, Harold F. "The Fenian Raids, 1866 and 1870." *Franklin Historical Review* 16 (1979): 39–44.

Brown, William Garrott. "The Tenth Decade of the United States." *Atlantic Monthly,* June 1905, 766–80.

Bruce, Susannah Ural. *The Harp and the Eagle: Irish-American Volunteers and the Union Army, 1861–1865.* New York: New York University Press, 2006.

Brundage, David. *Irish Nationalists in America: The Politics of Exile, 1798–1998.* New York: Oxford University Press, 2016.

Bryan, Frank. *Real Democracy: The New England Town Meeting and How It Works.* Chicago: University of Chicago Press, 2010.

Buckley, M. B. *Diary of a Tour in America.* Dublin: Sealy, Bryers & Walker, 1889.

Burleigh, Michael. *Blood and Rage: A Cultural History of Terrorism.* New York: Harper, 2009.

Burnell, Paul. "The American Civil War Surrender on the Mersey." BBC News, Nov. 7, 2015. www.bbc.com.

Burnside, Graham. "The Fenian Musket." *Gun Report,* Feb. 1990, 24–30.

Burrows, Edwin G., and Mike Wallace. *Gotham: A History of New York to 1898.* New York: Oxford University Press, 1999.

Bushnell, Mark. *It Happened in Vermont.* Guilford, Conn.: Globe Pequot Press, 2009.

———. "Then Again: Vermont Helps Launch an International Incident." *VTDigger,* May 7, 2017. vtdigger.org.

Busseau, Laurent. *"The Fenians Are Coming . . .": An Illustrated History of an Irish*

Invasion in the Early Years of Canadian Confederation (1866–1870). Stanbridge East, Que.: Missisquoi Historical Society Collection, 2016.

Busteed, Mervyn. *The Irish in Manchester, c. 1750–1921: Resistance, Adaptation, and Identity*. Manchester: Manchester University Press, 2016.

Butler, William Francis. *Sir William Butler: An Autobiography*. London: Constable, 1911.

Calkin, Homer. "St. Albans in Reverse: The Fenian Raid of 1866." *Vermont History* 35 (Jan. 1967): 19–34.

Callahan, John R. *Emerging Biological Threats: A Reference Guide*. Santa Barbara, Calif.: Greenwood Press, 2010.

Campbell, Christopher. *Fenian Fire: The British Government Plot to Assassinate Queen Victoria*. London: HarperCollins, 2003.

Campbell, Francis Wayland. *The Fenian Invasions of Canada of 1866 and 1870 and the Operations of the Montreal Militia Brigade in Connection Therewith*. Montreal: John Lovell & Son, 1904.

"Canadian-American Defence Relations, 1867–1914." Report No. 2, Historical Section, Canadian Forces Headquarters, Aug. 1965. publications.gc.ca.

Canadian Border Bard. *Canadian Border Songs, of the Fenian Invasion of Canada*. 1870.

Cavanagh, Michael. *Memoirs of Gen. Thomas Francis Meagher, Comprising the Leading Events of His Career*. Worcester, Mass.: Messenger Press, 1892.

Chambers, Ernest J. *The Queen's Own Rifles of Canada*. Toronto: E. L. Ruddy, 1901.

Chamney, William G. *The Fenian Conspiracy: Report of the Trials of Thomas F. Burke and Others for High Treason and Treason-Felony at the Special Commission, Dublin*. Dublin: Alexander Thom, 1869.

Chipman, George Fisher. "How Gin Saved Manitoba." *Canadian Magazine*, March 1907, 518–19.

Clark, Dennis. *The Irish in Philadelphia: Ten Generations of Urban Experience*. Philadelphia: Temple University Press, 1973.

———. "Letters from the Underground: The Fenian Correspondence of James Gibbons." *Records of the American Catholic Historical Society of Philadelphia* 81 (June 1870): 83–88.

———. "Militants of the 1860s: The Philadelphia Fenians." *Pennsylvania Magazine of History and Biography*, Jan. 1971, 98–108.

Clark, Joseph. "The Spy Who Came in from the Coalfields: A British Spy in Illinois." *Journal of Illinois History* 10 (Summer 2007): 90–106.

Cole, J. A. *Prince of Spies: Henri Le Caron*. London: Faber and Faber, 1984.

Coogan, Tim Pat. *Eamon de Valera: The Man Who Was Ireland*. New York: Harper Collins, 1995.

———. *The Famine Plot: England's Role in Ireland's Greatest Tragedy*. New York: Palgrave Macmillan, 2012.

————. *Wherever the Green Is Worn: The Story of the Irish Diaspora.* London: Arrow Books, 2002.

Corning, Amos Elwood. *Hamilton Fish.* New York: Lanmere, 1918.

Correspondence Relating to the Fenian Invasion, and the Rebellion of the Southern States. Ottawa: Hunter, Rose, 1869.

Correspondence Respecting the Recent Fenian Aggression upon Canada. London: Harrison and Sons, 1867.

Cowie, Isaac. *The Company of Adventurers: A Narrative of Seven Years in the Service of the Hudson's Bay Company During 1867–1874.* Toronto: William Briggs, 1913.

Crowley, John, ed. *Atlas of the Great Irish Famine.* New York: New York University Press, 2012.

Cumberland, Barlow. *The Fenian Raid of 1866 and Events on the Frontier.* Ottawa: Royal Society of Canada, 1911.

Dafoe, John W. "The Fenian Invasion of Quebec, 1866." *Canadian Magazine,* Feb. 1898, 339–47.

Dallison, Robert L. *Turning Back the Fenians: New Brunswick's Last Colonial Campaign.* Fredericton, N.B.: Goose Lane, 2006.

Darch, Heather. "For the Sake of Ireland." *Townships Heritage WebMagazine.* townshipsheritage.com.

D'Arcy, William. "The Fenian Movement in the United States, 1858–1886." Ph.D. diss., Catholic University of America, 1947.

Davis, Harold. "The Fenian Raid on New Brunswick." *Canadian Historical Review* 36 (Dec. 1955): 316–34.

Davis, Kenneth C. *A Nation Rising: Untold Tales from America's Hidden History.* New York: HarperCollins, 2010.

Delany, William. *The Green and the Red: Revolutionary Republicanism and Socialism in Irish History, 1848–1923.* San Jose, Calif.: Writer's Showcase, 2001.

Denieffe, Joseph. *A Personal Narrative of the Irish Revolutionary Brotherhood: Giving a Faithful Report of the Principal Events from 1855 to 1867.* New York: Gael, 1906.

Denvir, John. *"God Save Ireland!"; or, The Rescue of Kelly & Deasey.* Liverpool: John Denvir, ca. 1880.

————. *The Life of an Old Rebel.* Shannon: Irish University Press, 1972.

Department of Culture, Heritage, and the Gaeltacht. "National Famine Commemoration," June 21, 2011. www.chg.gov.ie.

de Trémaudan, A. H. "Louis Riel and the Fenian Raid of 1871." *Canadian Historical Review* 4 (June 1923): 132–44.

Devoy, John. *Devoy's Post Bag, 1871–1928.* Vol. 1, *1871–1880.* Edited by William O'Brien and Desmond Ryan. Dublin: C. J. Fallon, 1948.

————. *Recollections of an Irish Rebel: A Personal Narrative.* New York: Charles Young, 1929.

DK Eyewitness Travel Guide: Dublin. London: Dorling Kindersley, 2012.

Doheny, Michael. *The Felon's Track: A Narrative of '48.* New York: Farrell & Son, 1867.

Dolan, Jay P. *The Irish Americans: A History.* New York: Bloomsbury Press, 2008.

Donlon, Regina. "John O'Keeffe and the Fenian Brotherhood in the American West and Midwest, 1866–1890." *New Hibernia Review* 21 (Spring 2017): 86–103.

Doolin, David. *Transnational Revolutionaries: The Fenian Invasion of Canada, 1866.* Oxford: Peter Lang, 2016.

Dorney, John. *Griffith College Dublin: A History of the Campus, 1813–2013.* Dublin: Griffith College Dublin, 2013.

Driedger, Sharon Doyle. *An Irish Heart: How a Small Immigrant Community Shaped Canada.* Toronto: HarperCollins, 2011.

Duffy, Charles Gavan. "Four Years of Irish History, 1845–1849." *Westminster and Foreign Quarterly Review* 64 (July 1883): 71–94.

Edwards, Peter. *The Infiltrator: Henri Le Caron, the British Spy Inside the Fenian Movement.* Dunboyne, Ire.: Maverick House, 2010.

Egan, Timothy. *The Immortal Irishman: The Irish Revolutionary Who Became an American Hero.* Boston: Houghton Mifflin Harcourt, 2016.

Ellis, Peter Berresford, and Joseph A. King. "Fenian Casualties and Prisoners: Fenian Invasion of British North America, June 1866." *Irish Sword* 18 (Summer 1992): 271–84.

Ellis, William H. "The Adventures of a Prisoner of War." *Canadian Magazine,* July 1899, 199–203.

Emmet, Robert. *The Life, Trial, and Conversations of Robert Emmet.* New York: Robert Coddington, 1845.

Evans, A. G. *Fanatic Heart: A Life of John Boyle O'Reilly, 1844–1890.* Boston: Northeastern University Press, 1999.

Farfan, Matthew. *The Vermont-Quebec Border: Life on the Line.* Charleston, S.C.: Arcadia, 2009.

Feeney, Vincent E. *Finnigans, Slaters, and Stonepeggers: A History of the Irish in Vermont.* Bennington, Vt.: Images from the Past, 2009.

"The Fenian Brotherhood I.R.A. Belt Buckle." *American Fenians,* Feb. 2, 2018. americanfenians.wordpress.com.

Fenian Raid: An Open Letter from Archbishop Taché to the Hon. Gilbert McMicken. St. Boniface, Man., 1888.

The Fenian Raid at Fort Erie. Toronto: W. C. Chewett, 1866.

The Fenian Raid of 1870 by Reporters Present at the Scenes. Montreal: "Witness" Printing House, 1871.

"The Fenian Raid of '66." *Buffalo Historical Society Publications* 25 (1921): 263–85.

"Fenians Hide n' Go Seek." American Fenians, Sept. 1, 2015. americanfenians .wordpress.com.

"Fenians in Dakota." *South Dakota Historical Collections* 6 (1912): 117–30.

Finerty, John F. "Thirty Years of Ireland's Battle—V." *Donahoe's Magazine*, Sept. 1893, 275–80.

———. "Thirty Years of Ireland's Battle—VI." *Donahoe's Magazine*, Oct. 1893, 429–36.

———. "Thirty Years of Ireland's Battle—VII." *Donahoe's Magazine*, Nov. 1893, 539–45.

The First Report of the Missisquoi County Historical Society. Stanbridge, Que.: Missisquoi County Historical Society, 1906.

Forster, John. *The Life of Charles Dickens, 1847–1870*. London: Chapman & Hall, 1870.

Fredericks, Wanda Meryle. "The Growth of the Catholic Church in Anderson, Indiana, in Relation to National, State, and Local History." Master's thesis, Ball State University, 1966.

Frémont, Donatien. "Archbishop Taché and the Beginning of Manitoba." *North Dakota Historical Quarterly* 6 (Jan. 1932): 107–46.

French, Brigittine M. " 'We're All Irish': Transforming Irish Identity in a Midwestern Community." *New Hibernia Review/Iris Éireannach Nua* 11 (Spring 2007): 9–24.

Funchion, Michael F., ed. *Irish American Voluntary Organizations*. Westport, Conn.: Greenwood Press, 1983.

Galwey, Thomas Francis. *The Valiant Hours: Narrative of "Captain Brevet," an Irish-American in the Army of the Potomac*. Harrisburg, Pa.: Stackpole, 1961.

Garand, P. S. *The History of the City of Ogdensburg*. Ogdensburg, N.Y.: M. J. Belleville, 1927.

Gibson, Dale, Lee Gibson, and Cameron Harvey. *Attorney for the Frontier: Enos Stutsman*. Winnipeg: University of Manitoba Press, 2014.

Gleeson, David T. *The Green and the Gray: The Irish in the Confederate States of America*. Chapel Hill: University of North Carolina Press, 2013.

Goldman, Mark. *High Hopes: The Rise and Decline of Buffalo, New York*. Albany: State University of New York Press, 1983.

Goldstone, Lawrence. *Going Deep: John Philip Holland and the Invention of the Attack Submarine*. New York: Pegasus Books, 2017.

Golway, Terry. *For the Cause of Liberty: A Thousand Years of Ireland's Heroes*. New York: Simon & Schuster, 2000.

———. *Irish Rebel: John Devoy and America's Fight for Ireland's Freedom*. New York: St. Martin's Press, 1998.

Gordon, Michael A. *The Orange Riots: Irish Political Violence in New York City, 1870 and 1871*. Ithaca, N.Y.: Cornell University Press, 1993.

Grant, Ulysses S. *The Papers of Ulysses S. Grant*. Vol. 16, *1866*. Edited by John Y. Simon. Carbondale: Southern Illinois University Press, 1995.

———. *The Papers of Ulysses S. Grant*. Vol. 20, *November 1, 1869–October 31, 1870*.

Edited by John Y. Simon. Carbondale: Southern Illinois University Press, 1995.

——. *The Papers of Ulysses S. Grant.* Vol. 21, *November 1, 1870–May 31, 1871.* Edited by John Y. Simon. Carbondale: Southern Illinois University Press, 1995.

Gregg, George R., and E. P. Roden. *Trials of the Fenian Prisoners at Toronto, Who Were Captured at Fort Erie, C.W., in June, 1866.* Toronto: Leader Steam-Press, 1867.

Griffin, Brian. " 'Scallions, Pikes, and Bog Oak Ornaments': The Irish Republican Brotherhood and the Chicago Fenian Fair, 1864." *Studia Hibernica* 29 (1995–97): 85–97.

Guttman, Jon. "No Country for Lost Irishmen." *Wild West* 29 (April 2017): 58–63.

Gwyn, Richard J. *Nation Maker: Sir John A. Macdonald: His Life, Our Times.* Toronto: Random House Canada, 2011.

Gwynn, Denis. *Young Ireland and 1848.* Cork: Cork University Press, 1949.

Harmon, Maurice, ed. *Fenians and Fenianism: Centenary Essays.* Seattle: University of Washington Press, 1970.

Harnedy, Jim, and Jane Diggins Harnedy. *Campobello Island.* Charleston, S.C.: Arcadia, 2002.

Hart, H. G. *The New Annual Army List, Militia List, and Indian Civil Service List for 1875.* London: John Murray, 1875.

Haynes, L. Louise, and Charlotte Pedersen. *St. Albans.* Charleston, S.C.: Arcadia, 2010.

Herbermann, Charles G., ed. *The Catholic Encyclopedia: An International Work of Reference on the Constitution, Doctrine, Discipline, and History of the Catholic Church.* Vol. 5. New York: Robert Appleton, 1909.

Hill, Robert. *Voice of the Vanishing Minority: Robert Sellar and the Huntingdon Gleaner, 1863–1919.* Montreal: McGill-Queen's University Press, 1998.

Hill, Robert B. *Manitoba: History of Its Early Settlement, Development, and Resources.* Toronto: William Briggs, 1890.

Hodges, John George. *Report of the Trial of William Smith O'Brien for High Treason.* Dublin: Alexander Thom, 1849.

Hoffman, John T. *Public Papers of John T. Hoffman, Governor of New York, 1869–70–71–72.* Albany, N.Y.: J. Munsell, 1872.

Howard, Joseph Kinsey. *Strange Empire: A Narrative of the Northwest.* Westport, Conn.: Greenwood Press, 1974.

Hunt, Roger D., and Jack R. Brown. *Brevet Brigadier Generals in Blue.* Gaithersburg, Md.: Olde Soldier Books, 1990.

James Stephens, Chief Organizer of the Irish Republic: Embracing an Account of the Origin and Progress of the Fenian Brotherhood. New York: Carleton, 1866.

Jenkins, Brian. *The Fenian Problem: Insurgency and Terrorism in a Liberal State, 1858–1874.* Montreal: McGill-Queen's University Press, 2008.

———. *Fenians and Anglo-American Relations During Reconstruction.* Ithaca, N.Y.: Cornell University Press, 1969.

Jentz, John B., and Richard Schneirov. "Chicago's Fenian Fair of 1864: A Window into the Civil War as a Popular Political Awakening." *Labor's Heritage* 6 (Winter 1995): 4–19.

Johnson, Roy P. "The Fenian 'Invasion' of 1871." *Transactions of the Manitoba Historical and Scientific Society,* 3rd ser. (1950–51). www.mhs.mb.ca.

Jones, Wilbur Devereux. "Made in New York: A Plot to Kill the Queen." *New-York Historical Society Quarterly* 51 (Oct. 1967): 311–25.

Joye, Lar. "The Stone That 'Smashed the Van.' " *History Ireland* 25 (March/April 2017): 27.

———. "The Wearing of the Green: Fenian Uniform from Canada, 1870." *History Ireland* 16 (Nov./Dec. 2008): 51.

Junor, David. "Taken Prisoner by the Fenians." *Canadian Magazine,* May 1911, 85–91.

Kee, Robert. *The Green Flag: A History of Irish Nationalism.* London: Penguin Books, 1972.

———. *Ireland: A History.* London: Abacus, 2003.

Kelly, John. *The Graves Are Walking: The Great Famine and the Saga of the Irish People.* New York: Henry Holt, 2012.

Kelly, Mary C. *Ireland's Great Famine in Irish-American History: Enshrining a Fateful Memory.* Lanham, Md.: Rowman & Littlefield, 2014.

Keneally, Thomas. *The Great Shame and the Triumph of the Irish in the English-Speaking World.* New York: Anchor Books, 2000.

Kenna, Shane. *Jeremiah O'Donovan Rossa: Unrepentant Fenian.* Sallins, Ire.: Merrion Press, 2015.

———. *War in the Shadows: The Irish-American Fenians Who Bombed Victorian Britain.* Sallins, Ire.: Merrion Press, 2014.

Kenneally, Ian. *From the Earth, a Cry: The Story of John Boyle O'Reilly.* Cork: Collins Press, 2011.

Kenny, Michael. *The Fenians: Photographs and Memorabilia from the National Museum of Ireland.* Dublin: Country House in association with the National Museum of Ireland, 1994.

Kinealy, Christine. *Repeal and Revolution: 1848 in Ireland.* Manchester: Manchester University Press, 2009.

King, Joseph A. "John McMahon, Fenian Priest: Saint or Charlatan?" Unpublished paper read at the Western Regional Conference of the American Committee for Irish Studies, 1988.

King, Moses, ed. *King's Handbook of Boston.* Cambridge, Mass.: Moses King, 1883.

Kingsbury, George W. *History of Dakota Territory: Its History and Its People.* Vol. 1. Chicago: S. J. Clarke, 1915.

Kirk, Charles H., ed. *History of the Fifteenth Pennsylvania Volunteer Cavalry Which Was Recruited and Known as the Anderson Cavalry in the Rebellion of 1861–1865.* Philadelphia: Society of the Fifteenth Pennsylvania Cavalry, 1906.

Klein, Christopher. "7 Times the U.S.-Canada Border Wasn't So Peaceful." History Channel, June 30, 2015. www.history.com.

———. "When Washington, D.C., Gave the Pope a Truly Rocky Reception." *Mental Floss,* Sept. 22, 2015. www.mentalfloss.com.

Klohs, Abraham. "Once More Peace and Quiet Reigns." *Franklin Historical Review* 39 (2004): 33–36.

Kohler, C. Douglas. "For I Never Would Have Surrendered: The 1866 Fenian Invasion of Canada." *Western New York Heritage* 13 (Winter 2011): 8–17.

Kostick, Conor, and Lorcan Collins. *The Easter Rising: A Guide to Dublin in 1916.* Dublin: O'Brien Press, 2000.

Lacross, Jim. "The Battle of Trout River." *Franklin Historical Review* 51 (2016): 57–60.

Langan, Mary Martin. "General John O'Neill, Soldier, Fenian, and Leader of Irish Catholic Colonization in America." Master's thesis, University of Notre Dame, 1937.

Lass, William E. *Minnesota's Boundary with Canada: Its Evolution Since 1783.* St. Paul: Minnesota Historical Society Press, 1980.

Lawson, John D. *Defences to Crime: The Adjudged Cases in the American and English Reports Wherein the Different Defences to Crimes Are Contained.* Vol. 3. San Francisco: Sumner Whitney, 1885.

Le Caron, Henri. *Twenty-Five Years in the Secret Service: The Recollections of a Spy.* London: William Heinemann, 1893.

Lee, J. J., and Marion R. Casey, ed. *Making the Irish American: History and Heritage of the Irish in the United States.* New York: New York University Press, 2006.

Leslie, Shane. *The Irish Issue in Its American Aspect.* New York: Scribner, 1917.

Libby, Gary W. "Maine and the Fenian Invasion of Canada, 1866." In *They Change Their Sky: The Irish in Maine,* edited by Michael C. Connolly. Orono: University of Maine Press, 2004.

Lippert, Kevin. *War Plan Red: The United States' Secret Plan to Invade Canada and Canada's Secret Plan to Invade the United States.* New York: Princeton Architectural Press, 2015.

Little, J. I. "From Borderland to Bordered Land: Reaction in the Eastern Townships Press to the American Civil War and the Threat of Fenian Invasion." *Histoire Sociale/Social History* 45 (May 2012): 1–24.

Lormier, J. G. *History of the Islands and Islets in the Bay of Fundy.* St. Stephen, N.B.: Saint Croix Courier, 1876.

Macdonald, John. *Diary of the Parnell Commission: Revised from "The Daily News."* London: T. Fisher Unwin, 1890.

Macdonald, John A. *Troublous Times in Canada: A History of the Fenian Raids of 1866 and 1870.* Toronto: W. S. Johnston, 1910.

MacManus, Seumas. *The Story of the Irish Race: A Popular History of Ireland.* Greenwich, Conn.: Devin-Adair, 1979.

Martin, Lawrence. *The Presidents and the Prime Ministers: Washington and Ottawa Face to Face: The Myth of Bilateral Bliss, 1867–1982.* Markham, Ont.: PaperJacks, 1983.

Martin, Steven Henry. "Green Terror." *Canada's History* 96 (June/July 2016): 46–53.

McBride, Ian. *History and Memory in Modern Ireland.* Cambridge, U.K.: Cambridge University Press, 2009.

McCarron, Fidelma M. "Ireland Along the Passamaquoddy: Rathlin Islanders in Washington County, Maine." In *They Change Their Sky: The Irish in Maine,* edited by Michael C. Connolly. Orono: University of Maine Press, 2004.

McCartney, Donal. "The Church and the Fenians." *University Review* 4 (Winter 1967): 203–15.

McCollum, Ian. "Needham Musket Conversion." *Forgotten Weapons,* Oct. 15, 2014. www.forgottenweapons.com.

McCulloh, Burns E. *A Piece of Emerald: O'Neill—Nebraska's Irish Capital: The First One Hundred Years, 1874–1974.* O'Neill, Neb.: Miles, 1974.

McGee, Robert F. *The Fenian Raids on the Huntingdon Frontier, 1866 and 1870.* N.p., 1967.

McIntire, Suzanne. *Speeches in World History.* New York: Facts on File, 2009.

McKone, William L. *Vermont's Irish Rebel: Capt. John Lonergran.* Jeffersonville, Vt.: Brewster River Press, 2010.

McLean, John. "Competing Fenianisms: British, Irish, and American Responses." Ph.D. diss., University of Buffalo, 2010.

McManamin, Francis G. *The American Years of John Boyle O'Reilly, 1870–1890.* New York: Arno Press, 1976.

McMicken, Gilbert. *The Abortive Fenian Raid on Manitoba: Account by One Who Knew Its Secret History: A Paper Read Before the Society, May 11, 1888.* Winnipeg: Manitoba Free Press, 1888.

Meade, George. *Life and Letters of George Gordon Meade.* Vols. 1–2. New York: Charles Scribner's Sons, 1913.

Message of the President of the United States and Accompanying Documents, to the Two Houses of Congress at the Commencement of the Second Session of the Thirty-Ninth Congress. Washington, D.C.: Government Printing Office, 1866.

Miller, Bradley. *Borderline Crime: Fugitive Criminals and the Challenge of the Border, 1819–1914.* Toronto: University of Toronto Press, 2016.

Miller, Kerby A. *Emigrants and Exiles: Ireland and the Irish Exodus to North America.* New York: Oxford University Press, 1985.

Millett, Wesley, and Gerald White. *The Rebel and the Rose: James A. Semple, Julia Gardiner Tyler, and the Lost Confederate Gold.* Nashville: Cumberland House, 2007.

Missisquoi County Historical Society. *The Fenian Raids, 1866–1870, Missisquoi County.* Stanbridge East, Que.: Missisquoi County Historical Society, 1967.

Mitchel, John. *The Last Conquest of Ireland (Perhaps).* Glasgow: R. & T. Washbourne, 1861.

Moody, T. W., ed. *The Fenian Movement.* Dublin: Mercier Press, 1968.

Morgan, Jack. *Through American and Irish Wars: The Life and Times of General Thomas W. Sweeny, 1820–1892.* Portland, Ore.: Irish Academic Press, 2006.

Morley, John. *The Life of William Ewart Gladstone.* Vol. 2. London: Macmillan, 1903.

Murphy, Ronald Chase, and Janice Church Murphy. *Irish Famine Immigrants in the State of Vermont: Gravestone Inscriptions.* Baltimore: Clearfield, 2000.

Neidhardt, W. S. "The American Government and the Fenian Brotherhood: A Study in Mutual Political Opportunism." *Ontario History* 64 (1972): 27–44.

———. *Fenianism in North America.* University Park: Pennsylvania State University Press, 1975.

———. " 'We've Nothing Else to Do': The Fenian Invasion of Canada, 1866." *Canada Magazine* 1 (Winter 1973): 1–19.

Nevins, Allan. *Hamilton Fish: The Inner History of the Grant Administration.* Vol. 1. New York: Frederick Ungar, 1957.

Noonan, Gerald R. "A Characterization of General John O'Neill in the Light of His Colonizing Efforts in the State of Nebraska, 1872–1878." Master's thesis, Saint Paul Seminary, 1961.

———. "General John O'Neill." *Clogher Record* 6 (1967): 277–319.

Nowlan, Alden. *Campobello: The Outer Island.* Toronto: Clarke, Irwin, 1975.

O'Brien, Gillian. *Blood Runs Green: The Murder That Transfixed Gilded Age Chicago.* Chicago: University of Chicago Press, 2015.

Ó Broin, León. "The Fenian Brotherhood." In *America and Ireland, 1776–1976: The American Identity and the Irish Connection,* edited by David Noel Doyle and Owen Dudley Edwards. Westport, Conn.: Greenwood Press, 1980.

———. *Fenian Fever: An Anglo-American Dilemma.* New York: New York University Press, 1971.

Ó Dufaigh, Brendan. *The Book of Clontibret.* Monaghan, Ire.: B. Ó Dufaigh, 1997.

Official Report of the Investigating Committee of the Department of Manhattan, Fenian Brotherhood: A Full and Complete Report of the Investigation of the Management of Affairs, Financial, Military, and Civil, of Officials at the Fenian Headquarters. New York: Fenian Brotherhood, 1866.

O'Grady, Brendan. *Exiles and Islanders: The Irish Settlers of Prince Edward Island.* Montreal: McGill-Queen's University Press, 2004.

O'Kelly, Seamus G. *The Bold Fenian Men.* Dublin: Irish News Service & Publicity, 1967.

O'Mullane, M. J. *The Cruise of the "Erin's Hope"; or, "Gun-Running in '67."* Dublin: Catholic Truth Society of Ireland, 1916.

O'Neill, John. *Address of General O'Neill in Prison in Windsor, Vermont.* Oct. 1870. Pamphlet.

———. *Northern Nebraska as a Home for Immigrants.* Sioux City, Iowa: Sioux City Times Print, 1875.

———. *Official Report of Gen. John O'Neill, President of the Fenian Brotherhood: On the Attempt to Invade Canada, May 25th, 1870.* New York: John J. Foster, 1870.

Papers Relating to Foreign Affairs, Accompanying the Annual Message of the President to the Second Session, Thirty-Ninth Congress. Part I. Washington, D.C.: Government Printing Office, 1867.

Papers Relating to the Foreign Relations of the United States, Transmitted to Congress with the Annual Message of the President, December 2, 1872. Part II. Washington, D.C.: Government Printing Office, 1872.

Passewitz, Gregory R. "O'Neill, Nebraska: The First Quarter Century." Master's thesis, University of Nebraska at Omaha, 1973.

"Patrick Pearse's Graveside Oration at the Funeral of Jeremiah O'Donovan Rossa, August 1915." *Century Ireland,* July 2015. www.rte.ie.

Pender, Seamus. "Fenian Papers in the Catholic University of America: A Preliminary Survey." *Journal of the Cork Historical and Archaeological Society* 74 (1969): 130–40; 75 (1970): 36–53; 76 (1971): 25–47, 137–49; 77 (1972): 45–59, 124–36; 78 (1973): 14–26; 79 (1974): 1–13; 80 (1975): 61–73; 81 (1976): 120–33; 82 (1977): 127–38.

Plemmons, Michael. *Fianna: A Story Every Canadian School Child Still Learns, but One Conveniently Forgotten in America.* Chicago: 3A, 2009.

Pound, Louis. *Nebraska Folklore.* Lincoln: University of Nebraska Press, 2006.

Prince, Cathryn J. *Burn the Town and Sack the Banks: Confederates Attack Vermont!* New York: Carroll & Graf, 2006.

Pritchett, John Perry. "The Origin of the So-Called Fenian Raid on Manitoba in 1871." *Canadian Historical Review* 10 (March 1929): 23–42.

Proceedings of the First National Convention of the Fenian Brotherhood Held in Chicago, Illinois, November, 1863. Philadelphia: James Gibbons, 1863.

Proceedings of the Fourth National Congress of the Fenian Brotherhood, at Pittsburgh, Pa., February, 1866. New York: J. Craft, 1866.

Proceedings of the Ninth General Convention of the Fenian Brotherhood. New York: Council of the Fenian Brotherhood, 1870.

Proceedings of the Second National Congress of the Fenian Brotherhood, Held in Cincinnati, Ohio, January, 1865. Philadelphia: James Gibbons, 1865.

Proceedings of the Senate and House of Representatives of the Fenian Brotherhood in Joint Convention at Philadelphia, Pa. New York: D. W. Lee, 1868.

Proceedings of the Sixth National Congress of the Fenian Brotherhood, at Cleveland, Ohio, September, 1867. New York: J. Craft, 1867.

Proceedings of the Tenth General Convention of the Fenian Brotherhood. New York: Council of the Fenian Brotherhood, 1871.

Radforth, Ian. "Highly Promising Youths." *University College Alumni Magazine* 41 (Spring 2016): 16–23.

Rafferty, Oliver P. *The Church, the State, and the Fenian Threat, 1861–75.* New York: St. Martin's Press, 1999.

Ramón, Marta. *A Provisional Dictator: James Stephens and the Fenian Movement.* Dublin: University College Dublin Press, 2007.

Reid, James. *The Diary of a Country Clergyman, 1848–1851.* Edited by M. E. Reisner. Montreal: McGill-Queen's University Press, 2000.

Report of the Select Committee on the Causes of the Difficulties in the North-West Territory in 1869–1870. Ottawa: I. B. Taylor, 1874.

Reports of Cases Argued and Determined in the Superior Court of the City of New York. By Samuel Jones and James C. Spencer. *New York Superior Court Reports.* Vol. 37. New York: Diossy, 1885.

Richard family scrapbook. Private scrapbook compiled by descendants of Alvah Richard with newspaper and magazine clippings, photographs, and typewritten accounts of the events of 1870 from those who witnessed them.

Richmond, Randy, and Tom Villemaire. *Colossal Canadian Failures 2: A Short History of Things That Seemed Like a Good Idea at the Time.* Toronto: Dundurn Press, 2006.

Roche, James Jeffrey. *Life of John Boyle O'Reilly: Together with His Complete Poems and Speeches.* New York: Cassell, 1891.

Rogers, H. C. B. "Louis Riel's Rebellion." *Irish Sword* 2 (1954–56): 153.

Rosenzweig, Roy, and Elizabeth Blackmar. *The Park and the People: A History of Central Park.* Ithaca, N.Y.: Cornell University Press, 1992.

Rossa, Jeremiah O'Donovan. *Irish Rebels in English Prisons: A Record of Prison Life.* New York: P. J. Kenedy, 1899.

———. *Rossa's Recollections, 1838 to 1898.* Mariner's Harbor, N.Y.: O'Donovan Rossa, 1898.

Rowe, John G. "The Rescue of James Stephens, from Richmond Jail." *The Gael* 23 (Feb. 1904): 63–66.

Rowsome, Frank, Jr., and Joan Sten. "The Fenian Raid." *Vermont Life* 25 (Summer 1961): 34–40.

Rutherford, John. *The Secret History of the Fenian Conspiracy, Its Origin, Objects, and Ramifications.* Vol. 2. London: C. Kegan Paul, 1877.

Ryan, Desmond. *The Fenian Chief: A Biography of James Stephens.* Dublin: Gill and Son, 1967.

————. *The Phoenix Flame: A Study of Fenianism and John Devoy.* London: Arthur Barker, 1937.

Rykert, A. "Mr. Noyes and the Fenian Raid Cannon." In *Third Report of the Missisquoi County Historical Society,* 20–21. St. Johns, Que.: News Type, 1907–8.

Samito, Christian G. *Becoming American Under Fire: Irish Americans, African Americans, and the Politics of Citizenship During the Civil War Era.* Ithaca, N.Y.: Cornell University Press, 2009.

Sandborn, Ruth Ellen. "The United States and the British Northwest, 1865–1870." *North Dakota Historical Quarterly* 6 (Oct. 1931): 5–41.

Santos, Cory. "The Greatest Escape from Lincoln Prison." *Lincolnite,* March 14, 2013. thelincolnite.co.uk.

Savage, John. *American Citizens Prisoners in Great Britain.* N.p., 1870.

Sayers, Brian. "John O'Mahony: Revolutionary and Scholar (1815–1877)." Ph.D. diss., National University of Ireland Maynooth, 2005.

Scharf, John Thomas. *History of Saint Louis City and County: From the Earliest Periods to the Present Day: Including Biographical Sketches of Representative Men.* Vol. 1. Philadelphia: Louis H. Everts, 1883.

Schecter, Barnet. *The Devil's Own Work: The Civil War Draft Riots and the Fight to Reconstruct America.* New York: Walker, 2005.

Schmuhl, Robert. *Ireland's Exiled Children: America and the Easter Rising.* New York: Oxford University Press, 2016.

Schofield, William G. *Seek for a Hero: The Story of John Boyle O'Reilly.* New York: P. J. Kenedy & Sons, 1956.

Senior, Hereward. *The Fenians and Canada.* Toronto: Macmillan of Canada, 1978.

————. *The Last Invasion of Canada: The Fenian Raids, 1866–1870.* Ottawa: Canadian War Museum, 1991.

————. "Quebec and the Fenians." *Canadian Historical Review* 48 (March 1967): 26–44.

Sessional Papers. Fifth Session of the First Parliament of the Dominion of Canada. Vol. 7, no. 26. Ottawa: I. B. Taylor, 1872.

Sessional Papers. Fourth Session of the First Parliament of the Dominion of Canada. Vol. 4, no. 7. Ottawa: I. B. Taylor, 1871.

Shiels, Damian. *The Forgotten Irish: Irish Emigrant Experiences in America.* Dublin: History Press Ireland, 2016.

————. " 'The Lives of Her Exiled Children Will Be Offered in Thousands': Edward Gallway, Fort Sumter, and Foreseeing the Cost of Civil War." *Irish in the American Civil War,* April 12, 2016. irishamericancivilwar.com.

————. "Time to Move Beyond the Irish Brigade?" *Irish in the American Civil War,* Nov. 12, 2016. irishamericancivilwar.com.

Sim, David. *A Union Forever: The Irish Question and U.S. Foreign Relations in the Victorian Age.* Ithaca, N.Y.: Cornell University Press, 2013.

Slattery, T. P. *The Assassination of D'Arcy McGee.* Toronto: Doubleday Canada, 1968.

Smith, Gene. "In Windsor Prison." *American Heritage,* May/June 1996, 100–09.

Smith, Jean Edward. *Grant.* New York: Simon & Schuster, 2001.

Smith, Nicholas. "Ghosts in Green: Exploring the Fenian Raids and Vermont's Lost Irish Community." Bachelor's thesis, St. Michael's College, 2009.

Smith, P. G. "War at the Border." *Beaver Magazine,* Oct./Nov. 2007, 16–23.

Smyth, Major. *Records of the Sixty-Ninth, or South Lincolnshire Regiment.* Quebec: Middleton & Dawson, 1870.

Snay, Mitchell. *Fenians, Freedmen, and Southern Whites: Race and Nationality in the Era of Reconstruction.* Baton Rouge: Louisiana State University Press, 2010.

Somerville, Alexander. *Narrative of the Fenian Invasion of Canada.* Hamilton, C.W.: Joseph Lyght, 1866.

Sowles, Edward A. "History of Fenianism and Fenian Raids in Vermont." *Proceedings of the Vermont Historical Society,* Oct. 19, 1880, 1–43.

Speeches of Hon. Schuyler Colfax and General J. O'Neill, Who Whipped the Queen's Own in Canada: Delivered at the Great Fenian Picnic, Chicago, Aug. 15, 1866. Undated pamphlet.

Stahr, Walter. *Seward: Lincoln's Indispensable Man.* New York: Simon & Schuster, 2012.

Stanley, George F. G. "O'Donoghue, William Bernard." *Dictionary of Canadian Biography.* Vol. 10. University of Toronto/Université Laval, 1972. www .biographi.ca.

———. *Toil and Trouble: Military Expeditions to Red River.* Toronto: Dundurn Press, 1989.

Statement by Colonel Eamon Broy. Bureau of Military History, 1913–21. Document No. W.S. 1,284. www.bureauofmilitaryhistory.ie.

Stephens, James. *The Birth of the Fenian Movement: American Diary, Brooklyn 1859.* Edited by Marta Ramón. Dublin: University College Dublin Press, 2009.

Stern, William J. "How Dagger John Saved New York's Irish." *City Journal* 7 (Spring 1997). www.city-journal.org.

Steward, Patrick, and Bryan McGovern. *The Fenians: Irish Rebellion in the North Atlantic World, 1858–1876.* Knoxville: University of Tennessee Press, 2013.

Stewart, William M. *Reminiscences of Senator William M. Stewart of Nevada.* Edited by George Rothwell Brown. New York: Neale, 1908.

Strausbaugh, John. *City of Sedition: The History of New York During the Civil War.* New York: Twelve, 2016.

Swan, Ruth, and Edward A. Jerome. "'Unequal Justice': The Metis in O'Donoghue's Raid of 1871." *Manitoba History* 39 (Spring/Summer 2000): 24–38. www.mhs.mb.ca.

Taylor, Fennings. *The Hon. Thos. D'Arcy McGee: A Sketch of His Life and Death.* Montreal: John Lovell, 1868.

Taylor, John M. "In Queen Victoria's Secret Service." *Studies in Intelligence* (Winter 1985): 57–64.

Terrill, Frederick William. *A Chronology of Montreal and of Canada: From a.d. 1752 to a.d. 1893.* Montreal: John Lovell & Sons, 1893.

Towle, Martha Hanna. *A History of Franklin: Past and Present, Fact or Fancy, Legend or Folksay, 1789–1989.* Franklin, Vt.: Franklin Historical Society, 1989.

Trevelyan, Charles Edward. "The Irish Crisis." *Edinburgh Review* 53 (Jan. 1848): 229–320.

Trial of Patrick J. Whelan for the Murder of the Hon. Thos. D'Arcy McGee. Ottawa: G. E. Desbarats, 1868.

Tuttle, Charles Herbert. "The Fenian Campaign." *Old and New* 2 (Aug. 1870): 208–14.

Twain, Mark. "Unburlesquable Things." *Galaxy* 10 (July 1870): 137–38.

"The Untold Story of the Intelligent Whale." *Undersea Warfare* 38 (Summer 2008). www.public.navy.mil.

U.S. Congress. *House Executive Documents.* 39th Cong., 2nd Sess., 1867; 40th Cong., 2nd Sess., 1868; 40th Cong., 3rd Sess., 1869.

——. *Senate Executive Documents.* 40th Cong., 2nd sess., 1868.

Vesey, Maxwell. "When New Brunswick Suffered Invasion." *Dalhousie Review* 19 (1939): 197–204.

Victoria, Queen of Great Britain. *The Letters of Queen Victoria, Second Series: A Selection from Her Majesty's Correspondence and Journal Between the Years 1862 and 1878.* Edited by George Earle Buckle. London: John Murray, 1926.

Vronsky, Peter. "Combat, Memory, and Remembrance in Confederation Era Canada: The Hidden History of the Battle of Ridgeway, June 2, 1866." Ph.D. diss., University of Toronto, 2011.

——. *Ridgeway: The American Fenian Invasion and the 1866 Battle That Made Canada.* Toronto: Penguin, 2011.

Vroom, J. "The Fenians on the St. Croix." *Canadian Monthly,* March 1898, 411–13.

Walker, Mabel Gregory. *The Fenian Movement.* Colorado Springs: Ralph Myles, 1969.

Warner, Donald F. "Drang Nach Norden: The United States and the Riel Rebellion." *Mississippi Valley Historical Review* 39 (March 1953): 693–712.

Webb, Alfred. *A Compendium of Irish Biography: Comprising Sketches of Distinguished Irishmen.* Dublin: M. H. Gill & Son, 1878.

Weiss, John. *Life and Correspondence of Theodore Parker: Minister of the Twenty-Eighth Congregational Society, Boston.* Vol. 1. New York: D. Appleton, 1863.

Welles, Gideon. *Diary of Gideon Welles: Secretary of the Navy Under Lincoln and Johnson.* Vol. 2. Boston: Houghton Mifflin, 1911.

White, Ronald C. *American Ulysses: A Life of Ulysses S. Grant.* New York: Random House, 2016.

Williams, David Ricardo. *Call in Pinkerton's: American Detectives at Work for Canada.* Toronto: Dundurn Press, 1998.

Wilson, David A. *Thomas D'Arcy McGee.* Vol. 2, *The Extreme Moderate, 1857–1868.* Montreal: McGill-Queen's University Press, 2011.

Winks, Robin W. *Canada and the United States: The Civil War Years.* Baltimore: Johns Hopkins Press, 1960.

Yanoso, Nicole Anderson. *The Irish and the American Presidency.* London: Routledge, 2017.

Yeats, William Butler. *"Easter, 1916," and Other Poems.* Mineola, N.Y.: Dover, 1997.

Yost, Nellie Irene Snyder. *Before Today: The History of Holt County, Nebraska.* O'Neill, Neb.: Miles, 1976.

Young, George. *Manitoba Memories: Leaves from My Life in the Prairie Province, 1868–1884.* Toronto: William Briggs, 1897.

Zuck, Rochelle Raineri. *Divided Sovereignties: Race, Nationhood, and Citizenship in Nineteenth-Century America.* Athens: University of Georgia Press, 2016.

Newspapers

Age (Melbourne, Australia)
Albany Evening Journal
American Traveller (Boston)
An Phoblacht (Dublin)
Argus and Patriot (Montpelier, Vt.)
Army and Navy Journal (New York)
Atchison Daily Champion (Atchison, Kans.)
Auburn Daily Bulletin (Auburn, N.Y.)
Australian
Baltimore Daily Commercial
Baltimore Sun
Bangor Daily News
Belfast News-Letter
Boston Daily Advertiser
Boston Journal
Boston Post
Brooklyn Daily Eagle
Buffalo Commercial
Buffalo Daily Courier
Buffalo Evening News
Buffalo Evening Post
Buffalo Express
Burlington Free Press

Canadian Illustrated News
Charleston Daily News
Chicago Tribune
Christian Register (Boston)
Chronicle Herald (Halifax)
Cincinnati Enquirer
Columbian (Bloomsburg, Pa.)
Columbian Register (New Haven, Conn.)
Commercial Advertiser (New York)
Commercial Appeal (Memphis)
Connaught Telegraph
Daily Alta California
Daily Eastern Argus (Portland, Maine)
Daily Milwaukee News
Daily Missouri Democrat
Daily Ohio Statesman
Daily Phoenix (Columbia, S.C.)
Democrat and Chronicle (Rochester, N.Y.)
Detroit Free Press
Dublin Evening Post
Frank Leslie's Illustrated Newspaper
Freeman's Journal (Dublin)
Frontier (O'Neill, Neb.)
Geneva Daily Gazette (Geneva, N.Y.)
Globe and Mail (Toronto)
Harrisburg Telegraph
Hartford Courant
Idaho Semi-weekly World
Intermountain Catholic (Salt Lake City, Utah)
Inter Ocean (Chicago)
Irish-American (New York)
Irish Independent
Irish Times
Irish World
Lawrence American (Lawrence, Mass.)
Lincolnite (Lincoln, U.K.)
Louisville Courier Journal
Louisville Daily Courier
Maine Farmer
Malone Palladium (Malone, N.Y.)
Manchester Guardian
Manhattan Nationalist

Massachusetts Ploughman and New England Journal of Agriculture

Montreal Witness

Moore's Rural New Yorker

Morning Freeman (St. John, N.B.)

Morning News (Belfast)

Nashville Daily Union

Nashville Union and American

Nashville Union and Dispatch

Nation (Dublin)

National Labor Tribune (Pittsburgh)

National Post (Toronto)

National Republican (Washington, D.C.)

Newcastle Daily Journal

New England Farmer

New York Herald

New York Sun

New York Times

New-York Tribune

New York World

Niagara Falls Review

Observer (London)

Ogdensburg Journal (Ogdensburg, N.Y.)

Omaha Daily Bee

Omaha Daily Herald

Omaha World Herald

Ottawa Citizen

Philadelphia Evening Telegraph

Philadelphia Inquirer

Philadelphia Times

Pittsburgh Daily Commercial

Press Republican (Plattsburgh, N.Y.)

Pulaski Citizen (Pulaski, Tenn.)

Quoddy Tides (Eastport, Maine)

Rock Island Argus (Rock Island, Ill.)

Rutland Weekly Herald (Rutland, Vt.)

San Francisco Chronicle

Semi-weekly Wisconsin

Southern Star (Skibbereen, Ireland)

Spirit of Democracy (Woodsfield, Ohio)

Spirit of Jefferson (Charles Town, W. Va.)

St. Albans Messenger

Star Tribune (Minneapolis)

St. Johnsbury Caledonian (St. Johnsbury, Vt.)
St. Louis Post-Dispatch
Sydney Morning Herald
Tennessean
Times (London)
Times-Picayune (New Orleans)
Tralee Chronicle and Killarney Echo
Tri-Weekly Union and American (Nashville)
Vermont Daily Transcript
Vermont Journal
Vermont Phoenix
Vinton Record (Vinton, Ohio)
Washington Post
Waterford News
Weekly Nonpareil (Council Bluffs, Iowa)
Wheeling Daily Intelligencer
Yorkville Enquirer (Yorkville, S.C.)

Index

Page numbers in *italics* refer to illustrations.

Illustration Credits

ABOUT THE AUTHOR

Christopher Klein is the author of four books, including *Strong Boy: The Life and Times of John L. Sullivan, America's First Sports Hero.* A frequent contributor to History.com, the History Channel's Web site, Christopher has also written for *The Boston Globe, The New York Times, National Geographic Traveler, Harvard Magazine,* Smithsonian .com, and AmericanHeritage.com. He lives in Andover, Massachusetts.

3/19